#47-0108 Peel Off Pressure Sensitive

OUR COMMON AFFAIRS

Edited by Joan E. Cashin

OUR COMMON AFFAIRS

Texts from Women in the Old South

The Johns Hopkins University Press

Baltimore and London

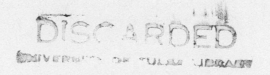

© 1996 Joan E. Cashin
All rights reserved. Published 1996
Printed in the United States of America on acid-free recycled paper
05 04 03 02 01 00 99 98 97 96   5 4 3 2 1

The Johns Hopkins University Press
2715 North Charles Street
Baltimore, Maryland 21218-4319
The Johns Hopkins Press Ltd., London

Library of Congress Cataloging-in-Publication Data will be found at the end of this book.
A catalog record for this book is available from the British Library.

ISBN 0-8018-5306-0

For Mary Lucretia Bond,

who lived and died in the shadow of one blue hill

CONTENTS

ACKNOWLEDGMENTS

MANY PEOPLE CONTRIBUTED to the completion of this book, and I am delighted to thank them here. Grants from the Center for Historical Analysis at Rutgers, the State University of New Jersey, and the Elizabeth D. Gee Fund for Research on Women at Ohio State University supported some of the research travel. For their expert assistance during the research phase, I thank the archivists and librarians at the Arkansas History Commission; the Earl Gregg Swem Library at the College of William and Mary; the Colonial Williamsburg Foundation Library; the Dallas Historical Society; the Special Collections Library at Duke University; the Filson Club Historical Society; the Georgia Department of Archives and History; the University of Georgia Libraries; the University of Kentucky at Lexington; the Library of Congress; the Hill Memorial Library at Louisiana State University; the Maryland Historical Society Library; the Special Collections at the University of Mississippi; the Southern Historical Collection at the University of North Carolina; the Ohio Historical Society; the South Caroliniana Library at the University of South Carolina; the Tennessee State Library and Archives; the University of Texas at Arlington; the Eugene C. Barker Texas History Center at the University of Texas at Austin; the Alderman Library at the University of Virginia; the Virginia Historical Society; and the Library of Virginia. I thank the staff at the East Tennessee Historical Society for their helpful information on locating some of the illustrations. Charles Arp, Fred Bauman, Jean Crescenzi, William Erwin, James Holmberg, Marilyn Bell Hughes, Marcelle Hull, Claire McCann, Lisa Oakley, Joseph Robertson, Gail Terry, and Gregory Williams were particularly helpful. As is so often the case, Henry Fulmer merits a special thanks for his cordial assistance.

My research assistants, Scott Flanegin, Nancy Long, Joon Park, and Mark Pitcavage, all did a fine job, and I appreciate their persistent sleuthing. I must also thank the colleagues who kindly took time from their own work to suggest possible documents: Steven Ash, Robert Brugger, Cita Cook, John McGuigan, David Moltke-Hansen, Thomas Price, and Lee Shepard. They pointed me toward fruitful, sometimes out-of-the-way, sources and opened up new avenues of inquiry. Roger Gilcrest's wise counsel was crucial in the last phases of finishing the book. I appreciated all the hard work of the staff at the Johns Hopkins University Press.

To Jane Turner Censer, Seth Koven, Jan Lewis, Reid Mitchell, Scott Sandage, and Warren Van Tine, I owe a heartfelt thanks for reading drafts of the introduction. All of them are superb critics, shrewd and fair-minded at the same time, and their clarifying, inspiring comments made the essay a much better one. Needless to say, any factual errors, stylistic blunders, or unwarranted speculations are my responsibility alone. Some of my obligations extend farther back in time. My early teachers encouraged my love of books, and for that I will always be indebted to Sister Mary Providence of the Sisters of the Sacred Heart, Elizabeth Fodor, and the late Dorothy Levin, a brave and generous spirit.

This book is dedicated to Mary Lucretia Bond, my great-grandmother's sister. Like most white women born in the rural South in the 1880s, she did not attend college. Like the black people W. E. B. DuBois encountered in the region in the late nineteenth century, she spent all of her days on a small compass of earth within a few miles of her birthplace. But she had many of the instincts of a historian: a keen sense of how communities change over time, a prodigious memory, and a talent for telling a story. Her knowledge of kinship relations was encyclopedic, dazzling in sweep and marvelous in the detail she could summon about generations who came before her. She was devoted to her stepmother, and into her advanced old age she revered her mother's memory. Miss Mary Bond died in 1984, but she would have understood the first chapter of this book.

OUR COMMON AFFAIRS

INTRODUCTION

Culture of Resignation

ONE JANUARY AFTERNOON IN 1861, Meta Morris Grimball entertained two of her favorite callers in her lavish home at the Grove plantation near Charleston. Mrs. Grimball was fifty years old, married to wealthy slaveowner John Berkeley Grimball, and the mother of ten children. Margaret M. Barnwell, one of her callers, was the spouse of cotton factor and slaveowner Edward Barnwell, who was even richer than John Grimball; Ann, one of Mrs. Barnwell's seventeen children, was unmarried at age twenty-two. Both families had owned plantations in the Carolina low country since colonial times, and their impeccable social position had also developed in tandem with extremely conservative political views. John Grimball and his sons were ardent secessionists, and among the many Barnwell cousins were Robert W. Barnwell and Robert Barnwell Rhett, two of the state's leading secessionists.[1]

Three weeks earlier, on December 20, 1860, South Carolina had hurled itself out of the Union, and since the first of the new year three other states (Mississippi, Florida, and Alabama) had followed in frenzied succession. But these privileged women, long-time close friends, did not even discuss such dramatic public events. Instead they began "talking of men," as Meta Grimball later recorded in her diary. Although she considered herself a happily married woman, Mrs. Grimball nevertheless announced to her guests that men did not listen to women. Even when a man asked for her opinion on a subject, "I never found my advice was attended to," she said. The conversation then turned to marriage and the power relationships embedded in the institution. Ann Barnwell declared that if a man ever went down on his knees to propose to her, she would "make him promise all sorts of things." Mrs. Grimball riposted that men never went down on their knees. When she asked Margaret Barnwell how her husband had broached the subject, Ann broke in to say that he must have proposed "as a passing remark between a conversation about the crops." Knowing Mr. Barnwell's dry, reserved manner, Meta Grimball burst into laughter. The visit concluded after further merriment, cleansing laughter chasing blunt remarks.[2] Despite their startling comments, none of these women had ever joined a reform society, published an article, or spoken in public to express their views of relations between the sexes. In fact, they had never taken political action of any kind on any issue.

This incident conveys much about white women's experiences in the Old South that has yet to be explored fully, namely, their wry skepticism regarding the opposite sex and the candid, joyful talk that women could have only in each other's company. This sense of commonality can be found even in the cockpit of secession, among women who were intimately acquainted with some of the movement's leaders. The incident takes us to what one anthropologist calls the "hidden transcript" behind the etiquette of social relations.[3] It also serves to introduce the central argument of this book, that a culture existed among many white women in the antebellum South. That culture might best be deemed a culture of resignation, and it flourished among women from property-holding families, who are the subjects of this study. Its fundamental premises were that women should accept inequity, not resist it, and that they should refrain from any involvement in partisan, electoral politics.

This question about a female culture has lingered unresolved since Anne Firor Scott's book, *The Southern Lady,* launched the field of Southern women's history in its modern phase in 1970. Much of the scholarly debate since then has pivoted on explicit comparisons with the North and on implicit assumptions about the relationship between culture and political activism. Both approaches, I suggest, may not serve us well as we attempt to understand women of the antebellum South. Anne Firor Scott's monograph was the first in a generation to focus on the South, and it appeared just as the profession was on the verge of an outpouring of scholarship on American women. Like most books on women's history published in the

1970s, it drew on the experiences of the prosperous and the literate. Scott documents how much work even affluent white women did in running households, raising children, and helping to manage plantations. Furthermore, she demonstrates that many women felt discontented with their poor educations, their work duties, and their lack of control over their fertility. Some also had persistent doubts about the morality of slavery. Scott does not argue for the existence of a women's culture—for that concept had not yet moved front and center in the scholarly debate—but she presents considerable evidence for its existence.[4]

The Southern Lady also performed a signal purpose by depicting white Southern women as historical figures in a specific context, releasing them from the stereotypes that pervade American popular culture. Salient among these images is the "belle," the young woman who is beautifully groomed, perfectly poised, and surrounded by eager suitors. She thrives on male attention and sees other women as rivals. This image is often elided with that of the "lady," who is well-groomed and well-mannered but older, married, and completely devoted to her spouse and children. Both women are apolitical, badly educated, and immersed in private life, and both are isolated from other women. Above all, they are supremely contented with the status quo. These stereotypes date from vaudeville, theater, and popular novels of the mid-nineteenth century and acquired new vitality when Margaret Mitchell's wildly successful novel, *Gone with the Wind,* appeared in 1936. Despite Mitchell's ambivalence about her own identity as a white Southern woman, her novel and the movie of the same title fixed the narcissistic Scarlett O'Hara (the "belle" who will not grow up) and the self-immolating Melanie Hamilton (the ideal "lady") in the national imagination. Few women in Anne Firor Scott's book match these stereotypes. Instead, they appear as harried workers in large households, tending many children, sometimes privately uneasy about the inequities of the society in which they lived.[5]

In the 1960s and 1970s scholars advanced the model of a female culture, which they discovered in the white Northern middle class. Barbara Welter's immensely influential article of 1966, "The Cult of True Womanhood," argues that women's cardinal virtues were defined in the antebellum era as piety, purity, submissiveness, and domesticity. Just as industrialization and urbanization began to transform the Northern economy, white families in the region underwent profound changes in gender roles and work responsibilities. Men began to leave the household to work for a salary, in the process creating a new middle class, while their wives stayed home to devote themselves to their "proper sphere," or separate sphere, the family. Welter portrays the cult as oppressive, but she adds that some of its tenets, especially piety, could inspire women to reform the world beyond the home.[6]

Carroll Smith-Rosenberg published an equally influential article in 1975 on the close friendships that antebellum white women forged with each other. Smith-Rosenberg calls these ties "homosocial," meaning that women identified strongly with each other and felt intense affection for one another. She implies that women could create a culture of their own that was not necessarily oppressive. In *The Bonds of Womanhood,* which appeared in 1977, Nancy Cott argues that white women in nineteenth-century New England shared so many experiences that they created a distinct "subculture." These experiences formed the preconditions for reform activity, according to Cott, particularly the woman's rights movement. This book remains the most elegant formulation of the women's culture model in the North. Both Smith-Rosenberg and Welter mention a few Southern women, but they concentrate on the white Northern middle class, and all three works have been taken as definitive statements on those women.[7]

It was not until 1984 that Suzanne Lebsock stated explicitly that a women's culture existed anywhere in the Old South. The long silence between Anne Firor Scott's book in 1970 and the monographs of the 1980s can be explained by the small number of women in graduate school until the 1970s, the scholarly focus on slavery throughout most of that decade, and the very persuasiveness of the Northern model. In *The Free Women of Petersburg,* Suzanne Lebsock investigates an impressive array of property records for middle- and upper-class women in that Virginia town. She discovers a female culture based on a standard of behavior called personalism, meaning "a tendency to respond to the particular needs and merits of individuals." These women identified with each other and in their wills left special gifts to white (and sometimes black) individuals. Occasionally they freed their slaves, and they emancipated individual slaves more frequently than did white men. They also formed charitable societies to shelter orphans and aid the poor, much as some Northern women did. It remained a white female culture, however, for few of these women could transcend racial divisions for long. Yet they emerge vividly as human beings, deeply flawed but free from stereotype. The book offers an entirely original perspective on Southern women's history.[8]

For all the skill of Lebsock's book, other historians have disputed its principal argument. In the mid-to-late 1980s, Catherine Clinton, Jean E. Friedman, Elizabeth Fox-Genovese, and George C. Rable published monographs on white women's educations, courtships, marriages, work duties, racial assumptions, class attitudes, and religious beliefs in the early national, antebellum, and wartime South. Written with panache and building on a variety of methodologies, all four books portray affluent white women as bereft of a female culture; they were also poorly educated, physically isolated in the countryside, and took no part in public life beyond contributing to the occasional charitable society. Rural women devoted themselves to church and family, and community norms shaped their very psyches, as revealed in their dreams. Urban women could not connect with one another because of class barriers and would not form meaningful bonds with free blacks or slaves. Most white women were blinded by racism or, if they were members of the planter class (the elite who owned at least twenty slaves), hobbled by their social and economic privileges. Most white women accepted the status quo, and most planter women celebrated it.[9]

Here the matter stood until 1992, when Victoria E. Bynum presented *Unruly Women,* the first monograph on free black, poor white, and yeoman women. Examining court records in three rural North Carolina counties, she finds evidence as rich as that Suzanne Lebsock discovered in the city. In fact, the book contains some of the most unforgettable portraits of Southern women yet to appear in print. Bynum describes an interracial "subculture" among free black and poor white women who drank, gambled, stole, and had sex with men of either race. Furthermore, she believes that "twisted strands of resentment and empathy" linked these women, for they were all subordinated to white men. But no female bond consistently transcended the barriers of race and class. Bynum declares that no female culture developed "comparable to that in the North" that produced reformers or activists in the woman's rights movement.[10]

The most recent scholarship has taken a promising new direction, exploring the intellectual context of women's lives. Christie Ann Farnham's work of 1994, *The Education of the Southern Belle,* argues that female academies in the antebellum era offered curricula similar to those in many men's colleges. Daughters of the planter class studied the classics, mathematics, and science long before most other American women and some American men. Filled with compelling material on student life, this work reminds us that there is still much to discover about Southern women. Farnham argues that the educational experience was distinctive in other ways, for these girls learned sociability and polished manners, not the restraint that Northerners acquired in school. She does not call this a women's culture but posits that Northern-born instructors successfully exported the doctrine of the separate spheres to Dixie. Whether or not the spheres took hold in the preindustrial, agricultural South, this monograph detaches white women's experiences from the reform requirement and examines them on their own terms.[11]

Scholarship in a closely related field, the white Southern family, has grown apace since 1980. These two fields together have made for one of the most exciting bursts of scholarship in the last thirty years, comparable to work on the colonial era in the 1960s and on slavery in the 1970s. Rarely has the profession seen such a swift accumulation of knowledge about long-neglected historical subjects. Daniel Blake Smith, Carol Bleser, Bertram Wyatt-Brown, Jan Lewis, Jane Turner Censer, Orville Vernon Burton, J. William Harris, Robert C. Kenzer, Steven M. Stowe, and Sally G. McMillen produced fine-grained, deeply researched, interdisciplinary studies of middle- and upper-class white families from all over the region. Drawing on the huge documentary record from the early national and antebellum years, these scholars discuss virtually every aspect of family life, from courtship to grieving rituals. Historians of the poor and the yeomanry have fewer sources to exploit, but Charles C. Bolton and Bill Cecil-Fronsman mined sermons, public records, and newspapers for valuable insights on marriage, child-rearing, work, religion, and migration patterns among the families who constituted the majority of white Southerners.[12]

Despite their contending interpretations of the family's structure and function, almost all these scholars find that white men and women led highly segregated lives. This seems to be the case for white families of all social classes. Steven M. Stowe goes so far as to argue that the configuration of planter family life alienated the sexes from each other. Some historians treat these differences as oppressive for women, and others as a natural part of family life. Although few of these scholars deal directly with the issue of a women's culture, most implicitly support the Scott-Lebsock view that the sexes had profoundly different experiences. Within the family, gender shaped destiny, expectation, and experience.[13]

How, then, does this body of literature affect the question of a white Southern female culture? Let us begin with terminology, for some confusion over language has clouded the debate, specifically the words *culture* and *counterculture* and their relationship to each other. The term *counterculture* is a historical marker in and of itself, redolent of the 1960s, one of the most turbulent reform eras in American history, and it surfaced in the popular press in 1969. A *culture* differs from a *counterculture,* of course. The *Oxford English Dictionary* defines the former as "the whole complex of learned behavior," (this use of the word arose in the mid-nineteenth century), while the latter is defined as "a radical culture, especially amongst the young, that rejects established social values and practices." The first term is neutral and descriptive, while the second requires a high degree of political awareness and a thoroughgoing critique of the social order. Indeed, Suzanne Lebsock observes that women of all ages in past societies may have created "counter-cultures" and adds that "as women come to power, a more humane social order will indeed come with them." Catherine Clinton, on the opposite side of the historiographical debate, also employs the term, arguing that white Northern women generated "a successful counterculture that under-mined patriarchal oppression." Both historians imply that Southern women must be not only reformers but also radicals if they are to have a culture.[14]

The standard is high, so steep that only a fraction of white Northern women would measure up if we applied it to them all. Among white South-erners, the defiant souls in Victoria Bynum's monograph would not meet it, because their resistance was personal and largely apolitical. Only Sarah and Angelina Grimké of Charleston might clear the hurdle. These sisters rejected their place in the planter gentry to build careers as abolitionists and woman's rights activists in the North. Both possessed a steely inner strength, anchored by religious faith, that enabled them to leave home, en-dure verbal abuse and physical threats for their views, and go on speaking tours advocating their ideas. Few white women in any region had this kind of fearlessness, and few whites, even among reformers, were so emanci-pated from racism. The Grimkés forged close, lasting relationships with their mulatto relatives when they discovered in the 1860s that their brother had two sons with a slave named Nancy Weston.[15]

I wish to suggest that historians of Southern women might put aside both the standard of a reform-oriented culture on the Northern model and a radical counterculture on the order of the 1960s. Let us no longer as-sume that white women had to be reformers to create a culture or, to phrase it another way, that the only culture worthy of the name had to result in political activity. Instead, scholars might return to the anthropo-logical meaning of *culture,* as a complex of learned behaviors. In the last thirty years, anthropologists have begun to take women's distinctive ex-periences seriously and have retreated from the assumption that all cultures operate according to coherent, universally accepted rules. They now por-tray a world of multiple cultures that are not always internally consistent, that have porous boundaries, and that construct "border crossings" where people from other cultures can exchange information. In the same spirit, historians of the South now describe a kaleidoscopic regional culture of many facets, while specialists in modern European history have discovered a female culture or consciousness among conservative, traditional, and apolitical women.[16]

Some American scholars have rightly criticized the women's culture model for overlooking the intellectual and political context, but these objections can be addressed while retaining the concept itself. Fortunately the literature on the political and intellectual history of the antebellum South is now so abundant that we can easily supply that context. This context so decisively shaped female culture that historians cannot understand women's lives properly without taking context into account.[17]

This is certainly the case for the issue of reform. A few causes, such as temperance, school reform, and charities for the poor, made some headway in the Southern states, but these movements remained weak, unable to overcome low literacy rates, an underdeveloped transportation system stretched across a vast region, and, especially, the presence of slavery. Most politicians and intellectuals feared that any broad-based reform movement might lead to an attack on this central institution that drove the economy and had enriched many thousands of whites since its North American incarnation in seventeenth-century Virginia. In the 1820s and 1830s, when a few Northerners attacked it directly for the first time and called for its abolition, white Southerners replied with a bold argument. Slavery, they proclaimed, was a benevolent institution. Bondage resembled nothing so much as an idealized family, they responded, for whites would care for childlike slaves like good parents, an argument called "paternalism." Proslavery writers reiterated the idea with increasing stridency for the next thirty-odd years, and in the 1850s they began to borrow pseudoscientific research to allege that blacks were inferior to whites. Politicians who wanted to stay in public life could not criticize slavery in any way; the only disagreement arose on how to defend it. The political climate became increasingly undemocratic, and free speech as we understand it ceased to exist, even for white men. We should take more seriously the tremendous pressures on the region's whites, including of course its women, to keep quiet about far-reaching reforms of any kind.[18]

This is not to say that white Southern women did not hold racist beliefs, for most of them were prejudiced to some degree. In their outlook on the world, all of these women were shaped by transatlantic currents in the world of ideas, from the Reformation to the Age of Romanticism, communicated verbally and in writing via the family, the school, and the church. Bigotry was part of their legacy as members of Western culture, for racism had a long, dishonorable history before the first Europeans set foot in the New World. Racial prejudice was also part of their inheritance as Anglo-Americans, for since the colonial era most whites of both sexes had assumed that they were superior to all people of color. We still know very little, however, about how antebellum white women related to blacks, Hispanics, immigrants, and Amerindians in daily life, and scholars have their work cut out for them on these issues. As historian Drew Gilpin Faust observes, the antebellum North no longer appears to be as progressive on race as earlier generations of scholars once believed. Even famous white reformers from the North were not free from bigotry. The novelist Harriet Beecher Stowe advocated the deportation of African Americans; the abolitionist Maria Weston Chapman insulted Frederick Douglass in racist language; and the educator Emma Willard favored servitude for black people as late as 1862 and opposed black male suffrage. The majority of white Northern women did not join reform societies of any kind, much less the most radical of them all, the abolitionist and woman's rights movements. In light of our current knowledge of the racial, ethnic, and class divisions that separated many Northern women, it seems prudent to view reform activity as only one expression of women's culture in the North.[19]

As we seek to understand women's lives in the South, we might adopt an interactive model that includes class as well as gender. We are just beginning to study the complex relationships between white women of different social classes. Thus far it seems clear that some yeoman women resented both male privilege in their own families and the class privilege of slave-owning whites. As to which they resented more, at what time and place, it is not yet possible to say. A few of the affluent women quoted in this book (Susan Wylie and perhaps Susanna Clay) are hostile toward the working and yeoman classes, but their comments are highly unusual. Class shaped work responsibilities, of course, for as hard as some plantation mistresses worked indoors, they did not do the grueling manual labor in the outdoors that poor white and yeoman women routinely performed. But the fact remains that all white women worked in this society, which lacked every convenience that electricity and running water now provide, and all white women did tasks in the household such as nursing the sick, cooking, cleaning, and sewing that white men rarely if ever did. Class may figure more directly in public life, for some elite white women were interested in politics and may have tried to exercise some influence on men by holding salons. But electoral politics remained irrevocably closed even to conservative women. Louisa Cheves McCord, the proslavery theorist from the top echelons of South Carolina society, was no more welcome than were the Grimké sisters. White men excluded all white women, regardless of class or political outlook, from the public arena.[20]

Based on what we know so far, I believe that gender should figure more prominently in our explanatory model. That part of a woman's identity remained constant throughout her life, while her social class could decline gradually over several decades or plummet suddenly in the wake of a father's bankruptcy or a husband's death. The selections presented here convey how ephemeral class identity could be in the unstable antebellum economy, as some families lost their fortunes (those of Nancy Deas, Sally Graydon, Mary Randolph, and Amanda Hughes) while a few rose swiftly in the world (Mary Franklin). Furthermore, it seems to be the case that some cultural values in the antebellum South transcended differences in social class. For instance, many white women from various social backgrounds treasured female friendship. Some experiences were so profoundly rooted in gender identity that they crossed class lines. Childbirth, for example, might be easier for the rich, if only because they enjoyed a better diet, but medical knowledge was so primitive that doctors and midwives harmed as many patients as they helped. Every woman, no matter how affluent, risked her life when she gave birth to a child.[21]

What is more, Southern white women and white men led very different lives. Even the most privileged white women could not attend universities or enter the professions; nor could most white women control their fertility; and most married women could not dispose of property. These bald facts alone suggest the conditions for a female culture, for identity is often based on shared exclusions as much as on shared values. But white women were also expected to comply with stringent rules on their private behavior. They had to be chaste and pure, to live for the family before and after marriage. They should be devout, pray, attend church regularly, and read the Bible. They should defer to their fathers, husbands, brothers, cousins, and ministers, who would protect them from harm and advise them on any matter pertaining to the greater world beyond the household. In return, women gave up their autonomy, but that was a small price to pay for acceptance, respectability, and security. White Southern women heard these admonitions all of their lives, from childhood into old age, from authority figures at home (including other white women), in school, from the pulpit, and in the statehouse. Nancy Conrad, whose letter is printed in this volume, believed that it was her duty as a woman to deny her own wishes, take up burdens, and serve others. These assumptions about woman's "nature" underlay the family and the entire social order.[22]

If we consider for a moment the recreational conduct that was tolerated among white Southern men, it clarifies this issue. Men could drink, gamble, engage in premarital and extramarital affairs, all behaviors that would have been scandalous if women engaged in them. Instead, women were expected to play the piano, visit relatives, or write letters. This is not to suggest that most women wanted to drink and gamble rather than play the piano (although some may have preferred that), only to indicate how deeply these gender expectations reached into everyday life to stigmatize certain kinds of behavior. The penalties for transgression were more severe for the distaff side of the household, for a white woman's reputation could be ruined by taking a carriage ride without a chaperone, while a white man might have mulatto children on his own plantation without being cast out of respectable society.[23]

It is worth noting that a white male culture coexisted with this female culture, a topic that scholars are just beginning to explore. In his excellent monograph, *Subduing Satan,* Ted Ownby argues that white men in the late-nineteenth-century South celebrated the "unrestrained exercise of will" in their recreational activities, such as hunting, drinking, gambling, swearing, and fighting, while evangelicals, many of them women, tried to protect the home from this conduct. Before the Civil War, white men had common experiences in politics, for almost all of them could vote; many took a zesty part in the politics of the day, which championed a "white man's democracy." Elite white men studied together at the university and sometimes developed lifelong friendships with one another. Family life required specialized roles for men; husbands, not wives, had all of the legal power and much of the informal authority in governing the home. Their sexual conduct was measured by different standards, for many white men committed adultery, sometimes with slaves, often with impunity, as white women could not. Furthermore, white males punished slaves of both sexes, as most white women did not, and they wielded the ultimate authority on the farm or plantation, as most white women did not. Young white men learned the fundamental lessons in exercising power from older white men. Ten-year-old Eliza Polk, daughter of a wealthy Tennessee planter, recorded without comment this exchange between her father and her teenaged brother: "Father said when my negroes run away I whip them when they come back, and George says that is right Father." [24]

But white men also had to conform to strict expectations on their behavior. They were constantly under scrutiny, because all white men had to support the slavery regime, and planters had to run it. Any show of fear, obvious signs of weakness, too much evidence of ordinary human vulnerability (all permitted among white women) would be ridiculed by other white men. Instead they learned to conceal such emotions and to develop an aggressive manner. Violent action, many came to understand, might be necessary in some situations. Moreover, it would be expected of them. These behaviors they also learned from older men. Whether a white man's personality fit this role was irrelevant, for he was expected to conform to it. Much remains to be done on this subject, especially on how evangelical men or individuals who were not tempermentally suited to the role handled its demands. Further study of white male culture promises to explain much more about family and gender in this region.[25]

The ideological pressures on both sexes to conform to their respective roles increased in the last three decades of the antebellum era, as the white South began to close ranks in the face of criticism from the abolitionist movement. White women were expected to play a part in the regime, as proslavery theorists reminded them, by managing households, feeding, clothing, and nursing slaves, and mediating relationships between whites and blacks in the home. Above all, white women had to be apolitical. Here we stumble on one of the paradoxes of gender in this society: great political pressures were exerted on women to show no interest in partisan, electoral politics. These pressures only grew stronger over time as the entire political and economic basis for Southern society—slavery—came under increasingly harsh attack. White women were expected to devote themselves to others within the family yet take no part whatsoever in debates on the public good. In general, the role called for continual, strenuous self-denial, and it silenced women and thwarted their talents in a society that was supposed to reward individualism.[26]

TURNING FROM EXPECTATION to experience, white Southern women's lives also diverged in significant ways from those of white men. First of all, they resided in a society filled with physical danger, and they were vulnerable to violence in a distinctive way. In the Old South, whites of both sexes mistreated slaves, but white-on-white violence was typically inflicted by one man on another or by a man on a woman and only rarely by a woman against a man. Yet historians have scarcely begun to investigate how racial violence and white-on-white violence may have influenced white women. Even witnessing violence could affect women, such as the Grimké sisters, who witnessed the brutal punishments of slaves before they left South Carolina. Sarah Grimké never forgot one especially gruesome sight, the decapitated head of a runaway slave stuck on a pole by the roadside. When white men deployed violence against other whites, much of it was expressly political. In 1836 the Charleston police warned Mrs. Mary Smith Grimké that they could not protect her two abolitionist daughters from mob violence if they came home to visit. In the 1850s, a gang of white men calling themselves Regulators beat up some North Carolina Methodists because they allegedly opposed slavery. The few who spoke out against bondage had their lives and businesses threatened. As historian William W. Freehling points out, Southern lynch mobs killed some three hundred whites for various offenses between 1830 and 1860. Almost all of the victims were men, but white women must have drawn the obvious lessons about the dangerous consequences of flouting community norms.[27]

The home could also be physically dangerous for white women in the antebellum South. Scholars have just begun to uncover evidence of domestic violence in private correspondence, such as Elizabeth Otey's letter to her son, published in this work. Substantially more evidence of abuse appears in the court records in every Southern state. The disturbing cases of Ann Cannon Powell and Harriet Henrietta Perry quoted here confirm what other scholars have found, that many courts did not take violence against women seriously. Even the proslavery writer Louisa McCord conceded that white men "frequently" abused white women; she also made some crude jokes about a "boxing match" between the sexes in which men might teach women a "striking lesson." (By the most convoluted reasoning, McCord also presented physical weakness as proof that women should not be granted the right to vote.) More research must be done before we can assess the regional distinctiveness of violence in the home, but it seems plausible that the frequency of Southern racial violence may have increased tolerance for violence against women, including white women.[28]

It is quite clear that the lives of white Southern women diverged from those of white Northern women in several important respects, starting with the miscegenation question. Throughout the antebellum era many white Southern men engaged in sexual relations with slave women (almost always coerced), just as abolitionists alleged, although most proslavery politicians and intellectuals vociferously denied it. White women grew up surrounded by a mulatto population, knowing and yet not knowing that their male relatives, friends, and neighbors fathered children with black women. But they almost never wrote about miscegenation, no doubt because they felt embarrassed about discussing any sexual matter on paper and because infidelity was so painful. Mary Boykin Chesnut, an outspoken planter's wife from South Carolina, was one of the few to write about it. Some of the entries in her Civil War diary seethe over miscegenation in general and her father-in-law's adultery in particular. She called him "as absolute a tyrant as the czar of Russia" and raged that white married women were themselves "slaves" and "surrounded by prostitutes." Slavery, she exclaimed, was a "*monstrous*" institution.[29]

Historians have taken due note of Mary Chesnut's elitism, her penchant for hyperbole, and her bigoted remarks about slave women. But her shortsighted fury about miscegenation may well be typical of white Southern women. Most of them probably could not rise above their feelings of betrayal or their racism to show any compassion for the victims, slave women. This seems to be true for Lucy Norman, whose divorce petition is included in this collection, for she threatened a slave even though her husband may have been forcing sexual relations on the woman. The high incidence of miscegenation probably made it more difficult for white women to forgive, for mulattoes constituted at least ten percent of the South's four million slaves in 1860. In Virginia hundreds of white women, such as Lucy Norman, named it as the cause for filing divorce petitions. The subject is worth attempting because it affected so many Southern women of both races, and, as scholar Nell Painter suggests, it may be crucial to our effort to understand relations between white and black women.[30]

White Southern women differed from white Northern women in another key respect, their demographic profiles. They married at younger ages (twenty as opposed to twenty-two or twenty-three) and had higher fertility rates (seven or eight surviving children as opposed to four or five) and higher rates of mortality in childbirth (an estimated one mother in twenty-five in 1850, twice the rate for New England and the Mid-Atlantic states). One study reveals that some couples in the Virginia gentry probably used some kind of birth control in the last antebellum generation, for the average number of surviving children in those families dropped from eight to six. Unfortunately, the historical record is completely silent on the methods these Virginians may have used. One woman in this book, a friend of Maria Marshall, may have known how to prevent conception, but few white women in the region at large were able to limit the number of their offspring. For reasons unknown, the majority did not practice effectively the ancient folk knowledge about contraception, and the advice literature, first published in this country in the 1830s, somehow did not reach most of them. Instead the typical Southern woman had a child at one- to two-year intervals for twenty-odd years from marriage to menopause. The responsibilities of motherhood came earlier and lasted longer for her than for other white American women.[31]

White Southern women also had flimsier legal rights and fewer legal protections than their Northern counterparts. The common law everywhere was harsh for women, but divorce could be harder to obtain in the South. Some states required petitions to the legislature, while others stipulated court action, and Virginia for a time required both. South Carolina did not permit divorce under any circumstances until the Reconstruction era. Regardless of the venue, the authorities often turned down a woman's request for marital dissolution because they wished to preserve what they understood to be social stability rather than individual happiness. Sometimes the courts did not believe a woman's uncorroborated account of her married life. Although the South enacted some of the nation's first married women's property acts, these statutes were designed to shelter a family's holdings from bankruptcy, not to advance sexual equality. A few women obtained separate estates through the equity courts, but most were wealthy and, one suspects, lucky enough to obtain shrewd advice from a good lawyer. Freedom of conduct in daily life is more difficult to measure, but white Northern women seem to have enjoyed more latitude here, too. During courtship, for instance, a proper Yankee could spend time alone with a suitor, while a respectable Southerner could not.[32]

It should not be surprising, then, that most white Southern women believed that only other white Southern women could comprehend fully their experiences. The assumption rings out from their writings, suffusing their letters from girlhood into old age. One middle-aged matron, Sarah Ann Finley, told her sister in 1853 that only another woman would be interested in what Finley called her "common affairs," the details of household and family life that absorbed so much of their lives, that they could not share with white men, and that white women in other parts of the country did not experience in the same way. As anthropologist Clifford Geertz astutely observes, common knowledge means a collection of shared understandings about what matters and how to survive in the world. These women felt that only other white Southern women could understand their complex code on how to live in a slave society. So this culture can be said to be distinctive on several grounds: difference from white Southern men, difference from white Northern women, and commonality with other white Southern women.[33]

WE MUST BEGIN TO DEFINE this culture and investigate its features with anthropological finesse. This book represents an initial attempt at describing its main characteristics, the first being its age, for the culture outlined in these documents had its origin in historical developments several centuries old: the Reformation that swept sixteenth-century Europe and eventually propelled thousands of Protestants to the New World; the agricultural, slave-based economy that took root in the North American colonies in the seventeenth century; and the American Revolution in the late eighteenth century, which raised literacy rates among all white women, first in New England and then more gradually in other regions of the country. One of many local cultures that persisted into the nineteenth century before giving way to a national, market-driven culture, this was a folk culture and flourished in the country, the village, the town, and the city. It may have thrived more easily in urban areas, where women had access to one another, but it was not limited to the city. Urban women could be isolated, as Susanna McDowell was in Lexington, Virginia, and rural women could participate in a buoyant female network, as Eliza Robertson did in Louisiana. Instead, this culture originated in the diverging experiences of the sexes, regardless of wherever women might happen to live. To paraphrase T. S. Eliot, the common bond between women arose from the sundry activities of ordinary life.[34]

In the allotment of cultural "space" of different kinds in the Old South, white women had some, but not many, places they might call their own. They created their own social space during family visits, at girls' academies, and at church services, when they interacted with each other most intensively. Some physical space in the home was designated primarily for women—the parlor, the drawing room, the hearth, the birthing chamber, the porch—where they spent much of their time, working together and talking to one another. But the rest of the house belonged to white men, literally, because most married women could not own property in their own names and, metaphorically, because white men controlled most of the cultural resources. Outdoors, white women might cultivate gardens, but white men typically owned the land itself. So this female culture, like many folk cultures, was both forced on women and created by them, for they made it out of the limited materials at hand. Yet it was vitally important to women themselves.[35]

The key philosophical assumption was reciprocity, deriving from the values of Protestant Christianity and from an even older survival ethic prevalent in many agricultural societies. Women assisted one another whenever possible in rearing children and managing households, and they expected other women to exchange time, care, and material resources toward that end. This expectation cleaved through class divisions, because all white women had family responsibilities that could best be carried out with the help of other white women. Even the affluent, such as Maria Marshall's sister, needed some assistance after childbirth. So this culture had a material base: women in property-holding families who had some resources to exchange could be included. The property threshold shut out poor whites and most Amerindians, who usually had no property of their own to offer. Free black women in prosperous families, such as Mrs. Decuir mentioned in Eliza Robertson's diary, might be included for the occasional reciprocal gesture, but they were not welcome.[36]

Neither were slave women welcome, although they might meet white women at a border crossing, an intermediate zone at the boundaries of slave culture and white culture. Northern white women and Southern white men did not enter this area as often or in the same way, for these encounters happened most often in Southern households (all over the region, I should point out, not only in the border states) where black and white women worked. Most slave women never met a white Northern woman, much less worked alongside one, and most did not labor with white Southern men in the household. In exceptional situations, individual Southern women might exchange resources across the color line. All of the circumstances were against it, of course, but human beings occasionally reached through the barriers of race. A slave woman might choose to offer some of her precious resources, perhaps some extra time, perhaps some kindness, to a white woman. This volume contains one account of a slave named Peggy who used her physical strength to protect her mistress Ann Powell from domestic violence. Neither woman left any direct testimony, however, so we can only wonder how these two women banded together against a common enemy in the household. But such loyalties, whether or not they were based on shared trauma, were rare. Elizabeth Perry's house slaves were more typical, for they would not approach the border crossing and offer the mistress one of their resources, the good will she wanted.[37]

Some women in this book approached the border crossing from the white side to practice "paternalism" with slaves. Virginia Cary's letter shows that some women thought it was their Christian duty, to be handed down from mother to daughter. As historian Peter Kolchin indicates, "paternalism" could also mean nearly constant interference in slaves' lives. Certainly Elizabeth Rives Early's account of a slave's religious conversion, suggesting the relentless pressure she put on this bondswoman, supports this interpretation. But a few white women, such as Maria Dyer Davies, could sometimes relate to individual slaves as human beings. Margaret McCue, who called bondage ungodly, expressed the subversive ideas uncovered by historians Anne Firor Scott and Suzanne Lebsock. The young Mary Starnes and the mature Mary Carter go beyond that to discuss slaves as an exploited people. Yet the great majority of white women did not willingly approach the border crossing and did not welcome a slave's approach. Most did not question American racism, and most imbibed it to the full. They viewed slaves with suspicion, hostility, condescension, or plain coldness.[38]

Moreover, this was a Protestant Christian culture, created by people of northern European descent, so these white women did not welcome practicing Catholics or observant Jews. Most women featured here belonged to the mainstream denominations, and some were actively evangelical, but almost all shared the religious prejudices of most Protestant Christians. They gravitated toward other Protestants and developed their closest ties with one another. These women were conservative Protestants, too, for the liberating message of the Second Great Awakening, which inspired some Northerners to reform this world, had little impact on them. Instead they tried to perfect their own souls, convert their families, and support their congregations. They absorbed Christianity's fatalism and tried to accept hardship, sudden illness, and heartbreaking death. Most would have agreed with Elizabeth Otey that sorrow was the lot of the human family. They did not always accept their burdens easily, as some of the angry outbursts in the book make clear, but their goal was to endure: submit to God's dispensations, as Nancy Conrad advised, or suffer and be still, as Jane Lomax put it. They admired women who trained themselves to be resigned. Nancy Conrad praised her friend Mrs. Strother for this trait, and Sallie Collins venerated her aunt Mary for the same reason. This life was precarious and unpredictable, so they tried to look forward to a better world to come, as Julia Gilchrist and Lucy Fletcher did.[39]

What is more, this culture fostered high expectations about expressing feelings in private relationships. We still know little about how white Southern women experienced the self, but these documents make clear how crucial it was for them to share their emotions with other white women. These exchanges alleviated loneliness, comforted the weary and the grief-stricken, and afforded them many moments of joy. The communications by Laura Cole, Maria Marshall, Sophia Springs, Henrietta Tilghman, and many other women all confirm this point. This female culture could not be called sentimental, however, for there is too much hilarity, indignation, and anguish here for that. Nor was there anything superficial about these relationships, for they were central to most women's lives. White Southern women raised their daughters to share their deepest feelings with other white women, especially family members, but to conceal them much of the time from white men. Jane Lomax develops this theme in her short story, and Henrietta Tilghman reveals the same dichotomy in contrasting letters to her female cousin and her husband. In fact, many of these women accepted a certain degree of incomprehension between the sexes. They expected husbands to father their children and support the household, and they hoped for affection and fidelity. But not many women had what scholars call a "companionate marriage," an intimate partnership between peers. Fewer still looked for romantic love, and some distrusted it.[40]

This women's culture derived from an oral culture, evident in the longing for face-to-face conversation that Lucretia Townes, Mary Jane Barton, and others described. It was in the midst of a slow, fitful transition from verbal to written communication, as literacy diffused gradually across the post-Revolutionary South. Because most of the women featured in this volume were born after 1800 and thus constituted the first generation of literate Southern women, they could convey in writing what used to be expressed only in person, as Margaret Manigault happily observed, and they took full advantage of it. As did most Americans, they benefited from the availability of mass-produced, cheap paper in the 1830s and better mail delivery from the construction of railroad lines in the 1840s and 1850s.[41]

A few women longed for more than the ability to write letters, however: they wanted a life of the mind. Although most remained provincials, focused on home, family, and neighborhood, a handful of the women in this book might qualify as proto-intellectuals. Sallie Graydon, for instance, valued knowledge for its own sake and urged her cousin to strive for academic excellence. Margaret Galbreath was given to reflection, while Mary Telfair read widely among transatlantic authors. Lizinka Brown hungered for conversation with other knowledgeable adults. But genuine intellectuals, the erudite who lived for ideas and wrote about them, continued to be extremely rare among white Southern women. They could not earn a living on the lecture circuit, for no respectable woman spoke in public or traveled alone, and the usual haven for intellectuals, the universities, would not admit them as students, much less hire them as professors. They also had to contend with the pervasive anti-intellectualism of nineteenth-century American society, which was even more pronounced in the South. Literary artists such as Jane Lomax and Mary Terhune were just as rare. (Their works are excerpted here because they portray in fiction the values that many white Southern women practiced in their lives.) Books were still expensive, beyond the reach of many households, and some of the major publishing companies did not even market their wares in the South because of the region's high illiteracy rates. Opportunities for learned or creative women remained bleak throughout the antebellum era.[42]

This female culture developed conflicted attitudes toward partisan, electoral politics, which may have derived from eighteenth-century Republican ideology. Descended in illustrious genealogy from the classics to Renaissance writers to American Revolutionary patriots, this political philosophy assumed that the survival of a Republican government depended upon a virtuous citizenry. In post-Revolutionary America, it alloted women a marginal role as "Republican mothers." As historian Linda Kerber notes, women were called on to raise virtuous sons to be good citizens and, as scholar Jan Lewis adds, to be helpful spouses for their citizen husbands. A few of the older women in this volume, such as Margaret McCue, were daughters of Revolutionary veterans, and Louisa Cunningham was distantly related to that most revered Founder, George Washington. Some white Southern women offered criticisms of public life that hark back to the Revolutionary era. They ridiculed fancy public ceremony (Maria Marshall, Susanna Clay) and pointed out the corruption of personal ambition (Louisa Cunningham) and its irreligious character (Hester Davis, Fanny Broderick). Others abhorred the violence inherent in the Nullification and secession movements (Julia Brown, Susan Wylie, Margaret McCue, and Amanda McDowell).[43]

But other white women withdrew from Republicanism altogether by rejecting any involvement in public life, for themselves or their menfolk. Susan Fishback disdained the scheming, self-deluding public men she knew, and Eliza Quitman and Mary Ann Cobb hotly informed their politician-husbands that politics had no "honour." As historian Bertram Wyatt-Brown cogently argues, manly honor in the antebellum South required brave, sometimes violent, defense of one's family and one's reputation, while womanly honor required family loyalty, chastity, and stoicism. Masculine honor did not necessarily require close involvement in family life, however, and women felt this distinction keenly. Quitman and Cobb thought spending time with the family mattered much more than public acclaim. A demanding political career took a man away from his family so much that it violated the Southern understanding of honor. Margaret McCue launched a similar criticism, that saving a man's soul was "much more Honerable" than winning high office. The concept of honor may well have meant one thing to most white men and another thing, or several things, to most white women. At the very least, it appears that the sexes disagreed on whether a man's public or domestic responsibilities should take priority.[44]

A few women departed from Republican ideology in another fashion entirely, by taking a genuine, if apologetic, interest in public life. Maria Campbell, Mary Telfair, Laura Cole, and Rebecca Smith felt a surpassing interest in the national crises through which they lived, although they all felt anxious about admitting it. Others made more pointed observations. Maria Marshall agreed with her husband's criticisms of President Andrew Jackson and made some unkind digs at Mrs. Jackson. Lucretia Townes was a zealous Nullifier, unique among all of these women for her unbridled partisan enthusiasm. Five of these six individuals (Campbell, Telfair, Cole, Marshall, and Townes) came from the slaveowning class, and three (Campbell, Telfair, Townes) were related to politicians, which may help explain their comments, while Lucretia Townes had an unusually forthright personality. But none of them engaged in political activity other than hazarding opinions in private correspondence, and by all accounts they did not contemplate doing anything more—or doing anything at all. Even these statements are atypical, for a historian could read dozens of women's letters before finding a single reference to public life.[45]

More typically, this female culture harbored a lasting discomfort with organized reform movements precisely because they required engagement with the political system. When many factors converged—literacy, religious faith, like-minded friends, and the intangibles of personality—it could produce reformers such as the sisters Grimké. Young Martha Gaston may be called a reformer-in-the-making. But Southern white women's culture rarely produced political activists of any viewpoint, and it would not sustain them. Even most conservative women did not want to get involved in such an all-consuming business as electoral politics. They were not so much politically immature, like the white women that historian John Mack Faragher studied in the rural Midwest, as acutely uncomfortable with public life.[46]

Therefore, the secession crisis of 1860–61 forced a crisis within white Southern women's culture, for it intensified their disgust for politics even as the threat of disunion aroused their profound love for the family. Two basic elements of female culture, discomfort with politics and love of the family, seemed to be set on a collision course. When women had to choose between the two, many felt paralyzed. As evidenced in these documents women decried secessionists as godless, faithless men, and many believed that disunion would inevitably result in war. They felt great fear — for their safety, the well-being of the people they loved, and the family's survival. (In Mary Starnes's case, this anxiety was somehow transformed into a fear of sexual violation.) To halt or at least delay the secession movement, they would have had to plunge into political life at its worst, when the public discourse in the South was anything but rational. Even if women had attempted to enter the debate, they almost certainly would have been unwelcome as speakers at public forums. As other scholars have observed about other women, they had yet to find a voice with which to speak in the public realm.[47]

Contrary to the bromides about fiery female secessionists, these white women had mixed views at best on the issue in the winter of 1860–61. In these documents they express much anxiety, considerable opposition to disunion, and finally some reluctant and qualified support. After the first cannons exploded at Fort Sumter in April 1861, many white women, such as Emma Mordecai and Lucy Fletcher, chose the family above all and followed their men into the Confederacy's folds, but even then some women were less than enthusiastic in their allegiance. Mary Hibberd decided that it was time to be "resigned" to secession's reality, and Emma Mordecai plaintively hoped that everyone in her divided family would somehow remain on good terms. When their menfolk began to join up, some women, such as Clara Dunlap, became the ardent Confederate nationalists, or "she devils," that Northern soldiers later encountered. Yet at the last hour a few independent-minded women, such as Amanda McDowell, could not bring themselves to support the war. The long secession winter of 1860–61, like other dimensions of the Civil War era, looks different from a female perspective.[48]

As the secession crisis reveals, this culture was riddled with evasions about the unpleasant, frustrating, and depressing aspects of white women's lives. This was a culture of resignation, not a culture of reform. The face it turned toward the outside world was defeatist, antipolitical, and pessimistic. As such it partook of an old religious tradition, more ancient than the sense of mission that had recently inspired some Northern activists after the Second Great Awakening at the start of the nineteenth century. Protestant Christianity, like most of the world's faiths, has taught men and especially women for centuries to accept suffering in this life. Like most of the world's women, these white Southerners expected little justice during their earthly existence. They had little or no confidence in engaging the public realm, much less redirecting the public debate toward the seemingly intractable problems of race and poverty. Some women were disgusted with public affairs anyway. Instead these women cherished each other, loved their families, and poured their considerable energies into their private lives. This female culture had a vital, white-hot center, crackling with energy at the core but decaying at the edges, losing confidence the closer it got to the public realm.[49]

It bears pointing out that there is a difference between accepting the status quo for these reasons and praising it as the best of all possible worlds. As these documents should make clear, white women did not embrace every value of Southern society or white male culture, and some realized that their society countenanced many wrongs. Margaret McCue, for example, believed that slavery was sinful and made bondsmen miserable, but it was up to her husband to free their slaves, just as it had probably been up to her father, not her mother, to decide to move from Virginia to a free state. In the meantime, Mrs. McCue prayed for God to influence her husband, just as her mother had probably asked for divine intervention. Like many white Southern women, she had little faith in her own capacity to effect change or, for that matter, in any one person's ability to change a sinful world for the better.[50]

Unfortunately this outlook led all too easily to an unwillingness to speak out against cruelty and name wrongdoing for what it was, even within the confines of the white family. Elizabeth Otey believed she could not help her daughter, who suffered "abuse" and other domestic sorrows in silence. With crushing finality, Elizabeth Randolph simply told her daughter Mary Carter to pray when Carter's husband (also Randolph's nephew) was unfaithful to her. Other women must have communicated this message to their daughters, directly or indirectly, in letters or private conversation, with a word, a nod, or a gesture: suffer and be still. Many women accepted that message. Both Harriet Perry and Lucy Norman apparently endured years of mistreatment before filing for divorce, and Ann Powell may have died from the long-term effects of domestic violence. Very few women even spoke up against legal inequity as Katherine Ambler did, when she declared that her daughters should share equally with the sons in her husband's estate.[51]

Charles Eliot Norton detected this resignation about the chief topic of slavery as he visited the luxurious estates of low-country South Carolina in

1855. Norton would later become an eminent literary figure, but then he was merely a young New Englander traveling for his health. If any population of white women might be expected to applaud slavery, it would be the plantation mistresses who resided here, but he described them as "bewildered" about it. Their efforts to do right, to uphold what they believed to be their Christian duty, were limited by "weakness, inexperience and opposition," meaning opposition from white men in their own families. Norton added that their "eyes fill with tears when you talk to them about it." For other white women it may have been easier to avoid this volatile, inflammatory subject.[52]

In fact, denial seems to have become a habit of mind for many white Southern women. Individuals in this volume (Leah Byrd Haynie, Mary Carter, the young Mary Starnes) broach certain subjects—loveless marriages, slavery's evils, frontier lawlessness—only to turn away from them. They shrank from confronting anyone about society's inequities, a way of thinking that seems to have been deeply engrained in most white Southern women. They probably learned it as children, and they maintained it as adults because it furnished them with a strategy to survive. Denial does serve a purpose, after all, and these women had to live with many fictions, surrounded by a mulatto population that was not supposed to exist and an authoritarian political culture that proclaimed itself the epitome of democracy. They did not learn to speak directly about trespasses in private or public matters, nor were they encouraged to communicate in that way. If they criticized the status quo, they did so implicitly, then shaded over their criticisms with rationalizations and a purblind determination to find something redeeming in the world.

Like most cultures, this one was not always consistent in its philosophical outlook or in the behavior it sanctioned. For one thing, these Southern women accepted the fatalism of Protestant Christianity but rarely followed the ethic of service to others beyond the family. Many distrusted personal ambition, as anyone would who believed in Republican ideology, but did not try very hard to be good Republican mothers or good Republican wives. Most embraced the Age of Romanticism and its attendant cult of friendship but not always the emphasis on romantic love with men. Typically they worried that their marital obligations would undermine close friendships with other women, not the other way around.[53]

How do we account for these strange disjunctures and inconsistencies? I believe that the existence of slavery may help account for them all to some degree. Bondage cast a long shadow over Southern life, brooding over every scene, as Julia Brown admitted, and it may have had the entirely unintended consequence of accenting differences between the sexes, because white men and white women played such specialized roles in the slavery regime. Its malignant influence also stifled reform, undermined truly democratic politics, and corrupted family life. As historian Margaret Ripley Wolfe wisely observes, four years of deadly warfare and all of the federal government's concentrated power were required to uproot slavery from American life. It is no wonder that the "peculiar institution" influenced white women's culture before bondage was finally destroyed. How slavery's demise affected the contours of this female culture is a momentous question for another book.[54]

This culture resembles others, too, in that it changed over time. Technological innovations reached into women's lives, such as when the sewing machine came into widespread use in the 1850s. In the same decade some mass-produced housewares ("ready made" goods, according to Sallie Collins) became available, at least to the rich. Similar transformations in racial attitudes marked the last antebellum decade. Some white women, like some white men, believed the rumors of slave insurrections that percolated across the region, and an unmistakable tone of fear crept into their letters. Just as important, an individual woman's racial attitudes could change over her lifetime. Witness for example the strange turn in Mary Starnes's outlook, as she shifts over the course of fifteen years from empathy to condescension to paranoid racism. These white women do not always fit the usual periodization in Southern history. The documents suggest that some women practiced "paternalism" before the 1830s, when proslavery theorists articulated the idea, while there is hardly a trace of the "scientific" racism popularized in the 1850s.[55]

Nor was this women's culture rooted in a biologically dictated difference in the natures of men and women, what is sometimes called essentialism. Relations between the sexes have always been fluid, subject to change over time and a variety of configurations from one society to the next, like most relationships between human beings. The contrasts between gender roles within the white population in different regions, or between blacks and whites within the South, amply illustrate this point. Nor did every white woman conform to every tenet of female culture. Mary Franklin put aside traditional gender roles in her drive to get rich, and "Mrs. C.," who is quoted in Eliza Wright's diary, made remarks that both women and men considered inappropriate in mixed company. But the documents assembled here suggest that most white women in this region of nineteenth-century

America, whose experiences and sensibilities are so foreign to our own, perceived themselves to be profoundly different from white men.[56]

THIS IS A PROPITIOUS TIME to explore the history of Southern women. Archives and libraries are filled to the rafters with manuscripts, and the next generation of scholars will extend the inquiry on a host of new topics. At the moment we are on the threshold of many publications on the Civil War and Reconstruction eras, making it one of the most promising fields in the entire profession.[57] Four additional areas may prove particularly fruitful for more research, beginning with the creative arts. Scholars have overlooked this dimension of female historical experience, probably because the field of women's history originated in the social history of the 1970s. For instance, what more can we unearth about the South's female writers? They were small in number but a few crafted successful careers, such as Augusta Jane Evans, whose works have just been republished, and Mary Terhune, the subject of Karen Manners Smith's dissertation. Jane Turner Censer's forthcoming work on novelists from the Upper South will illuminate more about these and other writers. What can we discover about popular transatlantic authors such as Madame de Staël, as Anne Firor Scott queried more than twenty years ago? What more can be learned about popular music? Singing together was a common ritual in schoolgirl friendships and sometimes in visits between adult women, perhaps because of music's capacity to stir emotion. We are just beginning to examine the symbols, both the written word and the lyric, that women chose to help make sense of their lives.[58]

Second, historians have scarcely begun to study material culture of the period, the objects that people used every day. We might begin with the houses in which women dwelled. What can we make of Calder Loth's observation that the mansion house may best be understood as the center of a small village of dependencies and outbuildings? How might this perspective affect our view of the plantation mistress's duties? What may we infer from Thomas Jefferson's design of Monticello, which allowed so little physical space for the white women in his family? Scholar Dolores Hayden has shown how crucial household design could be to women's labor in modern America. Many homes from the slaveowning and middle classes are still standing, so let us examine these buildings as historical artifacts for what they may disclose about time usage, household labor, and privacy.[59]

Interpreted as a feature of material culture, high fashion may also illuminate aspects of social class, health, and sexuality. Southern historians have neglected this topic, despite the enduring image of the "belle" as a fashion plate. Yet dress in this society may have had subtle political connotations. Is Susanna Clay's impatience with elaborate public ceremony related to her impatience with high fashion? How do we square fashion's dictates with the ill health and numerous pregnancies so many adult women experienced? How do we interpret the dieting and eating disorders one scholar uncovered among white teenagers? Why did so many women wear such uncomfortable designs, which seemed to grow more awkward in the late antebellum era, culminating in the unwieldy hoopskirt? This fashion took the entire country by storm, but it remains closely linked in the national imagination to white Southern women. Was there an element of truth in the old saying that hoops kept men at a distance—did they symbolize a white woman's inaccessibility? These skirts also implicitly devalued women's work, as does all high fashion, for no one could do housework or care for children in such an outfit. How does this immobilizing attire relate to other cultural changes in the late antebellum era, such as nativism, and to the booming cotton economy? Clearly this is a promising topic for scholars to pursue.[60]

A third exciting area for more research is the South's ethnic and religious minorities. Such scholars as George Brown Tindall, Grady McWhiney, and Randall M. Miller have made a fine start, but there is more to know about the Jewish and Catholic women who created their own subcultures and met other Southerners at border crossings. How did these women interpret such encounters? Jean E. Friedman's forthcoming edition of Rachel Mordecai Lazarus's diary will explain more about the women in this extraordinary family. There is a crying need for work on Franco-American women in the Gulf region, whose lives are illuminated incidentally in Michael T. Parrish's biography of Richard Taylor and Eli Evans's book on Judah Benjamin. Scholars have done outstanding work on Kate Chopin, an ethnic Catholic who wrote what may be the best novel by a white Southern woman, but this dynamic subculture invites more exploration. The legal rights of Louisiana women, based on the Napoleonic Code, were more advanced than those of other Southern women, and they may have enjoyed more autonomy in their daily lives.[61]

A fourth area for research, biography, is returning to popularity after languishing in obscurity for some years. Thus far historians have produced few biographies of Southern women for any period, despite estimable works on Mary Boykin Chesnut, the Grimké sisters, Mary Todd Lincoln, Jessie Daniel Ames, and Lillian Smith. Other women's lives are abundantly documented and deserve examination. Virginia Clay, the wife of a U.S.

senator and Confederate commissioner, became a woman suffragist after the Civil War. Would it be accurate to say that she conformed to scholar Carolyn Heilbrun's theory that women sometimes make dramatic changes in their lives during late middle age? In any case, Mrs. Clay left behind a memoir and a voluminous body of papers. Archives all over the region contain sources on other women, some of them famous and some not so well known, that await a biographer.[62]

THIS COLLECTION OF TEXTS focuses on white Southern women, for several reasons. It is intended to fill a long-standing gap in the historiographical literature. Dorothy Sterling and Gerda Lerner have already produced valuable document books on black women, including Southerners, part of a wave of publications on black women since 1980.[63] Nancy Cott, Nancy Woloch, and other scholars have published worthy document books on white women from other American regions. Many university presses have presented editions of family correspondence, and Carol Bleser's new series is devoted entirely to Southern women's diaries and letters. But this book is the first to bring together primary sources by and about white Southern women.[64]

Black people figure significantly in this volume, just as they figured in most white women's lives in the Old South. The 128 documents selected include some 130 references to African Americans, most of them slaves, and some fifty-odd women are mentioned by name. (Thirty-six men are mentioned by name, plus a few people whose gender cannot be determined, and the rest are called "the slaves" or "the servants.") The documents provide worthwhile material on black women's experiences, even though it is filtered through the warped lens of white women's perspectives. Those distortions are themselves part of women's history and the history of American race relations. All the chapters nevertheless make clear how important black Southerners are to any work on the region's history.

Our Common Affairs includes documents from every slaveholding state except Delaware and embraces the border states of Kentucky, Missouri, and Maryland. If the South is divided into its subregions, the border South is represented by nine authors, the Upper South by forty-seven authors, and the Deep South by forty-eight. The texts cover the years from 1811 to 1865, with most of the material clustered in the years from 1830 to 1861 (approximately seventy-five in the five antebellum chapters). Most of the material has never appeared in print before, and it includes letters, diary entries, a poem, a short story, recipes, and legal records. The authors are children, teenagers, young brides, middle-aged matrons, and the elderly, and most lived in villages, small towns, or the country. Only twenty-two of the authors lived in cities, and two (Susanna Clay and Floride Calhoun) were rural women who moved to Washington, D.C., because their husbands pursued careers in national politics. Their class backgrounds range from yeoman or artisanal (nine), the commercial middle-class (nine), upper-middle-class professionals (ten), and small-scale slaveholders (eighteen) to the planter class (fifty-two), with some overlap because, for example, some professionals owned house slaves. I determined a woman's social class by the wealth of her male relatives, her father's if she was single and her husband's if she was married. Therefore this collection is biased toward the literate and the comfortable, who generated the most documents.[65]

When I began researching this book in 1991, I simply wanted to close a gap in the literature. At the outset my methodology consisted of noting interesting documents that caught my eye. After a few years I realized that certain broad categories of experience kept emerging, such as the significance of friendship, so I began looking for texts that fit those categories. When I had at least twenty sources for each chapter, I stopped seeking documents on that topic. When the research was nearly done, I decided that these patterns constitute a distinctive female culture.

The book is organized into topical chapters, although there is considerable overlap here, too, because women wrote about more than one subject in their letters and diaries. The short introductions to the documents give the basic biographical information and highlight the principal themes. Within each chapter, the sources are arranged in roughly chronological order. To annotate the sources, I consulted biographies, biographical dictionaries, genealogies, family histories, county histories, state histories, community studies, atlases, monographs, reference works on many subjects, and the federal censuses (the schedules of 1850 and 1860 list details about every household member). Some references, such as names of family members, lines from hymns, or quotes from popular literature, could not be identified.

Editorial method being a subject of considerable attention these days among both historians and documentary editors, I want to make clear that I have faithfully transcribed the texts that make up this collection — including irregular spellings, antiquarian capitalization, and idiosyncratic punctuation. For the sake of readability, however, I have dropped raised letters to the same line as the rest of the sentence, regularized the length of dashes and hyphens, and rendered dashes as periods where the author clearly meant to conclude a sentence. In cases of undated or partially dated material, I have included in the headnote everything that can be ascertained about the date. Most authors noted where they were when they sat down to write, as well as the geographic location of their correspondents, but when they did not, the headnote provides what information we do know. Ellipses mark the omission of repetitive references to humdrum details like weather reports or scoldings for infrequent and tardy letters. Try though I did, I could not untangle a few garbled passages, which I have also marked with ellipses. Some repositories did not permit documents to be printed in full. Otherwise the texts appear as their authors wrote them, in all their provocative richness.

NOTES

1. Journal of Meta Morris Grimball, 12 Jan. 1861, Southern Historical Collection, University of North Carolina; federal census for 1850, South Carolina, Charleston County, Free Schedule, 154, Slave Schedule, n.p. (Barnwell); federal census for 1860, South Carolina, Charleston County, Free Schedule, 187 (Grimball); Stephen B. Barnwell, *Story of an American Family* (Marquette, Mich.: By the author, 1969); Randall C. Jimerson, *The Private Civil War: Popular Thought during The Sectional Conflict* (Baton Rouge: Louisiana State University Press, 1988), 8–11; Michael P. Johnson, "Planters and Patriarchy: Charleston, 1800–1860," *Journal of Southern History* 66 (Feb. 1980): 45–72. The Grove Plantation, where the Grimballs often spent the winter, was located in St. Paul's Parish, Colleton County. On the Barnwells in politics, see Eric H. Walther, *The Fire-Eaters* (Baton Rouge: Louisiana State University Press, 1992), 121–59; Laura A. White, *Robert Barnwell Rhett: Father of Secession* (New York: Century, 1931), 1–9. Edward Barnwell was the cousin of the Confederate captain Edward Hazzard Barnwell.

2. Journal of Meta Morris Grimball, n.d. Feb. 1861.

3. James C. Scott, *Domination and the Arts of Resistance: Hidden Transcripts* (New Haven: Yale University Press, 1990), 4–14, 4.

4. Anne Firor Scott, *The Southern Lady: From Pedestal to Politics, 1830–1930* (Chicago: University of Chicago Press, 1970), xi. Pioneering works in the field from earlier generations include A. Elizabeth Taylor, *A Short History of the Woman Suffrage Movement in Tennessee* (Nashville: Joint University Libraries, 1943); Julia Cherry Spruill, *Women's Life and Work in the Southern Colonies* (Chapel Hill: University of North Carolina Press, 1938). Because comparisons to the North have dominated the historiography, this essay focuses on North and South. Fine scholarship has been done on other regional cultures, such as John Mack Faragher's *Sugar Creek: Life on the Illinois Prairie* (New Haven: Yale University Press, 1986), and more remains to be done.

5. William R. Taylor, *Cavalier and Yankee: The Old South and American National Character* (New York: George Braziller, 1961), 162–76; Darden Asbury Pyron, *Southern Daughter: The Life of Margaret Mitchell* (New York: Oxford University Press, 1991). Historians have scarcely examined the image of the farm wife; see D. Harland Hagler, "The Ideal

Woman in the Antebellum South: Lady or Farmwife?" *Journal of Southern History* 66 (Aug. 1980): 405–18.

6. Barbara Welter, "The Cult of True Womanhood: 1820–1860," *American Quarterly* 18 (summer 1966): 151–74; Linda K. Kerber, "Separate Spheres, Female Worlds, Woman's Place: The Rhetoric of Women's History," *Journal of American History* 75 (June 1988): 9–39, 22.

7. Carroll Smith-Rosenberg, "The Female World of Love and Ritual: Relations between Women in Nineteenth-Century America," *Signs* 1 (autumn 1975): 1–30, 8, 27; Nancy F. Cott, *The Bonds of Womanhood: "Woman's Sphere" in New England, 1780–1835* (New Haven: Yale University Press, 1977), 197; Nancy Hewitt, "Beyond the Search for Sisterhood: American Women's History in the 1980s," *Social History* 10 (Oct. 1985): 290–321. On woman suffrage in the North, see Ellen Carol DuBois, *Feminism and Suffrage: The Emergence of an Independent Women's Movement in America, 1848–1869* (Ithaca: Cornell University Press, 1978); on political culture among white, middle-class, Northern women, see Paula Baker, "The Domestication of Politics: Women and American Political Society, 1780–1920," *American Historical Review* 89 (June 1984): 620–47. For the most recent statement that this female culture led to reform activity, see Kathryn Kish Sklar, "The Historical Foundations of Women's Power in the Creation of the American Welfare State, 1830–1930," in *Mothers of a New World: Maternalist Politics and the Origins of Welfare States,* ed. Seth Koven and Sonya Michel (New York: Routledge, 1993), 51–53.

8. Suzanne Lebsock, *The Free Women of Petersburg: Status and Culture in a Southern Town, 1784–1860* (New York: W. W. Norton, 1984), xix, 112–45; Jacquelyn Dowd Hall, "Partial Truths: Writing Southern Women's History," in *Southern Women: Histories and Identities,* ed. Virginia Bernard, Betty Brandon, Elizabeth Fox-Genovese, and Theda Perdue (Columbia: University of Missouri Press, 1992), 11–29. Cf. Harriet E. Amos, "'City Belles': Images and Realities of the Lives of White Women in Antebellum Mobile," *Alabama Review* 34 (Jan. 1981): 3–19, who applies Welter's argument to white Southern women.

9. Catherine Clinton, *The Plantation Mistress: Woman's World in the Old South* (New York: Pantheon Books, 1982); Jean E. Friedman, *The Enclosed Garden: Women and Community in the Evangelical South, 1830–1930* (Chapel Hill: University of North Carolina Press, 1985); Elizabeth Fox-Genovese, *Within the Plantation Household: Black and White Women of the Old South* (Chapel Hill: University of North Carolina Press, 1988); George C. Rable, *Civil Wars: Women and the Crisis of Southern Nationalism* (Urbana: University of Illinois Press, 1989).

10. Victoria Bynum, *Unruly Women: The Politics of Social and Sexual Control in the Old South* (Chapel Hill: University of North Carolina Press, 1992), 46, 90–110, 37, 56, 58, 8. For similar conclusions regarding women in literature, see Minrose C. Gwin, *Black and White Women of the Old South: The Peculiar Sisterhood in American Literature* (Knoxville: University of Tennessee Press, 1985).

11. Christie Anne Farnham, *The Education of the Southern Belle: Higher Education and Student Socialization in the Antebellum South* (New York: New York University Press, 1994), 11–120, 155–168.

12. Daniel Blake Smith, *Inside the Great House: Planter Family Life in Eighteenth-Century*

Chesapeake Society (Ithaca: Cornell University Press, 1980); Carol Bleser, ed., *The Hammonds of Redcliffe* (New York: Oxford University Press, 1981); Bertram Wyatt-Brown, *Southern Honor: Ethics and Behavior in the Old South* (New York: Oxford University Press, 1982); Jan Lewis, *The Pursuit of Happiness: Family and Values in Jefferson's Virginia* (Cambridge: Cambridge University Press, 1983); Jane Turner Censer, *North Carolina Planters and Their Children, 1800–1860* (Baton Rouge: Louisiana State University Press, 1984); Orville Vernon Burton, *In My Father's House Are Many Mansions: Family and Community in Edgefield, South Carolina* (Chapel Hill: University of North Carolina Press, 1985); J. William Harris, *Plain Folk and Gentry in a Slave Society: White Liberty and Black Slavery in Augusta's Hinterlands* (Middletown, Conn.: Wesleyan University Press, 1985); Robert C. Kenzer, *Kinship and Neighborhood in a Southern Community: Orange County, North Carolina, 1849–1881* (Knoxville: University of Tennessee Press, 1987); Steven M. Stowe, *Intimacy and Power in the Old South: Ritual in the Lives of Planters* (Baltimore: Johns Hopkins University Press, 1987); Sally G. McMillen, *Motherhood in the Old South: Pregnancy, Childbirth, and Infant Rearing* (Baton Rouge: Louisiana State University Press, 1990); Charles C. Bolton, *Poor Whites of the Antebellum South: Tenants and Laborers in Central North Carolina and Northeast Mississippi* (Durham, N.C.: Duke University Press, 1994); Bill Cecil-Fronsman, *Common Whites: Class and Culture in Antebellum North Carolina* (Lexington: University Press of Kentucky, 1992). On the planter family, see also Joan E. Cashin, *A Family Venture: Men and Women on the Southern Frontier* (New York: Oxford University Press, 1991).

13. Stowe, *Intimacy and Power,* xvii–xviii.

14. *Oxford English Dictionary,* 2d ed., prepared by J. A. Simpson and E. S. C. Weiner (New York: Oxford University Press, 1989), 121, 1025; Sara Tulloch, *The Oxford Dictionary of New Words: A Popular Guide to Words in the News* (New York: Oxford University Press, 1991), 72; and Raymond Williams, *Keywords: A Vocabulary of Culture and Society* (London: Fontana/Croom Helm, 1976), 77–79; Lebsock, *Free Women of Petersburg,* 144; Clinton, *Plantation Mistress,* 10. In a similar vein, two scholars argue that white women's culture in the North led to "heightened militancy"; see the introduction to Joanne V. Hawks and Sheila L. Skemp, eds., *Sex, Race, and the Role of Women in the South* (Jackson: University Press of Mississippi, 1983), xiii. Welter, Smith-Rosenberg, and Cott do not use the term *counterculture.*

15. Gerda Lerner, *The Grimké Sisters from South Carolina: Pioneers for Woman's Rights and Abolition* (Boston: Houghton Mifflin, 1967); Dickson D. Bruce Jr., *Archibald Grimké: Portrait of a Black Independent* (Baton Rouge: Louisiana State University Press, 1993), 22–32, 35. For the twentieth century, Jessie Ames and Virginia Foster Durr might also meet the standard; see Jacquelyn Dowd Hall, *Revolt against Chivalry: Jessie Daniel Ames and the Women's Campaign against Lynching* (New York: Columbia University Press, 1979); Virginia Foster Durr, *Outside the Magic Circle: The Autobiography of Virginia Foster Durr,* ed. Hollinger F. Barnard, foreword by Studs Terkel (University: University of Alabama Press, 1985).

16. Rayna R. Reiter, ed., *Toward an Anthropology of Women* (New York: Monthly Review Press, 1975); Rosan A. Jordan and Susan J. Kalcik, eds., *Women's Folklore, Women's Culture* (Philadelphia: University of Pennsylvania Press, 1985); Renato Rosaldo, *Culture*

and Truth: *The Remaking of Social Analysis* (Boston: Beacon Press, 1989), 25–45, 196–217; Ted Ownby, ed., *Black and White Cultural Interaction in the Antebellum South* (Jackson: University Press of Mississippi, 1993); Charles Reagan Wilson and William Ferris, eds., *Encyclopedia of Southern Culture* (Chapel Hill: University of North Carolina Press, 1989); Numan V. Bartley, ed. *The Evolution of Southern Culture* (Athens: University of Georgia Press, 1988); Ellen Ross, *Love and Toil: Motherhood in Outcast London, 1870–1918* (New York: Oxford University Press, 1993); Marion A. Kaplan, *The Making of the Jewish Middle Class: Women, Family, and Identity in Imperial Germany* (New York: Oxford University Press, 1991); Bonnie G. Smith, *Ladies of the Leisure Class: The Bourgeoises of Northern France in the Nineteenth Century* (Princeton: Princeton University Press, 1981).

17. Ellen DuBois, Mari Jo Buhle, Temma Kaplan, Gerda Lerner, and Carroll Smith-Rosenberg, "Politics and Culture in Women's History: A Symposium," introduction by Judith R. Walkowitz, *Feminist Studies* 6 (spring 1980): 26–64; Joan Wallach Scott, *Gender and the Politics of History* (New York: Columbia University Press, 1988), 37–50.

18. Bynum, *Unruly Women,* 52–56; Jane H. Pease and William H. Pease, *Ladies, Women, and Wenches: Choice and Constraint in Antebellum Charleston and Boston* (Chapel Hill: University of North Carolina Press, 1990), 122–26; Michael O'Brien and David Moltke-Hansen, eds., *Intellectual Life in Antebellum Charleston* (Knoxville: University of Tennessee Press, 1986); Drew Gilpin Faust, ed., *The Ideology of Slavery: Pro-slavery Thought in the Antebellum South, 1830–1860* (Baton Rouge: Louisiana State University Press, 1981); Harry L. Watson, *Jacksonian Politics and Community Conflict: The Emergence of the Second American Party System in Cumberland County, North Carolina* (Baton Rouge: Louisiana State University Press, 1981), 275–77; William J. Cooper Jr., *Liberty and Slavery: Southern Politics to 1860* (New York: Alfred A. Knopf, 1983), 208–9, 219–21; Lacy K. Ford Jr., *Origins of Southern Radicalism: The South Carolina Upcountry, 1800–1860* (New York: Oxford University Press, 1988), 183–84; Carl N. Degler, *The Other South: Southern Dissenters in the Nineteenth Century* (New York: Harper & Row, 1974), 1–96; Glenna Matthews, *The Rise of Public Woman: Woman's Power and Woman's Place in the United States, 1630–1970* (New York: Oxford University Press, 1992), esp. 94.

19. David Brion Davis, *The Problem of Slavery in Western Culture* (Ithaca: Cornell University Press, 1966); Winthrop D. Jordan, *White over Black: American Attitudes toward the Negro, 1550–1812* (Chapel Hill: University of North Carolina Press, 1968); Gary B. Nash, *Red, White, and Black: The Peoples of Early America* (Englewood Cliffs, N.J.: Prentice-Hall, 1974); Drew Gilpin Faust, "The Peculiar South Revisited: White Society, Culture, and Politics in the Antebellum Period, 1800–1860," in *Interpreting Southern History: Historiographical Essays in Honor of Sanford W. Higginbotham,* ed. John B. Boles and Evelyn Thomas Nolen (Baton Rouge: Louisiana State University Press, 1987), 117; Joan D. Hedrick, *Harriet Beecher Stowe: A Life* (New York: Oxford University Press, 1994); Catherine Clinton, "Maria Weston Chapman," in *Portraits of American Women: From Settlement to the Civil War,* ed. G. J. Barker-Benfield and Catherine Clinton (New York: St. Martin's Press, 1991), 149–67; Farnham, *Education of a Southern Belle,* 64. Chapman called Douglass "weak on account of his color" and doubted that one could "'expect better of a slave.'" See also Shirley J. Yee, *Black Women Abolitionists: A Study in Activism, 1828–1860* (Knoxville: University of Tennessee Press, 1992), 90–95. Histori-

ans need more scholarship on the order of Peggy Pascoe's *Relations of Rescue: The Search for Female Moral Authority in the American West, 1874–1939* (New York: Oxford University Press, 1990).

20. Stephanie McCurry, "The Two Faces of Republicanism: Gender and Proslavery Politics in Antebellum South Carolina," *Journal of American History* 78 (Mar. 1992): 1245–64; Susan Strasser, *Never Done: A History of American Housework* (New York: Pantheon Books, 1982); O'Brien and Moltke-Hansen, *Intellectual Life in Antebellum Charleston,* 32–33; Virginia Gearhart Gray, "Activities of Southern Women: 1840–1860," *South Atlantic Quarterly* 27 (July 1928): 269–70; Fox-Genovese, *Within the Plantation Household,* 243–46, 281–89, 360–62. On Northern households, see Jeanne Boydston, *Home and Work: Housework, Wages, and the Ideology of Labor in the Early Republic* (New York: Oxford University Press, 1990); Faye E. Dudden, *Serving Women: Household Service in Nineteenth-Century America* (Middletown, Conn.: Wesleyan University Press, 1983).

21. Several hundred women temporarily changed genders during the Civil War and disguised themselves as men to fight for the Confederacy. See Janet E. Kaufman, " 'Under a Petticoat Flag': Women Soldiers in the Confederacy Army," *Southern Studies* 23 (winter 1984): 363–75; Michael Fellman, "Women and Guerilla Warfare," in *Divided Houses: Gender and the Civil War,* ed. Catherine Clinton and Nina Silber (New York: Oxford University Press, 1992), 156. It seems most unlikely, however, that this happened often in peacetime.

22. All of the above-named scholars at least mention these strictures, but Anne Firor Scott, Catherine Clinton, and Bertram Wyatt-Brown explore them in the most depth. See also Kathryn L. Seidel, "The Southern Belle as An Antebellum Ideal," *Southern Quarterly* 15 (July 1977): 392–93.

23. Ted Ownby, *Subduing Satan: Religion, Recreation, and Manhood in the Rural South, 1865–1920* (Chapel Hill: University of North Carolina Press, 1990); Joe Gray Taylor, *Eating, Drinking, and Visiting in the South: An Informal History* (Baton Rouge: Louisiana State University Press, 1982); "Recollections of Letitia Dabney Miller," 9, Mrs. Cade Drew Gillespie Papers, Small Manuscripts, Special Collections, University of Mississippi. Wyatt-Brown, *Southern Honor,* 117–74, 226–53, 327–61; Clinton, *Plantation Mistress,* 101–22. Among the "respectable" white men who fathered mulatto children were Senator James Henry Hammond and thousands of lesser-known men, such as North Carolina planter Hamilton Brown; see Drew Gilpin Faust, *James Henry Hammond and The Old South: A Design for Mastery* (Baton Rouge: Louisiana State University Press, 1982); Joan E. Cashin, " 'Decidedly Opposed to *the Union*': Women's Culture, Marriage, and Politics in Antebellum South Carolina," *Georgia Historical Quarterly* 77 (winter 1994): 20. Women in the post–Civil War South also had to abide by higher standards of conduct; see John S. Hughes, ed., *The Letters of a Victorian Madwoman* (Columbia: University of South Carolina Press, 1993).

24. Ownby, *Subduing Satan,* 28, 103–4; Eliza E. Polk to Mary B. Polk, 24 Nov. 1851, Yeatman-Polk Collection, Tennessee State Library and Archives. On politics, see Ford, *Origins of Southern Radicalism,* 145–214; Cooper, *Liberty and Slavery,* 192–247; Steven Hahn, *The Roots of Southern Populism: Yeomen Farmers and the Transformation of the Georgia Upcountry, 1850–1890* (New York: Oxford University Press, 1983); Watson, *Jacksonian*

Politics, 282–314; and in the national context, David R. Roediger, *The Wages of Whiteness: Race and the Making of the American Working Class* (London: Verso, 1991). On friendship in the South, see Faust, *James Henry Hammond;* in the North, see Mark C. Carnes and Clyde Griffen, eds., *Meanings for Manhood: Constructions of Masculinity in Victorian America* (Chicago: University of Chicago Press, 1990); and Mary Ann Clawson, *Constructing Brotherhood: Class, Gender, and Fraternalism* (Princeton: Princeton University Press, 1989).

25. See especially Wyatt-Brown, *Southern Honor,* 129–74; Dickson D. Bruce Jr., *Violence and Culture in the Antebellum South* (Austin: University of Texas Press, 1979). See Stowe, *Intimacy and Power,* on ritual and self-control among planter men.

26. On women and politics, see Clinton, *Plantation Mistress,* 180–83; Rable, *Civil Wars,* 15–17; Bynum, *Unruly Women,* 54–55.

27. Lerner, *Grimké Sisters,* 34–38, 147; Bolton, *Poor Whites,* 56; Degler, *The Other South,* 56–79; William W. Freehling, *The Road to Disunion: Secessionists at Bay, 1776–1854,* (New York: Oxford University Press, 1990), 1:103.

28. Lebsock, *Free Women of Petersburg,* 34; Cecil-Fronsman, *Common Whites,* 135–36; Cashin, *A Family Venture,* 109–11; Bynum, *Unruly Women,* 14, 70; Thomas E. Buckley, ed., "'Placed in the Power of Violence': The Divorce Petition of Evalina Gregory Roane, 1824," *Virginia Magazine of History and Biography* 100 (Jan. 1992): 32–35; Louisa Susannah McCord, "Enfranchisement of Woman," in *All Clever Men, Who Make Their Way: Critical Discourse in the Old South,* ed. Michael O'Brien (Fayetteville: University of Arkansas Press, 1982), 349–51. Incest, which typically involved an older man abusing a young female, often included violence; see Peter Bardaglio, "'An Outrage Upon Nature': Incest and the Law in the Nineteenth-Century South," in *In Joy and In Sorrow: Women, Family, and Marriage in the Victorian South, 1830–1900,* ed. Carol Bleser (New York: Oxford University Press, 1991), 32–51. The best study of American domestic violence is Linda Gordon, *Heroes of Their Own Lives: The Politics and History of Family Violence, 1880–1960* (New York: Viking Press, 1988).

29. Elisabeth Muhlenfeld, *Mary Boykin Chesnut: A Biography* (Baton Rouge: Louisiana State University Press, 1981); C. Vann Woodward, ed., *Mary Chesnut's Civil War* (New Haven: Yale University Press, 1981), 262, 729, 29.

30. Fox-Genovese, *Within the Plantation Household,* 339–65; Drew Gilpin Faust, "In Search of the Real Mary Chesnut," *Reviews in American History* 10 (Mar. 1982): 54–59; Joel Williamson, *New People: Miscegenation and Mulattoes in the United States* (New York: Free Press, 1980), 63; James Hugo Johnston, *Race Relations in Virginia and Miscegenation in the South, 1776–1860* (Amherst: University of Massachusetts Press, 1970), 238–48; Nell Painter, "Of *Lily,* Linda Brent, and Freud: A Non-Exceptionalist Approach to Race, Class, and Gender in the Slave South," *Georgia Historical Quarterly* 76 (summer 1992): 258–59. Chesnut's much-discussed diary is not excerpted in this book to provide room for other voices.

31. Robert V. Wells, *Revolutions in Americans' Lives: A Demographic Perspective on the History of Americans, Their Families, and Their Society* (Westport, Conn.: Greenwood Press, 1982), 42, 92–99; Jan Lewis and Kenneth A. Lockridge, "'Sally Has Been Sick': Pregnancy and Family Limitation among Virginia Gentry Women, 1780–1830," *Journal of Social History* 22 (fall 1988): 5–19; McMillen, *Motherhood in the Old South,* 4, 81–88,

192; John D'Emilio and Estelle B. Freedman, *Intimate Matters: A History of Sexuality in America* (New York: Harper & Row, 1988), 59. For a hint that one woman did know how to limit births, see the Marshall letter in the chapter on work.

32. Margaret Ripley Wolfe, *Daughters of Canaan: A Saga of Southern Women* (Lexington: University Press of Kentucky, 1995), 92–94; Wyatt-Brown, *Southern Honor*, 283–91, 300–307; Suzanne D. Lebsock, "Radical Reconstruction and the Property Rights of Southern Women," *Journal of Southern History* 63 (May 1977): 196–216; Lebsock, *Free Women of Petersburg*, 54–86; Marylynn Salmon, "Women and Property in South Carolina: The Evidence from Marriage Settlements, 1730 to 1830," *William and Mary Quarterly*, 3d ser., 34 (Oct. 1982): 655–85; Cashin, *A Family Venture*, 108–9, 191–92; Ellen K. Rothman, *Hands and Hearts: A History of Courtship in America* (New York: Basic Books, 1984), 23–25. Cf. Jane Turner Censer, "'Smiling Through Her Tears': Ante-Bellum Southern Women and Divorce," *American Journal of Legal History* 25 (Jan. 1981): 24–47, who argues that divorce laws in the North and South were substantially the same. See also Norma Basch, *Framing American Divorce: Rules, Mediations, and Representations, 1770–1870* (Chapel Hill: University of North Carolina Press, forthcoming).

33. Sarah Ann Finley to Caroline L. Gordon, 17 Feb. 1853, Hamilton Brown Papers, Southern Historical Collection, University of North Carolina; Clifford Geertz, *Local Knowledge: Further Essays in Interpretive Anthropology* (New York: Basic Books, 1983), 73–93. See also Michael O'Brien, *Rethinking the South: Essays in Intellectual History* (Baltimore: Johns Hopkins University Press, 1988), 46–47, on communities of discourse. This female culture meets Geertz's criteria for "common sense," in that it was imminently practical, but it was anything but direct; see below.

34. T. S. Eliot, *Notes towards the Definition of Culture* (New York: Harcourt, Brace, 1949), 17–18; Ronald J. Zboray, *A Fictive People: Antebellum Economic Development and the American Reading Public* (New York: Oxford University Press, 1993), xv–xvi. I would not characterize this culture as an abstract "personalism," as should be clear below.

35. Scott, *Domination*, 118–21; James Clifford and George E. Marcus, eds., *Writing Culture: The Poetics and Politics of Ethnography* (Berkeley: University of California Press, 1986).

36. William Chester Jordan, *Women and Credit in Pre-Industrial and Developing Societies* (Philadelphia: University of Pennsylvania Press, 1993).

37. On interracial contacts inside and outside the household, see Sally G. McMillen, *Southern Women: Black and White in the Old South* (Arlington Heights, Ill.: Harlan Davidson, 1992), 98–127; Allie Bayne Windham Webb, ed., *Mistress of Evergreen Plantation: Rachel O'Connor's Legacy of Letters, 1823–1845* (Albany: State University of New York Press, 1983); George P. Rawick, ed., *The American Slave: A Composite Autobiography* (Westport, Conn.: Greenwood, 1972); Leah Fortson-Arroyo, "Black and White Women in Antebellum Tennessee, 1796–1865" (Ph.D. diss., Columbia University, forthcoming). On women of mixed race, see T. O. Madden Jr., with Ann L. Miller, *We Were Always Free: The Maddens of Culpeper County, Virginia, A 200-Year Family History*, foreword by Nell Irvin Painter (New York: W. W. Norton, 1992); Adele Logan Alexander, *Ambiguous Lives: Free Women of Color in Rural Georgia, 1789–1879* (Fayetteville: University of Arkansas Press, 1991); Williamson, *New People*.

38. Peter Kolchin, *American Slavery, 1619–1877* (New York: Hill and Wang, 1993), 108, 111, 118. I believe that slave culture was much more robust than this white women's culture, because slaves formed more powerful bonds out of their greater suffering and named their exploitation for what it was; see Leslie Howard Owens, *This Species of Property: Slave Life and Culture in the Old South* (New York: Oxford University Press, 1976), 217. Most scholars agree that some kind of slave culture existed; see Sterling Stuckey, *Slave Culture: Nationalist Theory and the Foundations of Black America* (New York: Oxford University Press, 1987); Lawrence W. Levine, *Black Culture and Black Consciousness: Afro-American Folk Thought from Slavery to Freedom* (New York: Oxford University Press, 1977); Herbert G. Gutman, *The Black Family in Slavery and Freedom, 1750–1925* (New York: Pantheon Books, 1976).

39. On the Southern drive to perfect individual souls or communities rather than reforming society, see John B. Boles, *The Great Revival, 1787–1805: The Origins of the Southern Evangelical Mind* (Lexington: University Press of Kentucky, 1972); Donald G. Mathews, *Religion in the Old South* (Chicago: University of Chicago Press, 1977); Anne C. Loveland, *Southern Evangelicals and the Social Order, 1800–1860* (Baton Rouge: Louisiana State University Press, 1980); and Lynn Lyerly, "When Worlds Collide: Methodism and the Southern Mind, 1770–1810" (Ph.D. diss., Rice University, 1995).

40. Elizabeth Fox-Genovese, "Between Individualism and Community: Autobiographies of Southern Women," in *Located Lives: Place and Idea in Southern Autobiography,* ed. J. Bill Berry (Athens: University of Georgia Press, 1990), 21–23; Stowe, *Intimacy and Power,* 192–223; Susan Phinney Conrad, *Perish the Thought: Intellectual Women in Romantic America, 1830–1860* (New York: Oxford University Press, 1976), 9–11; Lillian Faderman, *Surpassing the Love of Men: Romantic Friendship and Love between Women from the Renaissance to the Present* (New York: William Morrow, 1981). See also Mary S. Hoffschwelle, "Women's Sphere and the Creation of Female Community in the Antebellum South: Three Tennessee Slaveholding Women," *Tennessee Historical Quarterly* 50 (summer 1991): 80–89; and Nancy Long, " 'This Wilderness of Sorrow': White Women in Frontier Arkansas" (master's thesis, University of Arkansas at Little Rock, 1994). On sentimental culture in the white Northern middle class, see Ann Douglas, *The Feminization of American Culture* (New York: Alfred A. Knopf, 1977), and Karen Halttunen, *Confidence Men and Painted Women: A Study of Middle-Class Culture in America, 1830–1870* (New Haven: Yale University Press, 1982).

41. Zboray, *A Fictive People,* 11; Patricia Cline's forthcoming book on American women and travel. On the spread of literacy and print culture a generation earlier in New England, see William J. Gilmore, *Reading Becomes a Necessity of Life: Material and Cultural Life in Rural New England, 1780–1835* (Knoxville: University of Tennessee Press, 1989).

42. Clinton, *Plantation Mistress,* 123–38; Mary Kelley, *Private Woman, Public Stage: Literary Domesticity in Nineteenth-Century America* (New York: Oxford University Press, 1984), viii, ix, 35, 41–42, 93–99, 130–32; Zboray, *A Fictive People,* 12–13. See also Michael O'Brien, *A Character of Hugh Legare* (Knoxville: University of Tennessee Press, 1985), 19, 243, 276, for the dismal choices available to Legare's sisters Mary and Eliza. On "knots of interaction" within a culture, see Rhys Isaac, *The Transformation of Virginia, 1740–*

1790 (Chapel Hill: Institute of Early American History and Culture, by the University of North Carolina Press, 1982), 346.

43. Matthews, *Rise of Public Woman,* 52–71; Linda Kerber, *Women of the Republic: Intellect and Ideology in Revolutionary America* (Chapel Hill: University of North Carolina Press, 1980); Jan Lewis, "The Republican Wife: Virtue and Seduction in the Early Republic," *William and Mary Quarterly* 44, 3d ser. (Oct. 1987): 689–721.

44. Wyatt-Brown, *Southern Honor,* 25–61, 226–53. On public morality in the nineteenth-century North, see Mark E. Kann, *On the Man Question: Gender and Civic Virtue in America* (Philadelphia: Temple University Press, 1991).

45. On politically conservative women, see Cashin, " 'Decidedly Opposed to *the Union.*' " On what seems to be some unusual instances of fund-raising by Virginia elite women, see Elizabeth R. Varon, " 'The Ladies Are Whigs': Lucy Barbour, Henry Clay, and Nineteenth-Century Virginia Politics," *Virginia Calvalcade* 42 (autumn 1992): 73–83.

46. John Mack Faragher, *Women and Men on the Overland Trail* (New Haven: Yale University Press, 1979), 181. This discomfort lasted into the twentieth century; see Martha H. Swain, "The Public Role of Southern Women," in Hawks and Skemp, *Sex, Race, and the Role of Women in the South,* 37–57; LeeAnn Whites, "Rebecca Latimer Felton and the Problem of 'Protection' in the New South," in *Visible Women: New Essays on American Activism,* ed. Nancy A. Hewitt and Suzanne Lebsock (Urbana: University of Illinois Press, 1993), 41–61.

47. Faust, "Peculiar South Revisited," 114–15; Mary Field Belenky, Blythe McVicker Clinchy, Nancy Rule Goldberger, and Jill Mattuck Tarule, *Women's Ways of Knowing: The Development of Self, Voice, and Mind* (New York: Basic Books, 1986); Robin Lakoff, *Language and Woman's Place* (New York: Harper Colophon Books, 1975). See also Jimerson, *Private Civil War,* 8–11.

48. H. E. Sterkx, *Partners in Rebellion: Alabama Women in the Civil War* (Rutherford, N. J.: Fairleigh Dickinson University Press, 1970), 17–36; Mary Elizabeth Massey, *Bonnet Brigades* (New York: Alfred A. Knopf, 1966), 27; Katharine M. Jones, *Heroines of Dixie: Confederate Women Tell Their Story of the War* (Indianapolis: Bobbs-Merrill, 1955), 3–29; Francis Butler Simkins and James Welch Patton, *The Women of the Confederacy* (Richmond: Garrett and Massie, 1936), 1–13; Catherine Clinton, *Tara Revisited: Women, War, and the Plantation Legend* (Abbeville, N.Y.: Abbeville Press, 1995), 56; Reid Mitchell, *The Vacant Chair: The Northern Soldier Leaves Home* (New York: Oxford University Press, 1993), 89–113; Sara Ruddick, *Maternal Thinking: Toward a Politics of Peace* (Boston: Beacon Press, 1989), 155, 219. Drew Gilpin Faust, "Altars of Sacrifice: Confederate Women and the Narratives of War," *Journal of American History* 76 (Mar. 1990): 1200–1228, describes how many women lost faith in the Confederacy after the war began.

49. For parallels in the "culture of consolation" among workers in late-nineteenth-century London, see Gareth Stedman Jones, *Languages of Class: Studies in English Working-Class History, 1832–1982* (Cambridge: Cambridge University Press, 1983), 223–35, 237.

50. Scott, *Domination,* 85–91.

51. On the different ways that contemporary women and men use language, see George Steiner, *A Reader* (New York: Penguin Books, 1984), 375–82. On contempo-

rary mothers who teach their daughters to accept the status quo, including abusive treatment within the family, see Adrienne Rich, *Of Woman Born: Motherhood As Experience and Institution* (New York: W. W. Norton, 1976), 243–46.

52. C. E. Norton to J. R. Lowell, 6 Apr. 1855, in *Letters of Charles Eliot Norton with Biographical Comment,* ed. Sara Norton and M. A. DeWolfe Howe, (Boston: Houghton Mifflin, 1913), 1:126–27, quoted in Scott, *Southern Lady,* 50.

53. O'Brien, *Rethinking the South,* 5, 38–56, argues that Romanticism provided the framework for all of antebellum Southern culture. I wish to suggest that women may have interpreted the romantic ethos in a particular way.

54. Wolfe, *Daughters of Canaan,* 77–78. On a few devout white women from an earlier generation who spoke out only to be silenced, see Lyerly, "When Worlds Collide."

55. Anne Firor Scott finds considerable discontent within the South in the last antebellum decade; see "Women's Perspectives on the Patriarchy in the 1850s," in her *Making the Invisible Woman Visible* (Urbana: University of Illinois, 1984), 175–89.

56. Fox-Genovese, *Within the Plantation Household,* 42.

57. See, for example, Drew Gilpin Faust, *Mothers of Invention: Women of the Slave-holding South in the American Civil War* (Chapel Hill: University of North Carolina Press, forthcoming).

58. Augusta Jane Evans, *Macaria, or Altars of Sacrifice,* ed. Drew Gilpin Faust (Baton Rouge: Louisiana State University Press, 1992); Augusta Jane Evans, *Beulah,* ed. Elizabeth Fox-Genovese (Baton Rouge: Louisiana State University Press, 1992); Karen Manners Smith, "Marion Harland: The Making of a Household Word" (Ph.D. diss., University of Massachusetts, 1990); Jane Turner Censer, *The Reconstruction of White Southern Womanhood, 1865–1895* (forthcoming); Elizabeth Moss, *Domestic Novelists in the Old South: Defenders of Southern Culture* (Baton Rouge: Louisiana State University Press, 1992); Cashin, " 'Decidedly Opposed to the Union,' " 10–11; Jon W. Finson, *The Voices That Are Gone: Themes in Nineteenth-Century American Popular Song* (New York: Oxford University Press, 1994). See also Anne Goodwyn Jones, *Tomorrow Is Another Day: The Woman Writer in the South, 1859–1936* (Baton Rouge: Louisiana State University Press, 1981). On women and music, see the John L. Bailey Papers at the Southern Historical Collection at the University of North Carolina and the Sheet Music Collection at the Virginia Historical Society.

59. Calder Loth, "A Note on the Plantations and Architecture," in David King Gleason, *Virginia Plantation Homes: Photographs and Text by David King Gleason* (Baton Rouge: Louisiana State University Press, 1989), viii; Kenneth A. Lockridge, *On the Sources of Patriarchal Rage: The Commonplace Books of William Byrd and Thomas Jefferson and the Gendering of Power in the Eighteenth Century* (New York: New York University Press, 1992), 72–73; Dolores Hayden, *The Grand Domestic Revolution: A History of Feminist Designs for American Homes, Neighborhoods, and Cities* (Cambridge: MIT Press, 1981). See also John Michael Vlach, *Back of the Big House: The Architecture of Plantation Slavery* (Chapel Hill: University of North Carolina Press, 1993); Kenneth L. Ames and Gerald W. R. Ward, eds., *Decorative Arts and Household Furnishings in America, 1650–1920: An Annotated Bibliography* (University Press of Virginia, for Winterthur, 1989); Johanna Miller Lewis, "A

Social and Architectural History of the Girls' Boarding School Building at Salem, North Carolina," *North Carolina Historical Review* 66 (Apr. 1989): 136–40; Isaac, *Transformation,* 18–42; Charlene Boyer-Lewis, "Ladies and Gentlemen on Display: Planter Society and Gender at the Virginia Springs, 1790–1860" (Ph.D. diss., University of Virginia, forthcoming). On the Northern and Mid-Atlantic states, see Richard L. Bushman, *The Refinement of America: Persons, Houses, Cities* (New York: Alfred A. Knopf, 1992); Thomas J. Schlereth, *Cultural History and Material Culture: Everyday Life, Landscapes, Museums,* with a foreword by Kenneth L. Ames (Ann Arbor: UMI Research Press, 1990). On England, see Leonore Davidoff and Catherine Hall, *Family Fortunes: Men and Women of the English Middle Class, 1780–1850* (Chicago: University of Chicago Press, 1987).

60. Fox-Genovese, *Within the Plantation Household,* 212–16; Clinton, *Plantation Mistress,* 99–100; Shari Benstock and Suzanne Ferris, eds., *On Fashion* (New Brunswick: Rutgers University Press, 1994), 8; Margaret Jones Bolsterli, ed., *A Remembrance of Eden: Harriet Bailey Bullock Daniel's Memories of a Frontier Plantation in Arkansas, 1849–1872* (Fayetteville: University of Arkansas Press, 1993). See also Ann Masson and Bryce Reveley, "When Life's Brief Sun Was Set: Portraits of Southern Women in Mourning, 1830–1860," *Southern Quarterly* 27 (fall 1988): 33–56. On the marketing of fashion, see Neil McKendrick, John Brewer, and J. H. Plumb, *The Birth of a Consumer Society: The Commercialization of Eighteenth-Century England* (London: Europa Publications, 1982), 34–99.

61. George Brown Tindall, *Natives and Newcomers: Ethnic Southerners and Southern Ethnics* (Athens: University of Georgia Press, 1994); Grady McWhiney, *Cracker Culture: Celtic Ways in the Old South,* with prologue by Forrest McDonald (Tuscaloosa: University of Alabama Press, 1988); Randall M. Miller and Jon L. Wakelyn, eds., *Catholics in the Old South: Essays on Church and Culture* (Macon, Ga.: Mercer University Press, 1983); Michael T. Parrish, *Richard Taylor, Soldier Prince of Dixie* (Chapel Hill: University of North Carolina Press, 1992); Eli N. Evans, *Judah P. Benjamin, the Jewish Confederate* (New York: Free Press, 1988); Kate Chopin, *The Awakening* (Chicago: H. S. Stone, 1899); Thomas Bonner Jr., "Christianity and Catholicism in the Fiction of Kate Chopin," in *In Old New Orleans,* ed. W. Kenneth Holditch (Jackson: University Press of Mississippi, 1983), 118–25; Emily Toth, *Kate Chopin* (New York: William Morrow, 1990); Helen Taylor, *Gender, Race, and Region in the Writings of Grace King, Ruth McEnergy Stuart, and Kate Chopin* (Baton Rouge: Louisiana State University Press, 1989); Dolores Egger Labbé, "Women in Early-Nineteenth-Century Louisiana" (Ph.D. diss., University of Delaware, 1975), 51, 59–61, 143, 157, 158. See also Willard B. Gatewood, *Aristocrats of Color: The Black Elite, 1880–1920* (Bloomington: Indiana University Press, 1990); John Boles, "The Discovery of Southern Religious History," in Boles and Nolen, *Interpreting Southern History,* 524, 544–45.

62. Jean H. Baker, *Mary Todd Lincoln: A Biography* (New York: W. W. Norton, 1987); Anne C. Loveland, *Lillian Smith, A Southerner Confronting the South* (Baton Rouge: Louisiana State University Press, 1986); Virginia Clay-Clopton, *A Belle of the Fifties: Memoirs of Mrs. Clay of Alabama, Put into Narrative Form by Ada Sterling* (New York: Doubleday, Page, 1905); Carol K. Bleser and Frederick M. Heath, "The Impact of the Civil War on a Southern Marriage: Clement and Virginia Tunstall Clay of Alabama," *Civil War History* 30 (Sept. 1984); Carolyn G. Heilbrun, *Writing a Woman's Life* (New York:

W. W. Norton, 1988); Clement Claiborne Clay Papers at Perkins Library, Duke University. For a multigenerational biography of a family, see Bertram Wyatt-Brown, *The House of Percy: Honor, Melancholy, and Imagination in a Southern Family* (New York: Oxford University Press, 1994). On the preservationist Lucy Parke Bagby, see forthcoming work by Joyce McAllister, and on the Bagby family, see forthcoming work by Elizabeth Glade. On other subjects for biography, see Sandra Gioia Treadway, "New Directions in Virginia Women's History," *Virginia Magazine of History and Biography* 100 (Jan. 1992): 25.

63. Dorothy Sterling, ed., *We Are Your Sisters: Black Women in the Nineteenth Century* (New York: W. W. Norton, 1984); Gerda Lerner, *The Female Experience: An American Documentary* (Indianapolis: Bobbs-Merrill, 1977); Gerda Lerner, *Black Women in White America: A Documentary History* (New York: Pantheon Books, 1972). For other scholarship on slave women that emphasizes their alienation from whites, see Ann Patton Malone, *Sweet Chariot: Slave Family and Household Structure in Nineteenth-Century Louisiana* (Chapel Hill: University of North Carolina Press, 1992); Jacqueline Jones, *Labor of Love, Labor of Sorrow: Black Women, Work, and Family from Slavery to the Present* (New York: Basic Books, 1985); Jacqueline Jones, " 'My Mother was Much of a Woman': Black Women, Work, and the Family under Slavery," *Feminist Studies* 8 (summer 1982): 235–69; Deborah Gray White, *Arn't I A Woman? Female Slaves in the Plantation South* (New York: W. W. Norton, 1985); Paula Giddings, *When and Where I Enter: The Impact of Black Women on Race and Sex in America* (New York: William Morrow, 1984); Robert S. Starobin, ed., *Blacks in Bondage: Letters of American Slaves* (New York: New Viewpoints, 1974). Evelyn Brooks Higginbotham finds that black and white women's missionary groups occasionally worked together in the late nineteenth century; see *Righteous Discontent: The Women's Movement in the Black Baptist Church, 1880–1920* (Cambridge: Harvard University Press, 1993), 88–119.

64. Nancy F. Cott, ed., *Root of Bitterness: Documents of the Social History of American Women* (Boston: Northeastern University Press, 1972); Nancy Woloch, ed., *Early American Women: A Documentary History, 1600–1900* (Belmont, Calif.: Wadsworth Publishing, 1992); Joyce D. Goodfriend and Claudia M. Christie, eds., *Lives of American Women: A History with Documents* (Boston: Little, Brown, 1981). Among many letter collections and editions of diaries, see Michael O'Brien, ed., *An Evening When Alone: Four Journals of Single Women in the South, 1827–1867* (Charlottesville: University Press of Virginia, 1993); Virginia Ingraham Burr, ed., *The Secret Eye: The Journal of Ella Gertrude Clanton Thomas, 1848–1889,* introduction by Nell Irvin Painter (Chapel Hill: University of North Carolina Press, 1990); Thomas Dyer, ed., *To Raise Myself a Little: The Diaries and Letters of Jennie, A Georgia Teacher, 1851–1886* (Athens: University of Georgia Press, 1982); and Robert Manson Myers, *The Children of Pride: A True Story of Georgia and the Civil War* (New Haven: Yale University Press, 1972). At this writing, Carol Bleser's series contains ten titles.

65. I could not determine the class backgrounds of some women, such as those with common surnames whose documents did not provide any clues about their economic status. Sallie Collins, whose letter is excerpted in the chapter on friendship, is such a person.

FAMILY

THE FAMILY WAS THE CRUCIBLE for Southern women's culture. Here many women developed close ties across generations and within generations. From the time they were girls, they learned reciprocity, and throughout their lives they exchanged such household items as bonnets, peppers, dresses, and preserves. All of these transactions, no matter how small, helped households run more smoothly. With their conversations, letters, and visits, women also hoped to promote family harmony. Men expected them to take up this role, most women did it willingly, even joyfully, and they were glad to teach their daughters, sisters, nieces, cousins, and granddaughters to play the part.

Within the family, men's and women's interests sometimes diverged, however, whether it was on practical questions such as arranging a trip or legal matters such as writing a will. This chapter illustrates some of those private struggles between the sexes. But the documents also show how the family held conflicts in check and discouraged the expression of discontent. The family is a conservative institution in most societies, and in this society it was an especially powerful one. Why might this be the case? How were conflicts between the sexes resolved? What resources did this institution offer women?

Eliza D. E. Donelson to her niece Mary Eastin, 8 March 1826, from Florence, Alabama, to Nashville, Tennessee. Yeatman-Polk Collection, Tennessee State Library and Archives.

Eliza Butler was born into a prosperous family in New Orleans and married John Donelson in 1823, after an eight-year courtship. This letter throws into stark relief the gulf between the sexes: on the one hand, Eliza Donelson's lonely marriage, her husband's shady business dealings, and an absurd local duel and, on the other hand, the world of kinship revolving around her women relatives.

My Dear Mary,

Your affectionate letters came early to hand, and you will believe your Aunt, when she assures you that her wretched state of Health, is the only apology she has to offer for her seeming neglect to her Mother and many other conections and friends. our Conection together with my own little family, with the exception of myself are all quite well. I hird from Sister Coffee's Yesterday. as usual I am alone, my Husband having gone over the river to take possession of a set of Mills which have been erected by a Poor Old Man some two or three years ago on a place of your Uncle's. Brother William can tell you where it is, as it is the place on which Genl. Brown and his Brother have commenced to hire for sale. this Old Man was under the impression that the land was vacant and I suppose calculated on becoming purchaser at the land sales. the timber is very valuable as it is a Mountainous Country and thickly timber'd with pine. I expect my Husband home on tomorrow and shall go up to Genl. Coffee's to spend several days.[1] I wish you could see my Mary Bell Donelly as she calls her self. she can call you all quite distinctly, and for Music and Dancing, she can bear the palm from any Donelson that can be found.[2] You must not tell Sister Emily this, as I am told on good athority that she will dispute the point with me. our love to her and Andrew,[3] and say that they have our fervent wishes for their prosperity and happiness—To sister Catherine McMartin, Brothers William and Stockly, Uncle and Aunt Jackson,[4] and all other of our Conection that you may see, remember us, and to our Dear Father and Mother, say everything that affection can dictate. Your Uncle had late letters from Orleans. your Mother was then in pirfect Health. whin you see any of my Nashvill friends remember us to them in the moast affectionate terms—

particularly to the Judy and Mrs. MacNanney. the land sales will take place in May and previous to that time you may look for us, as your Uncle will take me to Mothers, and from thence go to Huntsvill to the sales. your acquaintances in this quarter are well, particularly Mr. Dawson. tis said he had a little fray the other day with Doct. Woodcock no blood was lost, nothing more than a little Genteel scratching—my Moll sends love to her Grand Father and Mother and to her dear little Cousins, and accept much for your self from your affectionate Aunt Eliza E. Donelson.

Mary Eastin

    1. Her brother-in-law John Coffee, who had moved to Florence ten years before.
    2. Meaning she can dance well.
    3. Probably her sister-in-law Emily Donelson, who had recently had a child. Her husband was Andrew J. Donelson.
    4. Other in-laws, including Andrew Jackson, who would be elected president of the United States in 1828, and his wife Rachel Donelson Jackson, who died that year.

Maria Louisa C. Marshall to her sister Eliza C. Gould, 7 February 1828, from Woodville, Mississippi, to Tuscaloosa, Alabama. Maria Louisa Chotard Marshall and Family Papers, Hill Memorial Library, Louisiana and Lower Mississippi Valley Collections, Louisiana State University.

Maria Marshall, Eliza Gould, and Sarah Dunbar were daughters of a planter, and all married well. But they, like many white Southern women, had to travel with male escorts whenever they wished to leave home. Marshall finds this custom frustrating, and she is particularly exasperated because her brother-in-law will not arrange a visit to her sister Sarah who has just given birth to a child. Here she also mocks Andrew Jackson's wife, Rachel, and the fanfare of his presidential campaign.

My dear Sister,

    Your last letter has been left unanswered (as usual) much longer than it should have been; but you do not flatter yourself your vanity prevents your attributing it want of Affections; for there is scarcely an hour that I do not think of your dear family, and indeed it often appears strange to me, that I am not fonder of it, but really my aversion to the pen is increasing daily. I have—however just trudged through a letter to our poor Sarah. I have not heard from her but once since the birth of her infant. Mr. Dunbar then wrote that she was doing very well; I wrote to Sarah about the 1st of December that I had no way of going to see her, that our gig was a mere wreck and there was no possibility of borrowing, but if Mr. D. would send for me I would go up and stay with her untill she recovered if it was [an] hour or month's.[1] Mr. D. replied that she was delighted to hear that I would go and would send down the carriage immediately, but "lo and behold" after being in readiness two or three weeks, here comes down a lame account, that the horses had the distemper, and that his driver was not trusty, and might break the carriage, and all that sort of stuff; but the next time I ask for his coach, it will be in readiness, with four horses if required.

I expect William had much rather have the money as a cashier than the honour as Director of the Bank. I do not think he need fear being made Governour, since S. L. Verry has been made judge, for you may depend they are bringing him along by degrees to the highest office of the state.[2] who knows but he may oppose our dear old General. I suppose you have seen the particulars of his visit to New Orleans, as you have a Jackson[3] paper in your city, but have you seen aunt Rachael's reply to the Governer of Louisiana, when he presented her the bedstead, a[r]moir, and table used by her "illustrious husband" during their visit to New Orleans, it is very much questioned whether the old lady put her wits to work on the occasion, but as you know her better than I do you may be enabled to judge whether it is in her style or now,[4] however be this as it may, the General's visit with all the parade of his party went off rather quietly, and it is very questionable whether after all the fine speeches and Big dinners, he gets the vote of Louisiana for that office to which he so modestly aspires.[5] We in this part of the country, that is my Husband and me, altho' always sensibly alive to gratitude, are a little sceptical upon that little item of qualification. . . .

1. William Dunbar, Sarah's husband, was a rich planter in Adams County, Mississippi.

2. William Gould, Eliza's husband. Neither Gould nor Verry were ever elected governor of Alabama.

3. Andrew Jackson visited New Orleans for a grand ceremony on January 8, 1828, to commemorate his victory over the British in the Battle of New Orleans in 1815. He was also campaigning for the presidency.

4. The gifts probably date from the Battle of New Orleans, in 1815. Rachel Robards Jackson (1767–1828) was barely literate and in her last years had a reputation for eccentricity. She also unwittingly committed bigamy when she married Jackson in 1791,

before her divorce from her first husband was final. Eliza Gould may have met her, because several of the Jackson nieces and nephews settled near Tuscaloosa.

5. Andrew Jackson did in fact win Louisiana (and Alabama and Mississippi) in the presidential election of 1828.

Will of Justina Maria Henrietta Campbell Taylor, 24 November 1828. John T. Coit Family Papers, from the Collections of the Dallas Historical Society.

A rich widow when she wed planter John Taylor in 1821, Justina Campbell shielded her property with a marriage settlement. Therefore she could distribute her estate as she saw fit. In careful language she makes allowances for contingencies in the lives of her daughter and mother, suggesting that Campbell either knew a great deal about the law or consulted a savvy attorney. She provides for her beloved daughter first and places that property beyond her son-in-law's control; then she bequeaths property to other relatives. For reasons unknown, she withholds a bequest from one nephew until his grandmother dies.

State of South Carolina
I Justina Maria Henrietta Campbell wife of John Taylor Junior of Cheraw in the said state Merchant under the power reserved to me in and by my marriage settlement before marriage dated the twenty-ninth day of December in the year of our Lord one thousand eight hundred and twenty one do make and publish this my last will and testament.[1]

Imprimis[2] whereas my dear and esteemed Husband has a life estate in all the property to which I am entitled and as by the blessing of God he is possessed of an ample fortune of his own I deem it of no consequence to him to leave him any of my property in perpetuity. I therefore give devise and bequeath direct limit and appoint all my Estate and property real and personal whatsoever to my dear daughter Anna Maria Coit her heirs and assigns forever to and for her own sole and separate use and without being in any manner liable to the debts contracts or control of any Husband who in she may have with full power and authority to my said Daughter notwithstanding coverture[3] to dispose thereof or of any part or parts therefore in her life time by deed or instrument under her hand and seal executed in the presence of two witnesses or in and by her last will and testament in the same manner and to the same effect as if she were a feme sole.[4]

But should my said Daughter die without leaving lawfully begotten off-spring at the time of her death and without having disposed of the said Estate real and personal or the proceeds thereof or of any part or parts thereof absolutely in her lifetime or in and by her last will and testament then and in that case I give devise and bequeath direct limit and appoint all my said Estate real and personal or the proceeds thereof or of any part of parts thereof and any and every part of the said Estate real and personal that may be in possession of my said daughter at the time of her death unto my dear and respected mother Henrietta Campbell relict of McMillan Campbell[5] my sister Margaret D. Campbell[6] the children of my sister Susannah C. King[7] and my son-in-law John Calkins Coit[8] of Cheraw to be equally divided among them share and share alike the children of my sister Susannah C. King exclusive of my nephew McMillan C. King taking among them the share which their mother if alive would have taken and at the death of my dear and honored mother I wish and direct that her share may descend and go to my said nephew McMillan Campbell King absolutely and forever.

I hereby make and constitute and apoint my dear and esteemed husband John Taylor Junior my brother Mitchell King[9] of Charleston and my son-in-law John Calkins Coit of Cheraw as my executors of this my last will and testament In witness whereof I have hereunto set my hand and seal this the twenty-fourth day of November in the eighteen hundred and twenty eighth year of our Lord. Justina Maria Henrietta Campbell.

1. A few wealthy women protected their dowries and other property with marriage settlements, which were roughly equivalent to prenuptial agreements. John Taylor owned seventy-one slaves in 1830, but the size of Mrs. Taylor's holdings is not specified.

2. Latin for "in the first place"; once commonly used to introduce the first clause in a will.

3. Meaning the usual legal assumption that a married woman's property belongs to her husband and is under his control.

4. Translates as "an unmarried woman," meaning that she could dispose of the property as she wished.

5. *Relict* is the archaic term for widow.

6. Her unmarried sister.

7. Her nieces and nephews.

8. In 1830 Coit owned seventeen slaves in Chesterfield County, South Carolina. He and his wife had one child.

9. Actually Taylor's brother-in-law, Mitchell King owned eighteen slaves in Charleston in 1830. He began his professional life as a headmaster, then studied law, and later became a wealthy judge.

Katherine Ambler to her sons John J. Ambler Jr. and Philip St. George Ambler, 5 May 1835, [probably from Richmond, Virginia] to Amherst County Court House, Virginia. Ambler and Barbour Family Papers, Special Collections Department, Alderman Library, University of Virginia.

In 1835 Katherine Bush Norton Ambler was sixty-two years old and the spouse of planter John J. Ambler Sr. The family was immensely rich—her husband owned thirteen farms and plantations—and their ancestors had lived in Virginia since the pioneers settled Jamestown in the seventeenth century. Although she brought a substantial dowry to the marriage, she did not make a marriage settlement as Justina Taylor did. When Mr. Ambler drew up his will in 1835, he confided in no one, not even his wife. That ignited several family quarrels, for his sons wanted him to exclude their two sisters from the estate. Mrs. Ambler has other ideas about equality between the sexes and between siblings in the family, as this passionate letter reveals.

My Dear Sons,

The day after you left us (which was a melancholy one to me, on more accts. than that of Parting with you) your Papa made Ella (poor Ella) write to Conway Robinson[1] telling him that he was content [and] he would decline writing the Will—and that niether of you, were at all Privy to the Contents of the Papers which he had entrusted to him (C. Robinson) no more than he, <u>CR,</u> was—now my Sons you know more on this subject than I do. all I know is, that I do not know, and may God grant in his infinite goodness I never may know the contents of those papers. I have often told you twenty years ago Mr. Tucker[2] the sinsearest Friend our Family has ever had Positively refused to write such a will as being inconsistant with his Idea of <u>right</u>—it rested for years, when another counsel was (secretly from me) consulted. God arrested that, for he[3] soon sicken'd and Died. again it is tryd, when the third Man who has been Solicited says the injustice which is intended compels him to decline being the Counsil —

my Belov'd Children — you are all equally near & Dear to my heart. I wish you all, with the other Children, to [be] equally dealt with.[4] you must know if you will reflect that this Intention is not just to your Sisters[5] — and if this injustice is done to them — who, my Dear Sons, is to reap the Benefit let me ask you, if you believe Father ever had Daughters or Brothers ever had Sisters more sincerely or afftly. attached than your Father & yourselves have — now my Sons, shew a disinterested love & that Blessed integrity & sound Principles which Christ advises & God approves — do to others as you w'd have others do to you — endeavor to have the benefit be equal and each will love and rejoice in the other — and be Satisfied, for conscience will approve — and the Bequeather in a Dyeing hour will feel no regret[6] — the time is gone Bye when the world approv'd of such inequality — think you there has ever such a thing transpired before of two Men refusing to write a will on acct. of the Glaring disparity — how did you feel, when it was suggested that there was one, to be more amply Provided for than you[7] — again I say I trust I shall never know the extant of the wrong intended to my Belovd Daughters — you both have much influence with your Father (my trust is in God) but do you do, what you can approve in a dyeing hour and contribute to a Blessed union upon earth securing to us, a Blessed union in heaven —

It has been my Pride to instill into your hearts and to mark in your lives that noblest Virtue, humanity can boast of a religious integrity of heart. that shall lay you unspotted in your graves — I thank God that I feel I have fulfilled my Trust and Duty to you both. May God give the Blessing thro' his Son, yr. affn. Mother K. Ambler.

P.S. notwithstanding my Dear Sons — I am agitated to trembling I cannot forgo the following acct. of Norbonne[8] — thare has been a great Baptist Convention here on Tuysday last. N. recived a note from a Mr. Fuller of who he became acquainted with, to the North — a gay young man saying he was now in Richd., as one of the delegates a Baptist Preacher — N. invited us to dine with him in conf. [conference?] with two English Preachers. Mr. Fuller and several other of the ministers Watkins Leigh, Mr. Call & Wickham[9] we were all pleased — when Mr. Fuller left him in the eveng. he told he wld Preach in the [Morning?] N. and most attended — he was in my estimation superior to Mr. Johns — I heard him tell N. he should see him again to talk with him on the important subject of his Soul — may God make it a day of

Grace to N. God Bless you my Sons—and let me see that day of Grace to you all—my very best love to my Dear Betsy & dear little John [10]—yr. K. A.

Mr. Leigh says Mr. Fuller was at the Bar a man of Tallant & Eminance.

1. "Ella" and Conway Robinson are somehow related to the Amblers.
2. Probably Henry St. George Tucker (1780–1848), a well-known jurist and lawyer who handled inheritance cases for other prominent Virginian families in the second decade of the nineteenth century.
3. The unknown lawyer, not Tucker, who worked on the will.
4. The Amblers had eight children who lived to adulthood, two daughters and six sons. Although inheritance practices varied in the antebellum era, the equitable division of the estate among all heirs was becoming the norm.
5. Katherine Ambler Moncure (1802–50), wife of Henry W. Moncure, and Elizabeth Ambler Nicholas (1804–77), wife of Robert C. Nicholas. Both sisters married well-to-do slaveowners. Neither Mr. Ambler nor his sons ever tried to justify their desire to treat the Ambler daughters in this way.
6. Meaning that her husband will feel no regret when he dies. He passed away the next year, in 1836. Unfortunately, the will went up in smoke when Richmond burned in 1865, leaving Mr. Ambler's decision a mystery.
7. John J. Ambler Sr. earlier considered leaving most of his estate to John J. Ambler Jr., who owned fifty-seven slaves in 1830, or to his youngest son, William Ambler, who lived with his parents. Philip St. George Ambler owned forty-seven slaves in 1830.
8. Daniel Norbonne Norton, her son from a previous marriage.
9. Watkins Leigh (1781–1849) served in the state assembly and the U.S. Congress; Mr. Call was probably a relative of her daughter-in-law Elizabeth Call Norton; John Wickham was a family friend and prominent attorney. His daughter was Leigh's third wife.
10. Probably Elizabeth Barbour Ambler and John Ambler, wife and son of John J. Ambler.

Eliza D. Eastin to her grandmother Mary Purnell Donelson, n.d. 1836, from Franklin, Tennessee, to near Nashville, Tennessee. Yeatman-Polk Collection, Tennessee State Library and Archives.

Eliza Eastin, the daughter of Rachel Donelson Eastin and William Eastin, was born in 1817. (She was also Eliza Donelson's niece.) Young Eliza was devoted to her maternal grandmother, Mary Purnell Donelson, a pioneer of the Tennessee frontier and widow of John Donelson. Eastin is already aware of divisions between the sexes in the family, as these ingenuous comments disclose, and the close attachments that mothers and daughters could develop for each other.

Dear Grandma,

I hope you will excuse my apparent neglect, altho I have not writen to you my dear Grandma, I have often thought of you in your late trials, & afflictions. I suppose Uncle Jack has told you Susie had another fine daughter. it is really a fine child. She has named it Emily Donelson after our dear Aunt.[1] Sister is very well, Rachel has been out for the last week, her health is not very good. She is very weak, & languid. sister is dosing her with bitters & I think she will soon be well again. Don't be uneasy about her Grandma. It is nothing serious. <u>I expect you can account for it.</u>[2]

We were <u>very</u> sorry to hear of John & Alex quitting college.[3] I expect they had no earthly excuse, just wanted to take a frollick. What does make boys so bad. I expect Aunt Coffees boys have given her more trouble than all the girls and everything else.[4] Sister Mary says she is perfectly satisfied with having girls.[5] She can keep them at home & teach them to knit & sew. but I hope & pray John may make a good & clever man. Brother is going to Carolina this spring. I don't expect Sister will be able to go with him. I expect she will go with as far as Nashville. I hope you will have a visit from Aunt Coffee soon. I was very sorry to hear of cousin Elizabeth's bad health, but I hope God in his mercy will spare her. It would be a grievous thing if she should be taken from her mother. Sister join with me in love to you Aunt Phila Uncle Stockly, & all our near relations. God bless you dear Grandma. Your affectionate child, <u>E. D. Eastin.</u>

1. Mary Donelson's youngest daughter, the wife of Andrew Jackson Donelson and the niece of President Andrew Jackson.

2. Meaning that Rachel is recovering from childbirth and that Mrs. Donelson, who bore thirteen children over twenty-seven years, will understand how she feels.

3. Probably John and Alexander Coffee, two of Eliza's cousins, who were in their teens.

4. Mary Donelson Coffee (1793–1871), wife of a planter in Rutherford County, Tennessee, daughter of Mary Purnell Donelson, and aunt of the writer.

5. Eliza's sister Mary Ann Eastin Polk (1810–47), who married Lucius Polk in 1832 and had several daughters.

Eliza L. W. Wright Journal. Wright-May-Thom Family Papers, MS 2416, Manuscripts Division, Maryland Historical Society Library.

Eliza Wright was thirty-six years old when she wrote this diary entry. Her spouse, William Wright, was a merchant, diplomat, and planter in the Chesapeake Bay area. She kept this journal for her daughters ("my dear girls"), which may explain her remarks about sexuality. The offhand tone of the entry suggests that such conversations may have been common between women when they were alone. Her caller violates custom, however, by making her remarks in front of men.

15 January 1836.

. . . She said, "Mrs. Wright, were you not very much frightened the night you were married? I am sure I should have died if my husband had not been <u>particularly</u> kind." She said here one evening that it was bad enough to have children by a man you loved, let alone one you could not—she said this before gentlemen and made Vic so mad.[1] Another time I said to her when she came up to put on her bonnet, "Why Mrs. C., you complain so much I shall suspect you." "That is it, Mrs. W., that is it. I am just <u>four weeks</u> advanced, and my belts are this much too small for me." Poor thing, I don't know whether she will be able to get in any of her dresses by the time she returns from Washington.[2]

1. One of Wright's sons.
2. "Mrs. C." may be the daughter-in-law of Congressman Jeremiah Crabb (1760–1800) of Montgomery County, Maryland. Nothing else is known about her identity.

Leah Byrd Haynie Reminiscences, 1837. MS 1837, Manuscripts Division, Maryland Historical Society Library.

Leah Haynie wrote this memoir in 1837, when she was a single woman in her forties. A native of Maryland, she grew up in Louisiana after her father, Richard Haynie, died in the 1790s. She obviously acquired a fine education and was ac-

*quainted with the classics, as many women were not. Haynie, who turned down
a proposal in her youth, makes observations about married life that are suffused
with fatalism about the range of white women's choices in the Old South.*

Oh! this married life, 'tis the ordeal for woman; or shall I call it a purga-
tory by which they are fitted for Heaven by having encountered all sorts of
horrors, until the spirit (if perchance it is not broken) is completely puri-
fied. . . . While I pity my own sex I would not seem to cast a slur on the
holy and indispensable ordinance of marriage. If she lives, woman must
make the choice to marry or become that shocking thing, an old maid. In
her wisdom she more frequently tries the first of the two, perhaps from,
often from, fear of . . . neglect & loneliness.

With some dispositions, this strait . . . between Scylla & Charybdis is
an exceedingly perplexing affair—the sum of the whole marshalled array is
fearful [1] . . . <u>affirmed wrecks</u> on one hand . . . while on the other . . . no
establishment—no consequence—no friends—nobody! Now for the ques-
tion—which side will you take?—there is no middle course. If you take the
right hand, there is <u>ten</u> to <u>one</u> you will add to the number already there,
but possibly you may escape the impending danger. On the left there is
nothing to impede. . . .

The history of both is this. They pretend <u>love</u> to be the base on which
the union must be formed. . . . This person to whom you unite yourself . . .
He may annoy you in every way but your lips must be sealed & you must
sigh to yourself for you are in his power. . . . With all the cares & anxiety
& endurance which this union brings with it for woman, she has to always
be guarded . . . against the approach of disgust. . . . Although it is seen so
plainly that this is a hazardous undertaking, with the alternative . . . pre-
senting so grim and dreary a prospect to the sprightly young beholder . . .
it is not wonderful she should hesitate and think and not know what to do.

Indeed woman's case is a hard one in this wilderness world of ours, but
let her not repine at a lot she cannot alter. . . . her condition is in itself . . .
more shielded from temptation than man's, and consequently . . . she is
more innocent and happy. These reflections she can find comfort in. Her
best way would be by times to inure herself to fall upon her own resources
for contentment, to bring her mind to the knowledge of its own powers to
amuse itself . . . by reading and reflection . . . and be true to her purpose,
then she is safe.

1. A reference to Homer's epic poem, *The Odyssey,* thought to have been written in the eighth century B.C. It describes the trials of the hero Odysseus as he makes a ten-year journey from the Trojan War to his home in Ithaca. At one point he must steer his boat downstream between two perils, Scylla, a monster, and Charybdis, a whirlpool. After Odysseus arrives safely home, he reflects on the dilemmas of human existence.

Anne Addison Carr Conrad to her sister-in-law Elizabeth W. Powell Conrad, 21 June 1838, from Martinsburg, Virginia, to Winchester, Virginia. Holmes Conrad Papers, Virginia Historical Society.

Anne (or Nancy) Addison Carr hailed from an accomplished Virginia family and married David Conrad, a lawyer who owned six slaves. When she wrote this letter, she had four small children. Her sister-in-law Elizabeth Powell Conrad was the granddaughter of a Revolutionary War veteran and the daughter of a planter. In 1838, Elizabeth was in her thirties and the mother of five children; her husband, Robert Y. Conrad, was also an attorney and owned four slaves. Nancy Conrad speaks eloquently on the supreme importance of a woman's relationship with her mother in her emotional life.

I was truly gratified at recieving your kind, affectionate letter, my dear Betty, and should have thanked you for it immediately, but for the press of my summer's work, which, being delay'd so much longer than usual, my family were really in want of; —The sympathy of our friends is indeed most grateful to us in the hour of sorrow, and it is a relief to pour out our hearts to those whom we know can feel with us.

The Lord has in his mercy, as yet, spared you the affliction of losing your Parents, altho, from the situation of your dear Father,[1] you know, in some measure, what the privation is, and, as you say, after seeing them for years, or even months, the victims of pain and disease, the thought that their beloved bodies are forever free from both, and their spirits rejoicing in the presence of their Lord and Savior, is one which ought to call forth our humble gratitude and praise, for we know that our loss is their infinite gain, yet, poor selfish human nature will often dwell upon the sad thought that there is none now left in the world to love us, to bear and forbear with us like those who are gone, for, dear as Husband and children may be to us, who is there that can fill a Mother's place? —In my beloved Mother's death we have every consolation, her own anxiety to "depart and be with Jesus," and the merciful manner in which it pleases our Heavenly Father to release her from this body of pain and death, never, I suppose, did any one die with less suffering or with more apparent peace and tranquility.

God grant that we may all die thus!!

How is your health now? Holmes[2] told me you did not look well, but you had hardly recover'd from your confinement then, I am glad to hear your baby is a strong healthy fellow, for it is a great blessing; this is about the time for your visit to Middleburg is it not?[3] remember me affectionately to your Parents and Sister, and to Ann Powell too.

When you see Millicent please give her my love and thanks for attending to my Bonnet which came very safely—Holmes can pay her for it when he has an opportunity—I presume she has paid Mrs. Searle. Please give my love to all our relations—& believe me, ever your afft. Sister Nancy A. Conrad.

I forgot to answer your enquiries after the children, they are getting through whooping cough very well, have never coughed violently, or been the least sick with it, so as to require medicine of any kind, more than a few drops of paregoric & antimonial wine to allay the cough at night.[4] Mr. Harrison & Jane are well, and would send their love if they knew of my writing, he was very much obliged to you for your kind invitation.

1. Burr Powell, a plantation owner in northern Virginia.
2. One of her in-laws.
3. Her parents' plantation, The Hill, was located near Middleburg in Loudoun County, Virginia.
4. Paregoric was an opium-tinctured camphor typically used to treat diarrhea, and antinomial wine, which contained traces of silver and other metals, was sometimes used to treat a bad cough.

Mary Virginia Early to her mother, Elizabeth Rives Early, n.d. May 1838, from Lynchburg, Virginia, to Richmond, Virginia. Early Family Papers, Virginia Historical Society.

Mary Virginia, the oldest daughter of Elizabeth and John Early, was born in 1824. Her father was a well-known Methodist clergyman and helped found Randolph-Macon College. Mary was devoted to her mother, who has just departed their Lynchburg home to visit a doctor in Richmond. But, as this letter indicates, her older female kin also "mother" her to some degree.

Saturday evening.

Dear Mother,

Papa started from home again today about dinnertime and you can form no idea how very lonesome I am. I disliked to part with him very much but we all are so anxious to see you that we gave him up cheerfully to what we would have done were the circumstances otherwise.[1] I have been reading the most of the day but have become quite tired of it and have come to the conclusion to commence my letter this evening and finish it early Monday morning. Miss Nancy wishes me to stay with her to night. I shall do so and dress early in the morning and go by aunt Irvine's as I go to Sabbath School. I will get my new calico dress this evening to wear tomorrow. I have taught Mrs. Nowell's class ever since she has been gone[.] there will be an examination of the Sabbath School schollars on tomorrow morning. I wish you could be here. The Miss Penns are boarding and going to school at Mr. Reid's. I have become very well acquainted with them and am very much pleased[.] they are very fine girls I think. I expect to spend the day with them on Monday at cousin Ann's as it is a Holiday and it is a wonder that Mrs. Reid has given us a holiday. Mrs. Reid has been very ill indeed. Dr. Pattison had almost given her up at one time but she is a great deal better at this time[.] as it is late and I have some preparations to make for Sunday I must conclude this scribble for the present. I will finish it on Monday and tell you all the news.

Monday evening. I heard an excellent sermon on yesterday morning[.] the text was so long that I really do not recollect it. I went to class meeting in the evening and as I came out of the gate I heard the Second Presbyterian Church Bell ring and Lelia Thurman and myself went down and heard an excellent sermon. at night I went to my own church and I heard again an excellent sermon[.] we had a crowded house and a very attentive congregation. I went down this morning to Mr. Reid's for the Miss Penn's, one of them had a sore throat and Mrs. Reid thought it most prudent for her to stay within doors[.] the other one came up and I have spent a very agreable day with her and cousin Ann.

Ann Markham has been to see me since you went away and they all treat me with such affection that I am going over there if nothing happens Friday week. I could go next Friday but it is a quarterly meeting and I should not think of leaving it[.] all of uncle Markham's family are in town and himself and Ann who have gone to the courthouse to the quarterly meeting.[2]

Lou has just come in to stay all night with me and that will prevent my writing you a long letter and my tooth is acheing so badly that I fear I shall not sleep much tonight, and I am sure this is the worst written letter I have sent you since you went away and I would commit this to the flames had I not promised papa so faithfully to write today. Your friends all send their love to you and I would mention their names but I am in such pain that I can hardly keep my chair. I have no mother to sympathise and cure me but I have some that feel like mothers to me. cousin Sends her best love to you[,] wishes you to write to her as soon as you are able. Pray for me that I may hold out faithful. Give my best love to papa[.] Your affectionate daughter Mary. I will write again soon.

My brothers are all well[.] all send their love to you[,] wishes you could be here to eat strawberries with them[.][3] some of them will write soon[.] papa will tell you all about Mr. & Mrs. Dogget and how she eats everything that comes in her way. cousin Ann says she would help me out by writing a postscript but she says has some mollasses candy on the fire and is afraid to trust us with it for fear we will let it run over. my tooth is a little better and I must try to fill up this sheet although I have no news of any consequence, cousin Ann says not to let papa forget her fish and you must give her love to every thing like a preacher.[4] give my best love to Lou Thrift and tell her Lou and Ann Markham send their best best love to her and wish to see her very much. My love to all enquiring friends, your affectionate daughter Mary.

1. Her father has gone to Richmond to bring her mother home. John Early (1786–1873) owned several house slaves.
2. The Early family's cousins, from Bedford County, Virginia.
3. Her younger brothers.
4. Meaning in an affectionate manner.

Anne Addison Carr Conrad to her sister-in-law Elizabeth W. Powell Conrad, 7 January 1841, from Martinsburg, Virginia, to Winchester, Virginia. Holmes Conrad Papers, Virginia Historical Society.

Nancy Conrad expounds on her theme of the centrality of the mother-daughter bond in another context, as her grieving sister-in-law is comforted by her mother.

My dear Betty,

I should not have suffer'd your last letter, and kind invitation to lay so long un-noticed but that, for several days after I recieved them, my Gudeman[1] was talking of taking Betty, & Rebecca up to spend part of their Holliday with you, and would probably have done so, but for Robert's letter,[2] proposing to meet him at Harpers ferry, and take a trip to Baltimore & Washington, which he accordingly did, and returned last night, after a very prosperous, and pleasant visit of a week, Robert left Baltimore for Richmond on Monday last, so that, I hope you have by this time heard of his safe arrival at his journey's end, tho, really, the many delays that the mails are liable to at This Season, are a sad trial to one's patience sometimes— I am truly glad that you have your excellent Mother to cheer and comfort you during your time of widowhood, your health too, I hope, from what I hear through others (for you do not say one word about it yourself) is quite re-establish'd, and that before the winter is over, you may make good your threat of coming down to see us, give my best love to our Mama, and tell her it would give us great pleasure to see her with you, and I will, promise her a snug, warm room.

It would have given me real pleasure to have spent my Xmas with you, and, but for the fear that bad weather might catch me from home with such a raft of small fry, I should certainly have attempted it. the children were very full of it, —I tell them now, if there comes a good snow, I shall leave them all, and dash up to see you, if it be but for a day.

Mr. Conrad saw our cousins Mrs. F. & Roberta frequently, the latter is to be married in about 10 days to Genl. Brown, member of Congress from Mississippi, he is a young widower without children, handsome, rich, and clever, so, I hope our cousin is doing very well.[3] they are going on a short trip to the North as soon as they are married.

All your friends here are well.

David Strother has gone to Europe [page torn] Miss Gordon is still here, she has been spending most of her time at Boydville with Mary Faulkner this winter. Mrs. Virginia Pendleton has another son about 2 months old. Mr. Harrison's family are well, but my Sisters eyes do not improve at all, and I fear, never will. Remember me afftly. to all our relations & friends— Do write soon. Your affte. sister Nancy A. Conrad.

1. A Low German endearment for "husband," used occasionally by German Americans. The Conrads migrated to America from the Palatinate states in the mid-eighteenth century.

2. Betty's husband, Robert Conrad (1805–75).

3. In 1841 Roberta E. Young married Albert Gallatin Brown (1813–80), a general in the Mississippi militia and a Democratic congressman, later the governor of Mississippi and a Confederate senator. The Browns had two surviving sons.

Jane T. Lomax, "Love Sketches," Southern Literary Messenger 8 (June 1842): *379–80.*

Jane Lomax was probably a daughter of Judge John Lomax of Spotsylvania County, Virginia. This well-crafted story, published in an eminent literary journal, illuminates the close ties between sisters, "familiar joys" in every way. Edith has recently broken off a courtship because her suitor deceived her in some way, while her beloved older sister is about to marry.

The sisters were together—together for the last time in the happy home of their childhood. The window before them was thrown open, and the shadows of evening were slowly passing from each familiar outline on which the gazers looked. They were both young and fair; and one, the elder, wore that pale wreath the maiden wears but once. The accustomed smile had forsaken her lips now, and the orange flowers were scarcely whiter than the cheek they shaded. The sisters' hands were clasped in each other's, and they sat silently, watching the gradual brightening of the crescent moon, and the coming forth one by one of the stars. Not a cloud was floating in the quiet sky; the light wind hardly stirred the young leaves; and the air was fraught with the fragrance of early spring-flowers. . . .

The sisters' thoughts were busy, as thoughts will be when some valued blessing is about to pass away. Their destinies were to be divided now, for the first time; and though not to be widely separated, they both felt that what they had once been to each other, they never could be again. With one, new associations were forming stronger and dearer even, than the lovely links of sisterly affection; but as the bride glanced at her companion, the future, with all its happily tinted visions, failed for awhile to soothe, and the familiar joys she was forsaking seemed more precious than ever. The other's look was composed, but it was the calmness of feeling too entirely subdued to gain refuge in outward grief. She had no sweet, tremulous anticipations, garnered up in the hereafter, no tenderness promising to repay a thousand fold the unnumbered ties it severed. Hers was the one trouble for which the lips have no expression, the gentlest sympathy no solace. For all other trials there are many comforts; for the deceived in love, this world affords no relief. We lose the balm friendship might have bestowed, in parting with the spirit of confidence; and when pleasures, like flowers, lie withered around us, prayer brings only the last and saddest wisdom of mourning—to suffer and be still. . . .

There were gay friends about the sisters later that evening, and kind wishes were whispered to the bride by those whose voices she loved, till the glow of hope and happiness revisited her cheek, and her brow was no longer sorrowful beneath that garland so pale with prophecies. Mordante's gaze followed Edith with affectionate solicitude, and he appeared surprised at her unruffled quietness and self-command.[1] He had anticipated some passionate demonstration of the woe pressing so heavily upon her; he could scarcely believe suffering existed beneath a smile so placid and a manner so composed. There was no visible sign of sadness, none of the petulance sometimes betraying the wound within; for her tone was kinder and softer than usual, and she was more than ordinarily interested in promoting the enjoyment of others. He judged, as men ever judge women, by the exterior tokens which evince so little of the inner truth; and with all his high-toned feeling and habit of observation he could not trace nor comprehend that mingling of pride and self-forgetfulness which make the mystery of a woman's love.

"Edith is looking beautiful this evening," he said to his bride, "and as tranquil as if the occurrences of the last few weeks had been already forgotten."

The sister sighed; the depth of her own devotion taught her to read more truly the secret history of another's. . . .

1. *Mordante* is French for mordant, biting, or scatching.

Virginia Meade Gordon to her sister Harriet Meade Browne, 8 August 1849, from Holmes Infirmary, Hinds County, Mississippi, to Pass Christian, Mississippi.

Whitaker-Meade Papers, Southern Historical Collection, University of North Carolina.

The Meade sisters grew up in a slaveowning family in Alabama, and both married slaveowners, Virginia just before this letter was written and Harriet, the older of the two, in 1840. This letter illustrates their love for their female kinfolk as well as their constant struggle for good health. They had chronic gynecological problems, as some women did in this era of primitive medical knowledge. Yet Gordon tries to be "resigned" to God's will.

My Dear Sister,

If you have not already heard it you will no doubt be surprized to find that I am here but my health continued to grow worse untill "Mama" became very much alarmed about me and made a desperate effort to get the man[1] to take me somewhere where I could have a chance to get well and concluded that this was the best place for me. Dr. Holmes lives seventeen miles from Jackson and has established an infirmary for sick ladies and has devoted himself for years to the study of female deseases and has acquired considerable eminence in that branch of the profession[.][2] he has upwards of twenty patients now and is receiving them (new ones) every day.

I have been told of some wonderful cures performed by him and cincerely pray that he may be be successful in my case although he gives me but little encouragement to hope that I ever will be entirely well again but I place such a firm trust in God, and have so much faith in his goodness that I can't help hoping that I shall yet be cured of my desease and I try to be resigned to His will whatever it may be and in your prayers dearest sister think of me and pray for me that I may be renewed in soul and body.

I arrived here three days ago almost worn out with fatigue. Mr. Gordon came down with me in the stage and we had dreadful roads and miserable coaches all the way untill we got to Canton. Mr. G— staid with me only one day so I am here among entire strangers with the exception of Mrs. Judge Gholson from Aberdeen.[3] she came down here four months ago in wretched health and will return in a week almost entirely restored— when she goes away there will not be a solitary face here that I have ever seen before. I feel lonely enough I do assure you and the Doctor thinks I will have to remain here six months and probably longer. but I am willing to put up with anything to enjoy <u>tolerable</u> health once more.

I intended writing to Brother Thomas now in a day or two and I am in hopes as I am so near him that he will come and see me.[4] please when you write to him beg him to do so it would be such a source of gratification to me to see him.

I left them all well at home except poor Fanny who had gone up the Morman springs for her health. she had been sick for a month before I left home with some female desease of course.[5] Mama's health is very good. she was to have gone up to the springs two days after I left. she suffers some times with disordered stomach and she thinks the water will make an entire cure of her. Brother Everard seem determined to move to Red river unless Mr. Browne can persuade him to go down to Pass Christian.[6] I expect we all shall make a little cotton this year as we did last. the crops have been very much injured by the constant rains and it is thought that they will make nothing atall on the praries and from the appearance of the crops as we came down I should think they would make very little.

the servants at home were all well except uncle Edmond who had been very sick with chills and fever but was recovering again. Mammy was with cousin Laura who had just given birth to another daughter much to cousin Bolling's anoyance I can assure you. her Mother and sister Mrs. Glidewell were both with her when I left but expected to leave in a few days for north Alabama. I am distressed at being obliged to leave poor sister Lizzy so near her confinement which she expects next month[.] I left her looking remarkably well and I hope she will get safely through her troubles. Doctor Smith and horrey were both well. horrey had gone up to the Morman springs to hunt. Bets was expecting to go to Blount springs every day[.][7] she is going with Lucy Randolphe.

Mr. Smith has determined to leave Columbus and go to Norfolk to teach with his brother[.] you may know it is a grief to us all to see them go. I feel sincerely attached to him and Mrs. Smith too[.] such good people are rarely met with in this world.

Lucy Randolphe is going on with him to stay untill her education is finished and Mama hopes to send Minny to him next year. you would be perfectly delighted to see the improvement in dear little Minny in ever respect. she is getting on well in her studies and really plays and sings beautifuly[.] she played at the concert given at the close of the session and I was really afraid that she would be spoiled by being so complimented but I think it would not be an easy matter to spoil her particularly when she has Teck to keep her down. Teck and Miss cunningham have gone to the springs with "Ma." they are quite as devoted as ever.

How is my poor dear sister Betsey? I trust that by this time Genl. Grant has returned. if he has not I know she is wretched. we hear that he has offered for the legislature. is it true? I feel so uneasy about her health but I pray that a summer at the Pass may restore her.[8] I will write to her in a day or two. How is cousin Sarah? give her my very best love and Mr. Lightfoot too not forgetting Sallie and Amelia and dear little Etta and Everard[.] kiss them for me a thousand times. I am almost crazy to see them. I do feel sincerely sorry for Mr. Browne but can't help think that as his general health is so good he will yet recover from this effect affection of his legs.[9] tell him I would write to him but I am always feeling so badly that I have written to no one for an age and find it a greater task than ever but tell him I have not forgotten him.

remember me most affectionately to Mr. and Mrs. Brooks if you see them this summer. give my best love to Bell and ask her to write to me. good bye my own dearest sister. I daily thank my God that you are yet left to me that amidst all my trails, he has blessed me in giving me such a sister and one whom I love so much. farewell and may God bless you. Pray for your poor sick "Sippy."

1. This may be her husband, her father Richard Meade (a physician), or another doctor.

2. Possibly Doctor Thomas G. Holmes, a physician in antebellum Mississippi.

3. Probably the former Miss Ragsdale, wife of District Court Judge Samuel J. Gholson.

4. Their brother Thomas, who lived near Hamburg, Mississippi.

5. Their sister-in-law Frances Meade, spouse of Richard Everard Meade and the mother of two young children.

6. Their brother Richard Everard, a farmer in Lowndes County, Mississippi, who was considering moving to the Red River Valley in Louisiana.

7. A resort in northern Alabama.

8. Meaning Pass Christian, a village on the Gulf Coast.

9. Gordon means "infection" here. Planter Richard Browne had been an invalid for several years, and he and his wife had no children. He died later in 1849.

Elizabeth Otey to her son James H. Otey, 31 July 1843, from Bedford County, Virginia, to Columbia, Tennessee. James Hervey Otey Papers, Southern Historical Collection, University of North Carolina.

Elizabeth Matthew Otey's husband, planter Isaac Otey, served in the Virginia legislature for thirty years. The couple had twelve children, one of whom, James

Otey, migrated from Virginia to Tennessee and became a bishop in the Episcopal Church. In this letter to James, Mrs. Otey tries to excuse her grandson's "abuse" of his mother and sisters with the observation that everyone in the human family has troubles to bear. Apparently she has taught her daughter to endure her mistreatment in silence.

Dear James,

I have seated myself to comply with your request as far as I am able and in the first place to say I am really Sorry to hear you say you are again afflicted with so Distressing a complaint as Dyspepsia[.] do you intend going to any of the Medical Springs[.] I know your Complaint from Observation is Distressing one but Resignation to the will of An All wise Benifactor [will give?] great paliation[.] was you to see yours [page stained] now for 4 yea[rs] Laboured under Disease of a Complicated nature and I fear without hope of release how Distressing he is quite emasiated has measurably Lost the use of one of his Legs, his mind is much the Same as when you saw him Last and I make no [page stained] would be pleased with A Letter from [page stained] for he is gratified when any attention is paid him but this I [tell?] you Before in answer to yours of the 12th of Agust which is the Last I had from you untill this by Mr. Aiken[.] your sister is as kind to him as she can be and I Believe he apricaates her endeavors to render him as Comfortable as she can—but he is not her greatest trouble[.] She has a grown Son that ought to be a Comfort to her but is a Source of many unhappy Hours[.] he hangs about Home Does nothing and is Dissapated and sometimes very abusive to his Mother and Sisters. She had to get an overseer this year and James will take her Horse and go of[f] without Leave which you know is provoking and she has to bear it all in Silence. I do pity her but can't help her out of her troubles, but troubles of different kinds seem To be the Inheritance of the Human Family. Still I am Led to Beleive we are often the cause of our own Difficulties in some Deegree

now their is your Bro. John's[1] [page stained] yet his own son[2] I suppose might be as Happy as this World could make every one, but trouble seems to Come in on them as [a] Whirlwind. During Convention[3] Van went of[f] unknown to his parents and came to Richmond[.] John [Sr.] came after him gave him Leave to go on to Philadelphia[.] he returned while I was in Lynchburg seem'd very Penitent how long it may continue don't know[.] Dexter has been sent Down[4] from university of Virginia. I can't [page torn] but report says Something a [page stained] for Begining now I write these things in Confidence not that [I] wish to wound or promulgate Family Brawls or secrets.

Well I went to Richmond very unexpectedly for as I was riase [page stained] Woods and was always at home I never had aspired to anything Higher but [illegible] People errs by absenting themselves so much from Socity[.] Fanny Cook was with and indeed was the moving cause of my going we made many new acquaintances but would that we was so much [prayerful?] with [page stained] Minor he appears to be a perfect gentleman and I told Virginia I was much pleased with her selection no Grandchild could have been more attentive and polite than he was to me met me at the Boat Landing and reconized me from the Family likeness[.] He had a good Deal of Company during Convention and I think both acted there part well and if was to Judge they get on first rate[.] Virginia is greatly beloved by those [page stained] in that place I told Virginia [page stained] what alike we Derived great respect from [Losing?] Alice d to the Bishop one old lady she must come and shake hands with the Bishops mother[.] I met with some old acquaintances an[d] Realations that was really kind to us but as Virginia has writen to you I shall say no more as I have no Doubt she has given you a [good?] Description of of The whole Affair. I left Mr. Cooks Last Friday Serahs Kentucky Beau [page stained] Stay Long after his arrival but as far as I was able to Judge think him a worthy Inteligent young Man he is said to [be] wealthy and of Worthy Parantage from Christian County but I [feel?] Serah wont profit by the good offer. Thare has been A Long Dry Spell here and peopl[e] very Sicklys Both in Town and Country[.] old Mrs. Beard Departed this Life yesterday she was in her 87th year [page stained] than me you Speak of my going on with you I cant promise to put you to that much trouble but if you come this way I will if alive and well go as far as Richmond with you[.] Robert is in Lynchburg at this time Walter is expected there shortly the Last he wrote me he was going to Mississippi[5] in the faul Mr. Conford's Famaly is [considerable?] Wealth I had [page stained] may all well at that Time but the Females of the Families much Dissatsified. Tom was teaching at [page stained] School well I have Complied with your request and writen a Long Letter but not an inteligent one and I think it is Doubtfull whether you can read it or not when you write say how does Mildred's Children Come on Frances and Children join me in Love to you and Family with sincere aff. Your's E. Otey.

1. John Otey was an elderly planter in Campbell County, Virginia. He and his wife, Lucy Mina Otey, had eight children, seven sons and one daughter.

2. John Otey Jr.
3. Meaning while they were attending a religious meeting.
4. A term meaning expelled, still used in England.
5. Her son Walter eventually settled in Arkansas.

Anne Addison Carr Conrad to her sister-in-law Elizabeth W. Powell Conrad, 26 May 1851, from Martinsburg, Virginia, to Winchester, Virginia. Holmes Conrad Papers, Virginia Historical Society.

In this letter Nancy Conrad now comforts her sister-in-law for the loss of her own mother. She counsels Betty Conrad to accept her grief and look forward to a reunion in the next life.

My dear Betty,

I learn'd on Saturday in a note from Mary B. McGuire to Becky, the death of your lov'd and honour'd Mother,[1] need I assure you my dear Sister how truly I sympathize in the feeling of affliction and bereavement with which, it is so natural you should for a time be oppress'd, for it is a loss which cannot be supplied; who can fill a Mother's place in the heart of her child? Whose love and tenderness is like hers, and when we feel that these are gone from us forever, there is a sense of desolation which will not be repress'd.

and yet, in cases like the present, how selfish is our grief, when we know that the beloved one whom we mourn, has exchanged a body of pain, and weakness and infirmity for the "glorious liberty of the children of God," that state of honour and immortality for which she has been so long preparing, and to which, like a "shock of corn fully ripe," she is now, so mercifully removed, without much previous suffering I conclude, tho' I have not yet heard any of the particulars attending her death. in this respect how much have you to be thankful for, that both she, and you have been spared the misery of a long, protracted, yet hopeless illness, such as generally precedes the death of old persons; After the first pains of separation are past, you will I know my dear Sister, be enable'd by faith to dwell upon this subject with thankfulness to that Heavenly Father who doesth all things well, and whose goodness has prepared in his "House, not made with hands," mansions for all his faithful children, that you may be enable'd to realize and apply his many previous promises is my earnest prayer.

Let me hear from you as soon as you can, any circumstances connected with the last hours of one whom I loved and regarded so highly, would be most interesting to me.

We have just hear'd again from my dear Bet, she is recovering slowly, but still very weak. All join in affectionate remembrances to you and your's, Your affte. sister, Nancy A. Conrad.

Please send the enclosed note to Ann Eliza.[2]

1. Catherine Brook Powell, a planter's wife in Virginia.
2. Elizabeth Conrad's unmarried sister. The note, which probably contained similar condolences, has been lost.

Caroline M. Gordon to her sister Sarah Gwyn Gordon Brown, 26 January 1852, from Gordon Springs, Georgia, to Wilkesborough, North Carolina. Hamilton Brown Papers, Southern Historical Collection, University of North Carolina.

Caroline Gwyn (1798–1880) of Wilkesborough, North Carolina, married James Harvey Gordon in 1823 and moved to Gordon Springs, Georgia, where they ran a plantation. In 1850, the couple owned thirty-six slaves, and they had five children. Deeply nostalgic about her youth in Carolina, Mrs. Gordon still feels a strong attachment to her female relatives. She evokes the world of "common affairs" that her niece Sarah Ann Finley would describe a year later in a missive to her own sister (noted in the introduction to this book).

Ever Dearest Sister, Think it not strange that I have at last taken my pen to write you, for the last four or five days you have been constantly on my mind, and in this time I have held you up in a more particular manner than usual in my prayers to a blessed and merciful God. And I have felt great concern fearing you were very ill and I should never see you again. . . .

O my sister how rejoiced I would be once more to see you[.] we are growing old—and ere long will be past traveling. . . . can't you come this coming summer to see us, you have now a strong inducement. Dear Ann's family is in sixty or seventy miles of us.[1] we are directly on the way, come do come to Gordon Springs and spend some time with us, and then we will if possible go with you to see Dear Ann, and then Rebecca, Oscar, and my

Brother Lorenzo. . . . [2] I think Col. Brown would enjoy the trip, and we all would be rejoiced to see you. . . . [3]

How are all of your dear Children[?] Write me all about them, tell Carrie to write me[,][4] give my affectionate love to all of them — O how I would like to see dear Martha and her children.[5] do you dear sister remember how I used to love Martha. O my poor Mother[6] and I thought she was perfection. O the days that are past and gone never to return, when I think of all these things it makes me so sad. . . .

my little Carrie sends her love to Cousin James[7] and Cousin Carrie too she says I remember Cousin Carrie very well. May heaven bless you and your dear family is the prayer of your affectionate sister Caroline M. Gordon.

Give my respects to Mrs. Martin, Mrs. Stokes. Mr. Wellborn etc. if they have not forgotten me.[8]

1. Sarah Ann Gordon Finley (1826–1907), called Ann, Brown's daughter from her first marriage, lived in Cherokee County, Alabama, with her husband John Finley and their children.

2. Her son Richard Oscar Gordon, her daughter Rebecca Gordon, and her brother Lorenzo Gwyn.

3. Hamilton Brown, Sarah's second husband.

4. The writer's namesake, Caroline L. Gordon (1828–91), Brown's daughter from her first marriage.

5. Martha Gordon Finley (1821–98), another daughter from that marriage.

6. Martha Lenoir Gwyn, who died in 1829.

7. Gordon's daughter Caroline Harvey Gordon, who was born in 1843, and Brown's son James Gordon.

8. Relatives and neighbors in Wilkesborough.

Annie S. Johnston to her sister Mary Wright, 23 June 1852, from Canton, Mississippi, to Red River County, Texas. George Travis Wright Papers, Eugene C. Barker Texas History Center, University of Texas at Austin.

In 1852 Mary Wright was in her early forties, the wife of planter George T. Wright (no relation to Eliza Wright in this chapter). She and her sister Annie Johnston wish to visit their widowed aunt in Tennessee. Johnston considers it a "sacred duty" because their kinswoman was in poor health and raising young chil-

dren alone. Johnston, who was usually quite subdued, erupts when her brother-in-law will not accompany them on the journey.

. . . Poor Aunt Betsy has no one with her now but cousin James. They have taken two orphan children to raise. Mary Hardy says she has been very cheerful all the time and attends to her domestic affairs as usual, but her sight is beginning to fail her now, so she cannot read as she has done. . . .

Mr. Wynn sold his negroes after cousin Sally A.'s death, and cousin Sam bought Aunt Sylvia and Malvinia; the former was very glad to hear from us and sent me a great deal of love. . . .

Tell Mr. Wright I shall consider him very unkind if he does not tell you exactly what he will do. I consider it a sacred duty we both owe her and if you will not go I will try to get some other person to go with me. . . .

Annie S. Johnston to her sister Mary Wright, [misdated 7] October 1852.

Dear sister,

I received your letter yesterday dated October 14th and sit down without delay to return an answer. Sam's came at the same time and Betty's a few days ago. I was much pleased to hear from you, for we had looked and looked for you until I had despaired of seeing you in time to go with me to Tennessee. Our poor old Aunt has I expect been as much disappointed as we were, for I wrote to her I thought you would come. Tell Mr. Wright I think it was so very unkind I scarcely know how to forgive him. . . .

Susan C. Stone Barton to her daughters Emily Barton Brune and Mary Barton Jones, 17 October 1853, from Fredericksburg, Virginia, to Baltimore, Maryland. Brune-Randall Family Papers, MS 2004, Manuscripts Division, Maryland Historical Society Library.

Susan Barton, born in the 1790s, was the mother of eight children. Her husband, Thomas Barton, an affluent lawyer, owned five slaves in 1850. Here she conveys the emotional significance of visits as well as the importance of exchanges between women in separate households.

My dear Mary & Em, I have been sewing on my patchwork & concluded you would think that was not so important an occupation as writing to you so have laid it aside, though have sewed very little lately, been busy about other things—so that there is little hope of its ready to use this winter— Mary Dowell came to day, expecting Carrie was here, but is a very agreable companion to Liz[1] your father & I—we have all been sitting round the table tonight & Fanny too, & have only part of the furniture in the room, Thurston put down the carpet, but was so busy cleaning the room that he could not finish—I had hoped we should have had rain before we put down the carpets, the dust is so disagreeable, but cannot wait longer for some of the rooms—I reckon Mary's being here will make the girls think they ought to come here & not stop with you dear Em, if you are not ready to come with Mr. D & Evy—but I do hope you will not have to suffer any more pain with the operations, & am rejoiced that one is out.

I have attended a funeral the two last evenings, our old friend Mrs. Greiman died Sunday night, I believe wrote you she had been taken ill a few days before—her family were all with her except Cornelia who has gone to England with Mrs. Wm K. Smith a few weeks ago—she was perfectly aware of her situation & expressed herself in the most gratifying way to her friends—Robertine was quite sick & after her death was carried to her mother's—

Dear little Sue Scott died early yesterday morning, & had really spent such a month of suffering, that I felt it was a mercy for her to be releaved, she has been prayed for at church the last three Sundays, & Mr. McGuire has seen her several times & seemed much interested for her, made one of the most beautiful addresses this evening I ever heard from him—& took such a delightful view of the short life of children being the commencement of an existence which would never end—I wish I could give you any idea of it. it was quite touching seeing the grief of little Hetty she made not the slightest sound, but wept all the time I saw her—Isabella has been there ever since she returned—& Hugh rarely left here—& Ann was as devoted & untiring in her attentions as a mother, & was wonderful in so young a person—cousin Fanny is poorly—Miss Susan Allison is with her & so cheerful that it is a comfort to her—

I feel so glad to say to every body that I expect both of you will be with us next week, & hope Mr. Brune[2] will be able to come, & he & Mr. Jones be here together. Barton insisted I must tell you the children here have had the chicken pox. I did not think of it when I wrote & all have gotten over it but little May Marye, & nine been sick with it but here. she had a cold which I think was the reason of her being sick—Maxwell is the only one to have it & Liz says she saw some little spots on him, which she hopes was it, & that he will not have any more — Thomas & Menard had a pox on their noses which have disfigured them, but they were not sick at all & I don't think there is any probability of Barton's taking it, & if he did, consider it too triffling to care about. he did not think it ought to interfere with his coming, but it was right always to let you know of any disease — but I don't consider that like hooping cough or any of those diseases, which I should not carry a child into — & they have been well so long I don't think it could be communicated now.[3]

I expect we shall get a letter tomorrow saying when Evy & Mr. McDowell will be here. the children are all well & give little or no trouble —

I was to see Mrs. Douthat & Mrs. McGuire yesterday, & they spoke very affectionately of you both & Mrs. D. hoped that you would be here before she left — Agnes was quite interested in a new carpet she was getting & said she wanted to see you so much — a Miss Marshall is there going to school —

Em be sure & bring your daguerreotypes for Thomas[4] — Mr. Bell left here to day & would have been a good opportunity of sending it — Thomas wanted it sent by mail — your father thinks he will come in after Mr. Bell goes out — Do you know not one of our children are in town with us — only Liz & two grandchildren — but I hope it will not be the case long — I suppose William told you I was quite well[5] — I have continued so — & beg you wont make yourself uneasy about me again dear Em — I should not have named my indisposition at all if I had not promised to tell you when I was at all unwell — & wrote you the whole at first —

Wednesday evening. Have just received both your letters, & feel so disappointed at the time being postponed for my seeing you that I don't feel exactly reconciled but my motto that it is "all for the best" will come to my aid — & I certainly want you to come at the time most convenient to you — but I think Xmas & summer the most disagreeable time here of any in the year to me, after the charm was broken of the first Xmas you being absent I cared less about it — but I want you all, all the time & shall be glad enough for you to come whenever you can — makes no difference to me when — only the longest time to be here — so sorry you are suffering with your face — No account from New York, & dont know when we shall see them think the girls had Art come on with Evy — as your coming is so uncertain.

Dear Mary, bring me a few red peppers.

All send love. your devoted Mother.

The girls[6] will be glad to see Molly, & I hope she will return with them.

1. Her daughter-in-law Elizabeth Genifer Barton, William Barton's wife.
2. Frederick W. Brune (b. 1813), Emily's husband, was a successful lawyer.
3. Chicken pox is of course a contagious disease.
4. Thomas is their younger brother, aged thirteen. In 1839 Parisian Louis Daguerre invented this primitive photographic process using silver plates. By the 1850s, daguerreotypes were popular throughout the United States.
5. Her son, a lawyer in his early forties.
6. Evalina and Susan, her unmarried daughters in their early twenties.

Private Journal of Mary Owen Sims. Small Manuscript Collection, Arkansas History Commission.

A native of Tennessee, Mary Owen married physician John Sims in 1850 and was widowed five years later at age twenty-five. She was raising her children alone in Dallas County, Arkansas. Her diary chronicles a family dispute over her husband's property and illustrates her close bond with her sister, who was visiting because her marriage was less than happy. It is perhaps not surprising that Mary Sims declined nine proposals before she remarried in 1861.

24 August 1855. This morning raining still. Mr. Sims had a long conversation with Judge Quillen about taking all the property from me and my children which he had given Doctor and got very angry, when he found I was not willing to give it up.[1] I tried to persuade Judge Q. not to take sister home, but he would not be persuaded. They got ready to start in the morning, but were prevented by a shower of rain. Soon after Mr. Sims came over again, and we made a compromise of the matter. After the writings were all drawn up and signed, he left very angry without speaking to me or the children and left the county without seeing us again. I am sorry he acted so badly toward me and my children, by trying to deprive us of everything he could.

This evening Sister and family left for home. How lonely and desolate I feel tonight. Dear Sister, I am sitting in our room, my little children are all asleep. How I now miss thy dear kind voice which always cheered me on and encouraged me not to give up to grief, but live for my children and look on high for strength and support in my lonely widowhood. While I sit here alone tonight while all around me are asleep and think of the many happy hours I have spent with the "loved and lost." Within this room I was first called mother. How well I recollect the time he sat by me with my hands clasped in his and said he ought to be a happy man and that he would try and be more contented in the future.

It was here we gave you to the stranger, dear Sister, to take you to his home. How he has treasured the gift you alone can tell us.

1 September 1855. [Sunday] Found Mr. Sims alone. He would not accompany us to church. We supped together and soon after retired to our rooms. We have but little congeniality of feeling—his hopes hardly ever to rise about earth and earthly things. He has lost his wife and all his children save one. Still his mind is entirely set on earthly things. . . .

1 August 1858. Sunday. Another year has rolled around and time in his silent course has brought my twenty-eight natal day. As I commence a new year, God grant that it may be dedicated to Thy service—that each step towards the grave may draw me nearer to thee. Three of my Christian brothers spent last night with me. Of course, our conversation was on Godly subjects. We all went to church this morning and listened to a very edifying discourse from Bro. Salley. After service returned home. Mr. Abbot and lady, Mr. W. R. and sister and Dr. Harris spent the evening with me. They are all young and gay and our conversation was not very edifying. Indeed, I felt that my conversation was not that of a woman professing Godliness; but I suppose it was such as suited the company. Really it appears sometimes when my heart is most sad that I am most gay. A letter was handed to me at church today from Judge Quillen informing me that Sister was seriously ill and the physician had advised to have me with her. Poor stricken dove—she conceals the wound that is killing her, mental anguish joined with her peculiar situation is more than flesh can bear;[2] but, Sister, if the humble and sincere prayers of a sister who loves you as her own soul can avail anything at the mercy seat of the most high, you will yet come through every trial and be a bright and glittering star in the New Jerusalem—for I know you are the puriest Spirit unwashed by the blood of the lamb that inhabits this mundane sphere.

11 November 1858. I left home the eleventh of August and did not return until the eight of October. Sister has been oh, so ill! She has barely escaped death four times in the last three months, but thanks be to God she was able to accompany me home. Since my return Ma has been quite sick; so I have spent half of my time with her, but as she is slowly recovering and I can stay at home awhile, having neglected my family so long I have spent

so much to attend to at present that I have no time to spare. I saw Sister at church last Sunday. She has improved so fast since she came home to us that anyone can see her mind more than her body was diseased.

24 November 1858. Sister and her children have been staying with me for the past ten or twelve days. She was immersed during the time.[3] I hope the word of God will be an anchor to her broken heart. Judge Quillen arrived yesterday on his way to Little Rock. He was very anxious for Sister to accompany him. At last she consented so they left this evening, leaving the children with me a charge. I was very willing to undertake [it] for her sake for her domestic horizon has been dark here of late that I am glad to add every ray of sunshine in my power. We all have most excellent health.

    1. Mr. Sims, Mary's father-in-law, had recently arrived from South Carolina and wanted her to give up ownership of her four slaves. Her children, William, Josephine, and John, were all under age five. Her brother-in-law John Quillen was a judge in Arkansas, and "Doctor" was her deceased husband.
    2. Her sister may be pregnant, as the phrase "peculiar situation" sometimes indicated.
    3. Meaning she was baptized.

Amanda M. Hughes to her daughter Mary Hughes, 12 January 1858, from Turnersville, Tennessee, to Nashville, Tennessee. Darden Family Papers, Tennessee State Library and Archives.

Even though Amanda Hughes's husband was a planter, she lost most of their property after his death in the 1850s and had to move in with relatives. Perhaps because of her swift decline in financial standing, the widow Hughes wants her daughters to learn as much as they can in school. She also highlights how trying it could be for daughters to leave their mothers to marry.

Very Dear Daughter, As I am entirely alone this evening, I will devote a few moments in writing to my own sweet Mary who occupies a large portion of my thoughts & affections.

    O Mary, you cannot tell how anxious I am for you to finish your Education and be at home but to judge by Ellen I would not have you with me very long.[1] But I do hope you will not find any one to win your heart so soon. I wish you when you are done going to school to have a select Library and go through a regular course of reading—and take an interest in home and the cultivation of your younger Sisters & Brother and not go out into the gidy world to seek admiration [2]—. what is it to be admired by the gay and the fashionable it only affords momentary pleasure, it is like a bubble floating on the sea it is soon passed and gone.

let your whole aim be while at school to store your mind with useful knowledge. Keep perfect control of your disposition never suffer yourself to become so fretted as to speak without thinking and weighing every word, and you will be very apt not to act imprudently—

Ellen left yesterday to go to housekeeping. I do hope she may find all the happiness she anticipates she is blessed with a kind husband and that should make her happy[.] she had a very bad cold when she left. I feel much anxiety about her she is so young, so child like when the time [came] for her to leave it was quite a trial for her to leave me. I do not think if they had not bought every thing she would have gone, but I think it will be the best for her to have some care[.] she will take more exercise and maby it will improve her health—

She will be a great pleasure to her Sister Emma. I hope they may remain near each other. Dr. Lockert is doing fine practice. Daughter I forgot to make you them cassafrass pills you can send them down and get five cents worth of cassafrass and take a piece as larg as a pea three times a day tell Emily she must take it to and if that does not improve your health you must let me know—do not neglect it—

Taylor has commenced his latter again. Sissie is going to school does not like to leave her Ma. Mr. Alley has bought Tom Mathias out and is pardner with Sam Mathias in the Store. I reckon it is Father and suninlaw now; but I believe Margaret is going to Clarksville to school the first of Feby[.] time will prove—

You must <u>write to your Sisters</u> often and to Mother tell Emily I think she might write to me. my love to Aunt Hughes Brother Lady & Family also to Brother Church & Family I have nothing more of interest Receive a Mother's warmest <u>love.</u> A. M. Hughes.

1. Ellen Hughes (1840–1910), another daughter, had recently married Andrew J. Allensworth.

2. Mary Hughes had four siblings in addition to Ellen.

Zelinda Ann Smith Payne to her daughter Mary Payne, 30 June 1858, from Lexington, Kentucky, to somewhere in Kentucky. Linda Neville Papers, Group II, Papers of Mary Payne Neville, Division of Special Collections and Archives, Margaret I. King Library, University of Kentucky at Lexington.

Zelinda Smith, born in 1809, married Daniel M. Payne, a lawyer and owner of thirty-one slaves in 1850. They had six children together, including their daughter Mary, who was nineteen. Mrs. Payne expects different kinds of behavior from her children, insisting that her daughter keep her company, if only through the mail, as her sons go out into the world.

My Dear Daughter,

I wrote you two letters last week and you only answered one of them I want to hear every day from you and feel greatly disappointed when the mail arrives and no news from Daughter. John is so much like Pa about writing that we would rather be astonished to get a letter from him, but with you it is different. if you are happy abroad you know that there are loving ones at home.

Tell Jim that I am afraid he has forgotten his Aunt Z. since he has that lovely wife and baby. I am so anxious always to see him when he returns to Ky. and cannot tell how it is that he dont come straight on to see me for we all feel that Jim belongs to us. I hope he will come to see us this Summer and bring his wife and boy to see us. Lizzy and Rich returned to day. I have not seen them. I went to see Cousin Mary Crittenden to day, her mind is much better. I hope you can prevail upon your Aunt Eliza an Cousin Lizzy to visit us this Summer with Upshaw and Harrence. if you see Cousin Sue tell her that I would be very much pleased to have her and Charley and the little ones to come and see us. I have had my fence made, and would have had some little work done in the back passage but Mr. Williams, has been too busy to wait upon me to much work on hand to do mine[.] Richard wrote to you yesterday and Sent your Aunt Parkman's letter.

write me word what you are doing and when you will return. You have been gone a long time and you must know that Mother is all alone. The boys all out attending to their business.

I do wish so much that I could spend this week with those dear dear friends of mine, with you[r] aunt John. tell them I often think and talk of the pleasant days we have spent together. My love to all of your Aunt Eliza's dear family. accept for yourself and John a Mother's love. Zelinda A. Payne.

Martha M. Miller to her daughter Louisa Miller Thum, n.d. 1859, from near Louisville, Kentucky, to near Louisville, Kentucky. Miller-Thum Family Papers, The Filson Club Historical Society, Louisville, Kentucky.

Martha Miller wed physician, planter, and politician Warrick Miller of Jefferson County, Kentucky. In 1859 she was in her mid-sixties, and her daughter Louisa was thirty years younger. This letter is notable for its ineffably tender, sweet tone and for the reciprocal exchanges between women, in this instance, bonnets for preserves.

Dear Daughter,

I am sorry to hear sweet Pattie has had three chills. I hope she will soon be well[.] I will send you some sage to make tea for her it is very good to prevent fever. I send her a little letter from Lou Cowgill. it came in a letter from her sister Mary to her Aunt Annie. tell sweet Pattie she must learn to write and write to her cousin Lou Cowgill.

I thank you for your nice presents but you must not spend your money for me, keep it for yourself my dear child. I had two new caps and when I have one I think I am quite well fixed I send you a Jar of plumb preserves & one of Blackbury Jam. I will make you some apple Jelly and preserves next week

Kiss sweet Willie, Pattie, & Mandeville for me and believe me your fond Mother M. M. Miller.

FRIENDSHIP

THE MODEL FOR FRIENDSHIP CAN be located in the family, in relationships between sisters, cousins, sisters-in-law, and other female kin. The devout faith of many women also encouraged friendship, for every soul needed fellowship, and the Age of Romanticism glorified it, with its emphasis on intimate ties with peers. As girls grew up, they formed close bonds with schoolmates, and after they married they became friends with their neighbors. Adult friendships contained some rituals such as visits after childbirth, but most visits were spontaneous, for one of their chief purposes was to give women an outlet for the emotions.

All adult women in the Old South had to contend with practical obstacles, such as the difficulties in travel, in keeping friendships alive, and mothers sometimes discovered that household duties prevented them from spending time with comrades beyond the family. Over the course of a woman's lifetime, most of her lasting friendships were probably formed with her kinfolk. Why would this be so? How did women express affection for their friends? And what practical purposes might these friendships also serve?

Margaret Izard Manigault to her sister Georgina Izard Smith (Mrs. Joseph Allen Smith), 8 August 1811, from Clifton, South Carolina, to Shrewsbury, New Jersey. Manigault Family Papers, South Caroliniana Library, University of South Carolina.

Despite her manifest pleasure in correspondence, Margaret Manigault longs to visit her female relatives. (Exactly fifty years after she wrote this missive, her granddaughter Margaret M. Barnwell and great-granddaughter Ann called on Mrs. Grimball, as described in the introduction.) The outing requires careful planning, even for a wealthy widow such as Mrs. Manigault. She, like other women, had demanding family responsibilities, and respectable white women did not travel alone.

If am not mistaken, my dear Sister, in my inference—I must congratulate you upon at least on the strong reasons which compel you to give up Carolina this year.[1] I shall myself frequently & sorrowfully feel the privation of your & Mrs. Smith's society which gave [joys?] to many hours last winter. You will I make no doubt spend your winter pleasantly where ever it may be—& as you say, nothing but the cold is to be apprended even at Black Point—Yet—I should rather have a firm persuasion that Solitude <u>would</u> be pleasant than experience it.

My time has been very completely occupied for some weeks, & every moment which was not necessarily devoted to my young children, has been spent in company. This will account for my not having been so alert a correspondent as usual. Your letters always give me great pleasure. Writing is a delightful invention—& the society which a little wafer affords to an intercourse of the most secret kind is a thrilling instance of the advantage of civilization. Is it not admirable that at this distance of thousands of miles we should be able to disclose with safety secrets of the utmost importance?

Let me tell you while I recollect it, that your green & chess men went to Town several weeks ago by my Brother Gerry who took them in his Gig. I hope you will one day or other receive them safe. You will be surprised to learn that I am at the eve of a great undertaking. Figure to yourself that I am going tomorrow to pay a visit to my Mother.[2] I shall be driven by my Son Horry who returned to us yesterday—accompanied by Charlotte & Darling & followed by the faithful Toby.[3] You don't know the preparations that I have been making for a week past—It is not easy neither I believe is it right for the Mother of a large family to indulge herself in excursions, however pleasant they may be to her. I do promise myself great pleasure in seeing my Mother, so happy as her late letters declare her to be. She has during the past year undergone great uneasiness. So many of her children absent & the health of some so precarious. Her mind is now at rest, & she seems grateful to enjoy the report & have had details of all this & of our little new niece's introduction into this world. If your residence, my dear Sister, was only within a day's distance from ours—I certainly should make an effort which if successful would so largely remunerate me[4]—but a night on the road is a terrific obstacle to a company of females. I feel the thorough inclination to indulge myself, & my daughters, but to speak sincerely I have very little hope of accomplishing this long desired visit.

Harry has returned highly pleased with his tour—he went to Boston, to Lebanon, to Ballstown, to New York—& acquited himself every where.

I am very glad to find that Mr. D. Loughton Smith has so far recovered his sight as to be able to read, & write a little.

Has Mrs. Dathkoff been to see you? Your friendly attentions would I should think be very acceptable to her. Her situation is truly pitiable, & she appears to deserve a very different fate.[5] As you describe your situation alone with so many gentlemen—you must at first have felt awkward in it—but with the support of a husband, with good sense, & without [notions?] a young woman may thus acquire a solidity which is [hard?] to be obtained among us. Sometimes you must feel the want of a female companion—But it is better to have none than a disagreeable one & an unexceptional one is a rare avis. I have experienced the kind of life you now lead—[felt afflicted?] I went during the first settlement of the place, & remained during a session of the Legislature at Columbia. Our house was the Rendezvous for the gentleman of our town—& although a Gay house, it was not I assure you [without?] its <u>defancies</u>[6]—it had two panes of glass by way of windows and many other lukuries of the same kind, & I never was happier in my life than I was there.

But Adieu—for I forget myself.

1811 Aug. 8th.

1. Meaning that her sister is pregnant and therefore cannot travel.

2. Alice DeLancey Izard, a New Yorker who married South Carolina planter Ralph Izard in 1767. Now a widow, she had homes in and around Charleston.

3. Charlotte and Darling are two of her several children, and Toby is a slave.

4. Manigault evidently means "remunerate" in the sense of compensate.

5. She is living apart from her husband.
6. Meaning deficiencies.

Mary Telfair to her friend Mary Few, 28 October 1814, from Savannah, Georgia, to New York City, New York. William Few Collection, Georgia Department of Archives and History.

Mary Telfair of Savannah led a life of extraordinary privilege. Financially independent since childhood, she was well read and well traveled, a cosmopolitan woman of the world. Like many women, she cherishes her female friends and distrusts romantic love, but unlike most women, she views a husband as an "encumbrance." Telfair remained single all of her life.

Feeble would be my attempts my dear Mary to describe to you the delight your charming Epistle created in my breast; never do I feel so happy as when conversing in idea with the friend of my youth. Oh how different from the <u>soul enlivening</u> intercourse enjoyed in the <u>third story</u> in Robertson Street,[1] but still there is a magic charm in receiving letters from those we love. The feelings certainly are less constrained than in conversation and we pour forth our whole heart without knowing it. I agree with that divine (though satyrical) Poet Pope in thinking that

> "Heaven first taught letters for some wretches aid
> Some banished Lover or some captive Maid."[2]

I have many Correspondents, but such is my disposition that I can never re-peruse their Epistles without being seized with a violent fit of the <u>blues</u> and to take a retrospect of the happy hours past in the society of my friends without engaging in all the luxury of grief. I am happy that you have proposed keeping a journal for me. I will do the same for you, though convinced that it will not be half as interesting as yours. Savannah does not produce a great variety, however, I will try my <u>prettiest</u> to afford you entertainment but my dear Mary it must be sacred from every eye but yours & <u>Fan's</u>.[3]

Oh! the dear soul. How I should like to hear some of her jokes and a few of her <u>brilliant</u> sentiments. Tell her the World has taught me the fallacy of some of mine. I begin to view things as I ought and instead of being charmed with <u>tinsel,</u> I await until a long acquaintance unfolds the merits of Persons, for I have been too frequently deceived. I once had a friend that I adored, but she married and forgot me, and all the protestations of friendship she so often made. If you knew the whole story you would think perhaps I displayed too much pride on the occasion, but I have never been accustomed to slights and can illy brook them.

The report of Sarah's engagement is without foundation. Her heart if analysed would be discovered to be formed of more adamantine materials than mine, which you well know is perfectly impenetrable to the wiles of sly little Cupid. I think Molly, you & I could <u>jog</u> through life without an <u>encumbrance,</u> which most women think absolutely essential to happiness. Are you serious when you excite the most pleasing hopes in me? Will you really visit me in April? Language is inadequate to express the happiness it would create among us all. I shall expect you, so beware how you disappoint me. Margaret has improved very much, she appears to be perfectly amiable and very well informed for her age[.] she is very fond of you & talks incessantly of the whole family. Accept our grateful thanks for the attention extended to her by every individual that bears the name of Few. Poor Miss Lewis! to have her fondest hopes crushed is dreadful indeed, and the dear <u>Youth,</u> how does he support the loss of such a <u>multitude</u> of charms. Miss Laight, still <u>gabbling,</u> her tongue must be nearly worn out in the service. does she know that her once loved Noble has two lovely children. they are beautiful as angels. So Henry has gone to <u>graze.</u> he was an ugly fellow, but <u>Gabe</u> your swain has he too sought the shades—and the <u>Fox Hunter</u> is he still extant? A young Gentleman of my acquaintance a Captain in the army saw him on the Louisiana. he enquired after his <u>Ballstown</u> Friends.

I am going to make a bold request will [page torn] get two mantles exactly like Margarets for [page torn] and myself. have them made to fit you and get them as soon as possible & send by the first Opportunity write at the same time, and I shall receive it safe. I am destitute of warm clothing and require Something to shield me from the <u>wintry blast.</u>

Do Mary, Mary write to me often. Tell Frances I have not yet finished her extracts of Verse & Prose. "The Lady of the Lake" is certainly a sweet little Poem. I know it almost by heart. Ellen is a wonder. I wish she had married FitzJames instead of Malcolm.[4] Adieu. I will write again very soon & a longer letter. Your friend, Mary.

1. The address of a school in Savannah the girls attended together.
2. The Englishman Alexander Pope (1688-1744), whose poem of 1717, "Eloisa to Abelard," describes unhappy lovers who parted and took religious vows.

3. Meaning compared to New York, where Mary Few's family moved at the dawn of the century. Fan is probably one of Mary Few's sisters.

4. In this very long poem by Sir Walter Scott (1771–1832), the heroine Ellen of the Scottish highlands must choose between two men. It is doubtful that Telfair memorized the entire work.

Sophia C. Springs to her sister Mary Springs Springs, 11 February 1818, from Mecklenberg County, North Carolina, to York District, South Carolina. Springs Family Papers, Southern Historical Collection, University of North Carolina.

In 1818, Sophia Springs was thirty years old, her sister ten years older; they were the daughters of a poor widow who owned no slaves. Like many adult sisters, they try, not always successfully, to maintain an intimate relationship despite their individual family responsibilities.

My Dear Sister,

I have seated myself at last, to perform a promise That I am almost ashamed to think of, by neglecting it so long. But I will not bother you with apologies for I believe they are unproffitable to those that make them, and sometime unpleasant to those that hear them. my pen is so bad that I can scarcely keep from it now—In the first place I shall let you know that Father in respects to health, is much as usual, his situation causes him to be a goodeal fretful, but that is nothing more than we might expect of any person in the same Situation.

When I get through the bustle of the day and retire to this little retreat, I often think of the little intercourses of tenderness which formerly existed betwixt us and how much on the decline they seem to be. What is the cause? I suppose that on your part it must be the increase of your domestic affairs, which of course will lessen your opportunity of keeping up a correspondence in some measure.[1]

But Friendship after all is the great medicine of life—we were born for society and the mind never so effectually unburdens itself as in the conversation of a well-chosen friend—happy the woman who finds such a treasure. It is more precious than thousands of gold or silver. What are the highest blessings unsweeten'd by society? How poignant are many sorrows of life without a friend to alleviate and divide them.

Our mother came up from Mr. Harris on friday last their family was well then—She went back yesterday and had a very cold ride I expect—She had promised to go back and stay with Sister Sarah until Mr. Harris's return from town—Brother John has been a good deal deranged for several days but I am told he is much better this evening.[2] I am Dear Sister Yours with Affection, Sophia C. Springs.

[in another hand] Grandmother's Sister Sophia C. Springs married Dr. Ross

1. Mary Springs married her cousin John Springs in 1806 and had five children.
2. Sophia Springs was single at this time in her life (she later wed Doctor Joseph Ross) and living with her parents and siblings. Her brother, who was in his twenties, was mentally disturbed.

Floride Colhoun Calhoun to her friend Elizabeth Pinckney Lowndes, 24 June 1820, from Washington, D.C., to Washington, D.C. William Lowndes Papers, Library of Congress.

Floride Colhoun of South Carolina married her cousin John C. Calhoun in 1811, when she was nineteen and he was twenty-nine. In 1820 her husband served as secretary of war in President James Monroe's cabinet, and William Lowndes, Elizabeth's husband, was a member of Congress. Mrs. Calhoun's quick temper was well known, but she also had a gift for friendship. Her letter to Elizabeth Lowndes shows that cordiality could be grounded in the common experience of motherhood.

I feel quite mortified, My Dear Mrs. Lowndes, at not acknowledging the receipt of your letter sooner; but hope you will pardon it, as it was my intention, to have answered it immediately, but preparing to leave home at the time and being absent some time, threw me into such an unsettled way, that I postponed it until now, hope you will think late is better than never. You can form no idea how bad I felt when you left me; I almost wished I had never been acquainted with you; it appeared to me when I went . . . [from] your Chamber, that I had lost a friend, and one that could never be replaced to me.

I hope the Children are well. Tell Rebecca she does not know how much

I miss her, but that I hope to see you and her next Winter.[1] I have done with your things as you requested, the clothes which the boys left I have put into the large ball[2] which I made; if there is yet any thing that I can do for you, let me know; as it will always afford me pleasure to serve you or yours, in any way. . . .

It will no doubt give you pleasure to hear of your friend Mrs. Wirt. She is well, but all of her Children have taken the whooping cough at the same time, consider what a time she must have of it and very much in want of a nurse which she cannot get.[3] All of your friends are well.

. . . Mr. Calhoun, Mama, and the Children are well. they join me in love to yourself, Mr. Lowndes, and the Children. Do remember me to Mrs. Joe Lowndes and all friends. I remain with great regard your affectionate friend Floride Calhoun.

1. Rebecca Lowndes, her daughter.
2. A nineteenth-century term for bundle.
3. Elizabeth Gambler Wirt, originally of Richmond, was the wife of William Wirt, Monroe's attorney general. They had twelve children.

Maria Louisa C. Marshall to her sister Eliza C. Gould, 12 April 1827, from Woodville, Mississippi, to Tuscaloosa, Alabama. Maria Louisa Chotard Marshall and Family Papers, Hill Memorial Library, Louisiana and Lower Mississippi Valley Collections, Louisiana State University.

Maria Marshall, wife of a successful banker, was devoted to her sister, and like most white women, she wanted female relatives nearby when she gave birth to a child. With mixed emotions of fear and joyful anticipation, she invites her sister to be with her through what could be a dangerous trial.

My dearest Sister,

Capt. Dyer delivered your letter, in New Orleans to Mr. Whitman who gave it to James Paul, as he was coming up this way so that thru the medium of your old admirer I had the pleasure of hearing from you. he seems to admire some of his old acquaintances as much as ever, yet he has found out a young lady in this neighborhood, who dwells in very <u>interesting woods,</u>

and withal a good many <u>chinking charms,</u> he returned from a visit to Miss Hooke yesterday in the finest spirits (and too Mr. M[1] who has been his confidant for the last 2 months) that he had <u>all sort</u> of encouragement, fool for luck, he has realized about 12,000 dollars and now very likely to be accepted by this girl, who must be worth a very considerable fortune.

Young Carter Beverly was here on his way to St. Francisville for his sister who went up with him yesterday. poor girl she is in wretched spirits owing to her Father's arrival in Natchez. he has been there two weeks and Dr. Randolph has not been near him neither does he allow his wife or her child to notice him. it was a foolish thing in the old man to come to this country, knowing the aversion the Dr. had for him, but I expect he was short of <u>allowance</u> and came for the 200 a year that Anne allowed him, but <u>that sum</u> the Dr. has curtailed to nearly one half, which was quite beneath him, the old Man is a piece of—imposition I have no doubt, yet when a man is doing so much for his own relations, he should not diminish any amount that his wife might have pleased to bestow on her Father, when she had the <u>liberty</u> and the <u>means</u>.[2] <u>Becca</u> told me that her sister had little Mealy yet, and that her health was very much improved. she says her sister will never give her up. I am glad to hear she is so much pleased to have her, as it will be a great advantage to that interesting child, and a releif to Mrs. Hogan.

What a melancholy situation the Abert family must be in. Mrs. Ramsey I am told has been sent to the hospital in Philadelphia, and it is supposed that Mr. Bary is entirely deranged at times.

I am sorry to hear that you and William behaved with so little philosophy on the decision of our claims. I am such a dont care body that I never formed many sanguine expectations, yet we both could have enjoyed the cash that a favourable decision would have brought us. it would have been enabled us to see you this summer, which would have been the greatest happiness that wealth could procure.[3]

I think William ought to go for his sister's, independent of the pleasure of taking care of them, his health might be much benefited. I hope however that as the summer advances he will be restored to that blessing. I could give you a full employment <u>about that time,</u> had I the resolution to leave my old man but I should suffer too much anxiety for him. his health is generally so delicate in summer that I should fear to leave him. The inquiry contained in your letter is on a subject that I have long wished to communicate to you, yet we all naturally feel reluctant to <u>commence</u> an acknowledgment of <u>that nature</u>.[4] My heart, however, is so closely bound to you that I shall be relieved to tell you the whole truth in August or September. my life may be endeared to me, or it may cease.[5] when I look forward to that moment I cannot believe that I am to be separated from you. I cannot look for the attentions of friendship, much less for those of affection. my intercourse with the people of this place has been of such a nature that I do not calculate, nor should I, of any attentions from them. But I have almost every blessing in an affectionate husband. It is one that enables us [to bear] our severest trials.

Tell Te[s] it is getting so dark, I can't see to write any more I'll go and eat my Supper. dear little soul how I should like to hear her chatting. Kiss them both for us,[6] and ask William if he never means to write to us. Give our love to him and all our friends, and believe me to be sincerely yours, Maria L. Marshall.

1. Levin R. Marshall, her husband.
2. It sounds as if Mrs. Randolph had an independent fortune or inherited property from a first husband, but the origins of this situation are obscure.
3. The two women were involved in an inheritance dispute, which was not resolved in their favor. William is Eliza Gould's husband. Despite Marshall's comments, she and her husband were already affluent, and by the early 1830s would be quite rich.
4. Marshall had difficult pregnancies and may have already had a miscarriage.
5. That is, she may give birth to a healthy child or she may die in childbirth. In 1833, Marshall died after giving birth.
6. Her nieces Tes and Sally.

Eliza Harriet Johnston to her friend Elizabeth Mackay, 18 July [1828], from Oakland, New Jersey, to Savannah, Georgia. Eliza Anne (McQueen) Mackay Papers, Special Collections Library, Duke University.

At the time this letter was written, Eliza Johnston and Elizabeth Mackay were in their late teens and both native Georgians. Johnston's family was moderately prosperous, and Mackay's father was a slaveowning merchant. Johnston's possessive, flirtatous remarks are typical of homosocial relationships that developed between some young women. A visit to her Northern relatives inspires further musings on the competing ties of friendship and family.

I have left all the beaux downstairs, the <u>interesting Charley</u> among the number, to come up and talk to you: Oh! when will the time come, when I can indeed talk to you without the aid of a pen — old Time has surely turned a lazy dog, or he has exchanged his fleet <u>airy</u> wings for a pair of leaden ones: for each week has seemed a <u>month</u> since I parted from you — Thanks, a thousand thanks, Dearest Girl, for your dear delightful letter, which I received yesterday. I cannot well express how much pleasure it gave me; notwithstanding Savannah's being as dull as a "<u>dry old stick</u>," I think you managed to make it extremely interesting. Tell me all about your own <u>dear self,</u> and all the feelings of your heart, and your letters will always be so to me.

And do you <u>really</u> miss me so much sweetest? But Bessy love you must not patronize the <u>azure deamons,</u>[1] they are not <u>fit company</u> for <u>you.</u> I used to be now and then troubled with them, but since I have been here, I have sent them all <u>scampering,</u> and am determined not to be pestered with them again; if they should ever ask for admittance I will sing out, "I am engaged Sirs, call tomorrow" and you do the same, lovey, for <u>George Waldburg</u> is the <u>only divil</u> I will ever allow you to associate with — and <u>young Nick,</u> not <u>old.</u>

I will deliver your message to Brother James <u>this night week</u> some time <u>after eight</u> o'clock — The Neyles, I suppose have returned. do give <u>all</u> of our best love to them, and to your dear Mother and Catherine, not forgetting your sweet Sister Mrs. Stiles, Mrs. McQuean, and Miss Cowper, and I suppose I can't leave out <u>Brother Ben,</u> but you can there if you like, substitute <u>compliments</u> or <u>respects</u> for <u>love,</u> and I am not done yet. Augusta before she went to bed <u>charged</u> me to give her love to <u>you,</u> and then Mary and Susan, I suppose, will wish to send theirs to Sarah and Anne, <u>and Brother George his to your brother William!</u> (What a loving letter! Loves are, generally, sent at the <u>end</u> of a letter, but somehow I never can find a <u>place</u> for them there, so I thought I had better write them while I have room.)

How you must have missed the Neyles when they were in the country and dear little poney, too (The image of a <u>friend</u> of <u>yours</u>) that would have been such a comfort to you, to be taken away at the same time. I am sorry you have been so unfortunate about your riding, and as to Bliss, he is mighty touchy. I think the <u>gunpowder pie</u> exactly suited him: pray did you give him that, faded rose bud? and what did he say? threw it away, I suppose, without any remark [2] —

Thank you for mentioning so particularly how my Sister, the doctor, and the baby were — Sister Bell received Sister's letter Monday, and it was <u>well</u> it came then; for I had begun to conjure up all kinds of horrors in my brain, first fancying one friend was sick, then another, and then every body must be sick; but her sweet letter dissipated all these ideas; that, and the delight of again having some converations with you, though it is by letter, has made me so gay, that I fear you will think me turned a mad <u>harum scarum</u> girl.

In my innumerations of loves, I forgot to mention Mary Bullock. do remember me to her. Good Night — I will <u>dream of you.</u>

Friday morning—

I was reading to Aunt P. all yesterday and could not resume my pen. Oh! this <u>tedious</u> summer will <u>never</u> wear out. dear Liz how I long to see you! there may be, for aught I know, some truth in the proverb, "<u>Absence</u> strengthens true love," but it certainly cannot <u>weaken</u> the sincere attachment I feel for you, Lizzie dear. I have forsworn <u>Love</u> (at least what is <u>generally</u> so called) and will, with your permission, devote my heart to you (with the exception of one hole so <u>deep</u> that it cannot be got at, where my <u>numerous quantity</u> of sisters and brothers are enshrined, and, where, also <u>you</u> have long <u>long</u> held a place besides that, there is another little corner, in which I have packed some odd <u>dozens</u> of <u>Aunts, Uncles, cousins,</u> and <u>friends</u>). Say, Lady fair, will you accept of it? Perhaps like Lady Caroline Braymore in "John Bull" you will be <u>surprised</u> at my offering you a thing of <u>so little</u> or <u>no</u> value, and will wonder what use you can make of it: shall I tell you?[3] help me to try and make it more worthy of you and whenever you are at a loss to fill up a letter, write me a catalogue of my faults and follies & I will try to correct them.

I met, in New York, that specimen of <u>Russian gentility</u>, Mr. Kramer; but he was so much engaged talking to some ladies that he did not observe me, which I was very glad of — he and Major Erving were the only persons I saw, that I knew — the Major called on us the day we left.

About the <u>wedding</u> I cannot tell you much, as it has not yet taken place — Next Wed [page torn] is the day fixed —

[page torn] tea very early here, and then take a deli[page torn] walk, whe[page torn] <u>ends</u> in a romp — the other evening we we[page torn] down to th[page torn] and the gentlemen rowed us out a long way the [page torn] engaged a boat to take us over to an island, opposite, to-morrow — I wish y[ou] were here, and the Neyles too, we would have so much fun —

Yes! Bonnie be a sweet blossom! I think we had better finish Hume[4] this summer — I forgot all about it until Monday I went to search for a book in my Uncle's library, & spied there, all ranged in battle array, however undaunted, like a good girl, I took my volume down and read immediately sixty pages, which I have done every morning since — My letters, you say, must be <u>funny, sweet</u> and <u>long</u>—they certainly are <u>long</u>—but I cry much fear, they fail in the two <u>first</u> & most essential requisitions.

Good bye sweetest—I put a kiss here for you—take care it dont fly out when you open this letter—Yours with <u>unbounded</u> affection, <u>Bouncing</u> Bess.

Weighing <u>one hundred pound and one.</u> I certainly think I have <u>some</u> claim to this appellation.

Brother George this morning drove Sister Bell, Jane, and Louisa in a barouche to spend the day at Bordentown,[5] with Miss Ritchie and the Miss Telfairs—they have taken a house there, and are very comfortably fixed— I declined going, wishing to finish my scrawl to you—I have so much more to say to you, that I could fill up <u>now</u> three pages more, but no doubt, <u>you</u> would rather be excused <u>reading</u> them—So Adieu once more—Eliza.

We expect to be in Northampton[6] Saturday the 28th—direct your letter to that place, care of brother George. I will remember my promise, provided <u>you remember yours</u> (of not showing each others letters)—So write me soon dearest—EHJ.

1. Meaning spells of depression.
2. This appears to be a joke about a rejected suitor, but the reference is not clear.
3. "John Bull" is an English play by George Colman, first performed in 1803 and popular throughout the nineteenth century. Lady Caroline Braymore, daughter of an impoverished nobleman, rejects a wealthy aristocrat to marry another man; his initial declaration of love surprises Lady Caroline.
4. Probably Lord David Hume (1711–76), who wrote dozens of books on religion, philosophy, and history.
5. A town in New Jersey.
6. A town in Massachusetts.

M. Hooper to her friend Julia Pickens, n.d. 1832, from "At Mrs. McLean's," in North Carolina, to Pittsborough, North Carolina. Chiliab Smith Howe Papers, Southern Historical Collection, University of North Carolina.

Teenaged Julia Pickens was the orphaned daughter of Martha Lenoir Pickens and Israel Pickens, the governor of Alabama. In 1832 she was living with her maiden aunt in North Carolina. Miss Hooper's father was a yeoman farmer, and until recently she had been one of Pickens's schoolmates. This letter's feverish intensity and physical references suggest that their relationship may have had some erotic component.

Twere vain my Julia to attempt to describe the anguish of this day. Sad inexpressibly sad have been my reflections—and when again and again the truth the bitter truth that we have parted, so far as we can judge, <u>forever</u>— arose, the blood has rushed to my heart until (<u>believe</u> me) I trembled and felt sick in body as well as mind.—

O' Julia Julia <u>now</u> my heart is throbbing with very agony—my tears are ever ready to overflow but what avail are they? Can they recall that dear embrace? those eyes of love? that brow (sweet brow) this very morning I kissed? the hand whose pressure now I feel–No oh no! now will they ever be recalled. O <u>this, this</u> is what breaks my heart—for it feels as if it was really breaking.

To look back <u>upon all your love</u> is vain to alleviate my sufferings. I can only say again and again in agony of Spirit,

> "<u>Jesus thy</u> timely aid impart
> And raise my heart and cheer my heart"

This does comfort me and when I recollect that <u>my Father</u> ordered it in <u>infinite love</u> for our <u>mutual</u> good I am comforted.[1] It cannot be a thing of chance. So <u>much</u> suffering must be intended for some good. I do not give you a romantic exaggeration but the <u>real</u> and literal state of my feelings. Why is it? Is it that I am more capable of feeling more <u>keenly acutely</u> than others? I [illegible] O happy are they who have less. Tis a relief to tell you— oh it is—and this privilege is worth worlds to me.

We meet not here but above—oh <u>there</u> in that bright land—<u>we shall</u>— yes we <u>shall</u>—and these sorrow will <u>then</u> be forgotten—My Julia forget me not—my sister forget me not, forget not my last request. Love my Julia seek her society and the many hours that would otherwise be wasted in frivolous company will be gained in imitiating one so estimable—so lovely.[2] Heaven bless you both, asks your almost broken hearted friend & sister.

Miss J. Pickens & Miss M. Hooper

Love to all <u>every Girl</u>—each has in my heart a large place. Kiss the little girls—Adelaide Euphenia Susan Frances Betsy—Sister sends my [page torn]. I value them—my darling farewell!

Sunday morning. With whom dear sister did you sleep? Tell me were you resting placidly on another's arm while I wept in bitterness that mine was not your pillow and this sabbath morning <u>whose hand</u> usurps the sweet place that mine was wont to hold and whose is first in that heart <u>now</u>— Is it your sister whose matchless love for your makes her wretched— <u>oh forget me not.</u>

Do not show this be sure. send my [illegible] from you—

1. Abraham Hooper of Wilkes County, North Carolina, a farmer who owned no slaves in 1830.
2. Probably another classmate at school. In 1832 Pickens married an army captain named Chiliab S. Howe.

Laura Cole to her cousin Camilla, 1833, from lowcountry, South Carolina, to somewhere in Georgia. Laura Cole Diary and Letterbook, Brumby and Smith Family Books, Southern Historical Collection, University of North Carolina.

Laura Cole was a planter's daughter living in Carolina low country. She is very fond of her correspondent, a teenager her own age whose mother has just died. Here, Laura Cole reaches out to Camilla and invites her to share her grief.

To Camilla,

Since receiving the fatal intelligence contained in cousin Alfred's last letter, twenty times, dearest Camilla, have I taken up my pen and as often resigned it, hopeless of being able to offer a single word, which would not rather augment than diminish the anguish in which we so deeply sympathize. Painfully as my own feelings are involved, how little ought they to be considered, in comparison of the great, the irreparable loss my dear cousins have sustained. What could be said which would in any degree console you under such an affliction? Sympathy is vain—words seem idle! Nothing but a firm reliance on our beneficient Creator, and the precious hope, the soothing convinction that the loved one we mourn, is now enjoying a rich reward for all her virtues can possibly soften the first bitterness of grief. Yes Camilla, let us believe she has changed a state of existence (where, even in the happiest situations, severe trials must often be endured), for one, where pain or sorrow can no more reach here; where her pure spirit, freed from the shackles of mortality participates in all the bliss of promised redemption, becoming brighter and more glorious as successive ages roll on. How uncertain is all human felicity! How often do the events of a few weeks, nay a few hours destroy the fairest prospects, the dearest hopes of our hearts. A few minutes before receiving cousin Alfred's last [letter], I had closed a letter to you, dear Camilla, the sprightliness of which, I then fondly anticipated, would be consonant with your feelings. How did the single minute it required to see the dreadful contents of his letter, crush all the buoyant sensations with which I was animated, while penning the one to you, and leave in their place a feeling of deeper sadness, because so utterly unlooked for.

It was a heart-rending stroke to my dear mother — A sudden withering up of all those hallowed and gentle emotions with which she had ever cherished the idea of that loved sister, whom she was destined no more to embrace. "I am the last!" she exclaimed; as if communing with her own heart. "Not one green spot, on which the aching heart may rest when memory bears it back to his early days of peace and joy."

Doubly now, do I regret our separation. Did we live near you, I would endeavor by the most affectionate and unwearied attentions to prove to you under your present bereavement, how deep an interest I feel in your happiness. But divided as we are, I yield to the painful convinction, that I cannot in any way contribute to your tranquillity.

Thursday morning.

How calm, how beautiful — and yet how melancholy is this evening! Events long past, and only registered in the heart, are stealing gradually over the memory — while the fairy hopes, the illusive dreams of early youth, are sadly mingled with more recent and distressing occurrences. Beautiful — Beautiful world! why does the bitterness of grief so often pass over the heart when we seem only to contemplate thy loveliness? when we hear the music of thy winds and waves, inhale thy fresh and balmy airs, or gaze upon the cloudless skies, and verdant landscapes, why do we associate with feelings produced by thy blandness and grace, the memory of sorrow over which we have no control, thus — destroying half their soothing influence. Why — but because an overruling Providence has so ordered it lest we should fix our affections too deeply on things earthly and perishable in their nature. . . .

Write to me soon, dear Camilla, as your feelings will permit, and write unreservedly. Experience has taught me, that from a sense of duty to those who are equal sufferers with ourselves, we often suppress the appearance of grief, though the heart may be throbbing with anguish. But when we are alone, then comes the sense of desolation which nothing can so effectively relieve as the communication of our feelings to another. Let that other be Laura, who as she has ever rejoiced in your joy, will now sincerely sympathize in your grief. Yours most affectionately Laura.

Anne Addison Carr Conrad to her sister-in-law Elizabeth W. Powell Conrad, 24 January 1835, from Martinsburg, Virginia, to Winchester, Virginia. Holmes Conrad Papers, Virginia Historical Society.

Nancy Conrad was a lawyer's wife in a small town, the mother of several children. She had many friends but singles out one matron for her exemplary self-denial and resignation to God's will.

I owe you many thanks for your last kind letter, my dear Sister, and shall always be delighted to recieve one from you, tho I did not intend in my note to reproach you for not having written sooner, because I know it is an employment which you dislike, and I am too often remiss myself, to estimate the affection, or interest of my friends, by the number of their letters; —

I am truly sorry to find that your time has been much occupy'd with nursing this winter, and above all, that you have yourself has been so much of an invalid. That same Influenza is a much more serious thing than people generally believe, especially if not arrested when it <u>first comes on.</u> I believe both Mr. Conrad and myself would have been very sick with it, if we had not been bled immediately and with that precaution,[1] we got well much sooner than most persons, some here, who neglected themselves in the first instance, became quite ill with pleurisy. Mrs. Hoge's little son had a violent attack (so much so as to spit blood), from exposing himself after having the influenza. I felt particularly interested for the poor little fellow as his Mother was so far from him. You know she is spending the winter with her old friends & neighbors in Richmond, and his aunt's health was hardly equal to the fatigue and anxiety of attending upon him.[2] he is now, however, quite recovered, and Mrs. Strother looks better than I have seen her since the death of her child. I understood she was very much shocked & agitated upon first hearing of her brother David's death, but when I saw her she was quite composed, and as cheerful as usual; She is a woman for whom I feel great attachment, and sympathy. how much affliction has fallen to her lot! out of <u>seven</u> healthy, promising children, but <u>two</u> remain, besides innumerable others, of her nearest & dearest relatives whom she has seen cut off from before her eyes, and repeatedly she has been herself brought to the brink of the grave.

But she has been taught this important lesson, "Set your affections on things above, <u>not</u> on things that are upon the earth," and oh! how difficult a one it is, to poor human nature!

—Mary Matthews has a Son, both she & her child are well. Thank you for your kind enquiries about my health. It seems quite restored, tho' of course my constitution will never be as strong again, and will require more care, but I feel well, and my complexion is healthy, but you would be shocked to see how old I look, with one of my front teeth gone.

I hope your dear children have gotten well. Rebecca is as fat & healthy as she can be, but Betsy's health is delicate, and I often feel uneasy about her, she has had an other severe cold which still affects her hearing a good deal, and she looks thin & badly;[3]

It is not in my power to visit you at this time my dear Betty, I do not feel disposed to go any where from home, tho' it would give me the greatest pleasure to see you here, and I do think you ought to come as soon as the roads will permit. ask Robert if he does not think so too?[4] and write me word when I may look for you. I am glad to hear our cousin's James & Frederica are <u>casting sheeps eyes</u> at each other,[5] I think they would suit admirably. I am pleased that F. is coming to our Town soon, and hope she will stay some time with us. Give my love to her, and tell her so I am told she is to be one of Betty's Brides Maids. Chloe is well. She desires much love, and many thanks for your invitation which it would give her pleasure to accept if it was in her power. She sends her respects to Robert and a Purse of her knitting, which she begs he will use for her sake.

Tell Danny the children were delighted with the "Bon Anne" he sent them.[6] The good things were soon demolished, but the papers are put away carefully.

Remember me afftly. to all my friends & relations. Your affte. Sister— Nancy A. Conrad.

1. Her husband is David Conrad. Antebellum doctors believed that cutting a patient's veins would rid the body of poisons. Contrary to Mrs. Conrad's remarks, it rarely helped patients and usually harmed them.
2. Meaning that the boy was staying with his aunt.

3. Her young children, all under age ten.

4. Elizabeth's husband, who would have to accompany her on the thirty-mile journey from Winchester to Martinsburg.

5. Nineteenth-century slang meaning they were infatuated with each other.

6. A dessert popular in the nineteenth century.

Henrietta Kerr Tilghman to her cousin Mary Ellen Wilson, 24 February 1835, from Plimhommon plantation, Talbot County, Maryland, to Hope plantation, Maryland. Tilghman Papers, MS 1967, Manuscripts Division, Maryland Historical Society Library.

Henrietta Tilghman, a middle-aged plantation mistress, anticipates a great deal of hilarity during a visit with her cousins. She plans to do some piecework, but her principal goal is the uninhibited fun — "carnival," as she puts it — that women can enjoy in each other's company.

My dear Mary: —

I rec'd your affectionate note of the 20th by a very <u>beloved hand</u> on Sat. last — We had hoped to see you all on Friday next, but this unexpected snow will render the roads impassable for a week or 2 & we must abandon the agreeable plan we had formed. I am however <u>bent upon</u> a jaunt as soon as all the roads will permit & you need not be surprised to see me at Myrtle Grove during your sojourn there [1] — I am exceedingly anxious to make an <u>old time</u> sociable visit there such as I <u>used to</u> in my <u>early youth</u> & if it is talked about as long as most of our jaunts are before they are executed Susan & Henny will be off for Boston without my seeing them again,[2] so I am determined to break through all minor difficulties & be off as soon as possible. Tell the Grovers so when you go,[3] with my love, I will endeavor to prevail on Grandma to accompany us but if she is not disposed I shall not delay for her — I have been so secluded this winter, I am determined to go forth & <u>see the world</u> a little. — I am very busy too just now in making up a set of shirts for my old man [4] — but I have a plan for <u>saving time</u> in the accomplishing of that job — <u>wh. is only</u> to carry some of the <u>wristbands</u> &c. along with me & engage <u>your</u> nimble fingers to assist me a little — I suppose you'll have no objections to <u>getting</u> yr hand in — as the time may not be far distant when such work will form a part of yr <u>pleasing</u> duty.[5]

ah Mary dear! I fear for this projected visit of yours (if the <u>danger</u> is not already past). Keep thine heart with <u>diligence</u>—These naval officers are <u>appropriate</u> fellows & make very good husbands I don't doubt—but then the months & years of trying absence—<u>Mary</u> a <u>landsman</u> "ma chere"— Some of my friends won't thank me for this advice, so as I would stand well with them, let it be "entre nous"[6]—

I was much satisfied at yr note & am sorry to have incurred the charge of neglect of you—

I have really <u>intended</u> to write to you for some time & have wished for you <u>not seldom</u> this winter. You will not surely object to returning home with me from Myrtle Grove—I don't wish to abridge yr. visit there either, & leave it entirely to <u>yourself</u> to fix our stay—I am looking forward to carnival with you <u>gals</u> & intend to be as wild as any of you.

My sweet boy is very well indeed[7]—His eyes are as clear & bright again as diamonds. He has lately cut 4 teeth at once wh. made him for a week quite feverish every night. If this shd. find you at Hope give my very best love to them all—I dare say Grandma will be for going to bring Cousin A. to a Bible Meeting before long & I shall not object to the opportunity of seeing them—I particularly regret this interruption to our plan on acct. of Aunt Maria & hearing about her Phila. jaunt. I hope however she will get down here before a great while—as I wishe to add a line or 2 to Uncle Wm. I have not the space to tell you much of a letter I have lately rec'd from Mrs. Cope relative to our poor friend Matilda R. Suffice it to say at present, she is as low as it is possible to be—or <u>was</u> at her sister's writing. I am pierced at the thought that there is so little probability of our connecting again in this world. Mrs. C. mentions that a teaspoon full of milk 3 times a day with small pieces of ice was her only diet so you may judge of her situation.

T. has not had an answer to his letter to judge P. yet you shall be informed of it promptly when it arrives—I must say adieu, dear Mary. Yr. affectionate cousin, H. M. Tilghman.

P.S. To W. H. T. Esq.

My dr Uncle, The roads will probably prevent me from meeting you; should you have anything to communicate on any subject shortly, drop me a line or make any appointment that will best suit yr own convenience—Remember that in hard scrabbles is indispensably necessary to have a <u>witness.</u> We should be delighted to see you both truly. Tench.

1. A nearby plantation.
2. Maria's sisters.

3. A pun on the inhabitants of Myrtle Grove.

4. Her husband, planter Tench Tilghman.

5. Meaning that Mary Wilson may soon be married.

6. The French phrases translate "my dear" and "between us." Her husband graduated from West Point, and several relatives served in the United States Navy.

7. One of her five children, probably William, who died later that year.

Diary of Eliza Ann Marsh Robertson. Eliza Ann Marsh Robertson Papers, Southern Historical Collection, University of North Carolina.

As a teenager, Eliza Ann Marsh of Louisiana composed this poem for Margaret (later Mrs. Ashbel Henshaw). Of debatable literary merit, it communicates her warm affection for her sister.

New Iberia   June 25th 1843—

To My Sister—

Look to the east when the morning is bright
When the purple is blending with rays of rose light!
My spirit shall then hold communion with thee,
And thy blush bright as morning, must whisper of me
And look to the west, when pavilioned afar,
Sweet love sends her smile from her own favored star,
and think of our friendship as pure as star-shine
My spirit shall then hold communion with thine
And at midnights deep hour, when the moon is on high
Should the angel of sleep leave unseal'd thy soft eye,
Look forth! The calm radiance is hallowed by love,
And then prayers for true hearts may mingle above.

Margaret.

Mary E. Starnes to her friend Sarah J. Thompson, 25 September 1846, from Harrison County, Texas, to Augusta, Georgia. William H. Kilpatrick Letters, from the collections of the Dallas Historical Society.

These women, all of them lonely, one of them desperately so, struggle to remain friends on the Texas frontier despite the conflicts between men in their families. The author is in her late teens, the sister of William Starnes, a slaveowning planter and physician with whom she lives.

Dear Sarah,

I suppose you have received my last letter by this time, & have the satisfaction of knowing you are not forgotten, if forgetfulness is the only sin we will have to answer for we are both sure of a high seat in heaven, & you may tell whoever has the insolence to accuse us of any thing of the kind, not to judge other people by themselves. I suspect it is no one but Mary Thompson that talks that way about us, & if silence is any sign of forgetfulness we have long since ceased to live in her memory, for I can neither persuade nor provoke her to say a word to me, but I will not be too severe this time, perhaps the poor child has not heard from Sammy lately & she feels disposed to quarrel with every one else, as for yourself you have no right to utter a single complaint, for you hear from me just as often as I hear from you. write oftener yourself & I will do the same, your letters are always answered. Since you heard from me I have been sick again, & have not yet entirely recovered from the last attack, while I was taking medicine I made so much use of cold water, that the first thing I knew, I was badly salivated, & for a week after the fever left me I was compelled to live on such light diet, & have been so unwell ever since, that I am looking quite delicate at present, & so ugly that Brother compares me to the Witch of Macbeth [1] & says if dont fatten soon he will have to get a quill & blow me up. While my mouth was at its worst I received Mr. Sallerstedt's letter & you must know I had the blues to perfection when ever a letter from him made me cry, as lively as he always is, but he touched a tender cord. he spoke of old times, & that with my sore mouth was more than I could bear without shedding a few drops, for two or three days after I felt like crying all the time, & had to look up some books & go to reading, to keep from thinking about you all.

We have a great deal of sickness in the neighborhood. Brother is gone nearly all the time, it is only occasionally he gets to spend a night at home. he was sent for last night & soon after he started a dreadful storm came up.

he had a dismal swamp to pass through & it was so dark it was impossible to see the road. I was very much alarmed about him, but he came home this morning safe & sound, changed his clothes & started again in the rain. as much as he is compelled to expose himself he enjoys better health than when he had nothing to do. I am glad to hear your Ma thinks enough of me to dream about me. I hope the good part of her dream will come to pass & that no stranger will get the kiss intended for myself. I will certainly obey her orders to come home as soon as I have an opportunity of doing so, but when or how such an event could be brought about, I have no idea. I wish she would tell me, for it I am ever so fortunate as to get sight of her again, I will hold fast to her apron strings as long as there is a piece left, provided no one else has a stronger claim to her & my affections.

With regard to the show you say Mrs. Newby is ready to witness. I can only say she had better hang her hopes upon some one better calculated to please her Beauty than your humble servant, we could not make it out when we were near each other it is not probable we will do it now we are so many hundreds of miles apart, however, I am much obliged to her for her good opinion. Sister[2] says you may tell the old Lady, to come along, she will insure her a hearty welcome, & you with her, if you think the poor old soul can ever reach Texas with such a load of sin on her back. I am afraid she will have to drop you by the way side. be certain to let us now when you think of starting, for we have only two rooms to our house yet, but Brother has commenced an addition, & if you will let us know in time, I will try & get him to have it finished for your especiall accommodation; we will treat you as well as we possibly can, but all I can promise you besides a hearty welcome, is red bugs, ticks, fleas, & hickory nuts. there are the only things we have in abundance.

Give my love to Mrs. Taliaferro, & tell her I would rather see her than the President or queen Victoria. I know she dont think of me as often as I do of her, but she has so much more to take up her time & attention. I will not complain if she will only send me a message occasionally so I may know I am not entirely forgotten. Mr. Sallerstedt says little Sarah is getting to be quite the idea. I suppose Lucy is the same old thing.

You may now prepare yourself to hear what I have long been wanting to tell you about Mrs. Green, in the early part of last winter Brother & Mr. Green had a falling out. after that our families quit visiting, though the females thought as much of each other as ever. in the latter part of the winter Mrs. Green was taken sick & was confined to her bed for a long time, & I suppose did not receive that attention from the neighbours she ought to have had. Mr. G. is one of the most unpopular men I ever knew, & that I suppose with her other afflictions affected her mind. She has been partially deranged for several months & thinks she has not a friend in the country. she seems to love Sister & myself very much. you know I told you in my last we had been to see her. She saw us before we got in, met us at the door, & kissed us, & cried when we left her. I intend going again when I get well enough.

I would have told you her situation before, but as we were not on very friendly terms I was afraid Mr. Green might think I was meddling in affairs that did not concern me, & it was his duty, not mine, to write to her Father about it. I heard the other day he had written to her Father or Brother to come for her. I would like to know the truth of it. If you find out you must tell me in your next. I hope it may be so. If you ever hear from Bishop Andrew's family let me know how they are.[3] I will always be glad to hear from my old but unfortunate friend Sarah. Mr. Tenn's promised epistle has never been received. tell her if she dont mind I will get mad some of these rainy days & write to her again. I am glad to hear Ann Christian is looking so well. I hope she will have better luck this time than she had before.

The papers you sent me got here at last. I would like to have some more. do send one whenever you can, let your neighbours borrow from some one else.

I had almost forgot to tell you about an army of worms (not Mexicans)[4] we had in our cotton fields a few weeks ago. they have cut some of the crops very short, but they were late getting Brother's & I don't think they have injured him much. the cotton presents a strange appearance for this time of year; it is almost entirely leafless, & looks as if there had been a hard frost upon it. this has been a very good crop year, & if the worms had let it alone I expect the Farmers would have made as much cotton as they could have gathered. I am told it is very sickly every year they make good crops, but that only happen in five or six years.

Aunt Gatsy says I must put her in [this letter] every way I can, and do it nicely.[5] she is on her sick bed, but is getting better, sends her love to all & says you must tell Ma's Joe that when he gets married he hopes from that day, he will live an independent life. I suppose from that she wants him to marry a fortune. she says too he must be a good boy. I like to forgot that part. I believe all you say about little Hannah, kiss her for me. Ella can talk a little, but can't walk, & is nearly 14 months old.[6] She calls Sister & myself Aarty, she means Aunty. give our love to every body. I would name them if I had room. Sister has been dreaming about Libby lately, & so have I. your Mary.

1. In Shakespeare's play, three ugly witches called the "weird sisters" prophesy (correctly) that Macbeth will win great power and then die a tragic death. Starnes's correspondent should not be confused with Sarah S. Thompson of Kentucky, also featured in this volume.

2. Mary's sister Sarah.

3. James O. Andrew (1794–1871), a native Georgian, was the bishop of the Methodist Episcopal Church, South, from 1846 to 1866; he believed that good Christians could also own slaves.

4. The Republic of Texas and Mexico had contested their boundary for several years, and in September 1845 rumors of an American invasion of Mexico were rife. In October 1845, President James Polk ordered Zachary Taylor to concentrate troops along the border, and in 1846 the Mexican War began. It ended two years later in an American victory.

5. Aunt Gatsy is a middle-aged slave woman owned by the Starnes household.

6. William Starnes's daughter from his first marriage.

Martha E. Foster Crawford Journals and Diaries, Special Collections Library, Duke University

Martha Crawford was born in 1830 and lived in Tuscaloosa County, Alabama; nothing else is known about her background. In her diary, she articulates the themes of friendship among young women: the anxiety about marriage, the homosocial overtones, and the deep understanding on "common" subjects. In the 1850s she married nevertheless and moved to China to become a Protestant missionary.

2 October 1847.

I have the blues—I can't help it. And why? I am continually haunted with the idea of <u>being married.</u> A change from a girl to a woman—must leave my beloved parents for—I know not what. Must leave the harbor where I have been wont to sport carelessly without fear of winds or tempest—and enter with a stranger upon the broad Ocean of Life—exposed to storms with one who perhaps may turn traitor, and shipwreck my poor frail barque.

Alas, poor human nature! How long since I thought to be loved, to be <u>engaged</u> must be the summit of happiness—that it would more than outweigh every sorrow—compensate for every thing. And do I find it true? I feel like a prisoner. I feel as if I knew the future—and therefore was not waiting for time to disclose any thing. I formerly felt <u>free</u>—that I was my own—and could stand aloof and moralize upon the creatures around me—could gaze as a spectator upon the Grand Drama performing on this world—but now I feel I have my part to act—that I am no longer independent. It is a solemn thing for me to take a step which can <u>never, never</u> be recalled—there will then be no drawing back.

25 July 1849.
In less than two weeks cousin Lou will be Mrs. Rush Gates. What will become of me? Cousin Nancy will marry tomorrow night—cousin Beck some time this year and only Lizz and I will be left. I could well give up all but cousin Lou—I can't see how it is possible to get along without her. Rob will stay only a week or two after she leaves, and then—Ah me! I have never done without her—when from home I could write to her and look forward to a reunion. I felt almost as if I could claim her. But I must give her up—content myself with only a passing thought now and then, for the sake of past joys, sorrows, loves and mingled sympathy. We have often wept together—have interchanged bright hopes for the future—we have laughed together. She has been an elder sister, guiding and warning me of danger. Oh! what a thought! that we must so soon separate— <u>never to be as we have been.</u> She will think of me sometimes, I know with feelings of pleasure—but it will be only of the <u>past</u> and as a small affair. . . . I am becoming more Stoical. "Expect little pleasures and great sorrows, and you will be spared disappointments."[1] Cousin Lou and Cousin Rob were my all. The latter cannot supply the place of both. There are so many common little subjects of sympathy which she alone can feel and appreciate. And Oh! I must do without her! It is too horrid to think of. I shall die of the blues. I can't stay here. I hope cousin Joshua will succeed in getting me a situation in the Judson so that I can have employment.[2]

1. Stoicism, a philosophical movement dating from the third century B.C., emphasized rational self-control. It took its name from the Painted Portico (stoa poikile) in the marketplace in Athens, where its adherents met.
2. Members of a Baptist church in Marion, Alabama, founded Judson Female Institute in 1838. It was a well-known, widely respected girls' academy.

M. S. Rucker and Mary Jane Barton to Elizabeth Taylor, 7 October 1847, from Washington, Texas, to Readyville, Rutherford County, Tennessee. Barton Family Papers, Special Collections, University of Texas at Arlington.

This letter testifies to the importance of friendship for both adult and teenage women and how much they all longed for personal conversation. M. S. Rucker's husband made his living as a druggist in a small town; he was Mary Jane Barton's uncle and guardian. Mrs. Rucker is in her early thirties, Mary Jane is nineteen, and Elizabeth Taylor is a widow in her sixties.

Dear Mrs. Taylor,

I received your letter dated sept. 22nd and was happy to learn that you were all well. I was forced to believe that you was not a going to write to me, but you have explained it so satisfactorily that I cant complain. We were all truly delighted to hear what an excellent camp meeting you have had and would have been extremely happy to have been with you and participated in your enjoyment. We have had several excellent revivals in the county attended by the most desirable consequences. Indeed religion seems to have exerted an influence upon all there are but a few who does not seem impressed with the necessity of religion. We have church nearly ever sabbath and attended by a flourishing Sunday School. My dear friend you cant imagine how happy it would make me to visit my native land and to see my friends once more.[1] I am very thankful to your father for his kind offer and would except of it[2] but the children have become so attached to their Uncles and Aunts and also to the country that [they] do not wish to leave it; yet they all express their pleasure and happiness to visit their Grandfather and relatives and spend a year or so, but there is one part of your letter that I dont understand in reference to the company you keep. I have never doubted but you have kept the best of company. In response Mr. Ferel I have not seen him but once since last Christmas and then but a few moments. I just di——— to speak to him and that is all. I would be glad if you would explain it to me in your next letter.

Joshua was delighted to think that you a going to send him a present and ask us about a dozen times a day what we think it is. He says he will visit you when he receives it but cant think of spending a night with you unless I go with him. He is going to school. His uncle bought him a reading book. He was so delighted with it he memorized a piece directly to speak on Friday last. They are all going to school here, the two girls and Joshua. James is boarding at Brenham.[3] Tell Mary Jane that we are all so much pleased to think we are to be at her wedding. We s[t]ill hold our selves ready to go. I am in hopes it will be very soon for I am desirous of visiting you and I know that I will never get there unless something of the kind happens. We are all well at this time.[4] The county is generally healthy. We all join and send our love to you and Mother, Father, Husband, Children, and all. Your affectionate friend, M. S. Rucker.

P.S. I saw Bob last week. He was very sorry to hear of his Brother in law['s] death. He was delighted to hear from his Mother and wishes to be remembered to them all. I should [have] concluded my letter as Mary wishes to address her cousin a few lines.

My dear Cousin[5]

It is has been a long time since I have written to you and I will state my reasons for neglecting to write. First I am going to school and have a number of difficult studies to attend and worst of all have a composition to write every other week which keeps me very busy. Secondly, I have been very unhealthy this summer and dilatory both mental and phisically but I have now regained my health and being at leisure I shall deliver you a short epistol and try to portray my thoughts to you as exactly as possible.

My dear Cousin it is useless of me to express my desire of seeing you seeing that it is impossible. We will content ourselves by imagining ourselves conversing with each other. When Aunt wrote how you were enjoying yourselves sitting by your fireside you know not how I wish to be with you and participate in your pleasure. I am rather confined at present having to attend school. I cannot get time to write you a long letter. I have no news to tell you No weddings no actves of importance from me was just a monotony of dullness. I wish you would write me a long letter with all the news you have. If you have nothing else describe your fathers residence and all pertaining to it and another thing I want you to eat a double portion of apples, one half for me and when you sit down by your fireside to eat apples think of me in Texas seating by a heeping log fire eating pecans for want of better. I have tasted an apple but three times since here I have been living and cider I have never taste a single drop since I left my native land. We have plenty of whiskey and brandy and ale such as I care the least about yet for all that I do not think that I could leave Texas to live. Cousin you must come to see me. You will be pleased I am sure. I will give you as many beaus as you can take care of and as many beautiful flowers to press and fill your album as you can wish. Do come it would give me inexpressible happiness. I see nothing to prevent you. Elizabeth and Joshua are standing around the table fixing some hair for cousin Frances. Joshua says the short piece is his the middle E. and the outside mine.[6] Elizabeth says that Frances must come with you. She sends her love to all. Tell Cousin Jane that it will not be long before our school is out and then I will—and you a long letter. In the meantime you must write to me every opportunity. Receive all our best love. Your affectionate cousin M. J. Barton.

I wish to say a few words to Grandpa and MaMa. Tell them I have written several letters to them and I will write to them often when my school is out. I would give anything on earth to see them but I fear that wish will never be granted. If it is not I will try to meet them in heaven where [parting?] will be no more. Where I will be with my Dear Mother and Sisters Father[,] and misfortune cannot enter. Give my love to all. The children send their very best love for your self. Your affectionate granddaughter Mary J. Barton.

P.S. Aunt Frances has been laying out every week to write to you[7] but she has so much company that she has not time to do anything. She has had company all day so she could not come down. She sends her love to you all and wishes you to write.

1. She was from Tennessee.
2. Meaning to accept it.
3. James, Joshua, and the two girls are her children.
4. Mrs. Rucker died a year later after giving birth to her sixth child.
5. Taylor was actually Barton's aunt, not her cousin. The comments about beaux suggest that she may have written this letter to another, younger relative not named here.
6. In the nineteenth century it was common to give wreaths, brooches, or bracelets of woven hair as gifts to family members.
7. Meaning stating her intention to write.

Divorce Petition of Lucy W. Norman, Legislative Petitions, Henry County, 20 December 1848. Records of the General Assembly, Archives and Records Division, The Library of Virginia, Richmond, Virginia.

Lucy Norman was in her early thirties and some ten years her husband's senior when they married in 1844. Her dowry contained a considerable estate in land and slaves, but she never learned to read or write. After some unhappy years with her husband, she filed for divorce on the basis of emotional mistreatment, physical violence, and his "connection with one not of his own color." The circuit court granted her petition without comment, perhaps because the defendant disappeared and three witnesses supported the plaintiff's charges. Most white women would have sought a divorce only as a last resort, because a failed marriage was usually blamed on the wife. Many would have been ashamed to file for a divorce, and many others would have dreaded appearing in court for any reason. For Elizabeth Murphey, it is clearly a labor of love to testify on behalf of her dear friend Lucy Norman.

Extracts from the Depositions referred to in the accompanying Petition, viz, from the depositions of Wilmouth Edwards, Catherine Carter, & Elizabeth Murphey in the order here named.[1]

Question. Do you know whether the charges or allegations purporting to be a statement of the Causes in which Lucy W. Norman intends to apply to the next General Assembly for a Divorce from her husband James B. Norman & hereto annexed are erronious or true?

Answer. Upon an inspection of each of the said allegations I think I can safely say that they are substantially if not litterally true. Not long after the intermarriage of the said plt. & dft.[2] I was introduced into their family & lived in the same for about five months, serving this Time[.][3] the dft. often manifested a strong dislike or aversion to the company of the plt. & frequently used insulting, indecent, abusive, & vulgar language towards her. During the same time he appeared to be strongly attached to a servant girl of the family whith whom he habitually had illicit & criminal intercourse. He frequently slept with her — said several girl sometimes in a pallet in his wife's chamber & at other times in an adjoining room of the house. He often embraced & kissed her in my presence, invited her to a seat at the dinning table with himself & family & appeared to be passionately attached to her. This course of conduct did not of course, escape the observation of Mrs. Norman. She often times in my presence feeling[ly] and earnestly remonstrated against it. But he generally turned a deaf ear to her entreaties — sometimes flew into passion & did not scruple to declare that said servant girl was as good & worthy as she said plt. I heard him on one occasion seriously threaten the said plt. if she laid her hands, in an angry way, upon the said servant girl—& generally in reply to her remonstrances he told her if she did not like his course of conduct To leave his house & take herself to some place she liked better. Since my residence in the family the said dft. has left his then place of residence & for a while lived in the neighbourhood apart from his wife with the said servant girl a member of his family.

Question. What was the general course of conduct observed by Mrs. Norman the plt. towards the dft. during your residence in the family?

Ans[wer]. I am sure she never said or did any thing in my presence to provoke or in any way instigate the course of conduct observed by the said dft. On the contrary, she conducted herself with the strictest propriety at all times, towards him, was remarkably kind & conciliatory under the circumstances & manifested the deepest solicitude for his reformation—of which she seemed to entertain hopes & to which every effort appeared to be directed.

And the said Catherine Carter saith That during the time referred to in the foregoing deposition I occasionally visited Mrs. Norman the plt. & frequently heard Mr. Norman the dft. use vulgar & abusive language in her presence & threaten her with bodily violence. On one occasion I spent a night there & when breakfast was announced the following morning I entered the dining room & on seating myself in company with Mrs. Norman at the table Mr. Norman called to Maria the servant girl above referred to & invited her to take a seat at the table with the family to which Mrs. Norman objecting Mr. N. insisted that she said girl should be so seated & said to Mrs. N. that if she touched her he would take the life of her Mrs. N.

And the said Elizabeth Murphey saith That upon an inspection of the annexed charges I believe them to be true in the fullest sense of the terms used. I have long been acquainted with Mr. & Mrs. Norman & prizing very highly the society of the latter I have been a constant visiter in her family ever since her intermarriage with the said dft. During these visits I have often heard him use the most scandalous & vulgar language in the presence of Mrs. N. & to indulge in epithets the most insulting & abusive towards her & to threaten her with great bodily violence. I can also & do hereby testify to his illicit & criminal intercourse with the servant girl Maria above referred to. On one occasion I spent a night with Mrs. Norman & am well satisfied that Mr. Norman spent the same night in the same bed with the said servant girl.[4] On the next morning when Mrs. N. & myself had finished breakfast he directed said servant girl to seat herself at the table from which [he] had just arisen—to which Mrs. N. objected & saying to the girl if she seated herself at the table that she Mrs. N. would have her severely punished. To this Mr. Norman replied that, in each count, he would visit her (Mrs. N.) with a like punishment. Mrs. N. then burst into Tears & asked me if it was not too much to stand? To which Mr. N. replied it was nothing to what he intended to inflict upon her. I could detail many such instances of cruel indecent & reckless conduct if desired. After living for a few years under the same roof with his wife Mr. N. left his former residence in company with said servant girl Maria & settled himself in the neighbourhood where he lived in open adultery with her until recently when he took the said girl with him to the southern country.[5] As to the conduct of Mrs. N. I am assured that it has been at all times, the most circumspect, conciliatory & forbearing & in no way calculated to provoke the opposite course of conduct on the part of Mr. Norman.

1. Only Elizabeth Murphey can be located in the federal census: in 1840 she was a widow in her thirties, heading her own household in Henry County and raising three young children. She owned no slaves.

2. Abbreviations for *plaintiff* and *defendant*.

3. Meaning he was a servant in the household.

4. This may indicate that Mr. and Mrs. Norman were sleeping in separate beds; that Mr. Norman had intercourse with Maria while his wife slept next to him in the same bed; or that Mr. Norman visited Maria in her own room.

5. Meaning the Deep South. By 1850 James Norman had moved back to Henry County, where he owned nine slaves; that year Lucy Norman resided in the county and owned ten slaves. By 1860 he had remarried a white woman and had a white child. Of the slave woman named Maria, there is no trace. By 1860 Lucy Norman had either remarried or left Virginia.

Sally Jane Hibberd to her aunt Jane Hibberd Keefer, 14 July 1849, from Martinsburg, Virginia, to Richmond, Indiana. Jane Hibberd Keefer Papers, MS 684, box 1, folder 4, Ohio Historical Society.

Sally Jane Hibberd and Jane Hibberd Keefer were Quakers and natives of northern Virginia, the daughter and spouse of yeoman farmers. Sally Jane, who was in her late teens, underlines the importance of reciprocity in women's friendship and in all social relationships.

Dear Aunt,

Father has not quite filled up this sheet therefore I will make an endeavor to do so tho the effort I fear will be a poor one for news is so scarce, or at least I have heard of none. Cousin Joe Hibberd & James Nelson, a friend of Cousin Joes paid us a visit a week or two since. We had a pleasant little fishing party while they were here & they seemed much pleased with the Berkely girls. the fun was, I had James for a beau until I got to George Tabbs & then gave him to Louisa thinking I would get one but all were taken up, so hope expired just at the Moment I saw Noble riding up on business, but I told him he must go with me. he said [he] had a dogged notion to go & I told him he must & away we went to take the lead, leaving Tace & yo[u]ng George Tabb behind. had it been a regular party I would have [been] in a fix dont I have no beaux but remember it was harvest times & all were engaged there were only ten of us. I know thee will laugh at me but I cant help I could find nothing else to say.

Oh how I would these pleasant evenings to sit with thee beneath the shade of the honeysuckle & woodbine as they twine their graceful foliage around the porch, but when I do this if ever it will be at some distant day. I think with such a kind woman as thee represents thy neighbor to be thee must live happy. it is such a nice way to get along when you can feel the freedom to ask to borrow & to lend, & I think it is the way we were designed to live one with another, as tho we were all one family of Sisters & brothers. write soon & excuse my brevity & look for more next time. All join me in love to thee. Thy Neice Sally Jane. remember us to any of our friends thee may see.

Elizabeth W. Cook to her friend Mary Wright, 10 March 1852, from Oak Grove, Texas, to Red River County, Texas. George Travis Wright Papers, Eugene C. Barker Texas History Center, University of Texas at Austin.

Elizabeth Cook, whose family has just settled on the Texas frontier, dilates on the significance of friendship, even for middle-aged women like herself. In her warm, chatty style we can almost hear echoes of the conversations women must have had when they met face-to-face.

My Dearest Mrs. Wright,

Perhaps you may have thought that I had forgotten you, but not so, no my Dear friend, for how often do I think of you & wish to see you. it is not for the want of that good feeling for you that has caused me to keep silent this long. as you may know, my cares of a family & several correspondents to write to which takes up my time pretty much. So I hope that you may excuse—.

Well, we all got here without broken bones, but I had a swelled face I'll tell you. then the cold settled through my whole body which caused me to be sick for several days but have enjoyed good health ever since. my white family suffered much with the influenza soon after we came here.[1] we can't forget the chills yet, as they visit us sometimes yet; but I hope from the appearance of our place that we shan't be subject to them long.

Well, Mrs. Wright I do not feel disappointed in the situation or locality of this place, & I hope with the blessings of the all wise Providence to make a plenty to eat.

I have plenty of neighbors, some that appear very pleased, but not one like yourself with me. no my friend, how I should like to see you—it is very pleasant to think, of the time that you set to come; well don't disappoint me if it [is] in your power, for it is only forty miles by becknal's bridge to come through Mt. Pleasant. I have not been to Daingerfield yet but want to go some of these days and then I will try and see you old friend.[2] Well how do you come on? You do not lack for company now I recon. This is one time that you like to see the Steam Boats coming is it not? If you do not I'll tell you that there is many a one here that does; for bread & meat is scarce in these parts about now.

Tell Mr. Wright that I have not found a place that would please him. so I fear I cannot get you for a neighbor here, but tell him to come with you & see.

we have churches convenient, of different orders; two baptist, so I can go as often as is convenient for me. I want you to write immediately on the reception of these lines & tell me what you are doing & expect to do; & how all the neighbors are getting on & whether you have been sick this winter or not.

Where is Sam? going to school yet? I suppose old Mr. Hunt is no more. poor man he has paid the debt that we all must pay sooner or later. Please let me know when his Nephew comes as I loaned the old man Mims eleven hundred dollars just before we left which he promised to pay at any time that I should wante.

Well as I have nothing interesting to write I will stop my scribbling. Lou often talks about You & says that you must come soon for she wants to see you bad. I will close by subscribing my self as ever your devoted friend, Elizabeth W. Cook.

Lou tells me to ask you if her cats have perished or where they are.

1. Southerners often used the phrase "white family" to distinguish their white relatives from their slaves.
2. Nearby towns in Titus and Morris Counties in northeastern Texas. A forty-mile journey by wagon would occupy two to three days.

Diary of Eliza Ann Marsh Robertson. Eliza Ann Marsh Robertson Papers, Southern Historical Collection, University of North Carolina.

Now married to planter William Robertson, Eliza lived near New Iberia, Louisiana. The couple had seven children together, and Mr. Robertson owned many slaves. Mrs. Robertson continues to relish the company of other white women, her kinfolk, friends, and neighbors.

13 January 1855. Weather a little cloudy & very windy. Slight sprinkle of rain[.] I spent all the morning in making a pound cake, three mince pies, & some syrup for my citron preserves. About three o'clock I went to dine with Mrs. Hopkins. We had a real woman's dinner 9 ladies and only one gentleman. I met there cousin Mary & Sarah, Mrs. Stubenger & the two Miss Cobbs. Mrs. Schriner & Mrs. Lourd in the evening. Cousin Mary Adelaide and I went down to sister's[1] and spent the evening. Expected to bid them good bye as they intended starting for Baton Rouge tonight, but brother Daniel was complaining of a bad cold & would not go[2] Cousin Mary left on the Jean Hebre for Port Gibson —

1. Sarah Marsh Avery (1818–78).
2. Daniel Avery (1810–79), Sarah's husband.

Julia A. Gilchrist to her friend Margaret Broyles Van Wyck, 22 June 1855, from Charleston, South Carolina, to Anderson, South Carolina. Maverick and Van Wyck Papers, South Caroliniana Library, University of South Carolina.

Julia Gilchrist and Margaret Van Wyck studied together in the early 1850s at an elite private academy in Charleston. Julia's father was a wealthy Charleston physician, and she married lawyer Robert Gilchrist, the son of a prominent judge. In 1855 she was nineteen years old. Her friend Margaret, age twenty, was a planter's daughter but had not married so well: her husband, physician Samuel Van Wyck, never truly prospered. The young women forged a warm friendship at school, based in part on their conversion experiences, and still feel a close and very private bond.

My dearest Maggie, my long cherished friend, how can a heart so full of love, so touched as mine has been to-day, refrain from laying it open to Some one, and that one must be you. . . . Will you call me childish, when I tell you your letter was wept over to-day? My mind reverted to days long gone, to the time when you took me to your heart of hearts . . . and for a moment I . . . imagine myself at dear old Church St.[1] again, but suddenly I start, and find that my condition has changed, that instead of the light-hearted Julia Whitridge I am the more sedate, but far happier Julia Gilchrist, yet knowing this, my heart is full of tears, and I indulge in a flow of them, that the "Past" is no more. . . .

It is hard to realize that I have been separated from you so long, nearly fourteen months. In that time we have met with many changes, have we not my darling? I have been called upon to give up an idol Sister. . . . [Then her infant daughter died.] I leave you to imagine the rest. You know me full well. . . . It <u>was</u> hard to give her up, but it was the decree of a kind heavenly Father. . . . I can never tell you what a trial it was to me not to be at your wedding. . . .

You say Maggie that Such love as ours has been, must always burn with undiminished brightness. It must indeed. I can not believe that God would allow us to waste such pure affections. . . . I know that in heaven we will continue to love one another, and in believing thus, I am comforted when dear ones are taken from me. . . . <u>you</u> and <u>I</u> both, gave ourselves to God on <u>the same day,</u> we neither of us knew it. . . . I remain as ever your devoted friend, Julia A. Gilchrist.

N.B. Do not let Mr. Van Wyck see this. You may read it to him if You think proper, <u>but no more.</u>

1. The address of their alma mater.

Marion Harland, Alone *(Richmond: A. Morris, 1855), 49–55.*

Mary Hawes Terhune, a slaveholder's daughter from Amelia County, Virginia, wrote this best-selling novel while she was still a teenager. Under the pen name Marion Harland, she went on to publish more than twenty novels, dozens of short stories, and a popular cookbook. The heroine of this novel, Ida Ross, is an orphaned teenager. While out for a stroll one day, she is caught in a sudden rainstorm and takes refuge on the doorstep of Mrs. Dana, whose sister Carry Carleton is Ross's schoolmate.

"How it rains!" said Carry, drawing aside the curtain. "It is lucky you came when you did. Did you know we lived here?"

"No, it was entirely accidental. I was walking and did not notice the clouds until the shower came; then I took refuge in the nearest house."

"A happy accident for me," said Carry. "I despaired of ever persuading you to visit me. This storm was sent for my express benefit. Sister and I never tire of each other's company; but the little ones demand much of her time; and brother John—Mr. Dana, often brings home writing, or is detained at the store late at night, in the busy season, and I am rather lonely."

[The two young women meet the Dana children, have supper, and go into Carry's bedroom.]

"Now," continued she, when they were in their room, taking from a wardrobe two dressing gowns, "I move that we don these and make ourselves comfortable generally."

And cozily comfortable they appeared, ensconced in armchairs in front of that most sparkling of coal-fires; a waiter of apples and nuts sent up by the thoughtful Mrs. Dana, on a stand between them; shutters and curtains closed, and the storm roaring and driving without.

"I no longer wonder at your cheerfulness, since I have seen your home," said Ida. "All the good things of life are mingled in your cup."

"You are right, I am very happy, but not more so than hundreds of others. . . ."

[They then debate whether human beings are inherently good, Carry arguing the affirmative.]

"You are a veritable alchemist," said Ida. "You would ferret out gold, even in the dross of my character."

"Try me!" replied Carry. "But bear in mind, nothing is to be secreted; no hard thoughts or jaundiced investigations. All must be cast into the crucible."

"And tried by what fire?" inquired Ida.

"Love!" said the warm-hearted girl, kneeling beside her and winding her arms about her waist. "Love me, Ida! and if I prove heartless and deceitful, I will cease to plead for my brothers and sisters."

The glad tears that impearled her bright locks replied.

Private Journal of Mary Owen Sims. Small Manuscript Collection, Arkansas History Commission.

Mary Sims, recently widowed, lived on a small farm in central Arkansas. She is being courted by several ardent suitors, her mother and brothers lived nearby, and she has many friends at her church, but her deepest connection is with her sister.

7 April 1857. Tuesday. April has come again with all its changes — sunshine and showers — but on the fifth nature took an uncommon freak, it rained hard nearly all day — faired off in the evening and at night the ground froze hard to the great distress of all farmers. The corn is all killed and wheat appears to be entirely destroyed and my garden is ruined. My peas in bloom the day before now appears as if they have been scalded. I reckon it is well that God puts forth his hand sometimes and smites the earth, in order that we may not be forgetful of his bounty. I received a letter yesterday from Sister which gives me much uneaseness on account of her ill health. She is my only Sister and the only being in the world who I can speak freely to.[1]

1. Her sister, Mrs. Quillen, was married to a local judge.

Sallie R. Collins to her friend Mary Brown Polk Yeatman, 24 October 1860, from Hillsborough, Tennessee, to Maury County, Tennessee. Yeatman-Polk Collection, Tennessee State Library and Archives.

Sallie Collins, recently married, once attended a girls' academy with Mary Brown Polk Yeatman, a planter's daughter who was about twenty-five years old in 1860. In this effervescent missive, she pays her friend a high compliment by comparing her to her favorite kinfolk.

Dearest Brownie,

I wrote to you a week ago, but the letter was not Sent—I mention the fact of having written it, to show I have not been unmindful of you— I know you must have been and must still be anxious to hear something farther of Sarah—

Both the babe and herself are doing finely—there never was such a good babe scarcely! She sleeps charmingly, and eats wonderfully! Just give her a sugar say and she's no trouble to anybody—she is not <u>very</u> pretty now, but we think she will be one of these days, when her face fills out—She is very bright looking, and is altogether a very promising child I think.

She has no name as yet—Sarah Says she is <u>deliberating</u> about one—Sarah has just had a letter from dear Em telling of her final engagement—I am so glad she feels <u>sure</u> of herself—Bless her dear heart! I do wish her <u>so much</u> joy and happiness! You must write us a long account of her appearance, parties, &c. &c. in Nashville—

I should so much like to see cousin and her babe! Since Sarah has told me you said the plague with it as she used to handle her pink bows I can fancy I see her with it! Dear cousin, I do love her a great deal—and Brownie, I love Aunt Mary more than I ever have. She does seem to bear her loss so nobly, so like a true Christian—

What of cousin Miss Brownie? Is she perfectly well now, and does she seem happy in her grand house?[1] How is her Mary's health? Do you keep house like a <u>city</u> lady, that is, do you have everything sent to you <u>ready made,</u> or do you attend to things yourself? I know you are capable of great things in the housekeeping line—

I should not be surprised if I went to housekeeping before this time next year, though I scarcely expect to do so now, that is we have no place as yet, and have not our eyes on any in particular.[2] Still, I think we will be apt to go to housekeeping sometime in the next few years, and <u>possibly</u> within 12 months—

Sarah says you asked her how I liked my lace—my dear, I think it the <u>most beautiful</u> I ever have behold in my whole life, with one exception—and I am <u>perfectly delighted</u> with it I do assure you—As for the bouquet holder you gave me, some persons consider it the most perfect of my presents—it is <u>just exquisite</u>—I think—I hope to use it a good deal this Winter, when brother George Collins is married to Annie Cameron, which event takes place on the 28 of December—Brownie, wont you write to me please? You owe me a letter, and if I dont hear from you shortly I shall feel as if you were forgetting me and I love you so dearly—I feel as if you and Em were <u>near</u> relations, near and very <u>dear</u> kinfolk—

When I have a house of my own I want you to come see me—I want you to <u>know</u> my husband. I know your generous heart would be glad to understand him, and oh! if you did but comprehend him, how you would admire him!

Give my love to Mr. Yeatman please and to Liza[3] if she is with you still. Think of me ever as your truly and <u>warmly</u> attached friend, Sallie R. Collins.

1. Mary Brown Polk (1841–97) married Henry Clay Yeatman in 1858 and lived on a handsome place in the country. The son of a wealthy banker, Yeatman was a trustee for a successful ironworks.

2. It was common for upper-class newlyweds to live with one set of parents, usually the bride's, for a year or so after the nuptials.

3. Mary Yeatman's sister Eliza, who never married.

Katherine Bush Norton Ambler

This demure pose is misleading, for Mrs. Ambler had strong
words about the inequitable distribution of property in her
husband's will. *Courtesy of the Virginia Museum of Fine Arts.*

Margaret Izard (Mrs. Gabriel) Manigault

Her enigmatic expression belies the great pleasure she
took in visiting her female relatives and friends.
Courtesy of the Allbright-Knox Gallery, Buffalo.

Mary Telfair

Independently wealthy and independent in spirit, Telfair
chose not to marry. *Courtesy of the Telfair Academy of
Arts and Sciences, Inc., bequest of Mary Telfair, 1875.*

Martha Brown Callendar Forman

Delicate bonnet, weathered face, gnarled hands:
Mistress Forman of Rose Hill. *Courtesy of
the Historical Society of Cecil County, Elkton, Maryland.*

Rose Hill

This grand house was also a workplace, a headquarters where
Martha Forman supervised the labor of many slaves. *Courtesy of
the Historical Society of Cecil County, Elkton, Maryland.*

Mary Randolph Randolph

After her husband lost his fortune, Randolph published a
cookbook for financially challenged landladies like herself.
Courtesy of the Virginia Historical Society.

Sarah S. Thompson

Middle age and great wealth did not spare Thompson a
round of duties on her plantation, including nursing slaves.
Courtesy of the Filson Club Historical Society.

Lucy Muse Walton Fletcher
Her eyes averted, Fletcher's anxious personality is captured in
this image. *Courtesy of Special Collections Library, Duke University.*

Virginia Randolph Cary

Another Randolph reduced to poverty, Mrs. Cary took up the
pen to advise young women on how to build character.
Courtesy of the Virginia Historical Society.

Jessamine Grove, Tennessee, home of the Maney family
In this house, Martha Maney taught her daughters
"paternalism," that distinctive mix of caretaking and racism.
Courtesy of the Tennessee Historical Society.

Eliza Turner Quitman

A politician's spouse who minced no words about her
disdain for her husband's career. *Courtesy of
Mississippi Department of Archives and History.*

Ann Miller
She measured a man's worth by his private conduct rather than
his public success. *Courtesy of the Filson Club Historical Society.*

Mary Ann Lamar Cobb
Another politician's wife, who penned witty, caustic
remarks about "honour" or the lack of it in public life.
Courtesy of Milton Leathers.

Lizinka C. Brown

Brown estimated the Confederacy's chances of survival in
1861 as poor; a canny face reflecting a shrewd intelligence.
Courtesy of the Filson Club Historical Society.

WORK

Most white women worked very hard in this society, for a great deal of toil was necessary to run even a modest household. Some women enjoyed their labor, especially the more creative tasks of cooking and sewing, but many found their daily portion exhausting. Their work was tedious, repetitive, and messy. Women sometimes did a man's work, too, such as laying a hearth. These selections also reveal how dramatically a woman's duties could change over time, for some had to enter new occupations when their households collapsed. At least one widow rebounded and made a tidy fortune from a gold mine, but this kind of rags-to-riches story seems to have been atypical.

White women of the middle and upper classes also worked, even when slave women assisted them. No matter how wealthy they were, all women did some household tasks, and the plantation mistress's duties required flexibility as well as meticulous attention to detail. White women sometimes worked alongside African Americans, and one individual in this chapter accorded a black woman some glancing respect as a fellow worker. But most of these women did not respect slave labor or even appreciate the fact that slaves spared them many distasteful chores. Whom did white women prefer to work with, and why might that be? What might a typical workday be like for a slaveowner's wife? How would her duties differ from those of a yeoman farmer's wife?

Alice DeLancey Izard to her daughter Margaret Izard Manigault, 27 April 1815,
from Lancaster District, South Carolina, to Philadelphia, Pennsylvania. Mani-
gault Family Papers, South Caroliniana Library, University of South Carolina.

Nancy Izard Deas, the subject of this letter, was in her mid-thirties when it was
written. She was the daughter of a wealthy planter, and she married William A.
Deas in 1798. Although Mr. Deas was a planter's son and had a promising career
as a lawyer and diplomat, he slid deeper and deeper into debt. As her mother
Alice DeLancey Izard relates, Mrs. Deas began preparing to earn some money
herself. She relies on another white woman to manage slaves, who overworks and
probably mistreats the black women. The hierarchies are clear—a lawyer's wife
hires an overseer's wife to supervise slaves—but everyone works.

. . . I was very desirous that she should come here, after the party [lef]t
us, for it is painful to me to know [her] to be alone, & ill, but I could not
[p]revail on her to come. She said she had just established her spinning business, that it was going on very well, & she knew if she left home it would
be overturned, & little, or nothing done. I saw her looking over Cotton
yarn sufficient to make sixty yards of cloth, & she is endeavoring to get her
Women taught the manner of preparing it for the loom & of weaving it.[1] I
am pleased at seeing her make these exertions. Mr. Deas hired an overseer
before he left her, who seems to be a worthy Man, his Wife is the civil-
lest, most obliging Woman that can be, & takes pleasure in giving the black
Women all the instruction in her power. Nancy says that if Mr. Deas does
not succeed in his Law scheme, she shall look on this Farm as their dernier
resort,[2] & make up her mind to living on it.

This is a wise resolution; yet it would hurt me to think that she was so
far secluded from the society she loves, & has been accustomed to. Farewell My Dear Daughter, that Heaven may bless you is the prayer of your
truly affecte. Mother A. Izard.

1. Meaning the female slaves.
2. French for "last resort."

Diary of Martha Browne Callender Forman. MS 1779, Manuscripts Division, Maryland Historical Society Library.

Martha Browne Callender kept a diary intermittently from 1814, when she married Thomas Marsh Forman ("the General"), to the 1850s. In 1821 she was thirty-three and lived on the couple's plantation in Cecil County, Maryland. Most of her duties involve supervising, feeding, and clothing the Forman slaves, whom she calls simply "the people." She has other responsibilities, however, such as attending the overseer's death and organizing his funeral, and she shifts easily from one task to another.

Dec. 12 [1821]
Wednesday the General went to Delaware.
I had my leef fat rendered, and put it in 4 large Crocks. Made our Sausages and put it in two large Crocks. Mr. Vanzant came and attended to the cutting up of our meet.[1] Thare is 34 hams, 2 Shoulders, 10 Midlings, 10 Jowls, 8 Chines, 4 Heads salted away for ourselves, and all the rest cut up in pork for the people.

Susan came to make the peoples Cloth.

Dec. 13 [1821]
Thursday I cut out the peoples cloth clothes. Cut John and Jacob Burk's and Boston's trousers, Moses and Philip Ant[igua?] Neds and Olivers Neilsons Coat Henry Allens Coat and trousers.[2] This has been a very windy day and night, the Irishman's Dam gave way last night.

Dec. 14 [1821]
Still cutting out the peoples cloth.

Feb. 20 [1824]
Friday I went over to the quarter early this morning to see the overseer. He is very low. Stayed until 12 o'clock, came home and dined with Mr. Vann Ribbe and returned immediately. Took the sheets to lay him out and all things that was necessary.[3] He died about three o'clock. I stayed by him until his last breath. It was a trial. His agony was very great. He has left a wife and four small helpless children. I made the necessary arrangements for his funeral, my husband not at home, to the best of my judgment, and if I erred it was an error of the head and not of the heart.

Feb. 10 [1825]
Thursday Hung up our meat to smoke, 80 hams, 18 fowls . . . 6 chives, 8 pieces of beef.[4] I went to the Cross Road and bought 12 blankets for the people, one dollar and 25 Cents each. Bought a small cotton coverlet and a small rose blanket for Harriott, the blanket one dollar and the Coverlid 75 Cents. Bought Minty and Julia each a flannel pack for three children.[5]

Mar. 24 [1827]
Saturday Old Rachel[6] brought home 10 hanks of Cotton for linsey of our own raising, three cuts in the old hank except one. I have got 116 hen eggs set and 77 Goose eggs set.

April 27 [1828] Sunday my husband and I went to Church the first dear sunday we have had for a long time. In the afternoon — drank tea at Mr. Ward's, very bad roads. Lewis left his wife this day. she has had two white children.

Dec. 17 [1828]
Wednesday. Killed 33 Hogs, weighing 4119 lbs. Rendered all my entrail fat, one tin can full and a small quantity in the other.[7]

1. Evidently a neighbor or kinsman.
2. Forman's diary lists all of their slaves (forty-three total in the early 1820s), including surnames and dates of birth. All of these men were born in the 1780s and 1790s.
3. Her overseer is called Mr. Webb, and Vann Ribbe is her brother-in-law. "Laying out" a body meant that it was shaved, washed, usually with vinegar, dried, and dressed.
4. The slaves undoubtedly smoked the meat while Forman supervised their labor.
5. All slave women: Harriott Belton, who was born in 1809; Araminta Gilmore, in 1784; and Julia Sewall, born in 1800.
6. Rachel Burk, a slave born in 1765.
7. Again, the slaves did the heavy labor while Forman supervised it.

Diary of Martha Tabb Watkins Dyer, 1823–39, Calloway County, Missouri. Samuel Dyer-Plain Dealing Collection, Special Collections Department, Alderman Library, University of Virginia.

Twenty-eight years old in 1823, Martha Dyer was a farmer's wife. She and her husband migrated that year from Albemarle County, Virginia, to Calloway County, Missouri. Although the Dyers owned several slaves, these laconic journal entries reveal that Mrs. Dyer performed some hard labor herself, both indoors and outdoors.

1823

2 September:	House raising here
5 September:	Well caved in
9 December:	Killed hogs
10 December:	Killed 2 beeves, one very fat
20 December:	Cut out my fat beef. Mr. Dyer sowed bed and brought sheep

1824

14 February:	Laid hearth
1 March:	Began to clear garden I planted peach ploms Damsons & cherry stones
6 March:	I [have been] doubling harness cotton set hen
13 April:	Fixed hen house
19 April:	Worked asparagus bed
20 April:	We sowed peas [this] even'g, got 2 ducks
21 April:	Set out turnips sowed parsley and another seed
12 May:	Plant cotton
2 June:	Set tomatoes
6 September:	I sewed netting on toilet
27 October:	I [am] making grape wine

1825

11 May:	Tremendous hail storm even'g. I lost most all my fowl.
31 May:	I tied up lettuce. My husband ploughing Prairie
10 September:	We gather'd plums off the lower tree
6 October:	Went to the garden and picked out cotton with the children.[1]
21 November:	Cut out beef
24 November:	I set asparagus roots

1. Meaning removing leaves and dirt from the cotton.

Mary Randolph, The Virginia House-Wife or Methodical Cook, *3d ed.
(Washington [D.C.]: P. Thompson, 1826), 85–86, 18–19, 24–25. Virginia
Historical Society.*

*Mary Randolph, born in the 1760s, was the oldest of the thirteen children of
Thomas Mann Randolph and Anne Cary Randolph. She grew up on a Virginia
plantation and married her cousin David Meade Randolph. After a series of
financial reverses, the couple opened a boarding house in Richmond in 1808.
This book, first published in 1824, reflects Mary Randolph's privileged youth,
for affluent women cooked with wine. It also draws upon her adult experiences
as a frugal landlady, for she advises women to use every item of passably "eatable" food.*

CHOWDER, A SEA DISH.

Take any kind of firm fish, cut it in pieces six inches long, sprinkle salt,
and pepper over each piece, cover the bottom of a small Dutch oven¹ with
slices of salt pork about half boiled, lay in the fish, strewing a little chopped
onion between, cover with crackers that have been soaked soft in milk,
pour over it two gills of white wine² and two of water, put on the top of
the oven and stew it gently about an hour; take it out carefully and lay it in
a deep dish, thicken the gravy with a little flour and spoonful of butter, add
some chopped parsley, boil it a few minutes, and pour it over the fish—
serve it up hot.

BEEF SOUP.

Take the hind shin of beef, cut off all the flesh of the leg-bone, which must
be taken away entirely, or the soup will be greasy.

Wash the meat clean and lay it in a pot, sprinkle over it one small table-
spoonful of pounded black pepper, and two of salt; three onions the size of
a hen's egg, cut small, six small carrots scraped and cut up, two small tur-
nips pared and cut into dice; pour on three quarts of water, cover the pot
close, and keep it gently and steadily boiling five hours, which will leave
about three pints of clear soup; do not let the pot boil over, but take off
the scum carefully, as it rises.

When it has boiled four hours, put in a small bundle of thyme and
parsley, and a pint of celery, cut small, or a tea-spoonful of celery seed
pounded. These latter ingredients would lose their delicate flavour if boiled
too much. Just before you take it up brown it in the following manner:

Put a small table-spoonful of nice grown sugar into an iron skillet, set it on the fire and stir it till it melts and looks very dark, pour into it a ladle full of the soup, a little at a time, stirring it all the while. Strain this browning and mix it well with the soup; take out the bundle of thyme and parsley, put the nicest pieces of meat in your tureen, and pour on the soup and vegetables; put in some toasted bread cut in dice, and serve it up.

SOUP OF ANY KIND OF OLD FOWL.
(The only way in which they are eatable.)

Put the fowls in a coop and feed them moderately for a fortnight; kill one and cleanse it, cut off the legs and wings, and separate the breast from the ribs, which, together with the whole back, must be thrown away; being too gross and strong for use. Take the skin and fat from the parts cut off which are also gross. Wash the pieces nicely and put them on the fire with about a pound of bacon, a large onion chopped small, some pepper and salt, a few blades of mace,[3] a handful of parsley cut up very fine, and two quarts of water if it be a common fowl or duck—a turkey will require more water. Boil it gently for three hours, tie up a small bunch of thyme, and let it boil in it half an hour, then take it out. Thicken your soup with a large spoonful of butter rubbed into two of flour, the yelks of two eggs, and half-pint of milk. Be careful not to let it curdle in the soup.

1. A large pot that was heated by placing hot coals at its base and on the lid.
2. A gill is four ounces.
3. An archaic term for nutmeg.

Maria Louisa C. Marshall to her sister Eliza Chotard Gould, 4 February [between 1825 and 1829], from Woodville, Mississippi, to Tuscaloosa, Alabama. Maria Louisa Chotard Marshall and Family Papers, Hill Memorial Library, Louisiana and Lower Mississippi Valley Collections, Louisiana State University.

Maria Marshall, a banker's wife in the Mississippi River Valley, relates to house slaves as workers but not as fellow workers. Her impatience and bouts of bad temper must have made her an especially demanding mistress. In these letters, she vents her frustration at her house servants in particular and at slavery in general.

My beloved Sister,

My superstitious feelings had almost led me to believe that some misfortune had befallen you, from a <u>dream</u> I had about my dear little <u>Tes.</u>[1] A
few nights ago I thought, I saw the little soul with a cap on, and looking very delicate, which made a great impression on me at the time, and
my apprehensions had increased with your silence. how welcome then was
your letter of the 23d, announcing the continued happiness of a family, that
is alone dear to my heart, for why should I share my love with those (tho
they may be near relatives) who are no longer interested in me. I have not a
heard a syllable from Sarah or Ann since I came home.[2] I commenced writing to Sarah a few weeks ago, but as I knew that she must be angry with
me, and I thought unjustly, I tore it up, for I could not muster up deceit,
enough to make a <u>sweet</u> letter, and I thought any other kind would be useless. I presume you have heard from Brother since his arrival in Natchez.
we saw a gentleman, who had seen him in Orleans, and mentioned that his
family had been restored by his trip.

Mr. M. had almost plagued me into a fit of jealousy by saying Eliza that
you were so busy writing to Brother, since his return, that you had no
time to notice me. the true cause however of your long silence is <u>almost</u>
as distressing. I regret to hear you have lost your invaluable David. I cann't
imagine how you make out with only Polly and Hanah.[3] we have three, and
I have to work after and follow them all day. I wish to gracious you had
some of them for I believe I could do better with two. One, however, is a
little boy who Mr. Ventress lent us (as long as we have use for him) to bring
water, which is some distance off. my old man had a well dug soon after we
got home, but we have never been able to use the water. it is so mudy and
has a horrid smell. Tell William I'll have green peas in about a month he had
better <u>ride over and dine with</u> us. The weather for the last two weeks has
been exactly like such as we have generally have in May. every person has
commenced gardening. indeed some have peas a foot high. I am told that
artichoke seed prospered this Spring, will yeald the Vegatable next fall—
year. you had better get some as William is anxious to have them. I am getting very much interested about my garden—it is a large one, and contains
a great many fruit trees. our neighbours however are so sociable and make
so free, with what they have no right to,[4] that I expect to get in a few tan-
trums about my garden <u>this summer,</u> for Heaven knows, I hope it will be
the last I have to spend in Woodville. there had [word missing; not?] been
a lady in my house except [page torn] for three month's, all my own fault
too, for I have not returned more than one or two visits, that even made
me on our arrival. but bless the people why should I care about them?

I am sorry to hear that the Hogan's have again forfeited the good opinion of their customers. what does, the gentleman Col. would be president does he not intend to make a living? poor little Nancy. she will have to take up her old trade again, in Fontaine's house. Little Garran is much with Sarah and Nancy that I [am] inclined to think he is smitten, which is it? that captivates's his little heart?

Tell old dady Cunningham that I am going to try and prepare myself to be a christian. Mr. Fox our minister spoke to me about it the other day as Mr. M. belongs to his church. I do not think it would be worth while to defer the ceremony any longer.

as I am afraid you will scarcely make the black lines intelligible I will not cross in red ink to William [5] but will take another opportunity to extoll his prudence and thoughtfulness, for which I render him many thanks. just two lines left for Sall and Tes, but they are enough—for language could not express what I feel for them. Old Man joins me in love to you and William. M. L. M.

19 December 1826
My dear Sister,

I do not feel at all like writing, but as I have neglected you so long, I must make an effort to overcome my bad humour—sufficiently to write you a few lines. you will naturally enquire—what has put me in such a fright and perhaps blame me.

but I think you would excuse me, if you could see the trouble I have in housekeeping. the servants have the highest finish of any that the Devil has imported lately. I think if we ever have good luck enough to leave Woodville, I shall never undertake to manage a house and negroes again, but I am afraid in the meantime my temper will be a good deal tryed. I haven't a very good stock of patience at any rate, but that little will be brought into requisition.

We returned from a visit to Nancy Buffer last evening, while down in that neighbourhood I saw your old friend E. Young she inquired particularly about you, and laughed a good deal on hearing that you had been so smart as to have two children in three years.[6] she has been in wretched health, but she looks now as usual. she appears to be very much attached to Ben Young's wife (Miss Semple that was) who is a very fine woman. they are all going up to Natchez tomorrow, and we have some idea of accompanying them—

Mr. Marshall intends going up for the purpose of getting Little's testimony which will cause him to be absent four days from home and as I do not think, I can remain that long by myself, I am willing to undertake the worst of roads.

In your last letter you don't mention my little darlings, you were too busy scolding my old man. he insist[s] upon it, that you are angry with him. tell William I am almost in hopes that he will not get well without coming to see us, as Davis say's I want to go see my people, mighty bad.

Give my love to Mrs. Hogan and kiss my little Sall and Tes for me. Mr. M. joins in love to you and William. Yours sincerely, M. L. M.

1. Her young niece Teresa.
2. Her sister and sister-in-law, with whom she is angry for some reason.
3. She and her husband, Levin R. Marshall, owned three house slaves.
4. That is, they take fruit from the trees.
5. Meaning she will not write a cross-hatched letter, a common practice in the antebellum era.
6. A tantalizing remark, suggesting, perhaps, that some women knew how to limit the number of pregnancies. Maria Marshall expired after giving birth to a child in 1833.

Sarah S. Thompson to her sister Virginia A. Shelby, 15 July [1832 or 1833], from Shawnee Springs, Kentucky, to Danville, Kentucky. Grigsby Collection, The Filson Club Historical Society, Louisville, Kentucky.

Sarah S. Thompson was a grandmother and the wife of George Thompson, who owned more than a hundred slaves. Despite her age and her family's enormous holdings, she still has obligations to meet, such as nursing a slave woman who is deathly ill and teaching a young relative how to manage her own household.

My dear Sister, . . . We are much distresed at the prospect of losing our favourite & valuable servant Lavinia. she had a child near three weeks ago, & Dr. Robertson says is a victim of the mismanagement of old Mrs. Jones. From the first there was difficulty, & we tried to get Robertson. He was sick & had Tomlinson with the midwife. she had a living child after five days labour & has been ill ever since, suffering more than I thought flesh could endure for such a length of time — she will probably not live through this day. . . .[1]

Letitia will I have no doubt aid and advise Mary in her domestic matters, & it was chiefly the object of my trip to arrange the business & work of the family so that Mary could go on without so much trouble.[2] Isabel is making up the negroes clothes. Salina has got a home, & Judy was hired out before Papa got back, at the rate of $30 a year to a man in the neighborhood. I wish we could hear of a strong young woman that would do in Ester's place.[3] Mary would then not have such an arduous task in keeping the house. I hope & pray that she may become more settled & steady, & in a short time she would become acquainted with business & not find or think of it as such a task—

I have got two long letters from Louisiana lately—her own health is quite good again & expects to be confined shortly. the children were well, & Mr. G. in better health than ever she knew him—I dread to hear again from [Maria?], for she says that the Cholera was on the next plantation to theirs where there were sixty or seventy slaves—25 had died & the sickness still <u>going on</u>.[4] do write as often as you can. My love to Cousin Susan and accept that of your affec. sister Sarah S. Thompson.

Could you without much trouble know of Mrs. Evan Shelby how much yarn it will take 8 cents out of the pound to make sixty three yards of double carpeting—1 yd. wide—. I am getting the yarn from S. Hill & do not want any more than will just do—And at some convenient time, will you please engage the weaving for me at Woods—it is all ready, & I only wait to know the proper quantity & when to send it up.

    1. Messrs. Robertson and Tomlinson are physicians, and Mrs. Jones is a midwife.
    2. Letitia is her daughter, and Mary is her granddaughter.
    3. All of these women are slaves.
    4. Maria is probably another daughter. A cholera epidemic swept the United States in 1832 and 1833, killing thousands of people.

Susan Polk to her son Lucius Polk, 13 March 1837, from Raleigh, North Carolina, to Mount Pleasant, Tennessee. Polk Family Papers, Library of Congress.

Susan Polk had fourteen children with her husband, William Polk, and when he died in 1834, he left two plantations and approximately one hundred and forty slaves in North Carolina and Tennessee. Mrs. Polk is unusually direct and tough-

minded, but she has a difficult time getting her husband's overseer, his business partner, and her own sons to cooperate as she settles the estate.

My dear Lucius,[1] I have been waiting for some time with the hope of hearing from You, something further in relation to our crop in the Western District,[2] whether Sales have been made of any part of it, and of how much. I think I requested of You as well as Leonie that the Cotton should be sold on Drafts on the East.[3] I find it will not do to have money deposited in the Western Bank. They do business in such a way that I can't dispose of their Deposit checks but at a great sacrifice. . . .

You know my anxiety to settle up the Estate, and still You do not say whether You have sold the Land near Franklin or collected the money the Franklin Lots sold for. . . .[4] I want him[5] to make a statement of it for me, of that part which is to be divided between <u>all the Heirs</u> . . . what he has done with Balch, whether that part of the business is likely to be shortly brought to a close.[6] I gave him instructions to bring suit against him and have not heard from him since. Mary writes me that William has made a Very good crop 118 Bales of Cotton and sold it well.[7] I hope he will now be satisfied with the Country and feel settled. . . . my continued Love to all, Your Mother Susan Polk.

1. Her son Lucius Polk had moved from North Carolina to Tennessee in 1823. In 1830, he owned fifty-one slaves in Maury County, Tennessee.
2. This phrase dates from the eighteenth century, before Tennessee became a state.
3. Leonidas Polk, another son, moved to Tennessee in 1833; by 1840, he owned 105 slaves in Maury County. Polk later became a noted Episcopalian bishop, and during the Civil War he served in the Confederate army, attaining a general's rank before he died in 1864.
4. A community in Tennessee.
5. One Mr. Fogg, an overseer.
6. Alfred Balch of Tennessee, William Polk's business associate.
7. Another son, William Polk (1790s–?), and her daughter-in-law. They moved in 1836 to Maury County, where William was a physician and planter.

Divorce Petition of Harriet Henrietta Perry, Legislative Petitions, Chesterfield County, 23 March 1839. Records of the General Assembly, Archives and Records Division, The Library of Virginia, Richmond, Virginia.

Harriet Perry was twenty-eight years old in 1839, when she filed for divorce from physician William Perry. (The couple was apparently not related to the South Carolinians featured in the chapter on race.) By that time Mrs. Perry had been working as a seamstress for five years. In 1840 the state legislature rejected her divorce petition without comment, despite a testimonial from her lawyer, the "young lady" mentioned below, and officers of the local circuit court, which found merit in her complaint. Even though she was still legally married, she set up her own household in Richmond, took in boarders, and supported herself and her children on her own.

To The Legislature of Virginia [1]

The Petition of the undersigned respectfully represents that she has been married to a certain William Perry more than eight years; that upon her marriage like all young people, she looked forward to years of happiness, prosperity, and joy to follow that event; but soon to her mortification and surprise her husband began to indulge in habits of intoxication and with these habits daily increasing all her fond hopes began to vanish and sorrow and sadness weighed heavily upon her mind. In the middle of the year 1834 your Petitioner's husband removed with his family to the town of Manchester in the County of Chesterfield at which time her husband's intemperance became so constant that it frequently made him almost a madman and the violence of his conduct with repeated threats of taking your Petitioner's life, caused her to have frequently the greatest alarm for her safety, nor was his conduct confined to her alone, but extended to the family and to a young lady who lived in it so that your Petitioner and this young lady had often to leave the house for the preservation of their lives,[2] it is this way alone that she was able to prevent the most violent injury to her person from being committed, if not her life taken, which she was continually in fear of, as in addition to these threats, the knife was often used in making them. Your honourable body can from this relation easily immagine perhaps the truly unfortunate and miserable condition and situations of your Petitioner, who instead of the peace, joy and social harmony which should attend the matrimonial state, was racked continually with a fear of her life's being taken so that she could not lie down on her bed with safety to herself; disquietude and weariness of spirit preyed upon her health, her home continualy the scene of uproar and confusion, and herself the subject of abuse from a man who was lost to all feeling and the insulter and persecutor of those whom it was his duty to protect. In the midst even, though of all that was heartrending and fearful to your Petitioner, she alone had to support by her daily labour her distressed family and to supply her children with food and raiment, and though she used all the affection that a wife could use towards her husband, yet it had not the effect of arresting him in his downward progress to ruin, nor could she induce him to provide in the least for his suffering family. Your Petitioner will now come to the last acts of his cruel career which took place some time in the month of July 1835[.] they had all come over from Manchester to the City of Richmond to the residence of your Petitioner's mother, where they spent the day, and on our return home the next day and for several days his conduct became so excessively violent and alarming that your Petitioner concluded that it was most advisable to return to her mother's, which she did in company of her brother-in-law; on this last occasion she was actually driven by the most cruel threats from his home and was compelled to seek to seek her personal safety in the house of her mother. Soon after she arrived at her mother's your Petitioner's husband left this place and has never been heard of since, having now been gone more than four years;[3] what has become of him, your Petitioner, cannot even immagine, but if he is alive, it certainly appears that he never intends to return; he left her under the most distressed circumstances without any home but that of a widowed mother, with her children to support[4] and no means to do so, but your Petitioner's daily labor; her mother very poor, herself[,] and family reduced to poverty by the intemperate habits and cruel conduct of her husband.[5] From this situation by the generosity of her neighbors in giving her work she has ever since been able to maintain herself and her children with respect. It is under these circumstances, that your Petitioner throws herself upon the clemency of your Honourable body to releive her from that marriage tie which has thus been the source of so much misery and distraction of mind and that you may in your wisdom and justice restore her to those rights and to that situation, which her cause, she humbly conceives deservedly merits, is the anxious prayer of your Petitioner and most obedient Servt. Harriet Henrietta Perry.

1. In 1840 the state gave jurisdiction over divorce cases to the circuit superior courts of law and chancery. Nevertheless many lawyers continued to submit petitions to the Virginia legislature, hoping that it might be more sympathetic than local courts.

2. This woman, who was not named in the records, was probably single and boarding with or working for the family.

3. Other legal records indicate that William Perry left the state for parts unknown.

4. She had three small children.

5. By 1840, when Perry set up her own household, she had somehow acquired an elderly slave woman. Perhaps the slave was an informal divorce settlement from her departed husband, a gift from her mother, or a purchase.

Henrietta Kerr Tilghman to her husband, Tench Tilghman, [1840s], from Plimhimmon plantation, Talbot County, Maryland, to Baltimore, Maryland. Tilghman Papers, MS 1967, Manuscripts Division, Maryland Historical Society Library.

Henrietta Kerr, a congressman's daughter, owned twenty slaves in her own right before she wed planter Tench Tilghman in 1832. Although she brought a large dowry to the marriage and performed her varied duties as wife, mother, and plantation mistress with dispatch, she must ask her husband for a few dollars to pay the bills.

Dr. husband, I have calculated as well as I could, without having Mrs. Bradshaw's assistance, the quantity of cloth for the servants' clothing. My recollection is that it took, of the single width after shrinking, 6½ yds. to a suit. For 8 men, Nick included who is so nearly grown, it will take 52 yards and I should say 53 or 4 to allow for shrinking. We have generally purchased a cloth rather lighter in quality & cheaper for the small boys. I have enough left of last winter's supply to make little Phil a suit and for the other 4 I think 17 yrds. would be a fair allowance [1] —

With respect to women's clothes I will write again — should like to have however samples with prices of linsey [2] —

The boys need cravats — suspenders — a silk handk. a piece — Arthur a pr of best shoes pr of gloves and a <u>tooth brush.</u> If you think it worth while to make any further addition to their cloathes for the time they will be absent, I think it should be a vest for Tench and pr of gem brown pants for Arthur. [3] The best pair which he takes will probably need washing on Sat. afternoon & <u>to be well dried</u> for him to wear clean on Sunday — unless you get him a pair — Tench will tell you about their winter cloathes — I wish you would take the boys or send them with Howell, to see Anna Handy and C. Lowry. —

You were in such a bustle this morning that I would not call your attention to the <u>circumstance</u> of my being in want of means to settle some accounts—thinking too they could be still deferred as you would use all yr money whilst absent—but I have been thinking this afternoon that before you get back I shall want to go to town to get my silk scarf made up in another form as I have intended to do against cooler weather—I shall then wish to pay Mrs. Thompson's bill—$8.42. Beside that I ought to settle with Mary 3 dols at the end of this week. She really sews so faithfully for me that I do not like to put her off for her wages. I have not settled yet a balance on Matilda's sewing account—& I have two small dues to servants—making in all about 15 dols. which if you can let me have, I shall be glad, but if you are low in funds & have it not to spare from yr present demands from home I can do with 3 dols. or even excuse you altogether.[4] Now that I have made my case known I leave it entirely to yr. convenience.

Dr. C. & his wife came over to day and I will let you know Aunt Anne's decision about the school. Yrs. ever affecionate H.

My obliging husband will please attend whilst in Balto. to the following things—viz—
The Cloth for men & boys as pr memo in his possession—
—to the purchase of 2 pieces of <u>blue</u> plaid domestic for women—
—To procuring samples of linsey for old women & children—
—Get also Buttons & thread for cloth—
1 yd. of cheap box muslin for linings
—cotton matrasses.

1. Mrs. Bradshaw is evidently the overseer's wife, and Nick and little Phil are slaves.
2. A coarse cloth made of linen, cotton, and wool.
3. Tench and Arthur are her sons, both in their early teens.
4. She is paying some of the slave women for extra work.

Diary of Elizabeth F. Perry. Benjamin Franklin Perry Papers, Southern Historical Collection, University of North Carolina.

Charlestonian Elizabeth McCall married Benjamin F. Perry in 1837, when she was eighteen and he was thirty-two years old. Her husband was a lawyer, journalist, and politician, notable for his strong pro-Union stand during the Nullifi-

cation crisis in 1832–33. In 1844 the Perrys lived in Greenville, South Carolina, with their three small children. The eleven Perry slaves loom large in Elizabeth's daily life. She works with them regularly in the household, believes she treats them well, and feels she knows them fairly well, yet she is unable to comprehend why they are discontented.

11 March 1844.

. . . <u>Servants</u> have given me great trouble & have been my only trials in my married life. I have come to the conclusion that servants are <u>happier</u> & more attached to owners who are <u>strict</u> than to <u>indulgent</u> ones. No one could be kinder to their servants than we are, & yet they are an unhappy, ill-natured, discontented set; always wrangling among themselves, & displeased with their owners. The fault is with us, that we give our servants too little to do & are not strict enough with them. It is entire[ly] out of our nature to be severe, & our servants think they can do as they please & the less they <u>have</u> to do, the less they <u>wish</u> to do.

Eliza is discontented, impertinent, immoral, & dishonest; but when she <u>chooses</u> is a smart servant; she is a first rate seamstress & can do anything well that she pleases. When she belonged to Mamma she was unhappy & wished she belonged to me.

She was always pretending to be sick, did nothing, & wasted away her life. Now she belongs to me, she wishes she was back again at Mammas, & though she does more work now than formerly, I have had no comfort in her since I owned her & am afraid I never will, & she is such a bad example to her children. They would do much better without her. Edward is a smart, useful boy, & considering his <u>training,</u> very good. I think he will make a fine servant. Clara seems smart, but promises to be pert.[1] Minerva is smart, honest, neat, & truthful, but has a violent temper & [is] often impertinent; on account of her many good qualities, I am obliged to put up with some counteracting bad ones & would be loth to part with her; she is very capable.[2] She & Eliza are generally at dagger's draw with each other.

Delia is truthful & honest, not very smart; but on the whole a good servant. Lindy is cheerful, & as far as I can judge, truthful, honest, & capable. Jim is faithful & honest & I think will prove a valuable servant, quite capable; attends to his business & can do almost every thing. James is <u>singular,</u> I cannot understand him. One thing is certain, he is <u>lazy</u> to an extreme. I am afraid he is of no account.[3] We read a prayer & chapter in the Bible every night to the servants, we let them go to the Sunday school, we feed & clothe them well, we gratify all their reasonable desires. We are kind to them, give them little to do, do not make a practice of inflicting corporal punishment on them, only reprove them when absolutely necessary. If any one is entitled to good, faithful, contented, grateful servants, we are. Sheriff, the boy my husband owned when we came to housekeeping, given him by his father, he was obliged to sell on account of his bad conduct. He robbed the Post office; he has twice run away from the person to whom he was sold & returned to Greenville. The last I heard of him he was in the Jail at Asheville. He was taken up and put there. Poor fellow, he did not know when he was well off & I expect has often bitterly repented his bad conduct. I have devoted more space to servants than I intended. They have proved to me so great a trial that they afford me an inexhaustible theme. However I will drop it for the present for a pleasanter & more profitable subject. The clock has just struck 9. I have read the chapter & prayer to Jim, James, & Lindy, all who made their appearance. . . .

   1. The slaves Eliza, Edward, and Clara were aged thirty, eight, and six years old respectively. Perry's mother was Elizabeth Haynie McCall.
   2. Minerva was twenty-one years old.
   3. Delia, Lindy, Jim, and James were sixteen, eight, twenty, and fourteen years old respectively.

M. L. Brown to her sister-in-law Agnes Jeffreys, 26 April 1845, from Howard County, Missouri, to Caswell County, North Carolina. Mrs. James M. Jeffreys Letters, Special Collections Library, Duke University.

Mrs. Brown's letter reveals how difficult it could be in a frontier environment to furnish a household or make it comfortable, even for a planter's wife like herself. The letter also suggests that white women continued to be responsible for nursing, clothing, and feeding slaves, just as they had been in the seaboard, and it communicates how much she missed her home and family in the seaboard.

My dear Sister,
   I had been waiting with much anxiety for an answer to the letters I had written back, and at length on yesterday dear Christina's letter arrived, but

how sad, and how grieved, I felt when she mentioned how sick our dear Mother had been. I was so much in hopes my dear Sister that the first intelegence I had from all would be cheering, but as she mentioned that she was about again I most sincerely hope, and trust in the Lord that she has entirely recovered. Do my dear Sister visit her often and cheer her up, you are so kind and gentle in disposition I know that your company will soothe her lonly hours. how often I have thought of her, and all of you since I have been in this distant land. my memory treasures up, and dwells on every recollection of you all. every little one of your household feels dear to me. I often find myself forgetting everything here, and my thoughts gone to the days and hours we spent together. I was much gratified to hear that all your family was well.

Since the spring has come, we have all had much better health than when we first arrived here. All strangers suffer more or less the first winter, they have to become acclimated. We were so much exposed travelling in the depth of winter from place to place before we could get settled, and after we reached this place the house was brick, large rooms, and rather open, had not been occupied for a length of time, which made it very damp. I had very severe colds, indeed all the family had them. Mr. Brown has had better health than he had in N. C., he used to be much afflicted with sick headache, he has not had a single attack since he has been at this place.

When I wrote to Christina we had seen so little of the desirable portion of [page torn] I could not give her much information as to how we liked, as we were not able from cold weather to get to the counties Mr. B. intended going to, but since then Mr. Brown has been out looking at the lands in some of the best counties, and returned much pleased with them. Saline and Lafayette, he thinks very good.[1] this County is very good but the land are high. the boys have also been out and appear well satisified with the country. I have seen nothing of the county only in travelling to this place through Boon[2] and a small part of this county. There was two farms in Saline which were very good, but only log houses we had some thought of purchasing one of them but we heard that those who lived there had chills and fevers so we gave it out. we have been advised by experienced persons to see the crops gorowing on the place before we perchase. The Lands are rich enough in all these counties but strangers have to be very cautious of the situation as many places are very unhealthy, all bottom lands here are sickly.[3]

We have hired our men out for this month and the next very well, as it is the season for breaking hemp, but they say it is very hard work. men generally hire well here, good cooks and very strong women without families also hire well. We have the most of our women and children on hand. Three of our women have been confined since we came here, one lost her child and has been sick in bed for two months, but is now better. I have commenced spinning our winter cloathing as I now have some experience about the winters here and I think negroes must be better clothed here than the country we left. They say here they never had so mild a winter as the last. I prefer the climate of N. C. to this and also the water. I do not like the water, and it washes very badly.

Since we have been keeping house, we have found things for our table very difficult to obtain more so than I could have supposed. we could not get a vegetable but Irish potatoes. I gave one dollar for a bushel of sweet potatoes to plant, and very indifferent at that, even butter is scarce in the winter. in the farming counties things are more plentiful. this [is] a hemp county. with all their good land I do not think they live as well as many persons in your part of the country. Plenty of meat and bread, which seems to be a consolation to the negroes. We have perchased no furnature except a bed, table and few chairs, as we do not know how far we will have to move them.

we have frequently had company mostly gentlemen. This neighberhood is composed of plain farmers, but very substantial peple, not [page torn; much visiting?] among them. some of the girls have visited me. they appear quite [page torn]. No person my dear Sister can realize the trouble and deprivation a persen has to undergo who moves out here, but those who try it, and then to start housekeeping from the begining even to the smallest trifle. I often sigh for the comforts of my old home. when I walk through these bare rooms. If I was at a home of my own I think I should feel some better satisfied. I feel no interest here —

My little girls are well. I have at last commenced fixing Laura to send her to Boonville, the only female school near here, but I feel not satisfied as to the health of that place, as it is on the banks of the Mo. river. Little Rosalie is often talking of Aunt Agnes — She seemed deeply interested about my writing to you. she sings a little song which she learned from some of these little western girls, very sweetly, "Long, Long Ago," which always makes me feel sad.[4]

We have had the direst weather here I ever saw. we came here in Jan. and we have not had a rain that completely wet the ground since we came here.

There are no vegatables in our garden scarcely to be seen but a few indiffer-ent looking peas—the plant beds just sprouting up, that is all. not a single thing has come up but those mentioned. long dry spells, then, as much rain as the way the climate is here. William and Livingston[5] are at home at this time. Law does not seem to be a very profitable buisness in this state. lawers and Drs. in abundance, overstocked. If we can have our health through the summer and made a good selection in a home I hope we shall be contented here. I never expect to go far from this, only to some county not distant for I am truly tired of travelling and my time of life requires repose if I am only comfortably fixed, that is all I desire.[6] I often regreat that I am so far away from My dear Mother and Sisters. what a pleasure it would be my dear Sis-ter to be with you again and dear Cristina tell her to take good care of her health. Tell her I love her for her kind remembrances to us all. Mr. Brown desires me to give his best love to Agbee and says that he misses you very much and how glad he would be to have your company. he also requests me to say that since he has been out explor[page torn] the cou[page torn] from what he has seen heard and formed an oppinion he thinks he shall be well satisfied with the country if we all have our health through the summer, and will perchase Land in some of the counties not far from this as soon as he is suited. and glad I shall be my dear sister to have a place again that I call home and cheer myself sometimes with the hope that if we get on well perhaps some of the family will at some time visit, us. by water they would come very soon. Dr. Garland sometimes travels for his health. I wish he would come out here and see this country. And Mr. Jeffreys also—When we came here we came one of the worst routes, the longest [page torn]ould be travelled and we had such a time as I should never wish [page torn].

I have written a long letter to you it is all the satisfaction I can now have, and I must now my dear Sister ask of you to answer it as soon as you recieve it, as I feel so anxious to hear from you and write me how my dear Mother is. O! I hope the Lord will bless and restore her to good health again, and give all the love of my heart to her when you meet. do not neglect to write us soon as this is recieved. and remember [me] to dear Eliza I was so grati-fied to hear that she was in better health give my love to my sisters and brothers and all their families—ever your affectionate sister M. L. Brown.

1. Counties adjacent to Howard County in north central Missouri.
2. Boonville, a small town near the county line.
3. Meaning all river valleys.
4. A popular ballad by Englishman Thomas H. Bayly, first published in the United

States in the mid-1830s. Some of the nostalgic lyrics go as follows: "Tell me the tales that to me were so dear / Long, long ago, Long, long ago / Now are you come, all my grief is removed / Long, long ago, Long, long ago / Sing me the song I delighted to hear / Long, long ago, Long, long ago / Let me forget that so long you have roved."

5. Some of her relatives, probably her sons.

6. Mrs. Brown is middle-aged and may be going through menopause.

Mary G. Franklin Account Book, 1853. Special Collections Library, Duke University.

Mary Franklin was a poor widow when she headed to northern Georgia in 1832 for the state land lottery. She won forty acres in Cherokee County, land that had recently been taken from the Indian nation of the same name, and set to work panning for gold. By the early 1850s she owned nineteen slaves, a farm, and a mill worth some twenty-five thousand dollars. Hard-bitten and barely literate, she nonetheless managed her property closely, as this account book from 1853 demonstrates. Franklin often disregards gender when assigning work to her slaves, putting women in the mill, men in the house, and both sexes in the fields — perhaps because she departs from traditional gender roles herself.

13 January.	Men at the [mill] Race. Women and Henry plow. M[ary]. M[artha]. Weave.
20 January.	Calihan, Dan, Aron salt suet. Unis Jane at lard and Sausage. Mining hands at their work. Dan, And[y] at Negro Houses repairing. Henry and Women plowing. Joe ha[u]ling wood and Boards.
31 January.	Send Joe to the Foundry hall, Mick with waggon. Sam, Roland and farming hands plowing.
28 February.	Rain all day, River rising. stop the Mill. Women in[side]. M[or]g[an]., Mat shell Corn. Mary at the Mill from Dinner too spin.
12 March.	all hand[s] working on Plot, repairing fence and Clearing out. Joe ha[u]lling rails, Peg weaves, Sam Jim, ha[u]ling slate. River stop the Mill. Leonidas, Cal go to Justis Co[u]rt to attend to my business.[1] rain at night.

| 21 March. | Rain last night, River up, too wet to Plow. all hands in new ground. Joe ha[u]l Manure, Dan at his Bench. Solomon came yesterday. |
| 27 March. | Jane in Garden. Unis washes To make Soap. Mary Wash at pounding Mill. Rain. Lary, Mg Spinning. I got no letters this weke. |

1. Leonidas and Cal are her adult sons.

Diary of Eliza Ann Marsh Robertson. Eliza Ann Marsh Robertson Papers, Southern Historical Collection, University of North Carolina.

Eliza Robertson matured into a serene, good-natured matron who handled her many obligations deftly. Her placid nature should not obscure how much labor she performed, however, as a planter's wife in coastal Louisiana. She works at a range of tasks, from poisoning rats to cutting out diapers; sometimes she works with a house slave, other times alone; she works every day, even on a Sunday (January 28, 1855). What is more, she was pregnant while she wrote these entries, due to give birth in July 1855.

29 November 1854. Weather still clear but warm. William left this morning for Lafayette.[1] I have been hard at work all day putting away my hog. Succeeded in trying out the lard stuffing the sausages & salting away the pork before dark. Sold one ham of it for $1.15 cts. feel miserably tired tonight. got Miss Walker to sleep with me to keep me company. Sister Sarah & Mrs. Sharp came up and spent the evening with me.[2] Commenced poisoning some rats tonight.

1 December 1854. Weather very disagreeable, rained a good deal during the day. finished stoning raisons. Chopped the meat & got everything ready to put together. ground my citron preserves & made the syrup. Cousin Dolly and Mary Avery came to see me after dinner.[3] William objects strongly to my writing a journal but I think I will keep it up a while longer.[4] received a letter today from D. Stone.

20 January 1855. Weather quite warm & very windy. I intended going to St. Martin's to day with Mrs. Stubenger, but could not spare time,[5] have been very busy all day. had the house thoroughly cleaned. Cut out four curtains. a dress for Eliza, & one for Leila, & four aprons for Georgy.[6] worked a little in my garden & spent the afternoon pruning the rose bushes. Set one hen today with 15 eggs.

22 January 1855. Weather intensely cold, hard freeze last night. William started to Opelousas this morning,[7] but was obliged to turn back on account of the cold. I have kept pretty close to the house all day. Cut out & nearly finished a plaid sack for Georgy. Made Betsy sew on Georgy's aprons. Louis[a] commenced Eliza's dress. Cousin Sarah called in the morning to get the pattern of my Alpaca sleeves. After supper I darned stockings and darned old stockings they are.

28 January 1855. Weather cold & very windy. Spent the morning reading my Bible and prayer book. Pa & Mr. Henshaw took dinner with us. as I let Ann[8] go to St. Martin's, I had a great deal of the housework to do myself. Uncle's negro man brought us 7 more cords of wood William paid him 18 more dollars & still owes him 5 dollars.

2 March 1855. Weather delightfully pleasant. I have been busy at a number of jobs today. Spent part of my time in the garden. assisted in cleaning my pantry thoroughly, & stopping up rat holes. I washed the breakfast things, so as to give Fan time to give the kitchen a good cleaning. Mr. Henshaw came to see us & staid to dinner. I made some nice jelly out of pigs feet for dinner. I washed the dinner things and made two pillow cases today. Caroline & Georgianna Cobb came in after tea. William received a letter from Mr. Goodrich to day, telling him that he sent him some freight on the Huron which is sunk in the Atchafalaya.[9]

21 June 1855. Weather very pleasant, this morning I altered some little coats that Mrs. Weeks gave Georgy, cut out two mosquitoe bars, & fixed the tops for Mrs. Johnson to make[,] cleaned my sewing machine, & commenced some baby night gowns.[10] Cousin Sarah & John Marsh spent part of the afternoon with me.[11] In the evening I went to see Mrs. Schriner.

23 June 1855. Weather showery all the morning but clear in the afternoon. having only Ann to work, I have been pretty busy all day. I put away the

clean clothes, mended Leila's pink muslin dress, finished hemming Johnny's muslin slip, cut out three chemises & one night gown for myself. Cut out 20 baby napkins[12] out of some old linen & prepared some old linen for use. Dr. Duperieur came this morning & prescribed a dose of calomel for Louisa tonight.

27 June 1855. Weather just the same. William went to Lafayette this morning, I have been so busy sewing all day that I have not had time to feel lonesome heard the children [say] their lessons this morning & did a great variety of sewing. Cousin Sarah, Mrs. Debucly came to see me this afternoon. Sister & the girls came up this evening, Sarah staid all night with me—Mr. Dyer hired Abe today.

16 July 1855. Weather quite pleasant fine shower this morning. I cut out two spencers[13] for Leila to day & finished one of them. Mr. Alexander came to see me this evening. Mr. Miller sent three of his negro women to look at my sewing machine.

17 July 1855. Weather still pleasant. I have felt much better to day than I have for some days past, but I don't think my hour of trial can be far off. God grant that I may get through it safely.[14] Miss Fanny Hunter call'd to see me early this morning with Nan's two little girls, but they all spend the day at Mrs. Moore's, she came back again in the afternoon. Sarah Devalcourt spent part of the afternoon with me, in the evening William & I took a ride. I nearly made Leila another spencer to day. Ann made the skirt of a baby dress—

1. William is her husband, and Lafayette a small town about twenty miles away.
2. Her sister Sarah Marsh Avery, of whom she was very fond, was a middle-aged plantation mistress. Mrs. Sharp is a neighbor.
3. Mary Avery is her niece.
4. It is not clear why he would be opposed to Mrs. Robertson keeping a journal.
5. A town about ten miles away on the Bayou Teche River.
6. Her young children.
7. A town about forty miles away.
8. A house slave.
9. The Atchafalaya Bay off the coast of southern Louisiana.
10. Elias Howe patented a sewing machine in 1846, but this is probably Isaac Singer's model, developed in 1851, which proved to be more popular.
11. Her nephew, age eleven.
12. Diapers.

13. Small tailored jackets then in fashion.
14. Many women feared childbirth and called it their "hour of trial."

Diary of Maria Dyer Davies. Maria Dyer Davies Papers, Special Collections Library, Duke University.

Maria Davies was in her mid-twenties and living with her sister and brother-in-law in rural Noxubee County, Mississippi. Here she recounts the household's move to the nearby town of Macon. Although Davies was the heiress to a small fortune, she does much of the physical labor during the move. She works alongside a slave woman named Delilah, upon whom the entire household seems to depend.

1 January 1856. We have been waiting anxiously all day to know whether Judge Ames would let us have Delilah. Bro. W. saw Sister Henny And she says, Henny wouldn't take 2000 $ for Delilah.[1] We have had the blues badly to-night. Not a servant, and none to be had; just moving; and so suddenly to give up the only one who knows all about every thing in & out of the house;[2] it is too bad. I don't know what we can do & none can do us so well as Delilah. She don't want to live where Judge Ames house is, in the country, in a swamp, and I expect she will be the only one to do anything. Louisa will be apt to go home soon; Diza says she can't do anything without her, & then there will be none but Mammy left.[3] We have it to bear, & look in the face; we can't help it; but we cannot but feel sad to hink of moving into such a house & have to put up with somebody, we will not want. If there is any <u>light,</u> to the picture, it is Yet to be discovered. How we are to do, is an unpleasant & difficult question. We have been packing some to-day. took down wardrobe & bedstead &c. Mr. Jim Dow, sent in a load of furniture & now we begin to relize our having to go too. Well—I hope there is some good in it all, for somebody: now—we sit and say over & over, "what can we do"; "what <u>are</u> we to do"; "we can't possibly do without Delilah" and then she don't want to go. And this is the state of mind in which we must lie down to sleep.

4 January 1856. Busy packing, ripping, moving every thing from this old place &c. Then Bro W. took little Molly & me, in the buggy for town. Poor

Billy came near choking. roads miserable, and the house, when we arrived, looked no better. I walked about mechanically: there was about so little to give one a "home feeling" as can be imagined: A muddy yard, broken-down door steps, dirty floors, dirty walls, dirty roof, no locks to doors, a bed of ashes in the fire-place; cob-webs; dirt dawbers, wasp-nests, no fire, a cold day, no broom to sweep as we arrived before any of the wagons, and more dirt on the floors than a broom could remove; no chair to sit on, and too long a list of evils to enumerate. I swept & swept with a borrowed stump of a broom, but to very little purpose, except a bad pain in my back. Delilah & I worked away & had the carpet down & beds made by the time Sister came. Delilah cooked, we ate in our room, and Bro. W. declared it "right comfortable." I was very tired.

5 January 1856. Wagons still coming & we were stowing away in the little room. No body felt settled & very little done, besides looking for the wagons & putting up the things. The Piano was brought & had to be put in our room. We live in one room, cook in the other, & the little room is is a pack room. We felt bad all day thinking of Delilah having to go away, & she seemed much depressed. Mammy came with the last load & most of the things had been brought, though the roads are almost impassable. There is a great amount of hauling done, wagons going all the time, & the roads are made worse by it.

7 January 1856. Rain during the night & misty all day. I haven't [felt] well for a day or two. Very weak today. Delilah is gone, at last. I fell as though some one was dead. We will miss her a long time. This is late in the afternoon. Bro. W. rode downtown to see something about the stable. Mr. Cromwell is drunk & has gone, no one knows where.[4] Bro. W. expected to leave for Mobile this morning, but rain & other things prevented & I feel sad—dejected. If I only was well I would not feel so, but I cannot but feel so until the cause is removed. Nothing so oppresses my spirits, enervates a body as Sickness.

1. Charles Ames, the brother-in-law of Maria's sister Mary Davies Longstreet. William D. Longstreet, another brother-in-law, was a forty-year-old judge and slave-owner. (He was also the brother of James Longstreet, later the Confederate general.) Sister Henny is Henrietta Longstreet Clemens, another sister-in-law. They apparently loaned Delilah to the household. Maria Dyer is not related to the Missourian Martha Dyer whose diary entry appears in this chapter.

2. A slave woman named Sally, whom her brother-in-law had sold or hired out in

November 1855. Maria Davies and her siblings inherited twenty-seven slaves from their father, and Sally may be one of that number.

3. Louisa, Diza, and Mammy are slave women.

4. Cromwell is evidently the landlord from whom the Longstreets are renting their house.

Diary of Lucy Muse Walton Fletcher. Special Collections Library, Duke University.

Lucy Walton was born in Virginia in 1822, the daughter of a well-known Presbyterian clergyman, William C. Walton. After attending Catherine Beecher's famous girls' academy in Hartford, Connecticut, she married a minister named Patterson Fletcher; a year later, at age twenty-six, she gave birth to the first of the couple's five surviving children. In the late 1850s, the family resided in Middleburg, a small town in Loudoun County, Virginia. Mrs. Fletcher works hard to meet the many demands on a minister's wife, but she is a lonely spouse and a frustrated, insecure housekeeper. She yearns for gratitude, even friendship, from her house slaves and cannot see why it is not available.

15 December 1856. . . . Sometimes when I think that I shall probably be subject to the trial of having servants about me as long as I live, I feel a kind of desperation that is difficult to overcome & I am ready to cry with the poet, "O for a lodge in some vast wilderness." It is impossible to inspire them with any gratitude—although I have been extremely kind to both Mary & her baby—a kindness to which I am sure she has never been accustomed for she bore a dreadful character. She manifests no interest either in me, or the children, & tries my patience sorely.

I had several visitors during the meeting—the first occasion on which I have succeeded in persuading any one to return with me from church—Indeed I have almost ceased to invite, & to make any preparation for them. Among those who came up, were Miss Snyder, & "young John's" wife who is a daughter of Abraham Snyder's—I took Mattie with me to church to keep him out of mischief & left the dear baby with Nannie [1]—trusting them both with a kind Providence, praying that He would watch over them & keep them from all harm—I sometimes found it hard to still a mother's anxieties about them but I felt that it was my duty to go. . . .

1 January 1857. This year commences a new era in our domestic history. We have hired only one servant, & having no more Mr. F. has undertaken to be his own hostler. I think when things are settled again we shall find it a more comfortable arrangment—tho' I shall be obliged to get some one to help me in the care of the children & my sewing. It is <u>impossible</u> for me to accomplish all that is necessary to be done without such weariness & suffering as at times to make life almost a burden. My new servant is a bride, not more than 17—of course very inexperienced. This is an advantage in one respect—she will probably not be so opinionated as my last,[2] but it gives me much more care, requiring a constant superintendence. So far I have been <u>very</u> much pleased with the disposition she manifests & hope we shall get along very comfortably. She has a great ambition to live with "high people" & seems anxious to do every thing just according to my wishes. She is much more cheerful, more like a rational being than any servant woman I ever had. We have great difficulty in getting water having to bring it ¼ miles—There has been so little rain or snow, our hogsheads are entirely empty & the servant men about us, are so lazy that it is very difficult even to hire them to bring wash water. Our residence here has certainly given an ample opportunity for letting "Patience have its <u>perfect</u> work." O! if I could only feel that I was becoming more patient, more gentle & humble under the trials & vexations to which I have been subjected, it would go far towards reconciling me with the lot assigned by me to Providence. Often, when thoroughly worn out by the incessant strain of mind & body to keep things in order the injustice of things expected of me, or charges brought against me, of neglect & indifference.[3] I give way to impatience & this hasty retort which shows that I am not <u>bearing</u> my cross as I should. Dear Mother![4] how often I miss her kind sympathy & words of encouragement & <u>counsel.</u> Knowing that I was subjected to a good many trials, she was just. Sent me a little book which she thought might bring me some comfort. The first lines I read in it, "Take heart! who <u>bears</u> the <u>cross</u> today Shall <u>wear</u> the Crown tomorrow," have been sounding ever since my ears, & will I hope be the means of stimulating me to greater watchfulness & earnestness. I do want to <u>forget my self</u>—to live more for the happiness of others—to <u>do</u> good & <u>thus receive good.</u> . . .

2 February 1857. Although I have Scarcely time or strength to write tonight I must write down an event that is altogether a new thing in our history among this people—Mr. Engle brought his wife[5] over to spend the evening with us. It really did me good, although it placed me in quite a dilemma.

Poor Sarah[6] has been suffering dreadfully with a gathering on one of the fingers of her right hand, & had with difficulty succeeded in getting up our frugal dinner. (We have had but 2 meals a day since Christmas.) It was after 3 when they arrived, & we were just finishing off our dinner—table was to be cleared off, fires replenished in both rooms—the baby to nurse, company to be entertained, & <u>immediate</u> preparations made up for an early supper, as they had several miles to ride. I had been almost worn out by the exertions of the morning—after making up 2 beds, helping to clear off the breakfast table, cleaning out my own room, washing & dressing the children, I had cleaned up in the study & <u>Robert's</u> room[7] which is always a <u>serious</u> undertaking, owing to the <u>quantity</u> & variety of litter (tobacco, ashes, &c) & the number & weight of books &c to be lifted & dusted—& I had to clear away the dust & dirt of plaster made by some men who came to cut a hole in the ceiling to the garrett. Stopping meanwhile to make up some light bread for dinner. (It was my first attempt at light rolls & I succeeded better than I expected.) As Nannie too was complaining I had the passages & stairs to swept & by the time I had finished I was aching from head to foot. When I seated myself to nurse the baby, I could scarcely raise myself up again. My back has been troubling me very much of late, indeed I have felt for the last month like a stiffened, over-worked horse. . . .

I do not wish to <u>complain</u> of any hardship or trial, but I so long for a <u>little sympathy</u> sometimes. My poor husband has so many demands on his time & patience in the performance of his responsibilities as man of all work, that I try to say as little as possible about my own trials of nerve & strength. It does trouble me to see so much of his time taken up with the care of horse cow & hogs, having to run thro' snow nearly up to his waist after an unruly cow, who has been more than usually well willed of late, or in full chase after some of the neighbor's hogs who have already ruined a large quantity of the fodder he was at so much pains to have put up, for the winter—

Our new cook is really very pleasant, more like a <u>human</u> being than any I have had. She is very careless in her habits, but not more so, than many, who are older, & as she seems conscious of her faults & wishes to have them corrected I hope to have some satisfaction in my Kitchen—which has always been a place of horror to me, except at intervals last year when Mary laid aside her contrariness for a time. Sarah has really had a hard time getting settled, for two or three weeks the weather was intensely cold, wells & springs nearly dry & it was almost impossible to hire any of the lazy negro men about here to bring wash water—one night, Antony a waggish black fellow belonging to Mrs. Neill took a large tub & a bucket in his hand, & returned from the Spring ¼ mile distant, over 2 or 3 fences, with the tub full of water—the next week no soap could be attained, after waiting as long as I could for some other opportunity to "turn up" I had to send Sarah off in a snowstorm 3 miles on a man's saddle—last week when Soap & water were plenty she was suffering so much with a gathering on the middle finger of her right hand that she could not wash at all or do much of any thing. I tried very hard to get a woman from one of the neighbors who has a number of servants about her, but was unsuccessful, & on Saturday had to set to work myself—as we had had so little washing done since Christmas, the children's wardrobes would not holdout—After making up bread to last over Sabbath, I washed on until Sarah seeing that I was very much exhausted <u>insisted</u> on washing (on the board) with her left hand while I rinsed, wrung them & hung them out, before bed time I had them all ironed aired & ready for use—The Sabbath fortunately for me was stormy & I could not go to Church, so that I had what I greatly needed a day of rest. . . .

1. Her infant son, who died soon after this entry was written, and her six-year-old daughter.
2. Mary, mentioned in the preceding entry.
3. Perhaps from her husband or other relatives, who may have felt neglected because of Fletcher's household duties.
4. Lucinda Walton of Alexandria, Virginia, who evidently died in the mid-1850s.
5. A neighboring couple.
6. Her house slave.
7. Possibly one of Mrs. Fletcher's brothers or a man boarding with the family.

Amanda M. Hughes to her daughter Mary Hughes, 27 April 1858, from Turnersville, Tennessee, to Nashville, Tennessee. Darden Family Papers, Tennessee State Library and Archives.

Amanda Hughes, a struggling widow in Tennessee in 1858, kept a garden and raised chickens on a relative's farm. While she was away visiting one of her daughters, she turned her projects over to a slave woman. Mrs. Hughes relates to her as a fellow worker, if only briefly, and praises her skill with poultry.

My Darling Mary, Agreeable to promise I have set down to write to you though I must acknowledge I feel rather melanchioly came from Clarksville two or three days ago when I left Ellen was doing very well though a slight imprudence might cause her to have another attact of feaver and the second one might be fatal. Mr. Allensworth[1] was to have bin here tonight on his way up to Nashville but he has not come, he intends comeing up to see you if he possibly can leave your Sister. I suppose it will depend on her health. I am sorry you try to keep your delicate health from me I am truly uneasy about your health if it is, as it was when you were at home, I am sure you will have to remain at home nex[t] Session and improve you[r] general health how much I wish I could travel like a gentleman, and I would come forthwith to see you. I do hop[e] I may be situated that I may not have to board the rest of the children a way from home. I stayed just one month with your sister would you have believed Ma could have ben kept away from home so long and no fa[r]ther than Clarksville.[2] The negroes all worked very well. A[u]nt Lydia kept hou[s]e. she has a fine chance of young chickens, has a great [d]eal better luck than I would have we had a heavy frost last night coat the beans, potatoes, corn and killed all the grapes. I think there will be peaches and apples enough if half were killed. my strawberris I think are not killed. My prospect for strawebries is very good. my ice is melting very badly that is the complaint generally the ice was very indifferent—this year, though I hope to have ice enough to give you a plenty of ice cream when you come home both of your Sisters are comeing up to spend some weeks with you I am look[page torn] forward to the time with much pleasure and I know you are in every one we hope we hope there will be no providential hindrance that all may meet around the Family board once more in health.

well I must not beg to call your attention to home pleasures to much for I am quite sure it is a trial enough for you to stay away from us all so long. well the children are do[w]n getting there lessons and are going to bed. Sallie [Marshall?] is staying with Sallie tonight well I must stop for tonight we have eat breakfast all are well this morning every apperance of rain this morning we are haveing a very wet spring. I fear there will be a great [d]eel of Sickness there is but very little yet. you must write me as soon as[3]

1. Her son-in-law, a physician.
2. A small town a few miles away, near the Virginia state line.
3. Here the letter ends.

M. J. Mathis to her children, 27 June 1858, from Dallas, Texas, to somewhere in South Carolina. John T. Coit Family Papers, from the Collections of the Dallas Historical Society.

In the midst of her litany of disappointments, Mrs. Mathis describes the grueling labor that women did on the Southern frontier even in the twilight of the antebellum period. The middle-aged wife of a yeoman farmer, Mathis is also homesick. While her husband praises Texas "pretty steep," she is eager to return to South Carolina.

My Dear Children, I received your kind letter of the 23 just one Month from the date this is the 2nd I have had from you since Mr. Mathis left, But I was writeing to him and I thought you would hear from me[.] I was glad to hear of his safe arrival at your house but if I could have gone with him I should have enjoyed it better than to be here writeing.

I expect he set Texas up pretty steep, well when he went away every thing looked promising for good crops but the Spring is a bad time to calculate for the first thing you know the drowth[1] comes on and everything dries up and looks as if fire had run through, garden's and all Spring crops come to an end, unless some particular pieces that stands the drowth they get half a crop. Some pieces of Corn lookes verry well yet but unless we have some rain soon there will not be a half a crop in this part of the Country our Corn was silked out a weeke ago[.] there has not been one drop of rain on it in 5 weeks and perhaps there will be none till August or September the streams and springs all so dry, our spring went dry this year by the middle of May and that would make me sick of Texas if nothing else to lug watter a half a mile is what I do not fancy much. You need not think I do not want to hear from or see you that is not so[.] I am no better satisfied nor do I like Texas any better than when you left nor I never shall there is not anything here to make me like it nor I will not stay here if I can get away. I would rather be there in the poore house than stay here. —

I had a letter from Sherman the other day I was verry glad to hear from them he wrote Roxania was married with no very flattering prospects[.] I am sorry to hear that. he did not tel me what a predicament Hull was in I hope he is out before this time[.] I do not know as I have anything more to write for James is a going to write[.] Morris sayes I must tel you he is to work like the verry Devil and he is a going to write as soon as he gets time.[2]

this from you affectionate Mother til Death M. J. Mathis.

1. An archaic term for drought.
2. Sherman, Roxania, Hull, and James are her in-laws, nephews, and nieces. Morris is her son.

Sallie Graydon to her cousin Lou Madden, 4 March, 12 March 1859, from Newton, Florida, to Laurens, South Carolina. Mabra Madden Family Papers, South Caroliniana Library, University of South Carolina.

Sallie Graydon grew up with her cousin Lou Madden in Laurens County, South Carolina. Their grandfather was a planter, but Madden's father owned only two slaves in 1850, and Graydon's family had fallen into destitution: she lived with two female relatives who owned no property of any kind. In 1859, at age twenty-four, Graydon migrated to Florida to work as a nurse and governess. Having been thrown on her own resources, she urges her teenaged cousin to study hard and be self-reliant.

My Own Dear Cousin Lou,

I received your exceeding[ly] kind letter yesterday which gave me much pleasure to peruse its pages. [March] 12th. Dear Lou I commenced this more than a week ago but owing to some sickness in the neighborhood I have failed to finished it untill another of your kind letters have made its appearance. Saturday was a week we were sent to go to see a gentleman who was suppose to be dying. We returned home on Sunday an Wenesday following went to see a sick lady, one of our neighbors, and found her so very ill we stayed with her untill she died. She died Thursday 4 Oclock in the eveng. She expressed a great hope beyond the grave Spoke of death often asked me to talk with her about death. She said she was happy and willing to give up all this world for the sake of Christ. She leaves three small children the youngest are twin girls about one year old, a husband and numerous other frends. It is an awful thing to die even when one is assured of eternal life. But to die in their sins must be a great deal worse. We should all be prepared for that fatal hour.

I feel somewhat melancholy today to think this is the last Sunday that I will spend at home in some time. The last of this week I expect to take charge of a gentleman's children who has employed me as a governess for the present year. The[y] live about twenty miles from here. Lou we are now mingling with the varied species of human nature—and do you not find as many different characters as faces. Some are very cold hearted & scornful whilst others are warm and generous to all. Which do you like best? Why of course the latter says you! We should ever strive to gain the friendship of all and if we have that generous and mild disposition we will never fail to do so.

Lou now is the time to improve the golden moments of youth and rise to the pinicle of fame. Do study diligently and you will receive a rich reward. Knowledge is something which cannot be taken from you wealth may be squandered but that never can be [1] I would be happy to hear that my cousin Lou had taken first honor in her class at Laurensville College. Dear Lou you must not think too much about the beaux. Wait untill you are done going to school and then you will be better prepaired to think of them. But I not mean that you shall slight the young men no[.] Some girls you know when in love with a young man can [not?] Study, nothing else. I would like to know who you are corresponding with. I have heard of a little preacher by that name.[2] I wonder if he is the one. If so I can't blame you for loving him. I can love a pious man much better than a weak one. My beau is a pious little Baptist though he says he fears if he stays in this wicked country he will become wicked too. I told him he must resist temptation and not follow the example of the wicked but set good examples for them to follow. I think he has resolved to do so. A friend of mine met him the other night in road and he was praying aloud for his patience[3]—but alas! poor fellow lost one and I don't think there is much hopes for the other.

Lou you need not be surprised if you hear of some of the girls about uncle Graydons[4] being off with some of the Florida boys. If you could take a peep Some Sunday evenigs you would see some half doz. horses tied at the gate and some handsome young men in the piaza. This is a great place for boys and few girls. We are living in a very pleasant neighborhood. There are several families living in sight of us. The Post Office is kept at our house and we have a church in half a mile of this place. The name of the P. O. is Newton. you must direct your next letters to Newton Fla. The people of this [place?] is having a new church built. I presume they will have it done buy Aug. You must come down to the dedication of it. Dr. Thomas has given then five acres for the church & graveyard from his land.

Cousin this is a delightful country the winters so mild & pleasant. We have flowers all through the winter and vegetables of all kinds. Corn is half leg high and cotton up very pretty. I was in the Orange groves a few weeks ago. Oh! it is the most disirable place on earth, a modern eaden. We spent a night there when the moon was shining all night in her grandest splendor. The Lake is an extended sheet of water and on the borders spontaneously grow the orange trees forming a perfect hammock of nothing but the tall heavy laden Orange trees. They are now in full bloom. They have very fragrant flowers. We have some trees in our yard which have some flowers on them if I can get one I will put it in this [letter] that you may see an orange flower. John has been staying with [us] a week he has had chills fever and did not feell like work. Mike Youstis came up for him today. I am to go on the Stage next Wednesday as far as Ocala then John will carry me out to brother Hodgkiss's. He is a precher. I recon I will be well pleased with my new home. Lou maybe I will pay you all a visit next fall if I can spare the time. I haven't decided how long I will teach perhaps till Christmas perhaps only six months. I will be making about twenty-five dollars per month if I succeed in my calculations. I must close my letter in hast[e] as the girls are going to walk out to see our neighbors and want me to go with them. Do write soon. I can get my letters from home.[5] Excuse bad writing and mistakes. Sue says she is going to write soon. Believe me as ever Your affectionate Cousin Sallie.

1. This remark suggests that perhaps Lou Madden's family had squandered its wealth.

2. Madden must have named him in a previous letter.

3. Graydon means "patients," for her beau is a physician.

4. Possibly Sterling Graydon, who owned three slaves in Laurens County, South Carolina, in 1850, before he moved to Florida.

5. Meaning after she takes her new job.

Elizabeth Maney Bowman to her sister Susan Maney Boddie, 19 December 1859, from Franklin, Tennessee, to somewhere in rural Tennessee. Douglas-Maney Papers, Tennessee State Library and Archives.

Elizabeth Bowman describes the various household tasks women performed, as well as one of the messiest tasks a plantation mistress had to supervise, killing hogs. She did some of the labor herself, at times trading jobs with a slave woman named Hetty. Her political views are just as interesting. A fervent Unionist, Bowman is worried about the regional tensions between North and South in the wake of John Brown's raid at Harper's Ferry in 1859.

My Dear Sue, I received your letter last week and was glad to hear from you. Sorry Mag has been troubled with risings—hope she will soon be well though—and never have any return of it—We all are only <u>tolerable</u>—nothing serious though—Hardy had a very bad cold—and has been in bed off and on for 2 days past—Eliza has a very bad cold, cough, and sore throat—I was sick for about 3 hours Saturday strongly threatened with the flux—but have gotten entirely over it—protected by cold I used remedies and kept quiet Saturday night and yesterday was well enough to resume my duties at Sunday School.

George is puny has been looking badly for 2 or 3 days and complains a good deal of his head—I must give him some medicine tonight and hope that will relieve him. Mag went up to Murfreesboro'[1] last week, and we expected Ma to return with D. Dick on thursday, but Fanny Dick was taken worse was very ill for some days and Ma preferred to stay till she was better so she wrote and sent him home Friday and said she would come today—yesterday I had a short letter from her—Fanny was better relieved entirely of pain and doing very well except in one place and the Dr. was leeching her there—she thought she would come home today but as it had turned so cold—she might not—but lo and behold this evening Brother went to the Depot and there was Mag come back—Ma was not satisfied to leave Fanny—said she would not be easy about her—so Mag came back—We were getting along well—no <u>need</u> for her to have deprived herself of the pleasure of her visit—but I suppose Ma & her would be better satisfied to have her at home—

Ma has not heard from Pa since his Uncle Jimmy and his folks got back has not had but one letter from him and <u>we</u> have not heard at all—I am very uneasy about him indeed—I dream of him at night and think about him all day—the gap in the railroad—is <u>horrid</u> traveling—but surely if he has written at all or if he is well and able to write—some of the letters would come. I know how he <u>hates</u> to write letters—but surely if he is in a condition to write he will do so in mercy to our anxiety, that he <u>must know</u>

we feel to hear from him when he is away from home—I don't know what to think and fear to hear, almost, as anxious as I am to get a letter—I wish Ma could have gone with him—

Larry has killed all the pork, and I <u>rendered</u> up the lard, the boiling of the <u>pigs feet,</u> and making cheese souse today and tomorrow (if Hetty cannot wash). I will have the last of the sausages stuffed and then it will be over for a year. —I have some Sunday school papers &c to send you—have only been waiting for Brother to go to Sumner, but I can't tell when he is going—I have asked you 2 or 3 times and shall not ask again—have you read Mr. Everett's speech?[2] What do you think of it? Good ain't it? Ought to be read by everybody I think North and South—Whig and [Demo]'Crat.[3]—

I think I will be able to write a letter to Martha Ann in [a] day or so—have intended it for some time—tell her all send love to her and hope Clint has entirely recovered—wish she and all her little ones were here—Martha says "tell her Ma howdy for her" she is well—There is a Cousin of Annie Maney's at Mr. James McGarock's—Miss Julia Southall of Miss. —daughter of James Southall—a very fine looking girl. I was in hopes that I should be able to get out to see her this week, but the snow coming this afternoon will stop it I fear—

Mr. Morey is <u>not</u> going away—all the Church are for his staying but 2 or 3 members—there are only 3 persons who do not like his preaching—viz. Mrs. Bostick, Mrs. Maury, & John B. McEwen—not <u>much force</u> either of them as judges—Mrs. B. dislikes <u>him personally</u> too—all this sub rosa—we had no idea of letting him go—but cant get more than $800 for him as two of these subscriptions are stopped—

Mrs. B. was very anxious for Mr. Harrison to come here—and asked him the question, taking a great deal on herself I think—to speak for the church in place of the session—She has not been to church for some time week ago yesterday was communion in our church—she was not there <u>at all</u> though she was in town Friday and her carriage was there again on Saturday—Wednesday night she was at Dr. Park's at a little tea drinking—she is not a <u>good Presbyterian</u> and I wish she was—or that she would join the Methodist church at once—Cannon & John come to our church nearly every Sunday pay strict attention and Jonny goes to Sunday School—Mag says with her best love that she will be up to see you in two or three weeks—says she will make Maggie some caps. I must close now as it will be a good opportunity. I will send you by Mag that white rain silk muslin whrapper (query—is that the way to spell it? I have sorter lost my wits) that I made so many summers ago and worked all down before. I promised to give it to you when I died! but it does me no good—large hoops making it too short & I dislike to have any dead capital[4]—so you shall have it now—ready to wear next summer if you like or do with just as suits you best. Our love to all the family & inquiring friends at home & in the bend. Love for the children and Brother Boddie. Kiss Mary for me—good bye— truly yours, E. M. Bowman.

1. A small town about thirty miles southeast of Nashville.
2. Edward Everett (1794–1865), a former U.S. senator from Massachusetts, traveled the country in the late 1850s giving speeches advocating the preservation of the Union. On December 8, 1859, he spoke to a large crowd at Faneuil Hall in Boston on John Brown's raid at Harper's Ferry and repeated his call for reconciliation. In 1860, he ran as vice president with John Bell on the Constitutional Union ticket.
3. The Whig Party had collapsed in 1854.
4. This may be Bowman's attempt at a pun about her wardrobe.

Mary E. Starnes to her friend Sarah J. Thompson, 1 November 1859, from Springfield, Limestone County, Texas, to Augusta, Georgia. William H. Kilpatrick Letters, from the Collections of the Dallas Historical Society.

Now a single woman in her late twenties, Mary Starnes lived with her brother William, who owned thirty-one slaves in 1860. Although he is a professional physician and tells her how to treat sick slaves, she is in charge of their daily care. The sick girl may be suffering from malnutrition or intestinal worms.

Dear Sallie,

I write to say because it is the appointed time, not that I have any news or any other communication to make that will in the least interest you. perhaps after I get started I may think of something you would like to hear, at any rate the attempt to write will prove to you that I am neither negligent nor forgetfulness of my duty.

Amanda received a letter from Isabell yesterday. Sister's family were all well excepting two of the children, one has sore eyes & the Baby I presume is teething, Isabell says she is nothing but skin & bone.[1] when I hear of sickness among the children I always wish to be with them, though I am not destitute of employment of that kind at home. I am giving Quinine every hour this morning to one of the grown negroes, & we have a little one who has been in delicate health for several months. Lately I have taken it on myself to attend to her particularly. I have been giving her tonics & medicines for worms, but she has not improved any. Yesterday I commenced with broken doses of Calomel according to Brother's directions.[2] if that don't bring her out I am afraid it is a bad case with her. she is very thin, her neck is not much larger than my wrist, her appetite is good, stomach very large & feels as tight as a drum.

You wish to know how I was pleased with the Camp meeting I told you all about that in my last, but omitted to mention the Beau I caught there. he is an old widower 60 years old, that will <u>take</u> you know, & when you come to see me I will introduce you to my grandchildren. The old Gentleman got in with one of our neighbors to try & find out if he could succeed. the Lady I presume felt a delicacy in broaching the subject to me, but spoke to Amanda about it, & requested her to tell me. I have not seen the Lady since, but if she ever mentions the subject to me I can very soon settle the hash, whether it will be to her satisfaction or not I am not prepared to say, but one thing I feel confident of, & that is, it will be settled to the entire satisfaction of his children.[3]

I must now tell you of a dream (or as the Dolefuls say a vision) I had a few weeks since, I thought you & Joe Newby had married each other I was very much astonished at the match but was not displeased. perhaps you can interpret the dream, if so let me have it in your next. I would like to hear something about Joe. where is he & what is he doing?

I heard from Cousin Camilla not long since, she says Ella[4] went back very well satisfied & Mr. Smith said all seemed delighted to see her at the Convent. we have had letters from Ella also since her return. she has been advanced in all her classes. Don't forget to mention Amanda Mann when you write. I hope if it is the will of the good One that her life may be prolonged for her Father's sake.

Let me know how Carolina Kelley is, remember me affectionately to Mrs. Oliver, & say to her I will be happy to hear from her. My best love to all my <u>dear dear</u> friends yourself included. Our white family are all well. Goodbye. Mollie.

1. Amanda is William Starnes's second wife, and her sister, the former Sarah Starnes, married her neighbor Sam Graves. Isabella is unidentified.

2. Nineteenth-century physicians often prescribed this white powder, a mercurous chloride, as a cathartic or diuretic.

3. In 1865 Starnes married another widower with several children, a physician two years her senior. She died in childbirth in 1868.

4. Mary Starnes's teenaged niece.

Elizabeth Peter to her niece Mary Hughes, 9 September 1860, from somewhere in Tennessee to Nashville, Tennessee. Darden Family Papers, Tennessee State Library and Archives.

In 1860, Elizabeth Peter was in her mid-fifties, the wife of a Methodist minister and slaveowner. Even though she was a grandmother and felt "old," she tends her garden, nurses the sick (both blacks and whites), does some housework, and between times hosts a visit from some of her numerous descendants.

Dear Sister, Yours of July 4th came to hand in due time but it found me in the busy time of harvest with a great deal on my hands. Emily's health very poor [1] and not help enough in the house for the work; hence I have had a pretty hard summer. Mr. Peter, Henry, Samuel, and Eva all had an attack of chills but are now pretty well again. Within the last 4 weeks we have had all our children at home to see us. Our grandchildren number 15 — Thomas who has no health lost 1 child this spring — poor fellow it is a mercy but I suppose he would not say so he is spending all we gave him cannot have any thing left — if he does not get able to do something in a year or two more he has 1 daughter named Lilian and son they called Edward Hamilton. I always feel sorry when I see the little ones — with such a helpless Father we try to help them what we can but O they are so dependent — Ann Blodgett has a Son by her present husband she is doing well.

Harriet has 3 Sons — Elisa has 6 children but Mary has never had any — I think I told you in my last that Richard belonged to the Itinerant ranks [2] — I hope he may do good he has 2 children —

Ann's little girl is now 7 years old (by Mr. Warwick) is I think very much like her Father, and I fear will give her Mother trouble — but I must hope for the best [3] —

Ellen told me in her letter that my old friends Mr. Bailey and sister enquire about me. do remember me to them. I have not forgotten them no the days of childhood and youth are fresh in my memory yet — you speak of the Farmers — yes we remember them too and time would fail me to speak of all the loved and remembered of goneby days but I trust we shall meet them all again in that eternal day.

I have now written u[n]til my h[e]adaches — I write but seldom. I feel old. I am going down the steeps of time fast, my poor bark will land on the other shore ere it be long —

but dear Sister you asked us once more to come to see you. I wish we could but how we can while we stay on the farm I cannot see. Samuel our youngest son will not be of age for three years[4] after that time if we live we may quit the farm then we might visit but I feel as though I would be so old by that time I could not enjoy a visit what shall I do — the times are hard here money sca[r]ce we can get along at home but to visit is impossible. Wheat crop here was almost a failure grass half a crop corn is good. —

Fruit rather scarce —

Prosperity in religion only in a few places —

Sickness in many localities — I must close by subscribing myself your sister[5] untell death E. H. Peter.

do write soon my love to all Farewell & may we meet in heaven.

1. Emily is a slave woman.
2. It sounds as if he is a traveling peddler.
3. In her other letters Peter said that her daughter Ann Warwick was unhappily married.
4. Meaning in three years he will be twenty-one years old.
5. An endearment for her niece.

RACE

In THIS CHAPTER A PICTURE OF exploitation, indifference, and overbearing "paternalism" unfolds before the reader. The devout women quoted here considered it their Christian duty to medle in slaves' lives. One advice maven felt this kind of interference was also evidence of good character in white women. Yet others saw slaves as commodities and would not even adopt the practice of "paternalism." Still others simply wanted to escape the daily contact with bondsmen that slavery required of a plantation mistress. One white woman, Mary Carter, struggled with the dilemma of being married to a planter who is unfaithful with slave women, yet she did not descend into bigoted fury in the spirit of Mary Boykin Chesnut.

Indeed, what begs for explanation, or at least some informed speculation, are the racial heresies in this chapter. One young woman felt compelled to share her egalitarian religious vision with slaves, despite threats from other whites, and several other individuals boldly approached the border crossing of the black community to exchange resources with people of color. Another young woman made the argument that proslavery theorists feared most of all: she called slaves an "oppressed" people. How do we explain these startling opinions? What might have happened to women who expressed these views in public? Perhaps most mysterious of all is the human connection between the slave named Peggy and the mistress Ann Powell. How might we explain Peggy's choices in that household?

Martha Gaston to her cousin Jane Gaston, 22 November 1824, from Wilcox County, Alabama, to Chester District, South Carolina. Gaston and Crawford Papers, South Caroliniana Library, University of South Carolina.

Raised together in South Carolina, Martha and Jane Gaston corresponded for many years, their friendship rooted in their ardent Presbyterian faith. Martha Gaston lived in the heart of the Alabama Black Belt in the 1820s as it was beginning to attract slaveowners from the seaboard. She believes that slaves should hear God's word, including the minister's bold message, and she acts on her convictions despite hostility from other whites.

Dear Cousin Jane,

With pleasure I take up my pen to write to you. It has been some months since I received your letter, but not having anything of importance to write I have pos[t]poned it till now. We have all enjoyed good health since we came here. Father I think is a goodeal fleshier since he came here. he and mother appear to be well pleased with their move.[1] Presbytery met at our church the first friday of this Ins[tant]. Oh cousin Jane it was a delightful meeting I think I never enjoyed a more precious time. My saviour brought me into his banqueting house and his baner over me was love.

> Oh the delights the heavenly joys
> The glories of the place
> Where Jesus sheds the brightest beams
> of his o'er flowing grace

Mr. Murphy opened presbytery with a discourse from these words[.] This is a true saying if a man desire the office of a bishop he desireth a good work. It was delivered to the clergy principly, but I thought it was aplicable to us all. It was a very finished course in the subject. They talk of geting it printed.

Mr. Cuningham preached in the evening from Psalm 133.[2] I was glad when they said unto me, let us go into the house of the Lord. Mr. Hillhouse preached saturday morning Psalm 113.[3] The entrance of the word giveth light. Mr. Alexander preached in the evning from those words[.] The disciples were first called christians at Antioch.[4] When he gave out his text I thought there was not much need for any comment upon it, but he had not long commenced, till he Convinced me to the contrary. He gave a particular discription of the christian character and wherein it consisted[.] after that they read their missionary reports. They had a two weeks tour apointed them the presbytery before. They were very satisfactory indeed. It was sundown when we left the meeting house. They apointed night meeting at brother John's. I thought I had been hearing so much that I had not room for much more, but when I got home, and took some refreshment and returned to brothers. the word seemed as sweet as ever. Mr. Mirphey and Mr. Hillhouse gave us two very weighty and impresive exhortations. I think they made use of some of the most weighty arguments in favour of confessing our Lord and savior before men that ever I heard. Mr. Mirphey said he thought one principle reason with a great many people was that they were affraid of testifying to the sons of belial[5] that they were not of their party; that they might be neutral and not distinguish themselves what party they belonged to but that would not do he said they were either of belial party or of God's and their not coming forward and confessing God was a plain testimony that they did not love him. We would think very little of one that would profess to esteem us in private yet would fail to do it publicly. Mr. Hillhouse preached the action sermon from romans 5 chap 1 vers.[6] Mr. Alexander opened the table serving. Mr. Cuningham preached in the evening from Rev. 3-11.[7] he that ever cometh shall not be [hurt?] with the second death. They preached until nearly the going down of the sun[.] I never saw people sit more patiently to hear preached and some of them had a great distance to go[,] a great many said they never had heard as soon preaching. one old lady said, when she heard some talking that they were hungry, that she was not in the least hungry; she had been feasting all the time, she was right full. Brother Boyd and sister had the pleasure of seeing their first born dedicating himself to God at that time he had been under serious impressions for some time before the meeting.[8] Mr. Cuningham had private conversation with him and afterwards he examined him publicly before the congregation. He answered him satisfactoraly, and was cordially received by the church.

Mr. Cuningham is the most engaged about the conversion of the negroes of any preacher ever I heard. He said on sabbath evening in his adress if ever his cold heart was refreshed in preaching that gospel he was commanded to preach to the poor that proclaimed liberty to the captives and the opening of the prison doors to them that are bound[,] It was in addressing those poor creatures, and he determined to presevere in it, though it should cost him his blood. In his reports to presbytery he gave several specimens of the hap[p]ly effects of his labour among them. he says that in the long days he generly preaches two sermons to the whietts and one to the blacks. He has a large sabath school in his congregation for the instruction of the negroes. They had one comenced in the pleasant valley,[9] but they met with so much opposition that they gave it up a while to see if they could have it sanctioned when the members of the legislature met. We have a small sabbath school in our congregation. We instruct both white and black. there has been some threats made, but no attempts to disturb us.

Those that attend with us learn fast. We had some of the good old presbyterians from the pleasant valley with us the time of the meeting. old Mr. William Morison and his son and the Mr. Bakey Mr. [illegible], and Mr. Alexander Marrow and his brother David Marrow. Mr. Alexander had three of his elder wi[page torn].

I am glad to hear that Martin John and Miss Me[page torn] have got a prospect of their adding to each others hapiness, and usefullness in the world. I hope they will be like good old Zachariah and Elizabeth.

My Dear cousin you have given me a detail of several marriages, and about your new house, all that I was glad to hear. But you never said a word about your trip, whether you were traveling to the Land of matrimony or not (though you may have traveled there before this time) [10] I hope at least you are traveling to the land of hapiness if you are in the land of matrimony I want you to let me know and how you are pleased with the country.

But my dear cousin we are fast traveling to a land from whence we shall not return to making any report to the inhabitants of this world.[11] Oh may we hope that assured confidence that Paul speaks of For we know that if our earthly house of this tabernacle were dissolved we have a building of God, a house not made with hands eternal in the heavens I sometimes get a sweet foretaste of the promised land.

While such a scene of sacred bliss My raptured eyes and soul emply Here I could sit and sing myself away To everlasting day. My Dear cousin I want you to remember me in your prayers I have great need of Divine assistance I have had a pretty constant visitor for sometime, but he has not come fuly to an exclaim[illegible] on the subject Though I dread it every day. I expect him to day. It is a matter of great importance to know how to act in such cases.[12]

Do not forget me in this matter. We are told where two agree touching any upon earth it shall be granted them. Brother Boyd and sister have arrived today from a meeting at Greensborough.[13] David saw Mr. Elias Wallis he has just returned from Carolina he states it has been very sickly there. Mrs. Wallis went a great way to be buried with her [family?].

Let me hear how cousin Jane Walker and her family do. Remember me to cousin McCrery and family. And to all your relations, and to Lucille. Gill how it would rejoice me to see you and her and have some sweet hours together. Brother Weir expects to be in Carolina about Christmas. If you have letters at brother Hugh's again that time he will fetch them to me. he does not expect to stay more than a day or two there.

This from your sincere though unworthy cousin Martha Gaston.

1. The Alabama federal census for 1820 has been destroyed, but the 1830 census for Wilcox County lists two men named Gaston, one of whom is Martha's father: John, who owned six slaves, and Hugh Sr., who owned five slaves. There is no information on Mrs. Gaston.

2. This psalm begins, "Behold, how good and how pleasant it is for brethren to dwell together in unity."

3. It reads in part, "Blessed be the name of the Lord from this time forth and forevermore. From the rising of the sun to its going down the Lord's name is to be praised."

4. A city in what is now Turkey; in ancient times one of the early centers of Christianity and the site of St. Paul's first mission to the Gentiles. St. Peter also preached there.

5. A biblical term for Satan.

6. The fifth chapter of Romans, verse one, reads, "Therefore, having been justified by faith, we have peace with God through our Lord Jesus Christ."

7. This verse from Revelations reads, "Behold, I am coming quickly! Hold fast what you have, that no one may take your crown."

8. Meaning he had been thinking of converting.

9. A nearby community in Alabama. Unfortunately, the historical record does not indicate what happened to Mr. Cuningham or the Pleasant Valley school.

10. Jane Gaston may already have gotten engaged or been married. She wed a Mr. Barkly in the mid-1820s, was widowed, and married a Mr. Crawford in the 1840s.

11. Meaning that one day all mortal beings will die.

12. It sounds as if her suitor is about to propose marriage and she plans to decline. Martha Gaston did marry a Mr. Gamble sometime after 1826.

13. A village in central Alabama.

Elizabeth Randolph to her daughter Mary Braxton Randolph Carter, 12–23 April 1825, from Germantown, Virginia, to Shirley plantation, Charles City County, Virginia. Shirley Plantation Research Collection, Special Collections, Colonial Williamsburg Foundation Library.

Elizabeth Carter Randolph was born in 1769 into one of the most eminent planter families in Virginia, and she married into another well-known family. A devout

Christian, by the 1820s she harbors doubts about slavery's morality. Her daughter Landonia shared her doubts and would try to free all of the slaves she owned, while Elizabeth Randolph supports "colonization," or the deportation of American slaves to other countries.

Your last past mine, which you no doubt have by This; so that in Fact you are in my debt, but as my gardening is almost over, as to its hurry & importance, I cannot deny myself the pleasure of chatting a few moments with my dear my darling child. Your lamenting your want of good preaching reminds me of the blessing the poor unworthy creatures in this county are to enjoy tomorrow & 3 suceeding days. W. M. will preach tomorrow — & Friday sat. & Sun. The Presbytery have a meeting. I hope to go tomorrow, but as the weather is rather unsettled I may be disappointed, indeed I know not that Land. can go,[1] as she has not been able to set up to dinr. for a long time before yesterday; but thank Heaven she is manifestly bettr. than for for months past.

You seem seriously to lament yr situation in respect to this great blessing — it is a favor withdrawn from many parts of the world, from the abuse & misimprovement of it; & perhaps was from that part of the World in which yr lot is caste,[2] be it so, yet blessed be God, all may have a Bethel[3] in every part of the Wilderness All will suit to place an Ebenezer for them; & when we humbly ask in faith, we shall find enough to support on the way to Zion. You think thus shut out from ordinances you may need somewhat more to feed your faith — but remember dr, He who fed the Prophet by Ravens, is the same, yesterday, to day, & forever — to him All look to him make our moan, & we shall not lack food — He that hungereth or thirsteth after righteousness shall be filled. O! these are precious promises! in them may we [illegible] & Amen! I know no place where there is more orthodox preaching than Warrenton,[4] or from the daily progress of sin that has appeared since the departure of Mr. Lemmon it seems as if a famine of the word prevailed among them, so we now see that in the midst of plenty people can starve & in the wilderness or barren desert God can feed his own —

O yes my child let us trust to him — let us love & serve him, & he will be our friend unto death. Your sisters like yourself are in every letr. I get making the same complaint concerning their loss & lack of public worship.[5] I hope it may to you all be a mean[s] of more watchfulness, as this is the only way in which good can be produced out of so great an evil.

— May you be brought to keep close to the word of God let it be the

Morn of yr counsel, look to the promises & guard against meriting its threats—never take this sacred Vol. up to read without a humble petition to have the perusal blest to you; as when laid by, return thanks for the privilege you have enjoyed, as you would after a comfortable repast of natural food for yr temporal support; but in a much higher degree. This will I trust prove the food that will support yr betr. part unto life eternal. Now dr let me recommend to you, the perusal of Teneton's extracts, I think if you have not got my copy you had best get one, also Doddridges Rise & Progress—These with yr Bible & Bickersteth on prayer,[6] will prove an excellent Library & be an excellent Society of spirited companions which is the best substitute I can recommend under the circumstances you so much lament—

Talking of books do in yur next tell me whether Lavinia took my first Vol. of the Children's Guardian, it is missen & we know not what to make of it & I am in hopes she has it.

My eyes are still very far from well but great are the mercies I enjoy as to the clearness of vision, as in all things I may say: my lot is, to read prayers of a night, & sometimes when they are sore pained & I think they cannot bear the light I am called on to read look at minute things cut nails &c &c all is done with more ease than could have been performed at an early period of life in short I feel so well & able above all desert or expectation at the evening of my day, that I feel as if I were becoming ungrateful to give way to any indulgence, & am rejoiced to say I am permitted to be more able & useful in most respects than I ever expected.

I am again seated to make another attempt to chat with you dr. after an interval of two days. on Wednesday I thought surely I should a lettr. to send to the P. O. on Friday but yr Papa suddenly appeared & told me he had sold his Slaves which had long been talked of[7] this was a shock that put an end to every pleasant idea & my pen has been laid aside till now, & now I am much hurried as I went to Church as I think I mentioned on thursday & yesterday was much engaged putting up little bundles &c for these poor Souls, which [page torn] all her Daughters & their Children, Celia & her [page torn]. I never saw people more distressed than one & all, & yr Papa not the least, he says he never was so much distressed in his life & determined never to part with any more.

Yesterday evening Mary Meade came down to spend some time with us, & I hope will be a means of drawing Landa. out, & helping her in her views of her progress; she left all well & is a sweet, mild, & amiable striver. I got yrs of the 8th Inst. last night & there you observe you have no tidings from this part of the world, were I not in the habit of trying to think all is well I should think hard that my letr. so often escape you.

O! I could write pages to my child but I must sit with dr. M. & do many other things, I tell you how delighted with the thought of yr health being betr & having more of yr company this summer should we be spared. O! that we could improve the time in a more satisfactory manner than we usually do. As to Chas. he is not married as yet I believe but it is not improbable that Randolph thinks, or says it will be a most advantageous Match to Chs & poor fellow I hope if he is married he may do well. I have never seen him since I saw you, he thinks himself forsaken by his friends & seems determined to forsake us — dr Soul I wish him all happiness & am pleased whenever I can be serviceable to him & long to see him. at any rate I think it an incumbeat duty that children should be attentive to their parents. You have not last mentioned my dr. W———r & I wish he may continue to amend. O! that he was fond of his books as Randolph. he is indeed an extraordinary child, but still one of failing educaSon. Kiss dr W———r for me & tell him I shall be grieved to see him behind any of my god-children in his education. O! who is with you that you can speak of the children. is it my dr litl. Bob?

If so give my love to him & tell him I still love him. Yr Papa, Mary, Landonia, Robert, & Lavinia all unite [with] me in affect. love to you.[8] My dr do write me in yr next whether Old Mother Betty is still in the land of the living.[9] My love to Hill tell him I hope he will not remain so long down the country on his own as well as yr account.[10] God bless you my beloved & grant you may reap the anticipated benefit from your trip to P[eters]burg. would it not be too late I should like my love to be offered to Mrs. Campbell.[11] Now dr Mother you will say I spare you this time. So dr. Adieu. Yrs ever E. A. Randolph.

Do write me how the colonization business goes on in Petersburg.

1. Her daughter Landonia, a young adult.

2. Randolph is referring to the fact that Mary Carter is separated from her husband. Because a white woman cannot travel alone, Mrs. Carter cannot attend church.

3. A holy place.

4. A small town in Fauquier County, Virginia.

5. The other Randolph daughters must be missing services for other reasons, for only Carter is separated from her husband.

6. Philip Doddridge (1702–51), a Presbyterian minister in England, wrote many devotional books; his *On the Rise and Progress of Religion in the Soul* (1745) was very popu-

lar. Edward Bickersteth (1786–1850) was an Anglican priest and published numerous books on prayer.

7. Planter Robert Randolph (1760–1825) served in the Revolutionary War as a teenager. In 1820 he owned eighty-seven slaves.

8. Mary Carter's siblings.

9. A slave woman on the Shirley plantation.

10. Hill Carter (1796–1875), Mary's husband, who was Elizabeth's nephew as well as her son-in-law. The Carters separated on several occasions because of Hill Carter's adultery.

11. Mary Carter's cousin Mildred Campbell.

Virginia Randolph Cary, Letters on Female Character, Addressed to a Young Lady on the Death of Her Mother *(Richmond: A. Works, 1828), 28– 34. Virginia Historical Society.*

Virginia Randolph was born in 1786 into a wealthy family in the Old Dominion. Among her twelve siblings was Mary Randolph, whose recipe book is excerpted in the chapter on work. Literary talent may have run in the family, but economic woes forced both women to take up the pen. Virginia married Wilson J. Cary, a man with persistent money problems; after he died, she wrote to support herself. Among her several advice books, all of them very popular, was Letters on Female Character. *Cary urges a young woman to follow the cue of older women in everything from the flow of a conversation to how to treat slaves. Both mistresses practice a form of "paternalism" by teaching their slaves to read and worship God, but they do so for distinctly conservative purposes.*

My Dear Mary,

Since I wrote last, both my feelings and taste have been accidentally gratified, by a call at the house of a lady, whom I shall call Emilia. She is a widow, who has devoted herself to the education of her only daughter. When I arrived at the house, the friend who had insisted on procuring me the pleasure of an introduction, politely requested permission to make me known to Emilia. She received me with dignified ease, and soon gave me that pleasant sensation, which arises from social intercourse among the true followers of the Redeemer: I fell into that sweet home feeling, which opens all the sluices of human affection.

Emilia spoke of her daughter, as the friend and companion from whose society she derived the greatest portion of her happiness. While she was speaking with kindling features, the subject of her discourse entered the room, having just returned from visiting a sick neighbor. "This is my daughter Emma," said Emilia, with an illuminated smile.

—My eyes fell upon a youthful form, of graceful size and proportions, plainly apparelled, and without the slightest approach to artifice in her demeanour. Her features at first appeared plain, but a smile diffused over them an irresistible attraction. She was grave, however, and her countenance exhibited traces of recent emotion. She entered into easy conversation, carefully falling into the subject selected by her mother, without showing any desire to dictate one of her own. In the course of a long morning's discourse, she developed rich stores of intellectual wealth, but showed no consciousness of the impression she was making on her auditors. I exerted my skill to draw her out, without betraying my design, and succeeded in fathoming a mind of no ordinary depth. The stream of literature had passed over this mind, fertilizing the soil, without leaving any pool for learning to stagnate in. There was moral beauty and grace in her conception, while her thoughts flowed with a freedom that betokened no small share of variety in her mental treasures. Her moral sense appeared pure from the slightest taint of worldly conformity. She had evidently taken, at the age of seventeen, that good part which was not to be taken from her; and her thoughts were exalted far beyond the impurities of earth. . . .

[The author describes Emma's Christian faith and purity at greater length.]

When the dinner hour approached, both mother and daughter quitted the room, "on hospitable thoughts intent," like our first mother. My companion took this opportunity to point out to me, several lady-like works which adorned the apartment. There were some beautiful landscapes finished with taste with skill and evidently taken from nature. An oil painting of the parting of Hector and Andromache,[1] displayed uncommon excellence in the art, but my friend informed me that Emma had applied herself to this branch of painting a few years ago, when her mother's pecuniary circumstances were embarrassed. "She then taught painting, by way of increasing her mother's income," said she, "and when their difficulties were removed, she gave up this arduous undertaking; at present, she rarely has recourse to her pencil, except to add to the funds of the Theological Education Society."[2] There were musical instruments also in the apartment, and my companion assured me that Emma touched them with skill and taste. "This accomplishment," added she, "she learnt in compliance with her father's desire; he languished many years in great bodily suffering, and music was one of his principal gratifications." . . .

[During dinner, a minister visits to thank Emma for converting a white woman to Christianity on her death bed.]

The eyes of Emilia glistened at this sincere and merited eulogium on her daughter. I could see that she prized it far more than she could have done personal praise. The evening past in social enjoyment, and I learnt yet more of the excellencies of both mother and daughter. It is Emilia's rule always to adhere to strict moral and religious propriety in her conversation. She keeps the spirit of religion always in operation, so as to pervade whatever subject she or her guests may wish to discuss. If the name is not mentioned, the essence of christianity is present in all her avocations and amusements; it sheds a halo light around the social circle. When night arrived, and the supper things were removed, the room was prepared for family worship; the servants entered, all comfortably and decently clad, with an air of respectful attention, that was infinitely pleasing. I was afterwards told that they were all instructed in the principles of christianity, and most of them professors of some standing.[3] Emma teaches them all to read,[4] and explains their christian duties to them; so that in obeying their heavenly Master, they perform all subordinate duties. "When we teach our servants to serve God," says Emilia, "they serve us of course, for obedience to their earthly master is one branch of their duty to their heavenly King." It is always better to give both children and servants a higher motive of action than mere subservience to our will. When this duty is involved in a more exalted one, there is a greater prospect of its being duly performed. I have never seen slaves look as they do in Emilia's family; and I am told, that she has the most moral and correct set in the country. This surely proves the propriety of her management, for I have often seen, in the houses of professors,[5] miserable examples of ignorance and vice among their slaves, while incessant complaints of their ill conduct made up the sum of social discourse. It is, doubtless, an arduous part of christian duty, to train this unfortunate class of our fellow citizens[6] in the way they should go; but it certainly must be <u>a part of christian duty,</u> and yet how seldom is it ever undertaken in any way! We hear complaints of our national misfortune, but see no efforts made to meliorate our condition. Surely religion demands and suggests some exertions in this obvious and imperious department of social duty. Emilia has among her dependants some characters who would not disgrace the higher walks of life. When she is questioned on the subject, she says, that she became aware early in life, that the ordinary behaviour of these people would destroy her happiness. She therefore set herself to arranging a method of management, which would have a tendency to remove these evils. "This method," said she, "I contested prayerfully, and if I have succeeded in enforcing it, the Lord has been pleased to bless my supplications, for I always knew the work was too great for my feeble powers to accomplish, and I have left it to Him who does all difficult things for his creatures. I never omit to pray that God may give me good servants."

. . . [Emma then attends the wake of a poor white woman, while another young white girl stays up dancing at a ball and sleeps late the next day.]

Let me entreat you, my dear Mary, to compare these two characters carefully, and tell me which of the two you wish to resemble? I know that both of your principles and taste will lead you to make a right choice. But I am far from wishing to confine you to an earthly model, when you have the fulness of perfection set before you, in Him who has commanded you to be perfect, even as he is perfect. Yet I do not at all approve the sentiment which is often exculpated by those who choose to entertain it, namely, that it is wrong to look at any character with the desire of imitation. If you see before you an example of practical excellence, it may save you the labour of embodying in your own mind the virtues to be copied. When you see, not only <u>what</u> good things may done, but also <u>how</u> they are done, you may set about them with greater confidence of success. The next letter I address to you, shall comprehend charity as a practical virtue. May the grace of God incline you fully to understand and practise it.

Ever yours.

1. Among the ancient Greeks, Andromache was married to Hector; when he died she married Pyrrhus and then Helenus. The artist may be Jacques-Louis David (1748–1825), whose painting *Andromache Mourning Hector* (1783) was widely copied.

2. A local charity.

3. Meaning those who profess Christianity.

4. For much of the antebellum era it was illegal in Virginia to teach slaves to read and write.

5. Here Cary means slaveowning whites who profess Christianity.

6. Slaves were not in fact citizens in any part of the United States.

Mira Lenoir to her niece Julia Pickens, 14 December 1829, from Fort Defiance, North Carolina, to Salem, North Carolina. Chiliab Smith Howe Papers, Southern Historical Collection, University of North Carolina.

The daughter of a planter, Mira Lenoir was a single woman in her thirties at the time this letter was written. Julia Pickens, her niece and ward, was a student at the well-known girls' academy in Salem. Lenoir may have owned the slave named Ginney, since an unmarried woman could hold property in her own right. Her grief is mixed with an unself-conscious racism that gives an ugly finish to her remarks.

Yours of the 21st of last month my dear Julia came to hand a week ago. we was very sorry to hear of our dear Louisa's indisposition & thankful to hear that the rest of you are well. I hope L. is well ere now I should be delighted to be with you Christmas but I have no hopes of it. Brother T. will want Dunganon & we have no other horse that I should like to ride, & mother requires much more attention than she did before she was hurt the last time. I have not stayed but 3 or 4 nights from home in 4 months. she can walk a little now till the crutch hurts her shoulder & I am affraid she will never walk as well as she did before. her health is good as usual. the rest of us are well. Mr. Davenports & Mr. Joneses familyes are well.[1]

you will have heard of the death of our favorite servant Ginney she was not well for some time but was not confin'd but 2 days before she died.[2] she did not seem to have any fear of death & I hope she has gone to [a] better world. I think she was the best servant we had, & we shall long feel her loss, but he that sent her, knowed best when to take her away. a good many of the neighbours came to see her while she lay sick & she was treated with as much respect by white & black as if she had been white.

You asked me if I have been to the Enchanted Valley.[3] I am a little ashamed to say no, but it is a fact. I have not been there. It is indeed a great piece of neglect but when you see a glowing description in some of the newspapers of the Sylvan Bower, the Cascade &c &c written by E. M. L.[4]— you will conclude that it is not for want of taste in such sylvan scenes, & admiration for the beauties of nature that has kept her away—

I have no news to tell you. I am glad to hear that you have lately received a letter from your uncle Samuel & that your dear little brothers are well &c.[5] I wish you to write to your uncle S. frequently I know it will be gratifying to him for you to do so, & he will take a pleasure in writing to you & giving you information about your brother & many other things that would interest you—

Capt. Dula will do me the favour to take you a pr of stocking & as I had a chance to write by him I thought I must scribble you a few lines, it is written in haste and I must beg you to burn it as soon as you can. I hope my Julia will make good use of her time & take care of her health. You all have our best wishes for your health & happiness. If I could take wings to fly to Salem how soon I would be there. Heaven bless and protect you Adieu Your Aunt Mira.

P. S. Give my love to every body you love that is if you are not in love with any of the Salem boys. E. M. L.

1. Relatives in western North Carolina.
2. Meaning she expired after childbirth. Lenoir later married and died while giving birth to her first child at age forty-five.
3. Members of the family sometimes called the Yadkin Valley in North Carolina, where many of their kinsmen lived, the Enchanted Valley.
4. She was christened Eliza Mira. These articles have never been found.
5. Julia's parents, Martha Lenoir Pickens and Israel Pickens, died when she was a girl, and one of her uncles was raising her brothers Andrew and Israel.

Susanna Preston McDowell to her husband, James McDowell, 22 December 1840, from Lexington, Virginia, to Columbus, Mississippi. James McDowell Papers, Southern Historical Collection, University of North Carolina.

Susanna Preston was related to a host of well-established planter families in Virginia and Kentucky. In 1818, when she was a teenager, she wed her cousin James McDowell. By 1840 her husband had served in the state legislature as a Jacksonian Democrat, and later he would be elected governor of Virginia and a member of the national House of Representatives. He was also sinking into debt and considering moving permanently to the Southern frontier. Mrs. McDowell did not want to separate slave children from their relatives, but out of self-interest rather than any regard for the bondsmen's feelings. In fact, she feels an aversion to slaves as individuals and slavery as an institution.

My dear Husband,

This sweet spring bursting upon us after weeks of gloomy weather, together with a leisure hour (as rare as a pleasant day) has roused me to the

<u>effort</u> of at least commencing a letter. it is really an exertion to turn my thoughts to any thing but what will add to the poor little baby's comfort, who is almost always in my arms, not that she is more unwell but accustomed to my nursing she is unwilling to be touched by any one else. she is very delicate and improves slowly, still looking pale and thin, but I hope by constant care to give her some health. The other children have been quite well,[1] the servants rather more complaining than usual so early in the season. Albert often layed up which of course puts me to inconvenience—if I were not so adverse to seeing another negro added to the family I would propose buying one of Calphurnia's boys, but as they are all together I should not to separate them, and we have troubles enough here. in a year or two the little boys here will be sufficiently large for the house, and I can do at present.

I do hope you have all your business settled before this[.] we understand from your letter to Mrs. Taylor[2] that you were able to save your land and purchase Watt's, but I cannot exactly see how this is to remove any of your difficulties. your extrication seems to me to depend upon a fortunate sale of the land again and The negroes.[3] This I suppose cannot be done immediately, Tho' I hear negroes are rising in This State. if you can save yourself I do hope you will sell out and be done with Missi———[.] I tremble at the thought of these long trips, and rather than see my son commencing life on a cotton plantation, I would prefer his turning up the rocks and scrawny cedars here all his days—

I do so long for your return. our family is too large and I too frail to be without an efficient head—James is working with all his might and is greatly interested in The farm. I am sorry to see him neglecting his studies. I urge him to his profession, but think any employment is better than idleness. Trent is industrious and doing quite well. Hill has failed in all he promised except The hogs—as for money I dont hear of any from any quarter and of course my funds are low or rather none at all. I still hope every Mail will releive my necessities, but hope deferred maketh the heart sick[4]—

Mrs. Taylor returned from The City a few days since, leaving your Mother and all friends well,[5] Mary better pleased than she expected, she left home very reluctantly but some changes in The school has reconciled her to it—

Sally is trying to content herself and while away time by making herself useful to me, indeed I am so closely confined with the baby I could not do without her, tho' I often wish she was somewhere enjoying refined and pleasant society—I fear a dull winter at home will make little change in her feelings. If we were not so pennyless I should be almost tempted to send her and James to meet you in Kentucky, but I feel every dollar used <u>unnecessarily</u> is taking from some one we owe (I write with baby in my lap), and cannot reconcile <u>such robbing</u> to myself—A mother's pride often whispers, we are <u>robbing Society</u> of a <u>charming ornament,</u> or <u>splendid</u> as cousin Ann would say—

I can give you no <u>town</u> news if there be any, as I never leave home, and since the Doc. has quit visiting the baby I rarely see any face that does not belong to the house.

I hope you will not let business engross you too much as to prevent your writing very often—May God protect you and bless you is the constant and fervent prayer of your wife S. P. McDowell.

Christmas gift father[6]
Cathy

Father I go to school and every day and can spell Christmas gift —Thomas

1. The McDowells had ten children, nine of whom lived to adulthood.
2. His sister Mrs. William Taylor.
3. James McDowell owned thirty-one slaves in 1840. His financial problems persisted until his death in 1851.
4. A quote from Prov. 13:12, which reads, "Hope deferred maketh the heart sick, but when the desire cometh, it is a tree of life."
5. Sarah Preston McDowell of Virginia, at this point quite old.
6. In the mid-nineteenth century, "Christmas gift" was a common holiday greeting.

Mary E. Starnes to her friend Sarah J. Thompson, 9 October 1845, from Harrison County, Texas, to Augusta, Georgia. William H. Kilpatrick Letters, from the Collections of the Dallas Historical Society.

In 1845, Mary Starnes was an orphaned fifteen-year-old girl living with her older brother William, a physician and slaveowner. Both natives of Georgia, they had moved to Texas about 1840. One of their bondsmen attacked an overseer, prompting her blunt remarks about the slaves she considers an "oppressed" people.

Dear Sallie,

I have waited a week after the appointed time for writing & still your letter for last month has not made its appearance. I see from the papers that the Yellow Fever is prevailing in New Orleans & several other large Cities. I hope it has not visited Augusta again. When your letters are so long coming I am apt to imagine something is the matter, though it may be owing this time to the irregularity of the mails, whatever may be the cause I hope the long looked for document will soon arrive & dispel all my doubts & fears.

Max Graves & the old Lady have returned at last after an absence of nearly 5 months. they traveled over a considerable portion of Texas, saw a great deal of rich land, fine stock, & every thing of that sort, but the most of it is too remote from navigation to suit Cotton planters, unless the people would build Rail Roads, then, it would be the very Country for them —

But I am afraid the present generation will die with old age before the iron bar will be seen puffing its way through that portion of Texas, that is, if the people are as dilatory there as they have been here[.] Two or three years ago I thought from the signs of the times we would have a rail road very soon, but they have talked & quarreled & squabbled, & speculated, & as yet accomplished very little towards building it. I believe they have cut down a few bushes & trees & done a little grading. The people have suffered privations enough this year for the want of Navigation to stir them up to greater diligence, & if it was to remain so, it is probable we would get a rail road after a while, but they flatter themselves with the belief that this has been an unusual year, & that it may not happen so again for a long time.

Sisters[1] Beau renewed the suit, but I believe she has decided it against him, though she is tired of a life of dependence she was a little tempted to accept of his offer & get a home of her own, but she has concluded six children is most too many to begin housekeeping with. Cousin Eliza Dickerson is still in Marshall but I believe she has not realized her expectation there, I think she intends going back to Austin. I have not seen her but the one time. Ella is at home at present, her eyes got so bad, her Pa brought her home to cure them.[2] they are improving. The crops generally have turned out much better than was expected, at one time last summer it really did look like starvation, but I think now we will all have bread enough to eat next year & Brother thinks his cotton crop will turn out about 50 bags, weighing about 500 pounds each, that is a very short crop for his force, but still it will be doing much better than he expected. The Overseer is getting well though he has but little use of his arm yet[3] — The negro is still on the place & has conducted himself very well since that time, but according to the laws of

Texas he has been guilty of a hanging crime, & should the Grand Jury take cognizance of it, I am afraid it will go hard with him. Brother is very uneasy & will be until Court is over. A white man would not be hung for such an offence. they hardly ever hang one when he is guilty of murder in the first degree, & I think the laws of our Country should allow a negro an equal chance with a white man for his life—They are an oppressed people any way & have more provocation to commit such acts than white people.

Let me know how Mr. Tuttle is. I am so sorry to hear that he is so afflicted. has he ever made a profession of religion? I feel anxious that he should do so before he dies. Sister is not very well. she has had a stiff neck for several days. I believe I have told you all the news, so good bye. Mollie.

1. Mary's older sister Sarah.

2. Ella is Mary's niece and William's daughter from his first marriage.

3. This may be one Mr. Crossley, also a Georgian, who worked as the Starnes's overseer in 1850; the slave's identity is unknown. The records are silent on their respective fates.

Elizabeth Brown Rives Early to her daughter Mary Virginia Early Brown [between 1847 and 1850], from somewhere in rural Virginia to Lynchburg, Virginia. Early Family Papers, Virginia Historical Society.

Elizabeth Rives married Methodist clergyman John Early in 1822, and she shared his fervent religious beliefs. Mrs. Early also shares his long-time concern for slaves' spiritual lives. (One of Mr. Early's first ministries was to Thomas Jefferson's slaves at Monticello.) In this account of the slave Matilda's conversion, we can detect a few flickers of egalitarian language—for instance, that God is no "respecter of persons"—but the letter has an overbearing, coercive tone.

My dear Mary, Join with us in praising God that another soul has passed from death into life. Today at ½ past 4 oclock Til was powerfully converted in my room.

Soon as I got here I discovered that her disease was as much of the mind as body. On Saturday I talked with her, & found she was earnestly seeking the Lord. I gave her all the instruction & encouragement I could.

Yesterday she was much depressed—I sang several hymns in my room which I thought applicable to her—"Jesus lover of my soul" &c. &c. read a part of our Lord's Sermon on the Mount. I left her in my room after dinner, & was sitting with Amanda in her chamber which is under mine. I heard her groaning & making a noise, and thought she was sick. Was about to go to her, when I heard her coming down the steps. I turned & said—"Til what is the matter"—The words were scarcely spoken when she fell on her knees at my feet—threw her arms around me, & exclaimed—"O Mrs. Early, I am so happy! O I love God & every body—Praise the Lord for what he has done for me." & many other expressions of joy & sung many hymns of rejoicing for her—she wept & rejoiced full one hour without cessation in the most rational manner. Nothing boisterous but one of the clearest, & most satisfactory conversions I have ever seen. Once she exclaimed— "Well, I reckon I'll get well now—Bless the Lord, I've nothing to trouble me now—O I never was happy before in all my life—" "I thought I was seeking the Lord for the last 6 weeks, but I never began in earnest untill Saturday." She is anxious to see you & all her friends & her Mars James [1] & I wish she was among them all—perhaps poor Margaret, & the rest of our careless ones [2] might be influenced to reflect & prepare to meet God.

Dear Mary! What great ground of encouragement have you & your dear husband—& how great will be yr crown of rejoicing to be able to say, when called to render an account of yr stewardship—"Here Lord are we, and the souls that thou hast given us." O may not all be missing. [3]

Till says—"Give my love to all at home and at yr house—to Ann & all & I want all to pray for me. Tell them all, I know I am converted now. My soul is full of love Love to God & all—Yes every body"—

She says she felt better this morning—but not fully satisfied—& when I left her—she fell on her knees to pray—but by the time she touched the floor, such a stream of love was poured into her soul, that she laughed out—says she put her hand on her mouth to keep from making a noise— she then bolted the door to lock herself in, but all would not do—She came down she hardly knew how; —she could not contain [herself]. O is not the God we serve a great God? No respecter of persons—but in every time & place, & in all nations—They that call upon him shall be saved. I wish you could see her. Her face beams with joy. Fannie says, "O Ma—what a bright face Til has—I wish t'was me." [4]

Give much love to all. Well! if we have not been to the meeting, [5] which I disliked to leave so much—the Lord has not suffered us to come without him, & I trust good will result to others. Til went out to the kitchen & gave all the servants a talk—all are unconverted, & I trust she may be made a blessing to them.

This evening Sally Langhorne & Miss Steptoe came to see me. Says Catharine Blair intends coming soon. If the weather continues as to-day we had better remain at least until Saturday—My cough is certainly better.

Till will now improve faster. But if it turns cold & rains—we had better return. Write often—And my love to dear Grace & all friends. The quiet of the country is very delightful. You must write to yr dear pa[6]—If I stay longer—will write to him when I know where to direct a letter. Bettie & Fannie are very happy—go fishing & Chiuquepea hunting every day.[7]

The Lord bless you <u>all</u> my dear children. Pray for us. Tell dear Tom to write often to his mother.[8]

Kiss the dear ones for me. "Howdy" to all the servants at home—I hope they will do all they can to get the house in order. Yr Mother—E. R. Early.

Monday night.

1. James L. Brown, whom Mary Virginia Early married in 1847.
2. Other house slaves, who are unconverted.
3. Mary's husband is a clergyman as well as a tobacco farmer, and the Browns own several house slaves.
4. Elizabeth Early's other daughter. She had seven surviving children.
5. A religious revival nearby.
6. John Early (1786–1873) would become bishop of the Methodist Episcopal Church South in 1854.
7. The family is visiting relatives, and the girls are digging up chickpeas.
8. Thomas Early, Mary's younger brother, was studying to be a minister.

Martha Ann L. M. M. Maney to her daughter Martha Ann Maney, 1 February 1848, from near Jackson, Mississippi, to Franklin, Tennessee. Douglas-Maney Papers, Tennessee State Library and Archives.

Born in North Carolina at the turn of the century, Martha Maney wed a planter and had ten children. She taught "paternalism" to her daughters, one of whom, Betty, practices it on her own plantation. Written while Maney visited her daughter Elizabeth Bowman, this letter shows her concern, laced with condescension, for her slaves.

My dear children,

I have no doubt you will be surprised to learn by this that we are still here, as I wrote in my last letter that we should start last monday, but so it is. That is the third time we have set for starting and are still stationery but I hope will not be long so now, for if it does not rain we will get off next week, unless something happens that we cannot prevent—

the reasons we did not leave was, last satturday we started to town your pa & Maj. B. in the barouche & I, Sally & Lavinia in Betty['s] carriage,[1] we got part of the way & the road was so hard that the horses could not pull out of the mud without breaking some of the harness of the carriage I was in, so we came back, and on monday your pa & Maj B went to town, your pa rode in the carriage, which had to go so as to have the harness mule good again, it took them three hours to get there the road was so bad, they staid all night at Cousin Mary & came home the next evening; your pa concluded that Maj. B. must go all the way with us to Ten[n], so he had business in Vicksburg & they have gone there to day; you pa to see old Zack T., Maj. B. & Mr. Thomas on business. they went to Cousin Mary's last night so as to be able to take the cars early this morning; Genl. Taylor stops there to day & they give him a ball tonight,[2] but our folks will come home to night, and they will have business & arrangemnts to make when they get back so it will take up the balance of the week, your pa says the roads have been so bad and are yet that we cant tell the exact time we shall get home, will have to take it slow & sure; I am in hopes though these 2 last weeks sunshine will dry them a good deal, we are very anxious indeed to get home, and would have started if the weather & roads would have permitted; you pa says every body says he is crazy to think of going now while the roads are so bad—our company will be large so we can help one another out of the mud; Maj B, Betty & children & us a Mr. Thomas who is going up to Nashville on business; Betty's trunks will be shiped on S Boat today, she will just carry enough cloths to do her & children on the road—Maj Bowman will return very soon, he goes on horseback; they talked very strongly of going by water, but gave it out, I told you pa that if we got in a mudhole we would crawl out but it would not be so easy in getting out of the Miss[issippi], my doctrine is not to anticipate troubles, but hope for the best & trust in a Divine providence, which has never yet failed the true believer.

We are all well. Sally Murfree is cutting her eyeteeth, which makes her rather fretful, she is quite fat and as sweet as ever—slow at talking yet, she will be as long learning to talk as Martha Ann was; Betty received Mag's letter last monday of the 16th it was two weeks coming on account of high waters I expect. I hope you were all well, if I may judge by what she says, the children were merry & playing, but she did not say (we are all well) that ought to be nearly the first thing that is said, and as those four little words are worth a great deal, and we are always very greatful & thankful to hear them, & I pray our heavenly Father you may all continue in health & peace till we meet again;

The negroes ask a great deal after each one of the children, and they quite loth to part from us; particularly Betty[3] as she is very kind to them and supplies their wants in sickness &c. The best of friends must part, and there is some of them (may be all) that I may never see again, particularly the old ones; old Sally['s] health is not very good at all. She has not recovered since she had pnemonia. Henry has got to walking about again. He was very ill before Christmas and came very near dying. The rest are all well, some little complaint, but nothing serious. Where there is so many together there will be some complaining of a pain or something; those that work out are busy preparing for another crop, some ploughing & others clearing up & burning stalks;

I wrote Dick a long letter last week & sent to Canton to be mailed, Mr. T. was going up there that day, so we sent it there; Betty will write next, and let you know when we are off. I will write frequently on the road, and hope you will get our letters; as I am writeing this to all of you I will direct to Martha Ann being the next oldest, as I thought perhaps William might not be at home; so I hope none of you will think hard of it, for I love you all alike, and never knew how much I loved you till I left you; and I hope & pray you may all live together in love & peace; I hope the little ones will be good and treat one another kindly. M. Ann, kiss the little ones for us. I dream about you all nearly every night, & such dreams. if you have got garden seed, better send and get some cabbage raddish I want the balance of the early peas sowed about 15 or 22 for Feb — they are sealed up in bottles in the press in the dairy.

Your Pa says he wants Isaac & Alex to move in the wash house (it will be right tight squeeze) but they can put their bed behind the door, & set the table between the loom & jam by the fireplace — put the other table in the cellar or under the shelter they put the hominy mortar in the kitchen;[4] he did not think of it when he wrote before; I hope they can make out; we think they would be better if any thing should be the matter, sick &c. my paper is most out & I have not said half but must draw to a close, give our love to Bursha, F. & all — to inquiring friends; my trunk is packed and ready to start, I forgot to say Georges feet are in a sorry condition to travel this week, but will be well in a few days—your pa and all join me in a great deal of love to you all, and I pray the Lord may spare us all to meet again is my daily prayer. M. A. Maney

give our love to Mr. N. P. & Lady.

give our best love to Betty & Mr. Frasier when you see them. Tell all the servants howdy and I hope each can give a good account of themselves when we get home. Make them take care of the fires in their houses. Remember us to Dr. Peck & Lady. you must excuse this poor letter burn it up—Tell Tommy & Dick to hold themselves in readiness for lots of fun when Willie comes—The Wind is blowing so strong from the South I am afraid it will rain, but hope it wont last long—hurts my feelings very much to lose all this good weather but hope the roads will be the better & we can travel the faster when we get on them for when we start there will be no turning back for us.

  1. Her daughter Elizabeth Maney Bowman, mistress of Tiger Bayou plantation.
  2. General Zachary Taylor, a national hero since his victories in the recently concluded Mexican War. The Treaty of Guadalupe Hidalgo, which ended the war, would be signed the next day, February 2, 1848.
  3. Her daughter Elizabeth Bowman.
  4. Meaning the mortar used to make hominy.

Mary B. Carter to her cousin Mildred Walker Campbell, 10 March 1849, from Charles City County, Virginia, to Petersburg, Virginia. Charles Campbell Papers, Earl Gregg Swem Library, College of William and Mary.

Mary Braxton Randolph Carter was born in 1800 into one of Virginia's most prominent slaveholding families, and after her marriage to Hill Carter she lived at Shirley, one of the state's most famous plantations located on four thousand acres along the James River. A visitor once described her as plain and unassuming, but she had quietly formed the heretical antislavery views evident in this letter, opinions she did not share with her husband.

My Dear Cousin,

I received both of your letters and the chair too with many thanks. I now tell you & think it will suit exactly. I have not seen Charlie since he tried it for last night & was laid up with one of my headaches and was not capable of thinking at all.[1] this morning I am better but still feel badly & have them oftener now than usual but I suppose they will pass off after a year or two if I should live and if they do not I shall be content if it be God's will, for I feel more each day of my life resigned to God's will in all things, and now I wonder how I could ever have felt differently for I always knew that all was working for my good, and this being the case why can we not always say "Thy will be done" —

I shall enclose you the money for the chair and for the <u>Herald</u> dear cousin I find no fault with the piece you complain of, in the <u>Herald,</u> for I think entirely with it, making allowances for the ignorance of the writer on the subject of slavery as it now exists; Josiah Quincy, Jr. (who by the way is with us at this time)[2] is not more prejudiced against slavery nor thinks it a greater evil than I do, and freely would I labour for my daily bread in preference to being the partner of one who owns 130 immortal beings.[3] O! the responsibility weighs me down to the earth. I feel that my duties are so great, and they are so imperfectly performed. O, I wonder how any one can approve of slavery, or not feel that in our enlightened age, it is a great sin, national and individual when it can be avoided, and I do think it could be gotten rid of if all would unite hand and heart to do so. So dear cousin please just let me continue the <u>Missionary Herald.</u> Hill does not read it, and it will do no harm here and is a great comfort to me. —

I am so glad to hear you are coming to see us at Ester but feel sorry that Calla will not be with you I hope Charles will come with you tell him I say he must come there was much delight expressed by all the children when they heard you were coming, and dear Charlie too was very glad to hear you were coming at Easter when he can see something of you he is a complete Overseer, and I never see any thing of him hardly.[4]

Mr. Quincy came down in the boat this morning with Mr. Carter to see the old Virginia plantations, and I hope he will not think as badly of them as I do—Cousin please bring me 2 copies of Charles History of Virginia. I want them for a particular purpose[5] —

God bless you I am called off by a number of persons so I must say good bye this is hardly fit to send you.

Yours, M. B. C. I enclose 10 dollars.

1. Carter suffered from migraine headaches. Charles Carter was one of her seven children; she bore ten others who died. Mildred Campbell, her cousin, was the widow of a businessman who owned six slaves before his death in 1842.

2. Josiah Quincy (1772–1864), the well-known politician and writer from Massachusetts, had long opposed slavery. His trip through the South may have been devoted to research for the antislavery pamphlets he published in the 1850s.

3. According to the federal census of 1850, her husband Hill Carter (1796–1875) owned 101 slaves.

4. Her son helped run the family's properties.

5. Charles was probably Mildred's brother-in-law, Charles Campbell. In 1847 he published *Introduction to the History of the Colony and Ancient Dominion of Virginia*, which reached a wide audience.

Reverend N. A. Okeson to Mary B. R. Carter, 11 November 1848, 30 January 1849. Shirley Plantation Research Collection, Special Collections, Colonial Williamsburg Foundation Library.

Mary Braxton Randolph Carter had seven surviving children with her spouse Hill Carter. In the 1840s and 1850s she wrote to Presbyterian minister Reverend N. A. Okeson, of New York City, for spiritual guidance. Her brief notations on his letters speak volumes about an aspect of married life that white women rarely described on paper.

Rev. Mr. Okeson on the subject of selling a female slave committing adultery with a view of putting a stop to it on a plantation. He is opposed to it. Nov. 11, 1848.

Rev. Mr. Okeson on the subject of a wife's separating from her husband for committing adultery. He is opposed to it. Jan. 30, 1849.

Ellen C. Blaettermann to her brother Richard H. Collins, 25 March 1850, from Keswick Depot, Virginia, to Maysville, Kentucky. Collins Family Letters, Division of Special Collections and Archives, Margaret I. King Library, University of Kentucky at Lexington.

Ellen Blaettermann's father had recently died intestate, and in 1850 sixteen of
his bondsmen were about to go on sale. Her husband, George, an engineer, owned
four slaves, and her brother Richard, a newspaper editor, owned none. Ellen, who
was in her mid-twenties, pities her father's slaves and objects to a Sunday auction
because she believes it violates the Sabbath. At the same time, she also wants her
mother to pay a low price at auction for other bondsmen who were not included
in her mother's share of the estate.

My Dear Brother,

I am going to write, not that I have anything that will be at all interesting, but I know that my friends will be anxious to hear from us.

Mr. Blaettermann left here last Saturday week to go to the Philadelphia
Trade Sales, too late for the Stationery Sales. We received Father's letter on
Friday afternoon[1] (we ought to have received it on Tuesday) and he started
from here that night at 1 o'clock for the cars and reached Philadelphia on
Sunday morning at 4 o'clock. I am looking for him to day when the train
comes up. I may be disappointed. He says that Philadelphia is crowded with
strangers, he does not give the cause. He heard Dr. Durbin preach last Sunday. I wish I could have been with him.

We have trouble enough about us. Yesterday (Sabbath as it was) the servants had their sale (you know negroes have no day but Sunday),[2] and it
was distressing to us to hear the auctioneer calling their things. They sold
them before our sale,[3] because poor things, they know not who will buy
them, and they thought best to be ready to go at a moment's warning. They
may be hurried off as soon as bought, and so they sold their things and
put the money in their pockets, so that they will take all they have with
them. Their things sold well, they are well supplied with things necessary
for housekeeping.

Henry Sichfried, one of the heirs at law, reached here on Monday last.
He stays at Mr. Stacklin's the administrator.

The sale of all the personal property together with the negroes comes off
tomorrow week, the 2nd of April, poor papa's birthday. I am afraid Mamma
will have to pay high for the servants she wants, for Stacklin has said he
will run them (that is the negroes) up high and has told the auctioneer not
to knock down until he got a nod from him. Mr. B. says he will expose him
if he carries things to extremes. It will be a sorry day to us especially to
Poor Mama. I am glad I came here. She seems much more cheerful since
we have been here. the children seem to amuse her. She takes it so to heart
that Papa left no will and that George gets nothing.

It is well that we took the Piano last Fall, so that though we gain nothing, yet we lose <u>nothing</u> that he <u>gave</u> us, except Aunt Lilly.[4]

We do not know when we will leave for home, not before the last of April, I presume, for the roads will not be in order for travelling before that time. We think of coming by wagon to Charleston.

I hope you will not need the money you loaned me before we return. Mr. B. would have sent it when he sent to Father but he had not enough to spare.

I received a letter from Margaret last Friday. I was glad to hear all were well.

Brother Joseph's wife will not be able to leave for California before next month not being able to obtain tickets for the Steamer before that time. Their little boy, Joe, was a year old the 15th of this month and very fine promising child so Louisa writes. I wrote a long letter to her on Saturday.

How are my little nieces? Lottie talks of Annie very often.[5] Kiss them both for me. Give my best love to Sister Mary and tell her I hope she will be nicely fixed before we come back, for I know she must be tired of living in a house and lot unfinished.

Remember me to Father Mother[6] and all the family to Mrs. Cox and family, Fanny Broderick, and all who may inquire for me.

Mamma sends her best to you and Mary and all the home folks. Tell Sue I will write to her next, you know I cannot write to all at once.

If Mary sees Mrs. Triplett or Mary Ellen I hope she will remember me to them with my sincerest sympathy in their deplorable loss—

Write soon my dear brother and believe me your ever affectionate sister—E. C. Blaettermann.

1. She calls her father-in-law, Mr. Blaetterman, "Father" and her deceased father "Papa."

2. Slaves had only one day each week, usually Sunday, when they were released from work.

3. Meaning that the lawyer and the auctioneer sold the slaves' possessions first.

4. A slave woman.

5. Collins had five surviving daughters (including Annie) and two surviving sons.

6. Her father-in-law and mother-in-law.

Mrs. Isaac Hilliard Diary. Hill Memorial Library, Louisiana and Lower Mississippi Valley Collections, Louisiana State University.

In 1850 Miriam Brannin Hilliard lived in Chicot County, Arkansas, on the banks of the Mississippi River. Her husband, Isaac, was a rich merchant and owned 131 slaves. Mrs. Hilliard nurses a slave child but makes cruel, obtuse remarks on the apparent suicide of another slave. Her further comments evince a deep distrust of African Americans. In fact, she wants to get away from the institution of bondage altogether.

June 17th [1850]. "Ike" received a handsome present this morning—a very large Velocipede.[1] Spent the [page torn]. Some man just from Louisville reports that Bush has run off. If it be true, and he should succeed in his escape, I dread the effect. When we change our residence, I cast my vote for a free state.

Returned home about 10 o'clock and found Melie's child in great suffering, from having swallowed as supposed a piece of china. Administered Ipecac,[2] oil, &c.

June 19th. Heavy rain fallen during the past night. Mr. Summers & Phrone obliged to defer their departure. Brother Abe sends an express, requesting Brother John to join him immediately in Cincinnati, to identify the body of Bush, who he learns is drowned. Captain states, he got aboard the mailboat Monday—remained undiscovered until they were nearing port—when he took him in custody and placed him in a yawl, with the intention of lodging him in jail. As they were nearing the Bank, Bush jumped overboard and sunk immediately. Strange story! Bush such a capital swimmer and drowned in 5 ft. water!

Deplorable state of things here. Negroes are nothing but a tax & annoyance to their owners—from fear, or mistaken indulgence, any degree of impertinence & idleness is tolerated. Within the last few months, Mr. Marshall's, Throckmorton's, Grey's and several other persons dwellings have been set on fire and burned to the ground. Idleness is the devil's workshop, and they have abundant time to hatch plenty mischief. I believe it to be my duty, so long as I own slaves, to keep them in proper subjection and well employed. So come what may, I intend to make mine do "service."

1. Ike is a male relative, and he received a child's tricycle, in the nineteenth century called a velocipede.
2. The dried root of a South American plant, often used as an emetic or purgative.

Martha Ann L. M. M. Maney to her daughter Martha Ann Maney, 25 March 1851, from Jessamine Hill plantation, Franklin, Tennessee, to Nashville, Tennessee. Douglas-Maney Papers, Tennessee State Library and Archives.

Martha Maney's letter reveals the unvarnished racism that coexisted with "paternalism" in her casual reference to a "nigger."

My dear child,

I now write to let you know how we all are, and to procure a letter from you; you pa has been unwell for some time, Kidneys out sick &c — he had the colic right bad last night, but is a great deal better this morning up & walking about, he cant yet wear his shoe on account of his little toe, it has healed up, but is very tender, and swells occasionally, so I dont know when you may expect him, he has been wanting to go to Nashville for the last three weeks but could not on account of his foot.

The rest of us are all well as usual, I hope this will find you with the rest of the family well; how is my dear little babe. I do want to see her so much, kiss her for me. Sally talks about her constantly, says she wants to go there to see her. I had your room cleaned up yesterday — I asked her whose crib that was she says, my babes; we heard from Betty[1] yesterday they were all well, she has not named her boy yet; Cousin Mary Hardeman is coming up in May; we heard from Dick last week, she was well, but some sick — uncertain when they will come home; Sue went home last Satturday, with your uncle Tommy — and Wm. went for her yesterday as he had business there, you pa intended to go tomorrow but was so unwell could not so Sue will come with your brother.

So Jenny Lind is coming to Nashville at last, are you going to hear her. I expect the people there are nearly crazed, about her;[2]

Mr. Cunningham got home last Satturday evening, with his new teachers, one is name[d] Fanny she is the music teacher. I dont know her other name. Eliza was telling me about them she got her information from

Louisa C. Sunday morning at S. School—the other two Christian names, one Martha for the hall & Miss Charlotte for the basement story, Eliza did not learn their other names. They had 63 scholars yesterday; a pretty good beginning; Marsha is plodding on with her little school, some that promised sent elsewhere, Davy Dick goes, so we have quite still times now nobody but Sally, & she is out nearly all the time, plays with her nigger.[3]

You must excuse this poor letter as I have the headache this morning;[4] I have no news to write as I have not been out much lately;

Anne Crockett has come home, she was out here the other evening with Mrs. Wm. Park & Mrs. Marshall. Mrs. has gone back home;

Has Clint caught any fish tell Harlly & Larry went to fishing Satturday, but did not catch any thing, I suppose the season has not fully opened, I want to see you both so much hope it will not be long before you will come, take good care of the dear little babe, the children all talk a great deal about her. Fanny D. wrote word she was making shirts I am too, I am determined your pa shall have a dozen (you know he spires to that number) so I have but two to make now; I will try to finish this week. I have to pick up & throw down so often, I have been slow in making them. I hired the making of five. Write soon & excuse this poor letter—this is my week to write. I shall write to Dick tomorrow & Betsy friday. you must remember us to Mr. Bodie—Mrs. A. D.—your pa, brothers, & sisters joine me in love to you. Mr. Douglass & kiss the dear babe for us—our love & respects to Mr. & Mrs. D.

and May the Lord bless you both is my daily prayer M. A. Maney.

This is written so bad but I have not time to write it over. Henry Monsons new goods has not come yet he has some beautiful silks & tissue—[packages?]—&c.

1. Another daughter, Elizabeth Maney Bowman.
2. The young Swedish vocalist who created a sensation when she came to America in 1849. Lind gave almost one hundred concerts before she returned to Europe in 1851.
3. Young children in slaveowning families often had slave playmates.
4. Maney occasionally had migraine headaches.

Judith Page Rives to her sister-in-law Mrs. J. F. Page, 23 June 1852, from Paris, France, to Albemarle County, Virginia. Page-Walker Manuscripts, Special Collections Department, Alderman Library, University of Virginia.

A native of Albemarle County, Virginia, Judith Page married William Cabell Rives in 1819. She inherited an estate called Castle Hill, where she and her husband lived for most of their lives. His political career included a stint as American minister to France from 1849 to 1853. As troubled as she is about slavery's many evils, Mrs. Rives can imagine no solution other than deporting the African American population. In the mid-1850s, the Riveses freed many of their slaves and arranged for their migration to Liberia.

. . . I have just been reading "Uncle Tom's Cabin." [1] I dare say you have seen it and cannot fail as I do to admire the wonderful talent with which it is written. The author is a perfect artist, and her paintings however terrible are splendid. I am sure we have half a dozen Mrs. Shelby's and Mas' Georges in our own neighborhood, and one of our dear angels now in glory might well impersonate to us the faultless Eva. [2] The dreadful part it is to be hoped is not every day occurrence but it is fearful to think that there are such abominations in our land, as I have too often heard from credible sources to doubt. [3] The author slaps up and down, right and left, North and South, so that we cannot quarrel with her for telling us dreadful though wholsome truths—I was delyhted to find so powerful a writer an advocate of colonization in Africa, the only reasonable solution of this vexed and troublesome question. [4] I feel quite "curious" to know what is generally thought of such a work in our country and neighborhood—do tell me when you write. . . .

Give our united and best love to each member of your dear family circle, and continue to remember us in your prayers as we never fail to remember you and yours. Offer our kindest rgards and best wishes to our neighbors and friends, and believe me as ever, my dearest sister, most affectionately yours, J. P. Rives.

1. The novel by Harriet Beecher Stowe, which was published in serial form in a newspaper in 1852.
2. Mrs. and Mr. George Shelby are slaveowners in Kentucky. They both feel uneasy about the immorality of slavery, especially the devout Mrs. Shelby, but neither can give up the material comfort that the institution provides. Eva is the pious daughter of Augustine St. Clare, a planter in the Deep South. She hates slavery even as a child, and her early death is usually interpreted as a punishment for her father's sins.

3. Rives is referring to the separation of slave families, or miscegenation, or both, salient themes in the novel.

4. Stowe (1811–96) was the daughter of a famous New England clergyman, Lyman Beecher, and lived for almost twenty years in Cincinnati. She advocated deporting, or "colonizing," the African American population.

Diary of Maria Dyer Davies. Maria Dyer Davies Papers, Special Collections Library, Duke University.

Maria Davies of Noxubee County, Mississippi, was twenty-two years old in 1855. An unmarried orphan, she lived with her sister and brother-in-law. Her racial attitudes show a mixture of self-centeredness and concern for an individual slave named Sally. She complains about losing a worker, but she is genuinely worried about the dangers the same woman will face as she travels a country road in an old carriage with a drunken man.

8 November 1855. . . . Bro. W. told us this morning that old Mr. Clemens had sent for Sally. And the boy came out, bringing the girl Mr. C. sent to sister Henny, and who takes Sally's place out here till Christmas.[1] This makes us feel worse, & indeed I can't tell when we have passed a sadder day. Sally is all packed up, starts by daylight, and I never expect to see her again. It seems to me I am more alive to depressing thoughts, and they sink deeper & stay longer than with most persons. I am not happily constituted in this. Grief is proper, but my feelings wear me out, and overcome me too much.[2] I have been going on as usual, but my heart is heavy. And Sister too is as bad. I dread to see Sally go away—to tell her good bye. And it makes the deeper impression, that I was so saddened at heart before. I could not realize either announcement this morning, Aunty's death or Sally's leaving—but I do to-night. I wish I could have more fortitude, more strength & faith & hope. Oh Lord, Thy Spirit can do all things, and I would come to Thee for strength, for grace. Oh, may we <u>all</u> live so that we may meet where there are no tears, no sighing, no wounded spirits, nor saddened hearts, but living & loving forever.

This is after supper, rather at bed-time. Sally has just been in & I told her she must live so as to meet me in Heaven. I pray that she may do it.

9 November 1855. Sallie started soon, though not by day-light, Gus[3] going with them & driving one of our horses through the bad mud. We passed a lonely day. The girl in Sally's place is excessively awkward & ignorant. She doesn't suit at all. Bro. W. at home all day & lonely. We walked out late, but the scene is dreary—dull—He was reading Childe Harold to us after supper reading in Byron generally & finishing C. H.[4] It was very dull to me. I cannot fix my attention when <u>listening</u> & working too, & not being in the habit of it. I enjoy reading to myself very much more, but I love for reading to be going on when I am at work, so I don't loose <u>all</u> of it. The piece though was quite unappreciated by me. Bro W. still talking of reparing the McCollum house though I object seriously—The day has been grey & gloomy.

10 November 1855. We have thought of Sally nearly all day. Ben, the man who carries her up, is not trustworthy. Gus said he was drinking & cursing all day. Bro. W. gave him a bottle of brandy, because the weather was so inclement, & his vehicle leaked badly. But the negro was drinking it all yesterday & swearing. Gus says he did not like his company, & that Sally was frightened. He staid with them last night, put them on sandy land[5] & came home. We have been thinking of Sally with such a man. Hester the negro girl says he was drunk coming down & that Jimmy Clemens was too—I prepared all my letters for mailing, have been cutting out Sister's worsted[6] dress. Bro. W. sent Louisa out this evening. Hester went back to town. A good exchange for us.

1. William D. Longstreet, a judge and slaveowner, who married her sister Mary. His brother-in-law Doctor Archie Clemens wed Henrietta Longstreet Clemens, "sister Henny."

2. One of her aunts had recently died.

3. Probably William Augustus Lucas, the young nephew of Maria's sister Mary Longstreet.

4. The English poet, Lord George Gordon Byron (1788–1824). One of his most popular works was *Childe Harold's Pilgrimage.*

5. Meaning he helped pull the carriage through the mud.

6. Made of a fine woolen cloth.

Diary of Eliza Ann Marsh Robertson. Eliza Ann Marsh Robertson Papers, Southern Historical Collection, University of North Carolina.

In 1855, Eliza Robertson lived on a plantation near New Iberia, Louisiana, the wife of a slaveowner and the mother of several children. She engages in reciprocal exchanges with a neighboring black family, whom she respects as "excellent good people" regardless of skin color.

13 December 1855. Weather cold & clear, but cloudy towards night. finished working the sides of Julius['s] pantaloons & cut & basted the lining. Miss Caroline Cobb & John Avery came to see me after dinner. John tells me that Pa came off the Island to day in a cart.[1] William bought 20 barrels of corn to day from Mr. Deciur on the Lake.[2] I sent some little presents to his children[,] if they have dark skins they are excellent good people, and many a white man might envy them their reputation for honesty.[3] After supper I took out my patch work that I commenced five years ago, & sewed some of it.

14 December 1855. Weather cold & clear. Finished my citron preserves this morning. Sewed a little on Julius's pantaloons, and after dinner I went down to see Sister Sarah. Found little Sarah suffering dreadfully with the toothache.[4] Mrs. Deciur sent me some peanuts, pecans, eggs, & two bottles of milk as a present. Miss Martha Johnson was married tonight to Mr. Eagleson of St. Martins. Leila & Julius went to the wedding with Ann. I sewed a little on my patch work after supper.

1. John Avery may be her nephew. Her father, John C. Marsh Sr. (1789–1857), owned a prosperous sugar plantation near New Iberia called Avery Island.
2. Her husband, William, a planter.
3. In the 1850s, four black or mulatto families named Decuir lived in St. Martin County, two headed by laborers and two headed by planters. One of those planters, Ovide Decuir, owned two slaves.
4. Her sister Sarah Marsh Avery and her teenaged niece.

Mary E. Starnes to her friend Sarah J. Thompson, 8 January 1856, from Harrison County, Texas, to Augusta, Georgia. William H. Kilpatrick Letters, from the Collections of the Dallas Historical Society.

Another slave on the Starnes plantation has gotten into another fight with a white man, but Mary Starnes's racial attitudes have undergone a pronounced change since a similar incident eleven years before. In 1845 she called slaves an "oppressed" people, but now she is more worried about the trouble the affair might cause her brother.

Dear Sallie,

I hoped to be able to write on the first day of the month this time, as it was the beginning of the new year, but was prevented from doing so, in the morning by business, & in the afternoon by sickness. Brother had been trying for several weeks to get ready to start out west with a portion of his hands, but did not get off until last Sunday.[1] He consulted a lawyer about that negro scrape, & he advised him to take his hands out west, for if it should be brought up by the Grand Jury, it would cause Brother a great deal of trouble & expense, even if the Negro was not hung. Court is in session now, but I have not heard whether they have taken any action in the case or not, as the Negro & all the witnesses are out of the way, we are in hopes nothing will be done with it. The Overseer will go as soon as he can settle up his business,[2] & Brother will return, I would like to have your company during his absence.

How did you spend your Christmas, pleasantly I hope. we spent ours at home. we had a few neighbors to dine with us, but the weather was so excessively cold there was not much enjoyment, we had to have big fires & draw close to them. We were at a party last thursday night at the house of one of our local Preachers, we had a nice little supper, & some of the young people seemd to enjoy themselves very much.[3]

I was at Church last Sunday & heard our new Preacher, his name is Stovall. I think I shall like him when I know [him] better. I will at least try to love him for his work['s] sake & if I am not mistaken in the man, it will not be a difficult task. The Preacher we had last year was one of my favorites. I had the pleasure of seeing & shakeing hands with him once more on last Sunday. Some kind friend is sending me two papers from Augusta, (The Cultivator, & Sentinel), if you know who it is, say to them, I thank them very much for these interesting tokens of their remembrance. I have given Joe the credit of it, at least I think of <u>him</u> every time I get one, if I have made a mistake you must set me right if you can. I was sorry to hear of the death of Mr. Tuttle, poor old man; I hope he has exchanged a life of suffering for one of happiness. How did he leave his property? I was in hopes he would remember you in his will, the Dr. has enough to do him, unless he has spent it, & if he has he dont deserve to have any more, a selfish old bachelor ought not to have much, does he make himself useful in any way? or is he only living to himself & for himself? I did not have a chance to send you a kiss for the Bishop, you must wait until next time. I heard he was coming back in the spring & would make a longer stay (but I cant vouch for the truth of that), if he should come, & I get a chance, you may look out for the kiss.

Your last letter was too short at one end. I hope paper will be more plentiful the next time you write, but I was thankful for that scrap, it was a heap better than mine.

Kiss dear little Buddy for us & tell him we are glad he thinks enough of his old Aunties to write to them. he is a smart little fellow & will soon be able to write by himself. he must be a good boy & learn his book, & love & obey his Mother, & God will love & take care of him.

Aunt Gatsy & Hannah are well. Noah & his wife are gone with the western party.[4] Sister is well & sends her love to you Ma & the rest of her friends. Her beau has not given over the struggle yet.[5] Sometimes I feel very uneasy about it, but I hope it will all turn out right. Remember me affectionately to your Ma, Dean, Libby, & all the rest of my dear good friends. Receive for yourself the warmest love of your friend, Mollie.

1. William Starnes moved to Limestone County, Texas.
2. Perhaps Mr. Crossley, who worked as an overseer for William Starnes in 1850. Whoever the overseer was, he simply disappeared from view.
3. Now twenty-six years old, she no longer considers herself one of the "young people."
4. All four individuals are slaves belonging to William Starnes.
5. Her sister Sarah eventually married Sam Graves, who may be the determined suitor.

Mary E. Starnes to her friend Sarah J. Thompson, 28 February 1856, from Harrison County, Texas, to Augusta, Georgia. William H. Kilpatrick Letters, from the Collections of the Dallas Historical Society.

Mary Starnes concludes her account of this incident, rationalizing the slave's sale to another master, and she describes another slave, Noah, in ways that smack of racist stereotype. She also protests a bit too much that he does not mind being separated from his mother.

Dear Sallie,

I have not been able to write to you this month, but I presume Libby has told you the cause. About six weeks since I took the sore eyes that have been prevailing in our family & Maj. Graves['s] for the last six months, & have not been able to do any thing scarcely since. I was not off the place but once in five weeks, & was in bed a good part of the time, my whole system seemed to be out of fix. Brother advised me to take calomel which I did, & that salivated me as usual.[1] I have suffered more with my mouth than with my eyes, my mouth is still very sore & my eye sight very bad. Amanda left last monday for Alabama, she has gone on a visit to her Sister who lives about 80 miles from Mobile.[2] Adam, her Father, Mother, & one of her Brother's little daughters went with her. her eyes were quite sore when she left, & Ada's were not well. Sister has escaped so far. she is very particular not to wash in the same vessel or wipe on the same towel with the rest of us. I am in hopes she will escape entirely, for her sight is not very good at best.

Brother returned from the west fat & well.[3] his health improved every day from the time he started, though the weather was excessively cold nearly all the time he was gone. He was delighted with the country, & so were the negroes. None of them were willing to come back. Noah sent his Mother word that he was living in a religious society. I suppose he thought that would please the old soul better than any thing else. he is as fond of fun as ever, will have his joke at somebody's expense. Brother says he afforded them all a great deal of amusement while they were traveling. The negro that cut the Overseer, he disposed of for land.[4] he gave 11 hundred for him & got at the rates of 14 hundred. the negro was well pleased. They say he has a good Master.

My kind friend sent me some more papers lately, on one of them was written a few lines, telling me you were allwell, a piece of information I have not received from yourself in nearly two months. where lies the fault with you or the mail?

Let me know who your Preachers are this year & how you like them, don't grumble & complain if you should not get the one you prefer. no Methodist should do that. leave it to the <u>good one,</u> he will do all things well, so he sends you "a man after his own heart" — it matters not whether he be eloquent or otherwise good will be done. I believe there is no sickness in the neighborhood at present. We have done but little gardening yet, it has been so cold & wet, though it is high time the seed were in the ground. I want you to let me know who it is sending me those papers. I gave Joe the credit of it at first, but I don't believe it is him now. I can't imagine who it is.

Ella is not going to school this year, we are still teaching her at home, she is well & sends her love.[5] I believe I have written all the news of any interest. Remember us to all our friends. Let me know how Mr. Tuttle left his property. Sister[6] joins me in love to Ma, Dean, & yourself. Do write to your friend, Mollie.

1. Antebellum doctors often prescribed mercurous chloride, a mostly insoluble salt, as a cathartic or diuretic, but a soluble form, mercuric chloride, was highly corrosive and could damage the skin or the mucous membranes.
2. William Starnes's second wife, Amanda Graves, whom he had recently married.
3. He had just purchased land in Limestone County, Texas.
4. Starnes's overseer on his plantation in Harrison County, Texas. There is no record of what happened to him after this incident.
5. William Starnes's daughter from his first marriage.
6. Sarah Starnes, Mary's sister.

Private Journal of Mary Owen Sims. Small Manuscript Collection, Arkansas History Commission.

At the time of these entries, widow Mary Sims was in her mid-twenties, living in the Arkansas Delta, and entertaining a visit from her hot-headed father-in-law. She owned four slaves in her own right, including the woman named Lu. Note the contrast between her common-sense reaction to an alleged theft in 1856 and her fear of a slave revolt a year later, symptomatic of the heightened anxieties of the late antebellum era.

28 July 1856. We need rain very much. Everything looks as if it has been seared with an iron. Lu is recovering slowly. The rest of us are well for which I feel thankful. I have been very busy in putting things to rights as I spent the last week at Ma's.[1] I would not have left home with Lu, but

Mr. Sims got into a mighty tantrum. Some of my negroes had stole his pocket book; so I sent for my brothers and went to Ma's, and left them to settle it as best they might.[2] He could not find it and went away very mad and I have not heard of him since.

24 March 1857. It has been nearly a year since I have recorded any of my thoughts. My time has been so much employed that I have scarcely had time to take the "sober second thought" about anything. I find after I have paid out all available funds I have that I am left in debt five hundred dollars; but I hope with the assistance of the good one to be able to say, "I owe no man." I have concluded to farm again this year and have employed Mr. E. again to oversee for me. I live a very secluded and monotonous life. I scarcely ever visit or receive visitors, but divide my time between housekeeping, instructing the children and reading. Mother spent two days with me last week and two of my uncles dined with me. One of them was on a visit from Tennessee and I had not seen in seventeen years. We have had great political excitement for the last year. I don't think I ever knew party spirit so fanatical. Mr. Buchanan was elected, and although I preferred Fillmore,[3] still I feel very much relieved for there was so much talk of insurrections among the slaves of the South that I felt I was in danger all the time and for three months I do not think I slept sound a single night. There was an insurrection contemplated in the little village in which Sister resided, but was discovered in time to stop it.[4]

1. Her mother, Ann Owen, a prosperous widow in her late fifties, lived nearby.

2. William and Benjamin Owen, farmers in their twenties.

3. Democrat James Buchanan (1791–1868) of Pennsylvania won the election of 1856, defeating Millard Fillmore (1800–1874), the candidate for the American, or Know-Nothing, Party and John C. Fremont, the Republican candidate.

4. Probably Princeton, in Dallas County, Arkansas.

Amanda M. Hughes to her daughter Mary Hughes, October 1857, from Turnersville, Tennessee, to Nashville, Tennessee. Darden Family Papers, Tennessee State Library and Archives.

In 1857, Amanda Hughes was a widow in her mid-forties, the mother of nine children. Now very poor, she lived with one of her relatives and helped run a farm.

She nursed slaves when they fell ill, a duty she shares with her oldest daughter, twenty-four-year-old Millie.

Mary Dearest, I received your very welcome letter yesterday was supprised to learn you had not received more letters from home, there is great irregularity in the Males, do tell me have you ever maled Mr. Allensworths letter,[1] he never has received a line from you, you said you had writin, to him, once before you come home, he is posed to think hard of you, says he does not know why his letters would not come, as well as ever, do write him a kind, and affectionate letter, for he is very kind and loves you as a Brother, and you are dependent on him, for the protection of a Father and Brother, and it is through his kindness that you will get home a[t] Christmas, write to him, if you do not write, to any one els[e], he will excuse all mistakes in a scholl girl,[2] it is the most simple words that you miss Spell, Margaret says you spell like you talk,[3] you lisp your words, she says your letters are so much like your own self, let me tell you now, Margaret is a sweet Girl, but do not trust her with any Secret, in a letter, about young gentlemen, but I do not suppose you have any. Mr. Allensworth is in Nashville, will be home on the coach to night, Ellen is at his Fathers, has bin to the Hopkinsville Fair, will be at home, in a week or two, to stay until she goes to housekeeping. Em has not bin up since the birth of her little Daughter, she is very well, expects to be up soon, her and Mag.

Lucy is very sick, I have bin going out to see her once a day for a week, sent Millie to stay with her and nurs her, untill she gets able to bring [her] home. I think with propper care we may be able to Save her, though she is very sick.

the health of our Families is tolerable good, nothing new in our little village worth speaking of. Oh yes, little Bob Alley, Sam Alley's Brother, is married to Mary Ogy. how does Cousin Em com on with her book. I am in hopes she is learning fast give my love to her also to Brother Hughs Family, Brother Church. this from your Mother A. M. Hughes.

1. Amanda Hughes's son-in-law and Mary's brother-in-law.
2. Mary Hughes is attending a girls' academy in Nashville.
3. There is no information on Margaret's identity, but she is apparently a relative.

Thomas B. Powell v. Samuel M. Cobb and others, December 1856 term of the
Supreme Court of the state of North Carolina. Hamilton C. Jones, annotated by
Walter Clark, North Carolina Reports, vol. 56: Cases in Equity Argued
and Determined in the Supreme Court of North Carolina, from Decem-
ber Term 1856 to December Term 1857 Inclusive *(Raleigh: E. M. Uzzell,*
State Printers and Binders, 1904), 13–16.

Ann Cannon married Thomas Powell in 1829, and she was evidently a battered
wife by the time she died in the early 1850s. At the time of her death, Thomas
Powell owned three slaves, which are the subject of this lawsuit. Mr. Powell, a
middle-aged farm laborer, alleged in court that he should retain ownership of the
slaves because his father-in-law deeded them to him. He won a suit in a lower
court against Samuel Cobb, the executor of his wife's estate; Joel Cannon, his
father-in-law; and his white, legitimate children. They in turn appealed to the
state Supreme Court, which upheld the lower court's decision and expunged the
underlined information as Powell requested. Black women rarely sympathized with
white women, much less tried to protect them from harm, but the slave named
Peggy chose to shield her mistress at considerable risk to her own safety.

. . . that the plaintiff ought not to have the said slaves for other reasons, to-
wit: <u>that he had abandoned his family and taken up with women of ill-
fame; that at one time he had left his wife and children for eighteen
months and gone to Lousiana, not having made any provision for them;
that the plaintiff was dissipated, careless, and wasteful, and was a spend-
thrift; that he had beaten his wife with a horsewhip, and that a certain
negro woman named Peggy had often protected her mistress from the
brutal violence of the plaintiff.</u>[1] The answer further states that the release
which the plaintiff had made was fair and bona fide, and that he never heard
of any dissatisfaction about it until <u>the plaintiff had married one of his
kept mistresses, when he became very anxious to get a negro to wait
on his wife and her children who had the misfortune to be born out of
wedlock.</u>

The plaintiff's counsel filed exceptions to the defendants' answer, setting
forth certain portions thereof as <u>scandalous, impertinent, and irrelevant,</u>
and specifying the matter above stated in italics as that excepted to.

1. This is probably the unnamed forty-five-year-old female slave listed in the 1850
slave census. At that time the Powells owned two other slaves, both of them children.

PUBLIC LIFE

PUBLIC AFFAIRS REMAINED PERIPH-
eral to most women's lives, except in time of war (the War of 1812, the
Mexican War) or when conflict seemed imminent (the Nullification and
secession crises). Public affairs then became central topics in their writings, pushing aside domestic concerns for the moment. Yet these women
had conflicted attitudes toward public life, views that seem to have been
refracted through traditional Republicanism, with various and unexpected
results. A few women exhibited a keen interest in politics, but most either
tried to uphold the ethic of disinterested public service, or insisted that
family obligations come first, or scorned political activity of any kind.

Furthermore, these women tended to see large abstract conflicts, such
as the Nullification controversy, in terms of how it might harm their own
relatives. They also held famous public figures, such as John C. Calhoun
and Zachary Taylor, to their own standards of ethical conduct, and some
feared that political activity would undermine the morals of the men they
knew and loved. Why would they worry about this issue in particular?
What threat might involvement in public life pose to domestic harmony?

Mary Telfair to her friend Mary Few, 19 October 1814, from Waynesboro, Georgia, to New York City, New York. William Few Collection, Georgia Department of Archives and History.

Mary Telfair, the daughter of merchant, politician, and Revolutionary War veteran Edward Telfair, was born in Richmond County, Georgia. When her father died in 1807 she inherited a large fortune. As a young woman Telfair read widely and had many friends. In 1814 she is absorbed in the course of the War of 1812, so much so that she briefly wishes she were a man and could participate in public life. Then she quickly disavows any serious interest in politics, even to her best friend, also the daughter of a Revolutionary veteran and distinguished politician, William Few.

Do not dear Mary infer from the length of time I have taken to answer your charming long letter, that it was not accepted for believe me the amusement derived from it was very great, several times have I perused it but the consciousness of a want of subjects for a letter in this remote place has thus long deterred me from writing, but now I am determined to make a <u>bold</u> attempt and should I not succeed your goodness will pardon me. Here we are immersed in a wilderness far removed from the Vortex of business and Pleasure where the "human face divine" never appears, and the only pleasure we enjoy is <u>looking</u> and talking to each other, the life we lead is similar to a monastic one only that we have no <u>Nuns</u> or <u>Confessions,</u> and are permitted to range unmolested through the gloomy pine trees whose dark green tops cheer the eye, and whose hollow murmurs <u>enchant</u> the ear, do you think <u>Molly</u> such a scene as this would please your fancy? bad as it is I should like to have you here and make "the unruly member" rattle a little, however I candidly acknowledge that I never found it deficient, <u>great</u> and <u>loud</u> talkers are my aversion, when in the society of a person of this description.[1] I always sigh for taciturnity, and feel every inclination to silence them. On the 28th of this Month we commence our journey to Savannah after an absence of nearly four months. I always return to town with pleasure and never leave it with regret, for even the most solitary abode where Hygenia dispenses her blessings, is preferrable to remaining in a place where the mind remains dormant from excessive heat, and the body liable to be effected by sickness. I am fond of the Country where

> "Boon Nature scatters, free and wild
> Each plant or flower, the mountains child"

and should take great delight in cultivating a little spot. What can be more pleasing than to watch the progress of a favorite plant. the interest we take in it bears a slight similitude to that which a Mother takes in her infant. What felicity could have been so perfect so innocent as that of our first parents before they tasted of the tree of knowledge. Yours and Frances garden I hope will flourish beneath your Loitering there like a little Eden. I made a beautiful collection of Vines and Shrubs last March, and put them into a Wooden box for you and have since regretted that I did not send it by Mr. Campbell as I fear the frost will rip their roots before my return. —

"Old Maids alley," "courting corner," and the Temple of Hymen — tell Fan I admire her wit and should like to know which of the three is her shrine.[2] I suspect she means to slip into the latter with some dear creature. I hope she will give me timely notice and not take me by surprise for the shock will be almost too much for my nerves. You and I will step boldly into the former and stand "the world's dread laugh," but Mary what report is this you alluded to, for I am all curiosity to know who you have been flirting with. Oh! you are a sly Girl and betrayed yourself without intending it, however. I will not believe it as you say there is no truth in it.

I agree with you my dear Mary in admiring Walter Scott, the wildness and enthusiasm of his verse is delightful, and then he possess so much amor patrie.[3] how beautiful his address to Caledonia is, in "the last day of the minstrel,"[4] but the Lady of the Lake is my favorite of all "his" productions.[5] the characters are so inimitably drawn, that of Broderick in particular, his virtues tho savage were very noble, and comes up exactly to my idea of the ancient highland Character, and Douglass though more polished and cast in a gentler mould, was equal in bravery, and still more to be admired. What a captivating fellow is Fitz James so much of the elegant man of fashion combined with a mind full of chivalrous deeds & romantic ideas, a heart replete with sensibility. Ellen, woman like, notwithstanding her predilection for Malcolm could not see him unmoved and refrain from bestowing a parting glance a little of the coquette in that. But if I continue undulating in my admiration for those "fictitious characters" I shall forget that there are real ones in Existence. —

I have read nothing this summer my mind has been wholly engrossed with needle work and inventing little trifles by way of amusement. The newspapers at this interesting period are to me more acceptable than the most beautiful poem, for I seize them with avidity, and my heart throbs with joy whenever I discover a successful action by the Americans, for instance the victory of Capt. Hull & Porter,[6] the gallant conduct of Captain [illegible] contrast it with the inglorious surrender in Canada which has cast a stigma on the American character which nothing but a conquest of that country can retrieve and how many valuable lives will that cost![7] The Southern States are in a defenceless situation, and should government authorise the conquest of Florida our troops will be sent there; the Spaniards and Indians together have commenced some depradations already. Several American soldiers & citizens have been inhumanly scalped.[8] The <u>sable</u> tribe flock to the Spanish standard and foolishly imagine that their freedom will be the result, little imagining that their bondage will be more rigid— .[9]

—I suspect all women are politicians now. Alexander accuses me of sporting federal sentiments because I abuse the administration.[10] Indeed a want of energy is very perceptible, and I only wish <u>I was a man</u> possessing talents either for the Cabinet or the field. I think I should be very active. Do not smile Mollie, for there is no danger of <u>Petticoat</u> innovations. Are you not tired of my nonsense I am of writing it so will bid you farewel not without a charge to write frequently. Do not let <u>the times</u> prevent you land conveyances will not I hope be stopped by the enemy.

—remember us all to the whole of your Family, and believe me unalterably yours, M. T.

19th October

1. Telfair may be referring to one of her relatives, several of whom had plantations in rural Georgia.
2. Fan is a mutual friend.
3. Meaning the poet Sir Walter Scott (1771–1832) and his love of his native country, Scotland.
4. Telfair misquotes the title of one of Scott's early works, "The Lay of the Last Minstrel," in which an aged minstrel describes the ancient rivalries between aristocratic families. In canto sixth, he addresses Caledonia (a romantic name for Scotland) as "Land of my sires! what mortal hand / Can e'er untie the filial band / knits me to thy rugged strand! / Still, as I view each well-known scene, / Think what is now and what hath been, / Seems as to me, of all bereft, / Sole friends thy woods and streams were left; / And thus I love them better still, / Even in extremity of ill."
5. "The Lady of the Lake," published in 1810, helped make Scott's reputation. It concerns the romantic dilemmas of a heroine named Ellen, who had to choose between suitors.
6. Probably Captain David Porter, whose exploits against the British in the north and south Atlantic made him a hero. Captain Isaac Hull also scored some naval victories in the war.
7. American forces made several forays into Canada during the war, but all of them failed.
8. The Seminoles and factions of the Creek nation, who allied with the British.

During the war the Americans and the British accused each other of inciting Indians to scalp their enemies.

9. Meaning runaway slaves. During the war approximately thirty-six hundred slaves ran away to the British, who had promised them freedom; some bondsmen escaped to Spanish Florida, where slavery was still practiced. As Telfair observes, bondage in the Spanish colonies could be more harsh than in the United States.

10. The Federalist Party harshly criticized the conduct of President James Madison, a member of the Jeffersonian Party, also known as the Democratic-Republicans.

Maria H. Campbell to her cousin Jefferson, 20 January 1815, from Abingdon, Virginia, to no address. Campbell Family Papers, Special Collections Library, Duke University.

Maria Hamilton of Virginia married her cousin David Campbell in 1799, when she was a young woman. Her husband served with distinction during the War of 1812, and she writes knowledgeably about state and local politics. Perhaps the fact that the marriage was childless gave Mrs. Campbell the leisure or the inclination to follow public events. Yet she, like many women, apologizes for discussing a verboten subject for "ladies" even when the nation is at war.

You must excuse me cousin Jefferson for not sooner answering your very friendly and acceptable letter of the 26th Nov. last, as my time has been much occupied since my return home with my domestic concerns. An absence of ten weeks with my friends in Tennessee and my long absence in the North had deranged them much, and cause[d] them to require my particular attention. —I do not like to commence political epistolary conversation with you, because you know we ladies are forbidden by the polite world to say much on this subject. Notwithstanding tho it is not our province to be politicians, yet I cannot avoid looking around me and viewing from my inaccessible mountains the important struggle in which my native and beloved Country is engaged—Her destiny is connected with the life blood of my heart; and altho I have suffered much in the separation from my husband[1] and acknowledge that I am nothing but [a] frail woman, yet I am willing to suffer more rather than see her savage and merciless foe triumph over her. —Our eyes here are now all turned towards New Orleans. Much depends I believe on our success there. If Jackson preserves that place, you may rest assured that it will place him on very high ground, let his enemies do and say what they will.[2] Those who act for their Country are the real patriots, not the flaming fireside politican who can find fault & do nothing else.

If you can procure a suitable Commission, and the war continues, accept it, and stand by your Country—She will one day reward you with interest.

Our Legislature has not yet risen that I have heard—Mr. Estill made a mighty <u>splash</u> in Richmond and is to be married to Miss Gay Robinson a very beutiful and accomplished young lady as I am told. He is now at Washington City, with her. The State of Virginia is about to raise troops—If she does I expect brothers Arthur & James will both go into the army.

Cousin David intends commencing the mercantile business shortly—I have heard that he intended going for goods this winter—

The Miss Prestons are gone to Richmond to go to school—I complied with your request in giving them your best respects—By the time you leave the army Susan will have finished her education—and then you know— you can—you can say, you can talk with her on literature, bell letters &c &c—While at Richmond, John can take care of her for you—Tho it may be trusting the lamb to the wolf—

We are as dull here, as you could wish if you were even wishing us all the [illegible] you could think of—No society except in our own families and I do not see any prospect of amendment.

Sheffey [3] I believe will have no opposition for Congress—Various persons are spoken of, but I expect none will come out. Mr. Russell has been named also Genl. F. Preston, Genl. Smythe, E. Campbell, Mr. Dixon &c [4]—Sheffey will be elected let who will oppose him. —Such is his influence here.

Edward has been lying with the rheumatism seven or eight weeks, but is recovered so far that he can walk thro his room.

Give my best respects to Aunt, Cousin Penelope, and my cousins generally. Your cousin Maria H. Campbell.

1. David Campbell (1779–1859), a lawyer and slaveowner, served in Canada and attained the rank of brigadier general before the conflict ended. A Democrat, he was elected governor of Virginia in 1837.

2. Andrew Jackson, who did in fact win the Battle of New Orleans in January 1815.

3. Daniel Sheffey (1770–1830), a Virginia lawyer, was elected to the U.S. Congress as a Federalist and served until 1817.

4. Francis Preston (1765–1835) served in the Third and Fourth Congresses from 1793 to 1797. After serving as a colonel in the War of 1812, he practiced law in Virginia; Alexander Smyth (1765–1830) became inspector-general of the army in the War of 1812. He served in the U.S. Congress during the second and third decades of the nineteenth century until he died in Washington, D.C.

Margaret Trimble McCue to her brother John A. Trimble, 25 February 1820, from Staunton, Virginia, to Hillsborough, Ohio. John Allen Trimble and the Trimble Family Papers, MS 249, box 1, folder 1, Ohio Historical Society.

Margaret McCue, a devout Christian, detests slavery on religious grounds, and she opposes the Compromise of 1820 because it permitted the Missouri territory to enter the Union as a slave state. She wants very much to move to the free state of Ohio but never could persuade her husband to migrate. Her brother-in-law Mr. Barry settled there in the early 1820s.

My Dear Brother,

I Received our letter too weeks after Date. I was verry glad to find you had not forgotten me although you Did not write. I thought when Reading your letter I would answer it immediately but its such a task for me to write it takes a week to get at it, but you will thats for want of Practice. I admits its so but my Domestic concerns Prevents my Practiseing much, & you must not neglect writing because I do not answer all your letters, but enough on this subject.

the friends are together with our own family well. we have Recieved no account from Brother W. since I wrote Mother.[1] I suppose his whole time is taken up with this greate Missouri question which was not Desided the last account. we hope it will be decided favourably On the side of humanity. Received a letter a few days since from Brother Allen informing us that a Bill had passed for opening a Canal from Lake Erie to the Ohio River. This cirtianly will be of greate importance to the People of Ohio, & ought certainly to Be a greate inducement among many others to emigration.[2]

I suppose it would surpris you all verry much to hear that Mr. Barry & myself have Been trying to Persuade our familys to move to Ohio, from Consciencious motives, but I fear the Difficultys are so great that I we will hardly Succeed. But there's nothing like Perseverance In a good Cause. the Difficulty of Disposeing of Property is verry great at this Time & the thoughts of moving scares Polly & James, Particularly when they Cannot see & feel the important advantage to Soul and Body, the Deliverance from the Perplexing trials which we must ever expect while holding these unhapy affricans in Bondage.[3] But we will try to Convince them that the

Remove would be to our temporal interest. Mr. Barrys arguments are so Strong & so Plain, there is no geting over them. I think he says if his incumberance was not greater than Mr. McCues and the advantage of a home to go to[4] he would be in Ohio before fall. But I meets waite with Patience untill the way is opened. Tell Mother she must pray for us Perhaps it is in answer to her prayers that our eyes have thus far been opened and if so they will be heard and the way opened.[5]

you mentioned in your letter it was gratifying to see our Brothers thought worthy to fill the posts of honour to which the[y] have been Called By their fellow sitizens to which I agree.[6] But O if we were all Members of the Church & House of God How much more Honerable, & that Crown of Glory which fadeth Not away than that of Princes. O My Dear Brother Seek the Lord in the Days of your youth Before the evil Days come.

write me often Give my Love to Mother — Brothers, & Sisters While I Remain your affectionet Sister, Margaret McCue.

N.B. Wm B.['s] Family Desires to Be Remembered to enquiring friends.

1. Her brother William A. Trimble had been elected to the U.S. Senate from Ohio in 1819; he died in 1821.
2. Another brother, Allen Trimble (1783–1870), was then a member of the Ohio state senate and later served as governor. The canal did facilitate travel through the state.
3. Polly is her sister and James her brother-in-law. Her husband, Mr. McCue, owned six slaves in 1820.
4. Meaning the homes of her brothers, mother, and in-laws, who have already migrated to Ohio.
5. Her mother, Jane Allen Trimble, opposed slavery even though she was a Virginian by birth.
6. Meaning the state and national offices her brothers held.

Margaret Galbreath Autobiography, 1825. Vertical File 2363, Ohio Historical Society.

Born at the end of the eighteenth century, Margaret Galbreath was orphaned and adopted by a wealthy merchant in Maryland. Her adoptive father's family had been Loyalists during the Revolution, and Galbreath grew up in a highly political and very conservative household. At a young age she was immersed in the international debate over Napoleon, and as an adult she continues to follow public events. She too disdains political women and grasps for a way to justify her long-time interest in public life.

About that time Nelson's victory over the French and the brilliant exploits of Bonaparte agitated the political world and were warmly discussed by our Junta of the fire side, and from continually hearing these things I became interested in them; though I never wished or dared to speak on the subject.[1] Carlos and Calculus were strong loyalists.[2] Calculus had once belonged to the king's guards. Carlos was educated with strong prejudices against rebels & republicans. this was the only point on which these two in the least agreed.

Gruflin[3] was a hot headed whig, a great friend of Bounaparte. Notwithstanding my partiality for the other two I agreed in opinion with Grufflin. —We are I think by nature idolators: there are proofs in all ages to show it. The temples of the enlightened Romans, the images of the Christian Catholics, the adoration paid to particular men who have appeared. Monuments both Ancient & Modern, strongly masks an propensity to worship something, and it is rather an enigma when we consider that ambition is the strongest of our leading principles as we should at the same time be actuated by one which would appear diametrically opposite.

On this subject I suppose others have written and handled the subject better than I am capable of, so I shall leave it and pass on the point which rise to the remark. —I now chose my Idol, in which was concentrated all I could conceive great and glorious; and what think you reader might it be so strongly fascinating to the mind of an innocent girl of 11 years old? Why it was on the last things one might suppose. Bounaparte became the object of my adoration! and with little variation so continued untill the present. Every thing that concern'd him interested me; but still it was not a blind admiration. I examined critically every tale I heard to his disadvantage, hoped it was false, endeavored to excuse, & when a sad truth came indisputably home I sorrowed with all my heart; At this time the English press gave me full exercise for these feelings as it constantly teemed with some scurrilous invective; some malignant fabrication of his cruelty and burning, promulgated by government for the purpose of inspiring the common people with a detestation & fear of the man whom they could not conquer nor subdue. I was then too young to understand this or to distinguish between probability and truth. —I believe no man ever lived who cost the English government more trouble and expence to calumniate than did he. —for which it has ever had my cordial hatred—Time, change, and my own trials little abated the attachment so early contracted for the mighty Corsican. I still think he was the only monarch I ever read or heard of who deserv'd to be a sovereign. Whatever cavillers may say about his ambition, I think his principle object was the honour & prosperity of France; which he in great measure attain'd, however mistaken he might be in some things, still every one will confess the French people were more happy under his administration than they have been before or since; He was torn from France against her will, and she will weep his loss in tears of blood. Bounaparte was my idol, but America the country I loved.

The company and conversation to which I was exposed at this early period may in some measure account for that taste which led to an acquaintance with and an investigation of national government and policy so much condemned by some of my friends as unbecoming in a woman, and stigmatized me with the name of "petticoat politician," which is a character I despise; and here beg leave to say I think there is a difference between a woman who makes herself busy about electioneering candidates, federal and republican parties,[4] and one who merely reads national history endeavors to investigate the causes which produce effects, & gain information of facts. Of this last class I think I am; about the other matters I never trouble myself; for it matters little to me what knave or what fool happens to be mounted on the government horse for a time, so that the people have him in their power; for it is my opinion that in a country like this the majority are very likely to be in the right.

1. Napoleon Bonaparte (1769–1821) proclaimed himself emperor of France in 1804 and embarked on a series of brilliant military campaigns until he controlled most of continental Europe. The British held him off, however, and Admiral Horatio Nelson (1758–1805) destroyed much of the French fleet at the Battle of Trafalgar in 1805. In 1814 Napoleon was forced to abdicate, and his attempt to regain power failed a year later.

2. Pseudonyms for her step-brothers.

3. Another pseudonym for another step-brother.

4. Meaning the Federalists and Democratic-Republicans, the chief opponents of the First Party System.

Susanna Claiborne Withers Clay to her sister Ann Eliza Withers, 16 December 1831, from Washington, D.C., to Petersburg, Virginia. LeVert Family Papers, Southern Historical Collection, University of North Carolina.

Susanna Withers married Clement Comer Clay in 1815 and arrived in Washington, D.C., from Alabama in 1829, when her husband began his first term in the House of Representatives. Mr. Clay supported Andrew Jackson, which makes Mrs. Clay's criticisms of fancy ceremony at the White House all the more interesting. In the same spirit, she mocks the extremes of high fashion visited upon another congressman's wife.

My dear Sister,

What is the matter? Why have you not written to me? I have in vain expected a letter from you? how am I to know what you wish or how you are? The weather has been very bad here and the Influenza has been prevalent in every part of the City. Mrs. Clay[1] was attacked with it and was quite sick for several days—I had some hopes of escaping as every one had been visited in the house—but my time had not arrived. yesterday I was taken very ill and part of the day compeled to keep my bed—had a high fever all night and but little <u>sleep</u>—but my anxiety to give you pleasure preponderated over every other consideration and I am now too unwell to receive company or go out of my room—notwithstanding—I have not made a purchase of a Bonnet yet I will not send you one till I hear from you—I could not [postpone?] for the river has, "and now is" frozen up—I fear to hear from Cousin Thomas! Do write immediately and tell me how [you] all are—I hope Aunt Mitchell did not suffer from her exposure when we were with her—I have met with many old friends—all of whom I am pleased to say, met me with much cordiality—and the only fear I have on that score is, that I shall not have the command of my time sufficiently to improve myself, as much as I wish.

We have received several letters from home—all were well—You will find one from James inclosed with I took the liberty of breaking[2]—I shall take the earliest opportunity of sending you you anything you wish provided you will write—I shall write to you at least once a week—and surely you can answer me!! Try, I know you have much perseverance when you think proper to escort it—and my dear Ann we all lack steadiness of purpose—I find that I have to force myself frequently to my duty—for example I hate to write—and the reason is that I have not been compel'd to do so untill a few years past—now my pride is frequently mortified But I know it is my own fault, and I think we are never too old to learn and have determined to write every day and try to do what I ought years ago.

I promised in my next to give you a sketch of my messmates[3] — Mrs. Gen. Speight of N. C. a very plain country woman who has little or no improvement and depends on her friends to judge for her in every thing[4] — Very anxious, as it regards appearance, with but little judgment to aid her. I have purchased every article for her since I came, at my own discretion, and if gratitude can repay — I believe I have hers. She is the second wife — and you may guess her simplicity when I tell you that she told me that his first wife was her sister!! I pity her, and I condemn him.[5] You see that I am obliged to avow a change of opinion — I have never had a case before presented, and did not know the effect.

Miss Wickcliffe of Ken.[6] A young, healthy, sprightly, girl of good natural understanding tolerably cultivated — plays on the Piano tolerably — perfectly easy, and unaffected upon all occasions. I admire her for her goodness she is as yet, artless and undesigning. I hope she may continue so — I have the good fortune to be on excellent terms with her also — The weather is still very bad and the snow covers every thing — I have in vain looked for good weather every day for three successive nights we have found snow, and the sun shineing in the morning —

You had rather I expect I would change the subject — Well, young A. Jackson is married!! It is said to a fortune and a beauty!!![7] I have not seen her yet — And the friends of the president say that there was more unnecessary parade there the night we reached the City than was ever heard of before — A party was given to the young married people, and the company invited to attend at eight o'clock — My informant did not get there untill half after eight, when the greater part of the company had assembled — There was no proper person — that is, none of the household visible — all at dinner!! — about nine or ten I have forgotten which the President was announced!! He appeared with young A. J. and wife, and they went round and was introduced to the company and were seated — next came Mr. & Mrs. Donelson — the same ceremony.[8] Then the secretaries and families, who were presented in the same manner!!! "Plain republicanism"!! and then the herd — Mr. Clay[9] called on the President he regretted that he did not know we were in the City that he might have extended the courtesy of an invitation to us — I should have gone I expect — But am glad he did not hear of it — H. Clay & Family are here — We shall have cards from them, haveing come last.[10] I have seen Mrs. Barnwell[11] Mrs. Poke of Ten.[12] Mrs. Seaman is here having changed her mind after we saw the Col. in Georgia.[13] She met with a very serious accident on the road having lost her trunk and cloathes — They are the ladies who messed with us[14] the winter I was here — Many others have called that I am fond of, and many that I shall to return cards.

I had written the above when I was called to see my good friend Mrs. Speight dress for the Presidents — A barber had the tortureing of her head and I was to put in the flowers — Poor lady, I pitied her — She suffered martyrdom — imagine the head in which, Pins, Wire, Flowers and combs, vied for ascendancy — She is off to dinner at 4 o'clock. — I have just had an admonition from Mr. Clay about writing after dark — Tell Cousin Dolly I will try and collect all the news, shortly and send her in the form of a letter — I have now many letters on hand tell my Ann [page torn] have not been to any other Church but Mr. Joneses, and that I hope Can [page torn] ill give me credit as I passed the Presbyterian with company who went there — I have not become reconciled to the made up worship. Tell me how you like it — Who has called to see you? Who do you like best among your relations? What have you bought? The river is still still frozen — I cannot send you any thing till it thaws — Should you think it necessary to get one do so — they are worn here like my summer one on my black have made one made to suit you stipulating the price — White feathers are worn to fall over in front — Adieu affectionately S. C. Clay.

1. One of her sisters-in-law or her mother-in-law.

2. Meaning breaking the seal on the letter.

3. Those who lived in their boardinghouse in Washington, D.C.

4. Susanna C. Withers Clay was herself a "country woman" by birth, although her family owned slaves.

5. Jesse Speight (1795–1847), a freshman congressman from North Carolina, was also a Democrat. He later served a term as U.S. senator from Mississippi. His first wife, surname unknown, died in 1826, and the next year he married her sister Louisa. Many Americans frowned on the sometime custom of marrying a deceased wife's sister.

6. Almost certainly a daughter of Congressman Charles Wickcliffe (1788–1869) of Kentucky, who served two stints in Washington (1823–33 and 1861–63) and various state offices; in between, he was postmaster general under President John Tyler.

7. President Andrew Jackson's adopted son Andrew Jackson Jr. (d. 1865) was the nephew of the president's deceased wife Rachel Robards Donelson Jackson. In November 1831 he married Sarah York (1805–87), a great beauty from Philadelphia.

8. Andrew Jackson Donelson (1799–1871), was the president's ward and secretary. His wife, Emily Donelson, was his first cousin; she died in 1836 of tuberculosis.

9. Her husband Clement Comer Clay (1789–1866), a lawyer and Virginia native who would be elected Democratic governor of Alabama in 1835. His oldest son, Clement Claiborne Clay (1819–82), would serve in the U.S. Senate and in the Confederate government.

10. Meaning that Kentucky Senator Henry Clay and his wife, Lucretia Hart Clay (1799–1864), would leave their calling cards; they then had six children. These Clays were Whigs and were distantly related to the Clays of Alabama.

11. Eliza Barnwell, wife and cousin of Congressman Robert Woodward Barnwell (1801–82) from South Carolina. (Her cousins are described in the introduction to this book.) He served in Congress from 1826 until 1833 and later served as president of the University of South Carolina and, in the 1850s, in the U.S. Senate.

12. Sarah Childress (1803–91) of Tennessee married James K. Polk in 1824 and accompanied him to Washington, where he served in the Congress for fourteen terms. In 1844 he was elected president on the Democratic ticket.

13. There was no Georgia congressman by the name, but this may be Mrs. Seaborn Jones, whose husband (a Georgian) served as commissioner to the Creek nation before he was elected to the U.S. Congress in 1833.

14. Meaning those who roomed with them.

Julia M. Brown to her cousin Jonathan Ralph Flynt, 12–13 October 1832, from Kirkwood plantation, near Camden, South Carolina, to Tolland, Connecticut. Julia M. Brown Letter, South Caroliniana Library, University of South Carolina.

Julia M. Brown was a native Southerner but attended school in New England. In 1832 she worked as a governess on a plantation in the South Carolina Piedmont. The furious internal struggles over the Nullification crisis have aggravated her disgust for partisan strife, but her thoughts on slavery are still confused. She fears a slave uprising but insists that bondsmen are unaware of their exploitation; her sympathies veer back and forth between master and slave. The entire letter is overlaid with a sense of hopelessness regarding how, or whether, the slavery issue might be resolved.

My dear Cousin Ralph, With a sickening heart, I this evening turn from the contemplation of the present dreadfully alarming state of Carolina and take my pen to answer your last kind letter. Tho' I am not a politician, you must not be surprised if this letter is <u>tinctured</u> with political feeling and strife, for this is the present theme of thought and consideration and conversation in Carolina. And for a few days past, our ears have been continually saluted with rumors of <u>fights</u> — quarreling — abuse &c. from the contending parties.

It has been the season of election of senators, and representatives — and such a struggle for precedence has been displayed, as I never before had the least conception of. In Camden the Union party carried the day by a large majority, and every one of their candidates was elected—which has inflamed the Nullifiers to the highest pitch—and they are venting their rage in quarrels—and challenges &c. War—duelling—and fighting are common everyday [phases?] here at present—. An extra meeting of the Legislature is convoked by the Gov.[1] and should the Nullifiers gain the preeminence in that body—a convention will be called and immediate Nullification will ensue—the result of which will inevitably be war—civil war—Oh if there was ever a period when Christians ought to to be much in prayer, it seems to me <u>now</u> is the time—for in God, the God of nations, as well as in individuals, is our help found.

[October] 13th. I had written thus far last evening when I was interrupted—and now this Saturday eve, I have retired to my room, that I might be <u>alone</u>—for I cannot wholly eradicate early prejudices, and predelictions for a <u>quiet</u> Saturday night. Yes, dear cousin R often, very often do I sigh for [the] luxury of a <u>home</u> Saturday night—Here, how wide the contrast—all is bustle—visiting and nothing indicating the near approach of the day of rest. And tho' I am not positive that this is <u>holy time,</u> yet I feel the propriety of spending this eve, in the preparation for the sabbath—in sacred duties tis a privilege to spend these hours—and I think should I ever have a family and home of my own, both Saturday and Sabbath evenings should be passed in sacred duties—the one as a preparation for the other, an improvement of the Sabbath—

You have little idea, cousin Ralph, of the vast dissimilarities both in manners, and feelings, between the North and South. The issue of slavery (than which there cannot be a greater) broods, and rests o'er every scene here— Oh how often does my heart bleed over the miserably degraded state of the slaves—but I am utterly at a loss to know, <u>what can</u> be done for the amelioration of their condition. T'would be death to emancipate them here—as to enlighten[ing] them, I am fully convinced, would be but to show them, what they now are mostly ignorant of, their degraded state—and I can only reiterate the inquiry which an eminent gentleman of this neighborhood <u>put to me</u> a few days since, when conversing on this very subject, "What can be done for them?" The Virginia insurrection has shown the South what they may fear, and expect at some future, perhaps not distant period.[2] As I pity the master, almost as much if not more than the slave. I have not been so unfortunate as to be placed in any situation where I see the poor creatures ill used—and I trust I never may be. I believe many aggravated tales of the general ill usage of slaves have been circulated in the North—they are tis true often a <u>stubborn</u> willful set, but who would not be, in their condition.

<u>Very many</u> of the Southerners <u>feel</u> the full weight of the curse entailed upon them, of which they are entailing on their children in turn.[3] Should the machinations of wicked men prevail and civil war ensure—there will be dreadful scenes presented in Carolina to the beholder. Oh my God avert these impending calamities and overrule all for his glory, the good of these United States.

You will pardon me, Cousin Ralph, for making this letter so uninteresting [with] political and slavery details—but did you see and feel what I have I am persuaded you too, would be aught to make it often a subject of remark—The present critical state of affairs here, and its being with us, a constant theme of conversation, would plead my apology for making my letter to political in its character—

Now I will turn to other topics—and first as respects your present situation my dear friend & cousin—I rejoice that it is one of pleasant nature—more so I should think than any one you have been in for many years, for permit to say to you, my friend, I am sensible that your previous situation, has been one of <u>trial</u>—and perplexity—Yes, were it not wrong to wish our beloved M. again below to struggle through this weary world,[4] I could desire, that she might now enjoy your present pleasant station—But she, dear M, is now far happier I believe, than if she were with us—free from sin, and its attendant sorrow—freed from her clayey tabernacle,[5] she roams the heavenly regions, and sings the praises of Immanuel—and can we selfishly wish her back? Oh no—rather let us live so as to unite with her in the employments of Heaven, when we shall have finished our earthly career of duty—How mysterious are the dealings of Providence with man—but infinite wisdom, directs them all—

You have probably heard of the long continued, and distressing illness of our friend Daniel—tho you are not aware of its full length—for you know not of it at home—. When last I heard from him, he had [not thus?] far recovered from another most violent attack as to sit up for two or three hours—he had lain eighteen days, in a helpless condition, twelve of which he was apparently near Eternity—He has indeed been most severely afflicted—and I need not say, that in this affliction, <u>I too have suffered</u>—as even now, I fear that his constitution has been so much shattered by disease that he will never gain be well—. What Providence has in store for <u>us</u>, is to us unknown—. Oh for a submissive spirit—Will you not cousin R remember us both, when you bow before the throne of grace—? And should our lives be spared, may we be more faithful, self-denying, and devoted Christians than we have ever been—. . . .

I shall offer no apologies for [my] letter—I have many letters to write—

numerous other engagements to occupy my time, and when I do write, it is ever in haste—Love to all my friends when you see them—and believe me ever your truly affectionate friend and cousin, Julia.

1. James Hamilton, a Nullifier, who resigned in December 1832 to lead state troops in case of war.
2. Nat Turner's revolt in Southampton County, Virginia, in 1831. He and his followers killed fifty-nine whites before they were captured.
3. Meaning the curse of slavery.
4. Ralph's deceased wife, name unknown.
5. Meaning her earthly body.

Lucretia Calhoun Townes to her sister-in-law Eliza Townes Blassingame, 5 December 1832, from Benlomond farm, near Abbeville, South Carolina, to Greenville, South Carolina. Townes Family Papers, South Caroliniana Library, University of South Carolina.

Lucretia Townes was the middle-aged wife of a physician, slaveholder, and farmer. She had an exuberant personality, and she intensely enjoyed her relationships with her female kinfolk, as this letter demonstrates. Her enthusiasm for the Nullification cause is equally vivid, although she neglects to mention that one of her uncles, politician John C. Calhoun, led the movement.

My dear Sister,

I received your letter dated 7th on the 15th. Though a long time coming it was nevertheless acceptable and highly entertaining. For a <u>man,</u> Frank writes a very interesting letter, but I must confess that a woman has a talent for <u>letter</u> writing in <u>my humble</u> opinion far above a man's.[1] There is not that stiffness and precision in a woman's letter, that <u>characterizes</u> that of a man, and I must say that <u>your</u> letters are always a source of great pleasure to me. You write just the kind of a letter that I like to read. it is almost equal to a verbal chit chat. it is when I read a letter from you, that I recall the many happy days that I have spent in Greenville, the pleasure that I always experienced when of a <u>saturday evening</u> we would go out to your Mother's.[2] You would dine with us on Sunday, and how sociable and happy we would all be. The change I know is for the better, but I spend many unhappy moments in wishing myself back. Dr. Townes frequently rebukes me for it, but I cannot help it.[3] I am not, nor never can be, satisfied here. true my family are all in Abbeville, but not near enough for me to visit them but seldom. in the summer I am always uneasy for fear that Dr. Townes or the children will be sick, but I must make the best of it.[4] Here I <u>am,</u> and here I <u>must be</u> for a time. <u>Fortune may</u> smile upon us, and <u>then, adieu to Abbeville.</u> There is one thing however which will always give Abbeville the ascendancy over Greenville. The people here are <u>Whigs.</u> In Greenville they are <u>Tories,</u> with but few exceptions.[5] Nullification has gone forth at last, and the names of her advocates will live forever. But a truce with politics, when I have other things to write about. We are all well and in pretty good spirits. Dr. Townes I believe fattens daily. he gets a little practice. I have weaned Samuel. he looks very well. Martha Eliza is as fat as a pig, so is Kate.[6] I assure you that it is with much regret that I will have to decline visiting you all this winter. Dr. Townes I expect will take Christmas <u>dinner</u> with his <u>Mother</u> and will explain <u>all things.</u> I shall visit you about the last of May or the first of June, and if nothing happens, tell your Mother that I will present her with <u>another grandchild!!!</u> in about the middle of April. Tell her that she and yourself must come down then. Now don't <u>joke</u> any of <u>your fun</u> at me when you read this, for you "done so before me," and pray how do you come on in that <u>line.</u>[7] I hear of nothing but weddings &c &c. there are I believe six or seven on the carpet. My <u>neighbour's</u> Brother, a Mr. Tullis, is to be married this evening to one of the Miss Bells that went to school in Greenville, & Mrs. Thurston knows her. Greenville must be getting scarce of girls. I hear of so many marriages lately. Poor Emily Hamblin, not off yet. she reminds me of the song, "Tis the last rose of summer left blooming alone." &c &c.[8]

I thought that Maria was to write to me, Soon after the wedding at old Jerrys. tell her it is not too late. Frank I suppose has given me up as a corispondent. And <u>Maria</u> my <u>friend</u> Maria spoke of me and the children to <u>you. take care</u> sister. don't be <u>too</u> friendly with <u>every</u> body. I may meet with someone that <u>you</u> don't <u>speak</u> to, and then[9] —

<u>Remember M.</u> and myself <u>do not</u> speak yet and if we <u>ever</u> do the advances must come from <u>her.</u> Tell <u>Frank</u> to look out too[10] —

If Dr. Townes goes up at Christmas I will send your Mother a dress ready made to put on Christmas day. I will make it very high in the neck and a tippet of the same. Tell her that I will make it by the dress of a good old Presbyterian lady as plain as herself, so she need not have any scruples about it. Tell her that I will get my friend Betsy Derricotte to stay with me while Dr. Townes is gone. You have already heard by Dr. Townes's letter to

Frank of the death of Aunt Mosely. it is an event that has long been looked for by all of her friends. Then you all were prepared for it, and <u>she</u> was well prepared in my opinion for the change. she had long resigned herself to the will of Providence. Lucretia Baker and husband were baptized some time since. —

We have commenced this morning to kill our hogs and have a tolerable good prospect for fine weather. I shall have a good seamstress in a few days.[11] McDuffie desired me to keep his [seamstress] while he was gone, which I shall gladly do.[12] He spent a night with us just before he left Abbeville. he is in fine spirits tell Frank and think[s] we can whip old Jackson.[13] he set off to Washington by way of Columbia on tuesday last. Governor Hamilton will send official copies of the proceedings of the Convention by the same stage that McD. goes in.[14] The Governor intends having the Ordinance, his addresses, &c. &c. written on parchment by a man in Charleston by the name of Morse and put into a handsome gift box and then placed in the office of the secretary of state for the benefit of posterity. And <u>our children's children</u> will read them and know that their ancestors were not <u>voluntary</u> slaves and <u>woe</u> be unto the <u>Tories</u> or submissionists in those days.[15] When the history of the present times is written <u>they</u> will be branded as <u>Tories, traitors,</u> and many other epithets equally deserving.

And what a proud place will South Carolina and the <u>Nullifiers</u> [page torn] <u>history pages.</u> —

I spent a few days with Aunt Nancy last week.[16] She is prodigiously alarmed at the thoughts of Jackson's having sent Genl. Scott and two companies [of] U.S. troops to Charleston with a supply of ammunition &c &c.[17] by the by what do you <u>scary Greenville</u> folks think of the <u>Ginerals</u> proceedings. I expect to hear soon of you ladies being all forted again the C[ourt]. H[ouse]. I will have all the <u>Jackleged knives old guns, clubs</u> &c &c hunted up and send them to you by the waggon.

Send Maria down if she is not going to school and let her spend the winter with me.[18] I insist on it. Give our love to your Mother, Mr. B., Frank, Maria, John, and the rest of the children.[19] Write soon a long letter. Margaret is expecting daily to increase her family. Your affectionate sister Lucretia A. Townes.

1. George Franklin Townes (1809–91), her brother-in-law, a journalist, lawyer, and farmer.

2. Rachel Stokes Townes, a widow living near Greenville.

3. Meaning she cannot help wishing she was back in Greenville. Her husband Henry Townes (1804–49) was a farmer and physician, and they moved to help his practice.

4. Her husband died in 1849, and she later married an Alabama physician.

5. During the American Revolution, some patriots were called Whigs, while loyalists were deemed Tories.

6. Several of her small children.

7. Eliza Townes married William Blassingame in 1818 and at the time of this letter already had six children.

8. An Irish melody, first published in 1813. Some of the lyrics go as follows: "'Tis the last Rose of Summer left blooming alone / All her lovely companions are faded and gone / No flow'r of her kindred, no rose-bud is nigh / To reflect back her blushes, or give sigh for sigh."

9. Maria may be a relative. Old Jerry is a slave, probably one of the thirty-odd slaves the Blassingames owned.

10. Apparently one of the women in the Calhoun family, at least three of whom were called Maria. The reasons for their falling out are not described.

11. In 1830 Henry Townes owned five slaves.

12. George McDuffie (1790–1851), a congressman in South Carolina, owned a plantation in Sumter County.

13. McDuffie was an outspoken supporter of Nullification and a bitter enemy of President Andrew Jackson. In 1834 he was elected governor, and he would later serve as a federal district judge and in the U.S. Senate. Lucretia Townes's youngest brother was named after him.

14. James Hamilton (1786–1857), governor of the state and an enthusiastic Nullifier. Hamilton left office at the end of December 1832 and became commander of the state's troops.

15. Rhetoric from the Revolutionary era, in which patriots called loyalists "Tories" and with considerable hyperbole declared that the British wanted to enslave them. Townes does not appear to believe that the federal government actually plans to enslave South Carolinians.

16. Probably Nancy Blassingame Sloan, Eliza's sister-in-law.

17. Winfield Scott (1786–1866), who had served with bravery in the War of 1812. President Jackson directed Scott to go to South Carolina to observe the situation, but Scott did not engage in any military action in the state.

18. Eliza's daughter Maria.

19. William Blassingame (1798–1841), Eliza's husband, was the former town sheriff.

Laura Cole to her cousin Camilla, 7 January 1833, from lowcountry South Carolina to somewhere in Georgia. Laura Cole Diary and Letterbook, Brumby and Smith Family Books, Southern Historical Collection, University of North Carolina.

Laura Cole was born in 1806 into a planter family living in coastal South Carolina. She supports Nullification and for the most part enjoys the novelty of discussing politics with men. Yet she fears the prospect of war and worries about her male relatives risking their lives.

I congratulate you, dear Camilla, on your brother's return home, although I was selfish enough to wish this happiness you feel in his society delayed a few months longer. I dare say, independently of the pleasure derived from a reunion with this dearest friend, he must feel a very sensible satisfaction in the exchange from this region of dullness to one of interesting festivity.[1] The Goddess of Mirth seems to have been frightened from this neighborhood for nearly two years; and I fear, the Genius of Superstition is usurping her place.

But these are spirit stirring times, and even the young, and the gay, feel no disposition to enter into mirthful scenes. We are now in a situation of powerful, all-absorbing excitement. The most inert dispositions, the most quiet families are roused into enthusiasm. Men, who a short time since, I verily thought would have been startled at the report of their own weapons, seem determined to risk life and fortune in the great struggle for civil rights in which we are likely to be involved. Even the ladies wear a brave air, whatever apprehensions they may feel, and we often, in private conversation, join the gentlemen in speaking of these deeply important affairs, with as much apparent calmness as if we were discoursing on subjects of minor consideration—In the event of war, my feelings must necessarily be deeply interested, but they become painfully so, when I reflect that my father[2] and five brothers are freely offering their lives in defense of our violated rights. I am surprised that the other southern states should be inactive in the present crisis. This is no bauble for which we are contending! It has become a question of liberty and slavery, and if they suffer Carolina to be crushed, where will be their boasted freedom? Liberty will be an empty sound, with which tyrants will mock their slaves, and this government a despotism as crooked in its maxims as Venetian policy itself.[3]

The state rights party strengthens me here, but our internal enemies are not yet entirely contemptible in number. We will probably have many volunteers from Virginia and Georgia, although those States have not declared themselves in our favor. The Virginians think they are disgraced by the measures of their state legislature,[4] and a Georgia paper says "Georgia is degraded by the conduct of her governor."[5] North Carolina has been aptly called the Rip Van Winkle of the south.[6] But I think even old "Rip" would rouse from her lethargies repose if she heard the roar of artillery from the shores of her sister state.

I must hope, cousin, that our affectionate wishes for my happiness may not prove unavailing though my present prospects are not very flattering. . . .

Tell cousin Alfred, Doctor Kill-pill is still besieging the fair Cornelia's heart. It is supposed that the fortress cannot resist much longer. But I am inclined to think this report a strategem of the besieger's to keep off other invaders; he thus gains time, and possibly his perseverance may obtain a capitulation. You perceive, I am becoming very familiar with military terms. You will be less surprised at this, when I tell you that our very drawing room is often devoted to military purpose. The war-like preparations which I daily witness cause many painful reflections; but I endeavor as far as possible to conceal, though I cannot subdue, the anxiety of my feelings, thinking it a duty we owe those with whom we associate, not to disturb their tranquillity by useless expressions of regret, or by yielding to fears which it is not in their power to dissipate. It is impossible to feel substantial satisfaction in our present situation, but it would be unprofitable to suffer the mind to sink into despondence. . . . your affectionate Laura.

1. Camilla and her family may be visiting Savannah.

2. Probably Richard Cole of Beaufort County, South Carolina.

3. A saying in the early nineteenth century, referring to the early modern Venetian republic, a naval power and mercantile center that had a reputation for crafty foreign policy.

4. The Virginia legislature sought a middle path by simultaneously opposing Nullification and President Jackson's policies.

5. The governor, Wilson Lumpkin (1783–1870), served from 1831 to 1835 and was a Unionist, although significant portions of the public seem to have supported Nullification.

6. A reference to the story by Washington Irving (1783–1859), *Rip Van Winkle: A Legend of the Catskill Mountains*. Set in colonial New York, the tale portrays a bumbling, well-meaning farmer who sleeps for twenty years and wakes up in the early nineteenth century.

Rebecca Anne Smith to her stepbrother John Jay Janney, 8 August 1833, from Kennett Square, Pennsylvania, to Springborough, Ohio. Janney Family Papers, MS 142, box 2, folder 1, Ohio Historical Society.

A Quaker from Loudoun County, Virginia, Rebecca Anne Smith has just begun teaching school in Pennsylvania. Here she playfully recounts her journey north-ward, including a visit to her aunt and cousins. She obviously enjoys the contro-versies over Nullification, although she makes the standard demurral for writing about it.

Good! Mine brother! —but do not take umbrage at the appellation. I have just received thy "yepistle" and hied me away to my dear little school room to reply to it while the spirit moves! is it right? be that as it may, I was truly gratified on the reception of thine but <u>indeed</u> it was so <u>querioulsy</u> folded that I fain had to tear it before I could come at the contents—I am glad to hear thee has arrived safely at the end of thy journey (if so be it)— Guess I was somewhat tickled at the description of Belmont the steamboat <u>Snorers!</u> Did thee ever see Paulding's description of those "creturs"—or has thee read much of Paulding's writings? if not I would advise thee when they spirits are a little dampened.[1] Just resort to them if they're to be had— and—if they don't banish the blues in little less than no time—take care of thyself—<u>Thy</u> journey was much more <u>tedious</u> than mine—maybe more pleasant too—but—I enjoyed myself quite enough. Only 'twas rather dull after the shades of night had settled <u>&</u> the cars so full of drab and brown <u>all</u> sitting with their heads adown waiting till the spirit moved 'em—We did not get started till half past three—I had to wait at Frederickstown an hour therefore we only got the halfway house just as the clock struck eleven— where supper was <u>waiting</u> for us—faith an' I was ready for mine—didn't get to Auntie's in Baltimore till half past two—found two of my lovely cousins there from Pa. who had not been awakened by my thundering knocks. So I very quietly ensconced myself in the same bed, and the way they were surprised & screeched & scrabbled for the first kiss wasn't a little curious.

Well! we had quite a goodly meeting of it—but it closed on fourth day— short and sweet—We staid two weeks in Baltimore visiting our friends re-ceiving visits &c &c—

We were at a party where there was a ventriloquist—The room was crowded to such an extremity that wherever a chair would sit there was a chair [2] — Guess we had a little sport — if 'twasn't that I have fear of thy patience being a little exhausted I would tell thee somewhat of his actions —

When our two weeks were up we sallied forth just at peep of dawn one beautiful seventh day morn to go on board what Paulding calls a "little sprinkle["] of the Steamboat [3] and glide rapidly up that beautiful bay the Chesapeake so <u>beautifully</u> described by some author — I don't recollect who — but thee has read it. Twas a glorious day I do assure thee, and we had a most glorious time <u>though lone females.</u> — We landed at Frenchtown about eleven where we got in one of the eight cars all connected together and standing in readiness for passengers — and crossed from Frenchtown to N-castle the distance of 16 miles in an hour and three minutes and that three minutes we stopped to take in passengers — Much swifter than horse power I think — I heard somebody speaking the other day of an accident I <u>may</u> call it that happened on the Germantown R. . . .

What do the <u>Sciones</u> say to the nullifying system? [4] There are more than a few in Pa. who will willingly take part with them. The turncoats are quite numerous since Jackson's proclamation! The "President's Message" was read as farce in the Baltimore theatre some time since! [5] Think it was pretty cutting — I forgot it was not for me to talk about these things — but really I take an interest in them. —

Its time I should look over and see what I have written for really I dont know the half I have rattled away at such a rate.

Well I have read it — I dont know what thee will think of it its just what come uppermost — I will leave it for thee to view and correct. Tell me of whatever thee thinks proper and will [re]ceived as a favour — Oh! I just wish thee had some of the many books I have been reading for thy perusal may be tho' the[e] has better — I cut my finger so badly that I had a sort of holiday for a couple of weeks — and during that time I read 3 of the "Waverly," <u>De Vire,</u> The Disowned — The Legendary [6] but enough I read what will have to last me for one while — "Where my friend did thee learn to say show"? Among the pretty Quaker girls of Belmont? I'm sure I didn't <u>tell</u> thee all as I have done — except some of the adventures I have had with the <u>beaux</u> &c &c — but next time I will tell thee <u>all.</u> I have already written enought to tire the patience of Job — Tell Mary Ives she that was to write — How could she expect me to write when I did not know how to direct a letter. [7] Give my love to them and tell I would give much to see them in their own happy homes — but think quite out of the question — here comes the end of my paper. its a good thing for I should say a somewhat more I reckon if there was more paper—I shall put this in the stage to-day to go to the next post-office for our post boy does not come again till next week and I am afraid if I leave it till then 'twill be consigned to the flames—Write soon a long letter to thy sincere friend and well-wisher—Anne.

1. James Kirke Paulding (1778–1860), an American writer and politician, had published fifteen books by 1833. Among his humorous works, *John Bull in America* (1825) and *The Lion of the West* (1830) are usually considered the funniest.

2. Probably meaning that every available space was filled.

3. Possibly a reference to one of Paulding's travel books or his "local color" books on the Hudson River Valley.

4. Meaning the sons, or scions, in the family. Her stepbrother later became a prominent antislavery Whig in Ohio.

5. Either Andrew Jackson's Anti-Nullification Proclamation of December 10, 1832 or his second inaugural speech of March 4, 1833.

6. Sir Walter Scott (1771–1832) wrote a series of twenty-six books known as the Waverly novels, named after the title of the first one, published in 1814. One was called *Legend of Montrose* (1819), but evidently none were entitled *De Vire* or *The Disowned*.

7. Meaning she did not know her address.

Eliza Turner Quitman to her husband, John Quitman, 14 February 1836, from Monmouth plantation, Mississippi, to Jackson, Mississippi. Quitman Family Papers, Southern Historical Collection, University of North Carolina.

Eliza Turner, the daughter of a judge in Mississippi, married John Quitman in 1824, when she was a teenager. Her husband served in the state senate and would be chosen acting governor of Mississippi in 1835 and governor in 1849; in the 1850s he would spend a term in the U. S. House of Representatives. The Quitman marriage had its share of tension. She ran their plantation during her husband's many absences, while he second-guessed many of her decisions. As this communication shows, she does not share his eagerness for public service.

My dear John,

I had the happiness to receive your letter by Major Petrie the day before yesterday. You still my dearest John complain of my neglect in writing to you. this is the third letter I have written you since I expected your return home. where they are, and have been, all this time I cannot say—I have never had, like you my dear, a private opportunity of sending you a single Letter [1]—Since my last letter to you, our dear little babe has had a violent attack of flu. She is now quite well again, except a little cough which makes her a little angry sometimes—Little Mookie has likewise suffered from a cold. she is quite playful again, and the rest of us are very well.[2] You must dear John believe exactly what I say in regard to the health of our children. You know me, I hope, too well to think that I would disguise or conceal their illness from you if they were indeed sick, but they are quite well—It is now nearly seven weeks since you left home. it seems to me like an age—I hope you may never again be tempted to become a candidate for any political office whatever. there is no honour to be gained by it, besides the great sacrifice of time, and everything else. I am sick and tired of being alone—I heard from Springfield today Neely wrote me his wife was very ill—he did not mention what was the matter. Peyton has recovered—My Mother also, has been very sick with this cold, and is still confined to her room.

Little William Griffith has the scarlet fever. —I heard that he had been quite ill, but was much better since. Mrs. Smith has lost her only son with it.

Dear John I hope your next letter may contain some inteligence of the adjournment of the Legislature shortly—You do not know how much I wish to see you, but I am [ever?] saying so, for I do hope that my dear husband, anxiety to see me is as great as mine is to see him—Do you think you could receive another letter from me? I do not think it worth while to write again—Adieu dearest John and believe me ever truly and affectionately your wife, Eliza Quitman.

1. Meaning that state legislators sometimes employed messengers who delivered mail for them.
2. Eliza Quitman had a child approximately every twenty-four months between 1824 and 1836, but only four survived to adulthood. The "babe" is Antonia, born in 1835, and "Mookie" is Sarah Elizabeth, born in 1834.

Louisa Bird Cunningham to her nephew Benjamin C. Yancey, 16 March 1836, from Waterloo, South Carolina, to Athens, Georgia. Benjamin Cudworth Yancey Papers, Southern Historical Collection, University of North Carolina.

Soon after she was born in the 1790s, Louisa Bird's family migrated from Virginia to South Carolina. There she grew up and married planter Robert Cunningham. She had long admired her ancestor George Washington, so it may be the president's example of disinterested public service that she wishes her nephew Benjamin Yancey to follow.

Dear Ben, . . . A portion of ambition is good—without it I do not believe any thing of much moment will ever be accomplished. it is the spur of life—and John,[1] I would like to possess more of a certain kind, such as you have, than he has—but Ben such as you have—if it is fed, will be the canker of the soul—it will be the bane of all happiness or peace of mind in this world—and may be, make a shipwreck of it in the world to come.[2] I speak somewhat from experience Ben—for what I have let destroy my own peace, I cannot but know and see in others, and wish and advise them to beware of the fatal enemy, as he gets his great grasp upon its prey.[3] I only will call to mind one individual, who has fallen beneath its fatal influence—John C. Calhoun.[4] Yes I view him as the most restless and miserable man in existence. His conduct shews it—all from unbound ambition. . . . your interest is near my heart as well as my children's. . . . yrs ever L. C.

1. Her son John Cunningham was in his twenties and studied law intermittently in the mid-1830s.

2. Benjamin Yancey is enrolled at Franklin College, later the University of Georgia. He went on to hold several public offices, but he became best known as a journalist in Alabama. His brother William Yancey (1820–63) later became an outspoken secessionist.

3. It is not clear to whom Cunningham is referring here. Her son John had not yet begun his political career, which was later undermined by his unsavory private life, not by excessive ambition. Her husband served for a few years in the South Carolina legislature but was devoted primarily to running his plantation. Two of her aunts married Supreme Court justices, however, and a number of her South Carolinian relatives were active in politics.

4. Calhoun (1782–1850) had a long career in national politics. In 1836 he was serving in the U.S. Senate. The families had once been on better terms. Robert Cunningham had read law with Calhoun years earlier, and Benjamin C. Yancey Sr. was his friend in the early part of the nineteenth century, when he practiced law in Abbeville, South Carolina.

*Marianne Gaillard to her brother John S. Palmer, 29 May 1846, from Claiborne,
Mississippi, to Pine-Ville, St. Stephen's Parish, South Carolina. Palmer Family
Papers, South Caroliniana Library, University of South Carolina.*

*Marianne Gaillard was a native South Carolinian whose family migrated to Mis-
sissippi in the late 1820s. In her early fifties at the time this letter was written,
she lived on a large plantation, and her adult children had settled nearby. Her
anxiety about the Mexican War is mixed with pity, bordering on contempt, for
Mexican soldiers. Although she approves of how President Polk is prosecuting the
war, she longs for peace and is not completely sure that the war is worth fighting.*

My dear Brother,

I would have written sooner and acknowledged the reception of your
letter and the likeness sent on by Mr. Gaillard—had I not been in great
tribulation, as to the result of the War movements[1]—I was never more
anxious to see Mr. Gaillard. Our Boys all wanted to go—And I thought
then that matters would soon have been brought to a close but it appears
that a heavy blow is meditated—it is generally believed that the President has acted wisely in raising a Sufficient number to bring the business
to a speedy close[2]—I fear the climate, more than the Mexicans, poor miserable, deluded wretches; they had to be forced to fight, one officer was
shot, he ordered his men to advance, he could not get them to move on he
commenced cutting and slashing with his Sword when he was shot down
by his own men—Genl. DiVega the Mexican Genl. who was made Prisoner & sent to N. Orleans was received & treated So courteously by Genl.
Gaines that he Says he means to make the United States his Home[3]—he
said if he had 50 Thousand men like those which captured him, & such as
he saw in New Orleans, he would not fear the World—Howard[4] was on
a visit to New Orleans and while there, it was discovered that the British
houses had been shipping Flour to the Mexicans, and in every Barrel there
was a Keg of Gunpowder there was a Schooner taken and these were found
in her among the papers of the Captured Genl. —they got some clue to
it. H[oward] says the populace was so excited that had they discovered the
names they would have been torn to pieces by the Mob—Genl. G. wisely
concealed the names to prevent any act of violence[.] it is not known what
he did with them—it is generally thought they are compelled to leave—

Tomorrow, I was told, that the Star Spangled Banner would be Raised
in our little Town—and there will be a call for Volunteers. Richeboury &

Saml.[5] say they are ready to respond to the Call—it is thought there will be no difficulty in raising a company—they say a draft must not be permitted in the county—I have lost pounds of flesh, since all this commotion, I knew that out of the number of Boys we had some would go—R. has given the whole business into Howard's hands. they have, they all say, the finest crop of both Cotton & Corn that has been planted since we have been here—

My dear Brother these exciting times does not suit me, I have become so nervous, that I don't believe I could have done with so little sleep— Mr. G. is as ready for the War as any of them—I believe if they would let him do as he pleas'd he would buckle on the Armour[6] I wish it was all over and peace once more restored—Oh! what a blessing Peace is, we have not been thankful enough for it. Betsey[7] was very ill last Saturday & Sunday she took a cold and it fell on her bowels—nothing but Strict attention, prompt treatment, & God's mercy brought her out—I was forcibly struck that there was no trouble but it might be worse—

Bet is much better and says you must present her thanks to her Aunt for the neat dress she sent the Baby—he is our Boy he is indeed a fine child, & is named T. Gaillard—my first exclamation on looking at your portrait was that you looked much older[8]—I forget that fourteen years had elapsed since we met—I think it is a good likeness, so does Richeboury—I shall prize it very much you could not have sent me anything that would have pleased me better—I wish you would bring yourself on—

how much pleasure it would afford me to pay you all one more visit— Richeboury says I must tell you they expect to make a first rate Crop— remember me affectionately [page stained] Simmons—& your family also to Marianne Sam & their [page stained] M L thank her & her Sister for the Quilts—they are not yet arrived but Suppose it will not be long—write soon & believe me ever Yr Affte. Sister M. G.

P.S. In confirmation of what Marianne has written touching the war excitement, I will add—that nothing prevents me from offering my services in some shape—but the pleasing task I have undertaken of writing a history of the Huguenots of So. Ca.[9] Could I procure an appointment in the writing department I believe I would, nothingstand the cause of my French Ancestors, volunteer, & proceed to Texas—I am not able to wield the sword, & I am a sorry Marksman—but I could occupy the place of one who might have physical strength to fight. I write this in serious soberness. T. G.

1. The Mexican War began in April 1846 and ended less than two years later with an easy American victory. The Treaty of Guadalupe Hidalgo, signed in February 1848, transferred huge territories from Mexico to the United States.

2. President James K. Polk, a Democrat who was elected in 1844. A slaveowner and staunch advocate of territorial expansion, Polk was eager to go to war with Mexico.

3. Don Romulo de la Vega, a colonel when the war began, did return to his troops and remained in Mexico when the conflict ended. Edmund P. Gaines (1777–1849), a professional soldier from Virginia, was in command of the western department of the U.S. Army when the War broke out.

4. One of her adult sons.

5. Two other sons.

6. Her husband, Thomas Gaillard, is in his sixties.

7. Her adult daughter, who has children of her own.

8. Her brother had recently mailed his daguerrotype to her.

9. Mr. Gaillard, a descendant of these French Protestants, had been working on the book for some time. His son Theodore Thomas Gaillard (1832–1903) evidently finished it for him. In 1887 he published *A Contribution to the History of the Huguenots of South Carolina, Consisting of Pamphlets.*

Ann Miller to her mother, Martha M. Miller, 12 April 1847, from Beargrass, Kentucky, to near Louisville, Kentucky. Miller-Thum Family Papers, The Filson Club Historical Society, Louisville, Kentucky.

Teenaged Ann Miller was attending boarding school when she penned this letter to her mother. She respects General Zachary Taylor more for his personal qualities, specifically his condolences to a grieving father, than for his military success in the Mexican War.

Ma Chere Mere,[1]

I have anxiously awaited the arrival of a letter from you, but I have not yet had that pleasure. I hope you will at least honor me with an answer to this when you get it. I wrote to Johnny yesterday, he was well the last time I heard from him as he had missed his chill a day or two before. I wish he could get well once more. How happy it would make us all if we could see you and Johnny well again. When did you hear from Sister Mary? I suppose Sister Maria's family are all well as I would have heard of it before now. We repeated our peaces of poetry last friday. It was done very well indeed as you might know as Mr. Thornton's school said it. There were a great many persons here. As it happened none of the girls fainted as it was prophesied by some. Four of the girls went home to spend their Easter holiday and they stayed to keep from saying their poetry. They did not come back until last Sabbath, but Mr. Thornton says he will fix them. The next lecture we have to write compositions. Mr. Thornton says they shall repeat their poetry and write compositions too. They are sorry now they did not come back.

We had so much after it was all over. We were honored with the presence of two of the handsomest gentlemen in the County of Jefferson. You can't guess who they were. I will tell you when I come home if you don't guess before. I went over to Aunt's saturday as I suppose Papa told you. We went up to hundly's church Sunday and Mr. Thornton preach[ed]. I was very much interested indeed. Tell Sister Louisa she must not forget to do what I told her. She must make haste and send it to me, and I will make her something so pretty. I left the memorandum in her silk dress pockatt Monday morning. Tell Papa please to have the Lady of the Manor[2] bound new for me, and I will be very much obliged to him. Mama do not make up my clothes or get my Bonnet until I come home. I want to get it myself. I am very much obliged to you for the dress you sent me. We are reading a very interesting and instructive history of England by Goodrich. It is his last literary production and worthy of his precious reputation, as a fine writer for the youth of our Country.[3] I think when he is called to a better world. the American's should rear a handsome monument over his remain's in gratitude for the useful manner in which he has devoted his fine talents, to the service of the rising generation. He may truly be termed the Children's Friend.

I suppose you have read a full account of the late tragic scenes in Mexico. Our success has been miraculous but so many hearts have been made to bleed; so many have been bereaved of the dearest objects of their affection, That we can scarcely rejoice. Have you read General Taylor's affecting and appropriate letter to the Hon. Henry Clay on the death of his gallant son? In my humble opinion it does him more credit than all his splendid victories over Santa Anna.[4] Oh Mama how much joy it would give me to hear that the war had ceased and we were victorious. I need not say any more about the war. I expect you know more about it than I do. Write to me soon. Give my Love to all the Pond Frog's. I remain your affectionate and obedient Daughter, Annie Miller.

1. French for "My Dear Mother."
2. Probably Martha M. Sherwood's advice book, *The Lady of the Manor, Being A*

Series of Conversations on the Subject of Confirmation (Philadelphia: B. Toward, J. & D. M. Hogan, 1831).

3. Charles A. Goodrich (1790–1862) wrote many books for young people on history and geography, including several published after 1847.

4. Taylor wrote to the Whig senator from Kentucky on March 1, 1847, to extend his sympathies at the death of Henry Clay Jr., who fell at the battle of Buena Vista in February. Antonio Lopez de Santa Anna (1794–1876) became president of Mexico in 1833 and led the fight against the United States in the Mexican War.

Sarah Potts to her aunt Ann Potts, 23 January 1849, from Pope County, Arkansas, to Bordentown, New Jersey. Potts Family Letters, Small Manuscript Collection, Arkansas History Commission.

Sarah's father migrated from New Jersey to Arkansas in the 1820s and there married Pamela Logan. In 1830 the couple's daughter was born, and she grew up in Arkansas. Sarah has recently returned from a year at a boarding school in New Jersey, where she did not feel entirely welcome. In fact, her letter shows a growing awareness of her regional identity. She is both proud of and defensive about her Southern roots and tries to justify slavery with a "paternalistic" argument. Her own stereotype of the cold, boorish Yankee emerges between the lines.

Dear Aunt,

As I have not written to you since I left Belle-Vue I will now scribble you a few lines that you may know I yet think of you though the distance between us is great. I should have written to you long ago but father wrote and I thought if I wrote too our letters would be much of a sameness and therefore would not prove interesting to you.[1]

In your letter to father you said you thought I ought to have written to cousin Jane.[2] I thought you were aware of the reasons of my silence. A few days before I left Belle-Vue some one (I do not now recollect who) asked me in cousin Jane's presence if I would write to her. I do not remember what reply I made but cousin Jane said if I would write to her she would get some one else to answer my letters. I said I would write to her if she would answer them herself. she said she did not have time. I thought nothing of this at the time but afterwards when I would think about writing to her I would always think of this and it occured to me that she did not wish to correspond with me or else thought my letters would not be interesting enough for her to devote a few minutes of her leisure time to writing an answer. I do not know whether Cousin Jane intended this for a hint for me not to write to her or not. I would not say not knowing but it seems perfectly natural that I should construe it in this way. What other construction could I put upon such a remark Knowing cousin Jane has correspondence and writes letters herself but perhaps she only writes to her most particular friends.

I received a letter from Mary Bergh a few days ago. I do not think she likes the situation at Flushing[3] as well as she did Belle-Vue. Indeed she said she did not. I am truly thankful that I am not there at school now. I was told before I left I would wish myself back again when I had been at home a few months but I have now been at home six months and I have never wished myself back yet. I loved my teachers and schoolmates all very much but I do not know whether I shall ever see any of them again or not. That would be a pleasure I could not even dare hope for at present. I have no desire to go north, nothing could induce me under any other circumstances than to see you and the rest of my relations and friends. I prefer the South the place of my nativity of which I think I might well be proud and in fact I am. I rejoice to think I was not born and brought up in the north. If I had been perhaps I would always have resided there, and never have known there was any better place but now I am very well satisfied here in and you would be too if you would come to Arkansas, or at least I think you would. The most of northern people object to the south on account of the slavery.[4] Why should they object to having black servants when they have white ones who are treated just as we treat our slaves. White people here are too independent to hire themselves as servants even the poorest could not be had.[5]

One evening since I came home when we had some company I was talking about Bordentown and told about people there taking pennies to Church to throw in the basket. They laug[h]ed very much at the idea of taking one cent to Church only and asked me if that was the way I did when I was there. I said yes and told them how the girls laughed at me the first sunday after I got to Belle-Vue when Mr. Gilder asked me if I had a penny and I said no I never had one in my life. I then told it was a common thing in Bordentown for people to take pennies to Church. I seldom saw anything else at the Methodist Church where I attended. People here are afraid of being laughed at if they throw in less than 25 cts. and coppers are not known here we have no such thing. I brough[t] some home with me last summer for a curiosity. The children think they are very large to be worth only one cent. I have no doubt but what you think this a very strange fact, but it is true. I could tell you of a great many strange circumstances but I will wait till you come to Arkansas and then you can see for yourself. If I tell you everything now you will have no curiosity in coming and besides I must save something new to tell you when you get here to keep you from thinking too much about Jersey.

Father is now very much in the notion of going to California but Ma is opposed to it and we are all trying to prevail on him not to go.[6] He is not at home to day he went to Dover this morning[7] and I have no doubt what he will return fully determined to go regardless of consequences. The road is long and difficult and the wild indian will kill them if they can as they pass through their territory.[8] But father does not seem to apprehend any danger of the Indians for there are a great many going from this and the adjoining states the most of whom will meet on our western frontier and organize in such large companies that the indians will be afraid to attack them. There are some from this State who are going to take their families but father says he cannot think of taking his until he has seen the Country and knows something more of it than mere newspaper reports. It will all be a wild goose chase I fear. Do you not think it will? Arkansas is a dear old spot, if it is backwoods (as cousin Maria said) and I think it a place good enough for any one to live and be contented without risking their lives in search of a better place which I do not believe can be found anywhere. If you could be here once and become acquainted with all of our good neighbours and see the Sociability Hospitality Charity Liberality Sympathy and independence that reign throughout our state all of which are emblematic of it, I do not think you would ever wish to leave it and go back to Jersey. Do you?

We experienced a considerable loss a few days ago in the death of one of our negroes a man who was not worth less than seven hundred dollars.[9] He was sick only a few days and had the best medical aid the Country affords all the time, but none of the medicine he took had any effect, and therefore he could not be saved. Everything was done for him that could be <u>done</u> but all to no effect. His death was occasioned by cold. We are all very well at this time except Mary[10] and she is able to be up all the time but she has something like a white swelling (you know) about a year ago which has never got well yet. I fear it will make a cripple of her.[10]

Aunt Lydia's family are well. I am going to see her as soon as Mary gets able to go with me (she has a very bad cold now). I wish you would come over and go with us. I know Aunt Lydia would be glad to see you.

This has been the worst winter I ever knew for the last three months it has been cloudy and raining almost all the time. It has not been cold but wet and very disagreeable. Since I began to write this letter it has cleared off so the sun is now shineing and we are all glad to see it for it has been twelve days since we even had the glimpse of it until to day. It is quite warm for I am writing in a room where there is no fire and I do not feel cold.

Please give my love to Mrs. Pearson Uncle Danny the Miss Thompsons and all of my Bordentown friends who have not forgotten me, and accept a large share for yourself. It is getting late and Ma and I are going out this evening so I must begin to think about coming to a close, but not without asking you to write me an answer. father says you do not seem to think it worth while to answer his letter which he has been expecting an answer to so long. I hope mine will not meet with the same <u>fate</u> if it does I will be dis- appointed for I think you will answer this letter as soon as you <u>receive it.</u> I would write you a long letter if I had more time but I guess these few lines will do for a beginning. <u>Be sure to write. I shall expect it.</u> Please not show this to anyone. I wrote it in haste. Your affectinate neice Sarah Potts <u>Esqr.</u>[11]

I wish I had time and room and I would tell you something about my t[r]avels coming home. I had a very nice time and if I had been in good health would have enjoyed myself very much. We laid By several days at different on the way. We stoped three days in Little Rock a great many of my friends and acquaintances called on me and I spent two evenings out. One at Governor Drew's and the other at ex-Governor Adams.[12]

Pa Ma and all the children send their love to you. they are all very anxious to see you to know if you look like Aunt Lydia. If father does not go to California which I do not think he will, He will go to New Orleans next winter and has promised to take me with him. I am very anxious to go there. I have always had a curiosity to see that City. If father goes to Cali- fornia he will start the first of April. Write so we can receive a letter before they leave. Good-bye.

1. Her father, Kirkbride Potts, died soon after this letter was written, leaving his wife a small farm and nine slaves.

2. Mrs. Ann Potts was in her late twenties and had four young children at home in 1850. Her husband, Daniel, a farmer in Hunterdon County, New Jersey, owned some three thousand dollars' worth of real estate.

3. A town in New York state near New York City.

4. Potts may be referring to the recent uproar over the Wilmot Proviso, which was introduced in the Congress in 1846. If it had become law, it would have barred slavery in any territory the United States acquired in the Mexican War (1846–48).

5. Many affluent whites in the antebellum North hired domestic servants, usually immigrants, who worked very hard for low wages. But even the most badly treated servant was nonetheless free, a crucial distinction that Potts chooses to ignore. Some whites did work as house servants in the South, although most affluent employers preferred free blacks, to whom they could pay lower wages, or slaves.

6. Mr. Potts may be considering joining the prospectors, or "forty-niners," who streamed into California after gold was discovered there in 1848.

7. A village nearby.

8. Many white Americans feared Indian attacks in the trans-Mississippi.

9. The high price suggests that this man was young and highly skilled. Slave prices rose in the late 1840s as the cotton market finally recovered from the Panic of 1837, and by the 1850s a slave man could be worth as much as a thousand dollars.

10. Her twelve-year-old sister Mary, one of her seven siblings. The nature of her illness is not clear.

11. For *esquire*, an honorific term for a man.

12. Thomas Stevenson Drew (1802–79), elected as a Democrat in 1844 and re-elected in 1848, resigned later in January 1849 because he was almost bankrupt. He ran unsuccessfully for the U.S. Congress in 1858, his last attempt at public office. Samuel Adams (1805–50), a wealthy planter and a Democrat, was president pro tempore of the Arkansas state senate when Governor Archibald Yell resigned in April 1844. Adams served as acting governor until November 1844, when he was elected state treasurer. He held that position until he retired from office in January 1850; he died a month later.

Mary Ann Lamar Cobb to her husband, Howell Cobb, 8 January 1850, from Athens, Georgia, to Washington, D.C. Howell Cobb Papers, Hargrett Rare Book and Manuscript Library, University of Georgia Libraries.

In 1835 teenaged Mary Ann Lamar married Howell Cobb, a law student who later became a congressman and cabinet secretary. She was the only child of a Georgia planter and inherited her father's vast holdings in land and slaves. One of her contemporaries, Mary Boykin Chesnut, said she was as mild as a violet, and most of her correspondence shows the wry, affectionate tone evident in the first paragraphs of this letter. That tone deserts her, however, when she discusses her husband's public career.

My dear Husband—

We have had unsuitable weather since Saturday. The first part of New years week was as beautiful as spring—Friday there was a change—Saturday was very cold—and Sunday morning began with a sleet which continued off and on thru' the day—thru' the night there was much rain—and yesterday we had rain in torrents with thunder—and a dark day—The boys[1] came home thru' the rain and did not return to school in the afternoon, as their boots were out of repair and the rain continued thru' the afternoon—They have the tooth ache so often by turns that I will not let them expose themselves to the wet. Their Rabbits pen was nearly a foot deep in water—and the poor little inmates were perched up on a dry point near the palings where the ground was shelving—They had to abandon their burroughs as that was floating—this morning the water has sunk more or less but still they have no dry footing yet they nibble very heartily at the Cottage leaves which John A.[2] has thrown to them—

After breakfast—As the ground is very wet, I had the buggy and Old Jim harnessed up for the boys to go in to school.[3] I prepared their dinner in a nice little tin bucket much to their delight—so they can take their dinner at school and not paddle thro' the wet so often—At breakfast they proposed to John to take a ride with them and they all three started off with the buggy with Tom walking behind—but Huck has just announced to me the unpleasing news that Jim had returned with the buggy as his Uncle John said the horse was too <u>stiff</u> to drive down town—Oh! have we not the luck of it—[4]

We have one broken down horse—one stiff horse—one colt nearly blind in one eye—our duck that Junius crippled our drake that got his feet mashed by a tread of one of Bro' Johns new horses—one Rheumatic negro—and another negro in Dr. Moore's hands—as I had to turn Aggy over to him almost in despair of her being well again—but the Dr. Says she will be very shortly—We've all then Seen enough of calamities for one small town lot.[5]

. . . I shall send this letter to the office and as there will be two mails due I have some right to hope for a letter from you particularly as none has come since Lamar's on Thursday last—You need not [give?] up the idea that I will let you off from writing as frequently as a man should whose wife is eight hundred miles distant, and her situation very precarious—Business or honour is all the same as you had none with me and since you occupy a position in which you are more than ever the <u>people's servant</u> my demands upon your attention will be more exacting in proportion—least you might forget in the press of business ever increasing for one from so lofty a station, that you have at home an humble little wife in an humble home.[6]

By the by I am getting our cottage home so comfortable that I shall feel little inclination to quit for a new home in Washington—tho' you are the housekeeper—My upstairs room is almost "unique" as Richard says. A warm looking <u>cotton</u> carpet ($13.12 ½) on the floor—Calico Bed & window curtains—My two sets of book shelves are filled and neatly arranged—also for the <u>denouement</u>—which Sophia <u>prognosticates</u> will take place at the next change of the moon on the 15th. If that is passed she thinks the next change on the 15 Feb. will bring matters to a crisis[7]—

Under these circumstances, I shall have to exercise a little patience do you not think so—? I have not all my arrangements quite ready—and would very cheerfully postpone the event till next month—Now as to my coming in as early as possible in the Spring—I give you fair warning that I will not stir hand or foot towards my journey north until I feel perfectly restored in strength of body and <u>mind.</u> I am now what I was when I commenced my winter journey in '44—my constitution has been shattered and now that it is patched up, I will take care that it gets no worse by forced journey—by your leave.[8] . . . Your affectionate wife Mary Ann Cobb.

1. The Cobbs had four surviving sons, John, Lamar, Howell, and Andrew.

2. The oldest son, John Addison.

3. Old Jim is a horse.

4. John, Tom, Huck, Jim, and Uncle John are slaves. The Cobbs had approximately ten house slaves.

5. The family home in Athens was actually a handsome new edifice constructed in the Greek Revival style.

6. Cobb, a moderate Democrat, had just been elected speaker of the House of Representatives. In 1851 he would be elected governor of Georgia; in 1853 he would return to the Congress; in 1856 he would serve in President James Buchanan's cabinet as secretary of treasury; in 1860 he would make an unsuccessful bid for the Democratic nomination for president. During the Civil War he served in the Confederate military and then died in the late 1860s.

7. It sounds as if Sophia is a slave.

8. Howell Cobb was first elected to the U.S. House of Representatives in 1842, so it is unclear why Mrs. Cobb refers to this particular journey. Nor is it clear why she was ill.

Hester Ann Wilkins Davis Diary. Allen Bowie Davis Papers, Manuscripts Division, MS 285, Maryland Historical Society Library.

Hester Davis, a forty-one-year-old planter's wife, lived in Montgomery County, Maryland. An ardent Christian, she waxes indignant about her cousin's absorption in his legal career and his violations of what she believes is a holy day of rest.

9 November 1851.

Cousin William Dorsey to dinner. Enroute to court. The Holy Sabbath profaned by conversation on politics which is at present the all absorbing topic of conversation. The Democrats have swept nearly the whole ticket at the recent election on the fifth for offices under the New Constitution.[1] [William Dorsey] Started in the afternoon for Rockville to be in time to attend to some business before court hour. No apology whatever. Surely the long suffering forbearance, the goodness of the Almighty, should lead men to repentance. . . .

1. In 1850, the state of Maryland revised its constitution, and Davis's husband, Allen, a Whig, attended the convention.

Susan Wylie to her sister Mary Wylie Mobley, [1851], from Lancaster District, South Carolina, to Chester District, South Carolina. Gaston, Strait, Wylie, and Baskin Families Papers, South Caroliniana Library, University of South Carolina.

The daughter of a judge and planter, Susan Wylie was twenty-five years old in 1850. Her male relatives had already divided over the secession movement, for her father Peter opposed it while her brother Richard supported it. In this letter to her sister, Wylie paints an acid portrait of a secessionist rally in upcountry South Carolina.

Mary,

We are tolerable except Hannah. She has continued sick since you left — not dangerous but very weak — when we sent for Wm. it was not altogether for Hannah. Teresa had been in labor the better part of the day & we were a little frightened & Sent for Wm. instead of Alexr. thinking Alexr. was sick as he had passed the evening previous from the meeting saying that he was taking the fever. I think Hannah will get along now. Teresa has the largest child she ever had—a boy. I attending the meeting. such a place great many. It undoubtedly was more like a corn husking than anything I can compare it to. in the morning Pressley was pushed forward to speak before the company had assembled & made quite a short speech. then beast Rhett[1] was cheered forward by things in shape of man. Such as G. Ragan & John Carrol & the bellowing of mules, & he went Illustrating the advantages of Secession & how we would roll in wealth & the most unheard of argument. His gaping gang gulphed it down and even applauded him for every puke anecdote he told. I don't think he spoke less than two hours & a half. they went so far as to have a flail[2] the beat the floor[,] the stand to applaud the villain. & in the afternoon Chesnut[3] spoke & made a very good calm argumentative Speech & used up <u>Mas</u> Rhett equally & as well as McEllery did at the village, but in a more smooth manner & was highly applauded but in a more genteel manner. Then came Adams[4] amidst the loud cheering of the horde & the greater part knew no more what they were making a noise about than the animals that brought them there. I could tell you [a] great deal but have neither time nor space. The wedding comes off tomorrow & I feel very sorry that Hannah cannot attend. . . .

1. Robert Barnwell Rhett (1800–76) attended a secession convention at Nashville in 1850 and came home to begin campaigning for disunion.

2. A wooden instrument used to harvest wheat.

3. James Chesnut Jr. (1815–85), a member of the South Carolina General Assembly and later a U.S. senator, perhaps best known today as Mary Boykin Chesnut's husband.

4. James Hopkins Adams (1812–61), a Whig member of the South Carolina senate, had supported the Nullification cause in the 1830s and began advocating disunion in 1851. He was elected governor in 1854.

Diary of Keziah Goodwyn Hopkins Brevard. South Caroliniana Library, University of South Carolina.

A childless and very rich widow, Keziah Brevard resided on a plantation in Richland County, South Carolina. Her husband, A. Joseph Brevard, had been committed to an insane asylum before he died in 1842, and she never remarried. Aged fifty-seven when she wrote this letter, she ran her plantation without an overseer. She was deeply, somewhat morbidly, religious and tried to be a "paternalistic" slaveowner. In this diary entry of October 24, 1860, she seems to conclude that believing Christians could have ended the slave trade, made slaves contented, or, perhaps, ended slavery altogether. The last weeks of the presidential campaign, in which Democrats Stephen Douglas and John C. Breckinridge both defended slavery, may have inspired these thoughts.

Wednesday 24th [1860]. This is another beautiful morn—every thing to invite man to purity—but I fear there are very few who think for themselves in these exciting times—God does punish his people for sinning against his commands—& have we not as a people made riches our God—I feel it is ever a sin with me—& I know I do not dwell on these things as I have known others to do—"Judge not lest ye be judged" I add here—for I know my trespasses are mountain high, but I do try to avoid commiting those sins God plainly forbids—anger & unpleasant thoughts often rise in this breast of mine—but all that is filthy I immediately call on God to help me put down—I do hate mean thoughts as well as bad acts—<u>I abhor sins of low degree.</u> Lord God—Almighty!! Save this our <u>dear—dear country</u> & pity thy poor unworthy servants—they know not how good thou has been to them—& those Northern cut throats—Oh Change their wicked hearts—they know no God or they never could have the feelings they have towards us—I must now stop or give way to feelings I should not—how can a southerner love those whose highest glory would be to know we were exterminated to give place to a people far inferior—I wish every vessel that would go to Africa to bring slaves here could sink before they reached her soil.[1] I would give up every [word missing; slave?] I own on earth if it could stop the slave trade.[2] My reason is this—we have a hard time with them & I feel for those who are to come after us. We never would have been unhappy with slaves if white people had been true to their white brethren & our negroes would have been happy if all & every one had made the religion of Christ their <u>North Star,</u> but religion is in show—Vanity & show <u>Man's God.</u> I too have [added?] a shade to the sins that beset us—Lord help me?

1. The international slave trade to the United States officially ended in 1808, but smuggling continued right up to the eve of the Civil War.
2. In 1860 she owned more than two hundred slaves.

Fanny Cox Broderick to her sister Mary Cox Collins, 14 January 1861, from Maysville, Kentucky, to somewhere in Kentucky. Collins Family Letters, Division of Special Collections and Archives, Margaret I. King Library, University of Kentucky at Lexington.

Fanny Broderick, the wife of an insurance salesman, was in her late thirties on the eve of the Civil War. She supplemented the couple's income by working occasionally as a dressmaker, and neither she nor her husband owned any slaves. Regarding the "all engrossing subject" of secession, she appears to be neutral. Her letter highlights the paralysis many women felt during the secession winter; she waits and prays and attends camp meetings, hoping for the best.

My Dear Sister,

As Lizzie has not written for some days (at my request) I thought I might venture to write a few lines without giving you news already told which is always insipid, but the past week has been dull and unfavourable for news gathering. Mr. Broderick says it has been the most disagreeable of the last fifty two, so that we have had to make great effort even to get to prayer meeting, you know Mr. B. thinks me a pattern of perseverance in this respect and yet I should have had to be absent from two of the meetings but Lizzie would generally start in the afternoon take tea with some friends up town, so that she got to all of them.

The meetings were attended as our usual prayer meetings are.[1] Mr. Crow assisted at some of the meetings and gave us some very interesting talks on the all engrossing subject, the condition of our country at this time. There were very few gentlemen attended the meetings. Many were prevented by business, and others are so much excited on political subjects that they have to be in readiness for the boat that they may get the papers immediately the boat reaches the landing.[2]

Phebe came home on Saturday, we had not expected her as she intended staying three weeks but she got a little home-sick I expect and it is so little trouble for her to get home that Lottie Rodgers and herself concluded to give us a surprise, she brought home some drawings she had finished and she expected to get paints &c so that she could commence painting this week, but we cant get the materials she will need here and she will Sketch in crayon until I can get what she needs in Cincinnati; I expect now to be with you next Thursday night two weeks. Ed sent me word that he wanted me to come down about that time and I could not get ready much sooner. Mr. B. will go down to night and wished me to go with him but I could not get ready and I prefer waiting until the last of this month.

I suppose you have heard of the death of Mrs. McClung. what a loss this will be to Sue & Nan! Mrs. McClung's brother sent her recently about $1200 and I heard he intended buying her a home in St. Paul. I hope he will show as liberal a disposition toward her daughters as I hear he is wealthy. Mrs. Whiteman Wood [rest of line missing]

I have no doubt her remains will be brought here. they should be, as she said before she left here that she had but one request to make of her friends and that was she might be buried by the side of her husband.

I am going to give you some work when I come down. I want to make some shirt bosoms and it will save me much time to have them done on the "machine"[3] so don't be planning too much visiting for the last time I was with you it was go, go, from morning till night and you know I am making my visit to see you all and not to be visiting all the time.

I expect to go to the country for a [page torn] days the latter part of this wk so I shall not write again. Mother was well when I heard from her a few days since. Mr. Blattermann is expected home the last of this week. All are well at Mr. Collins's and at Ellens. My love to all Yours. affect. Fanny.

1. Meaning that most of those present were women.
2. The landing nearby on the Ohio River.
3. The sewing machine, which was marketed nationwide in the 1850s.

Susan H. S. Fishback to her niece Susan P. S. Grigsby, 8 July 1861, from Lexington, Kentucky, to somewhere in Kentucky. Grigsby Collection, The Filson Club Historical Society, Louisville, Kentucky.

The redoubtable Susan Fishback, born in 1791, outlived four husbands. In 1861 she was married to a Baptist minister who owned several slaves. Her niece Susan Grigsby was in her early thirties and a stepdaughter of Robert J. Breckinridge from the powerful Kentucky clan. Susan Fishback's remarks about Beriah Magoffin, John C. Breckinridge (Robert J.'s nephew), John Letcher, and others indicate a withering contempt for politicians and their handiwork as the Union shattered.

My dear Susan,

   . . . Poor Ann Magoffin has been up a week, very much depressed and heartbroken for the loss of her dear little boy.[1] He was indeed a lovely boy. I don't know that I ever felt a stronger attachment for any child than I did for him. There was something very engaging, and attractive about him. A most affectionate warmhearted child. Poor Ann, if she ever sees the threats that are constantly made against her husband, it would be enough to crush her. I think it makes her very unhappy. Ann was formed for domestic life, and is not calculated for the wife of a politician, does not enter into any of his schemes of ambition. I am afraid he will ruin himself. It is impossible he can carry the State with him.[2] Beriah complained to me of the way he was treated. I told him he laid himself liable to be suspected of treason. The people did not want to leave the Union, and I thought he did wrong to send to the South for arms, instead of the Federal Government, that it was committing the State to the South, when they did not want to join the South. I wish he had other advisers than John Breckinridge & Tom Monroe.[3] Neither of them have anything to lose. Beriah has, and I am truly sorry for him, for he is kind and would do right under other influences. I told him candidly that we did not agree, that we differed fundamentally. . . .

   Kate got a letter from her Mother a short time since, telling her that she could not spare her any longer, that her two oldest Sons had started to Boonville at the call of the Governor, and she was in such distress about it that she wanted her at home. The idea of any one running after that miserable, cowardly Governor. . . .[4]

   O how I should love to be with you all in that sweet, cool gallery, for at least a month, calling about, and listening to the dear children's voices, and doing nothing but what was pleasant & agreeable. Until then, give my love to Mr. Grigsby and all the dear little children and believe me dear Susan your affecnt. Aunt S. H. S. Fishback.

   1. Ann Nelson Shelby married Beriah Magoffin in 1840, when she was twenty-two, and the couple had eleven children. She was Susan Fishback's first cousin.
   2. Beriah Magoffin (1815–85) had been governor of Kentucky since 1859. A Democrat, he supported the Crittenden Compromise and then refused to supply state troops for either the Union or Confederate armies. In May 1861, the state declared its neutrality, but in the summer of 1861 Magoffin was beginning to favor the Confederacy. In September he vetoed a resolution by the state legislature ordering Confederate troops out of the state. Magoffin was forced to resign in 1862.
   3. John C. Breckinridge (1821–75) ran for president in 1860 on the Southern Demo-

cratic ticket. On July 4, 1861, he gave a speech in the U.S. Senate attacking Lincoln's war policy and later that year joined the Confederate army. Thomas Bell Monroe (1791–1865) was a distinguished jurist and well-known Democrat. He advocated Kentucky's secession and later served in the Confederate Congress; his son became a general in the Confederate army. Breckinridge was not on good terms with his uncle's stepchildren, which may explain why Fishback criticizes him with such starch.

4. John Letcher (1813–84), who was elected Democratic governor of Virginia in 1859. He opposed secession until the firing at Fort Sumter in 1861 and then became an ardent Confederate.

SECESSION

AFTER THE PRESIDENTIAL ELEC-
tion of 1860, political events in the South moved swiftly, and women's fears
accelerated accordingly. Over the course of the winter of 1860–61, most of
the women in this chapter interpreted the national crisis in terms of their
Christian faith. Class affiliation, even slave ownership, did not necessarily
predict whether a woman supported secession. Most women excoriated
disunion as a reckless, sinful measure, and most of them had a realistic
understanding of the consequences: secession meant war, and war would
be terrible. Why did these women fail to act on their private doubts during
this crucial hour?

Over the course of the secession winter, public events gradually dis-
rupted the rhythms of private life. Unlike previous crises in national affairs,
this one rent the country in two and threatened to reach into every Southern household. Women had to make some hard choices about their ultimate
loyalties, and most of them choose flesh and blood over the Union. By
the summer of 1861, some were becoming the Confederate nationalists of
legend. Why does this "conversion experience" take so long? Why do some
women never convert to the new cause?

Mary E. Starnes to her friend Sarah J. Thompson, 28 July 1860, from Spring-
field, Limestone County, Texas, to Augusta, Georgia. William H. Kilpatrick Let-
ters, from the Collections of the Dallas Historical Society.

Mary Starnes's views have been transformed since 1845, when she described slaves
as an oppressed people. Fearful to the point of paranoia, she now believes that
abolitionists, slaves, and white "rascals" may attack her family. In 1860, her
brother William, with whom she lived, owned thirty-one bondsmen.

Dear Sallie,

Your letter for this month has not made its appearance yet & the month
is nearly out, but I have no right to complain for you will see by the date of
this that I am a long ways behind the time. I have been very busy this month
helping Ella make up her clothes before she leaves for school.[1] Brother has
concluded to send her to Waco, a town about a days travel from home, the
Methodist denomination have established a female college there. it has the
reputation of being a good school & several Girls from this neighborhood
have been going there. they are home at present spending their vacation.
Ella has become acquainted with them & is very much pleased with them
& delighted with the idea of having them for schoolmates.

I have no good news to tell you only that we had one delightful rain last
month on the 26th. we were very thankful for it, but we need another now
almost as badly as we did that. the rivers and streams are drying up & the
people have to drive their stock a long ways to get water, but as long as we
can live in peace & safety we should be thankful, for there are others who
are suffering not only from the drought but from the acts of wicked men
who seem determined to bring ruin upon us, & the whole South if they
possibly can.

In some of our northern counties the abolitionists have been tampering
with the negroes & caused a great deal of mischief to be done. a few weeks
since, Dallas, a considerable town, was burnt to the ground.[2] only one
house, a drug store, was left in the place. I understand that some wealthy
persons have been reduced to poverty, as very few had any insurance on
their property. Report says about a hundred negroes have been implicated,
the last accounts they had hanged 2 white men & 10 negroes. What trouble
those white rascals are bringing upon the poor negro, if they had half the
sympathy for them that we of the South have, surely they would not seek
their destruction. An attempt was made to fire two other places the same
day but without success. a store & perhaps a house or two was burned.

Ella received a letter from Isabel a few days since, all were well. I was in hopes Sister had got through with her trouble as she was on the look out the last of June,[3] & Beth's letter was dated the 16th of July, but I presume she was still on her feet as nothing was said about a new arrival.

From what I can learn they have suffered more than the drought in Harrison than we have. I wish you would send me some of your fruit. I have not seen a peach this year & don't expect to (only some in cans that were put up last year). Let me know how your fair came out. I am pleased to hear the Church & sabbath school is in such a thriving condition. I wish we had a Mr. Derby out there. Mollie.

My love to all. If Ella was at home she send must love to all. How is Amanda Smith? I have not forgotten the rest of the family. tell Ma—I am silent about them because my paper is out.

    1. Her teenaged niece, William Starnes's daughter from his first marriage.
    2. In the summer of 1860, rumors swept through Texas that abolitionists or slaves had started fires in Dallas. Newspapers throughout the South carried the story.
    3. Her sister Sarah Starnes Graves was expecting a child in late June.

Mary E. Starnes to her friend Sarah J. Thompson, 20 September 1860, from Springfield, Limestone County, Texas, to Augusta, Georgia. William H. Kilpatrick Letters, from the Collections of the Dallas Historical Society.

Mary Starnes's fears escalate in the last weeks of the presidential campaign of 1860, as she calls for spying on and opening the mail of suspect Northerners. Her comments underscore the irrational dimension of the secession movement, especially the fierce hostility toward outsiders and the increasing demand for conformity within the white population.

My Dear Sallie,

When this month came in I had no idea so much of it would pass, before I could make it convenient to write, but so it is, and as you have not been very punctual yourself of late, I can ask with a good grace to be excused.

I have the pleasure at last of informing you that we are in our new house. it is not finished yet, but we have three good rooms and a wide passage we can occupy, more room than we have had in a long time; when finished the house will have six good rooms, four fire places, and a piazza in front—The situation is a very pretty one, for some distance round us the land is level and perfectly green with grass, in the yard and all around the place are a great many forest trees. the only shade we have is from natural growth. The house dont present a very fine appearance outside, as it is made of logs, but I assure you we find it very comfortable inside—it is uncertain whether we will get it finished this winter or not, as Brother has more negro cabins to build before cold weather, and we must provide for their comfort as well as our own. he has done nearly all the buildings, and improvements about the farm with his own force, and as his crop is very short this year, he is unwilling to hire workmen to finish the house when he can do it with his own hands by waiting awhile, and save a great deal of expense, for white men work slow and charge high for their labor in this country.

Our camp meeting will commence the last of next week. it was thought for a while they would not have one, on account of the general excitement in our State, but as every thing seems quiet in our county and the vigilance committee, and patrols have not detected anything wrong among the dark-eys, they have concluded to hold one. —

It is true we have some suspicious characters among us, but they are watched and I presume will attempt nothing while the people are on the alert—A few weeks since the Committee arrested a fellow that hailed from Vermont, and brought him to Springfield for trial, but did not get suffi-cient proof against him to do anything with him. they let him go, and told him he might stay here, but if any thing occurred they would hold him re-sponsible. he acted wisely and left, or at least he was gone the last I heard of him. he may come back, as he has been in the habit of making trips off and returning—

We believe him to be the abolition agent sent out for this county, but somehow our committee got wind of him before he got fairly to work, and I presume frustrated his arrangements very much, that is, if he really is the character we believe him to be; I think the Committee should have kept quiet a while longer, given him a little more rope, intercepted his corre-spondence and watched him closely without letting him know they were at all suspicious of him. as it is, it is not probable he will attempt any thing here, but he may go to another county where he is not known and do mis-chief.

Ella is very well pleased with her school. we hear from her often, as she is only one days travel from home. When I heard from Sister's last, all was well but Tom he was suffering with his old disease (the piles) again. The crops in Harrison are very short. they had less rain there than we had here. I understand there was not corn enought made in the County to bread them until Christmas—

I am very anxious to pay Sister a visit, but dont know how I will manage to get there. Let me know how Martha Stack is. My love to Ma, Libby, Dean, Bud and my little Mary. Let me know who has Sarah Crump's child. Your loving friend, Mollie.

Margaret Trimble McCue to her brother-in-law John A. McCue, 11 September 1860, from Mount Solon, Virginia, to somewhere in Virginia. John Allen Trimble and the Trimble Family Papers, MS 249, box 2, folder 2, Ohio Historical Society.

Margaret McCue, who hated slavery in 1820, not unexpectedly opposes disunion forty years later. Like many other Southern women, she uses the family metaphor to describe her alarm about national affairs. She also reveals a lingering distrust for politics itself, which her daughter shares.

Dear Brother,

I have treated you so badly that I cannot make any apology. Your kind and affectionate letter was received in Culpepper, and I should have answered it immediately.[1] could I have given that kind of assurance of my deep Sympathy which your Situation & Sorrows has made me feel, So anxious have I been to know in what way or what I [could] do to relieve you. Oh how I wish you were near to me in many things & in many ways. I could Sympthasise & comfort you my Dear Brother & Sister but this cannot be. If I had If I had the means in my power that my Brother how Could I withold. Could I witness his privations in so many ways who is bone of our bone & has so many claims and was the Benjamin of our onc[e] happy family. O me thinks would our Dead Departed Mother witness the coldness and distance manifested toward each other if there could be Such a thing as Sorrow in heaven is it not enough to caus[e] Angles to weep over our inSensitivity & want of affection for each other in this Cristian land of Bibles & Churches. Has our family relations & Kindred degenerated with our country & society at large.[2] is there no ties to bind us together as family, moraly & politically? Oh we have reason to mourn in deep humility for our Self and friends &

our country. And cry to <u>God</u> that he would Save us from destruction as a nation. he alone can divert the evils of <u>disunion</u> and place Such men at the head of affairs that will be honest & true to their country, that can be trusted! All our trust is in overruling providence which does all things well!

We are all well as a family. Thare is Some cases of fever in the vicinity. Dr. L is quite Sick with typhoid fever Some Sore throat. I fear we are to have a Sickly fall after Such a dry hot Summer. there has been much hard rain lately Some freshets & Some losses Sustained. Marshall[3] has been very little at home Since last winter & now talks of going to Europe what will be the result God only knows!

And were it not I and am assured he may have it in his power to do Something for you & Sister, I could not consent to his going. And what would you think of Jack going with him. It might be the means of the restoration of his health — intirely. he would like to go very much — yet I have not Said any thing to him 'Cous[in]' Marshall yet. Dear little fellow I do not know how I could do without him. he is all my dependence & all my company.[4] Marshall has lost all relish for home & matters in the farm were it not for Jack I do not know what I would do. We are puting up a kitchen at this time w. Gravel & Mortar.

My cares are great for one of my age & I Should like to Spend the balance of my days in more quiet yet I would not murmur at my lot but try to do my duty in the best maner I can[.] we have many mercies for which we are not thankfull. Mr. & Mrs. Peck are great comfort to me. She is on a visit to her friends in the mountains and will remain some weeks. when I go she stayes and keeps house for me & does it so well. My visit to Elisa W. was in harvest the we[a]ther was hot & dry. Elisa is not Satisfied over there & she has reasons for it. there is no church of her choice. nor convenient [s]chool for her children. Not the right kind of Society & I fear she may become gloomy unless there is a change in her Situation. I wish you would write to <u>her.</u> I Showed her your letter she seem'd to feel very much in your affliction.

She was very fond of Dear Ella & Was shocked to hear of her death. She has only two children and is very much devoted to them. her adopted daughter is quite grown & is great company to her. D. is taken up with Politics, which is not pleasent to Elisa or profitable to himself.[5]

Our friends are all well. Lizzie Vardear is on a visit to the mountains at this time. what has become of Anna Barry[6] tell her I think She has forgotten her Virginia friends since Cou[sin] is married. tell her she would like Nannie very much. tell her Maggie Harris talks a great deal about her. Says she must come to Virginia again.

I do hope my Dear Brother you will Soon get a Situation which will be profitable. If you are elected to an office of profit, it would reconcile me to your voting for Douglas.[7] I hope my friends will stand up to the Whig cause to a man, not one to be found wanting.[8]

Tell Cousin Jennie I would be delighted to See her and Brother James this fall. I think the old gentleman could stand the trip quite well. I was disappointed in not seing Brother Allen in Virginia untill I heard he did not [try?] to see Cam. I suppose C. was very much distressed in the death of their little Son being absent So long from him. How is Cousin Elisa Sampson. I should like to to be there to Symphasise with you.

'Cous[in]' Elise Lidy has been berieved of her little Jewell. he was sertainly a bright & sweet little child yet of Such is the Kingdom of heaven. You must excuse this as a family letter as I write So few letters I want my friends to know none are forgotten at the throne of Grace—may they all remember me who have an interest there. Give my love to all my Dear friends. Kiss dear little Alice for Jack & I. and Roddy too Dear little fellow. Kiss Dear Lavenia[9] for Jack & I also and Kiss each other. not forgetting, Your affectionate Sister, M. T. McCue.

1. A county in northern Virginia where some of the McCue relatives lived.
2. When McCue's husband quarreled with John McCue over a business deal in the 1850s, the two families stopped writing to each other.
3. One of her adult sons.
4. Her husband died in the 1850s, and she lived with her son.
5. David Gatewood, who lives in Virginia, is married to her daughter Eliza.
6. A sister-in-law.
7. Stephen A. Douglas (1818–61), who ran for president on the Northern Democratic ticket after a distinguished career in the Senate. In 1860 he won one and a half states (Missouri and part of New Jersey). John McCue is in financial difficulty and needs a job.
8. The Whig party disintegrated in the mid-1850s after the Kansas-Nebraska Act became law, but McCue still supports it. John Bell of Tennessee, a former Whig and a Unionist, was one of the four presidential candidates in 1860, and the state of Virginia went for him in the November election.
9. Her sister-in-law Lavenia Trimble and her two children, Alice and Rodney.

Diary of Keziah Goodwyn Hopkins Brevard. South Caroliniana Library, University of South Carolina.

Keziah Brevard was widowed in the 1840s after a short marriage, and she lived alone on her South Carolina plantation for most of the next two decades. Perhaps because of her solitude, perhaps because her temperament has soured, her fears accelerated during the secession winter more rapidly than those of most other white women. In November 1860 she is already terrified of emancipation, while she simultaneously envies and resents the North.

Friday Morning the 9th [1860]. Oh my God!!! This morning heard that Lincoln was elected—I had prayed that God would thwart his election in some way & I prayed for <u>my Country</u>—Lord we [know?] not what is to be the result of this—but I do pray if there is to be a crisis that we all [word missing; lay?] down our lives sooner than free our slaves in our midst—No soul on this earth is more willing for justice than I am but the idea of being mixed up with free blacks is <u>horrid!!</u> I must trust in God that he will not forget us as unworthy as we are—Lord save us —<u>I would give my life to save my Country.</u> I have never been opposed to giveing up slavery if we could send them out of our Country—I have often wished I had been born in just such a country—with all our religious privileges & liberties with none of them in our midst—if the North had let us alone—the Master & the servant were happy with our advatages—but we had had vile wretches ever making the restless worse[1] than they would have been & from my experience my own negroes are as happy as I am— happier[2]—I never am cross to my servants without cause & they give me impudence, if I find the least fault, this is of the women the men are not half as impudent as the women are. I have left a serious & what has been an <u>all absorbing</u> theme to a common one—but the die is cast—"Caesar has past the Rubicon."[3] We now have to act, God be with us is my prayer & let us all be willing to die rather than free our slaves in their present uncivilized state.

1. Brevard seems to believe that some slaves deliberately stirred up discontent among other bondsmen.

2. She was actually not very happy. In other entries she regrets that she did not have children, laments her bad education, and wishes she had more friends.

3. In 49 B.C. Julius Caesar defied an order from the Roman senate and crossed this small river in central Italy, thus precipitating a civil war.

Diary of Lucy Muse Walton Fletcher. Special Collections Library, Duke University.

In the fall of 1860 the Fletchers moved to Richmond, Virginia, where Lucy's hus-
band took a pastorate at Duval Presbyterian Church. During the winter, Lucy
Fletcher began to retreat from her initial condemnation of secession. By the eve of
the Battle of First Bull Run, which took place on July 21, 1861, she has become
an enthusiastic Confederate. Yet she realizes that the war might involve a long,
cruel struggle.

25 December 1860. Richmond. We went to housekeeping in the fall—have
quite a comfortable double brick house on Third Street—but the times are
so unsettled that we do not feel justified in going to much expense. Our
people have shown very commendable energy in going to work to raise
Subscriptions for building a new church in a different locality (which my
husband felt was indispensable to success) but the excitement now rag-
ing all over the country is not favorable to church progress & the prospect seems dark indeed. The election of a <u>sectional</u> President, Lincoln, in
November seems to have exasperated the South & there is no telling what
will be the result. O South Carolina was off on a tangent & boldly seceded
on the 20th & I doubt not others will follow—I think a terrible responsibility rests upon those fanatics who have so long been stirring up strife in
our church[1] & those politicians who have availed themselves of such strife
for party purposes—If as seems probable now, this once glorious Union
should be dissolved, on them will rest the blame. May God in mercy save
our country from the evils which threaten her!

20 July 1861. The Confederate Congress meets today in Richmond! On the
15th April Lincoln issued a proclamation requiring all the States to furnish
a quota of men for the subjugation of the seceding states. This, of course,
left us no choice—We can have no faith in a Union that must be enforced
at the point of the bayonet, and will not in any event turn our arms against
our Southern brethren. On the 17th Virginia seceded. I cannot describe my
feelings when for the first time I saw the Flag of our <u>State</u> waving from the
Capitol which was the signal of Secession & realized that the old Flag of
our Union, in which we had so long gloried, would be to us, henceforward,
only a symbol of tyranny & oppression. The perfidy by which the Yankees
<u>forced</u> us to fire the first shot at Fort Sumter was in keeping with Seward's
treacherous policy.[2] War—<u>civil</u> war, the most cruel of all wars is now in-

evitable & our noble old State will have to bear the brunt—We know that our soil must be drenched with the blood of our bravest & best—but we have no alternative. The Northern people boast that they will make short work with the Rebels—in "ninety days the Rebellion will be extinguished."

1. The Presbyterian church was riven with sectional tensions in the late 1850s, and in the spring of 1861 Southerners organized a separate denomination; it was not until the 1980s that the churches reunited. In 1860, Fletcher seems to blame individuals in both regions for the division.

2. William Seward, the secretary of state in the Lincoln administration. It was actually the president, not Seward, who made the key policy decisions, but Fletcher is correct in that Lincoln manuevered the South into firing the first shot.

Mary E. Starnes to her friend Sarah J. Thompson, 1 January 1861, from Spring-field, Limestone County, Texas, to Augusta, Georgia. William H. Kilpatrick Letters, from the Collections of the Dallas Historical Society.

By New Year's Day 1861, Republican Abraham Lincoln was president-elect of the United States, and South Carolina had seceded from the Union, with other states soon to follow. For Mary Starnes, the political crisis has stirred profound sexual and racial fears. Now a thirty-year-old spinster, she convinces herself that abolitionists are persuading Indians to rape white women. There is no evidence for such a conspiracy, of course, but Starnes is prepared to believe the worst.

Dear Sallie,

Another Christmas with its amusements is numbered with the past, and we are as far apart as ever. The hope that we will ever meet again in this life is a very faint one, but I trust there will be a happy reunion in heaven where parting will be no more.

We spent Christmas day at home and a sad, sad one it was to me, if I could only be with Sister or some dear friend I think I would not feel quite so miserable. I have nothing of interest to write about, but as it is the first day of the month and the year I thought I would commence a letter to you if I did not finish it. I have been busy sewing all day, until a few minutes ago and as the sun was not down I thought I would improve the time by writing at least a few lines. Your letter for last month has been received.

I hope you will send the papers you spoke of. I would like to see them very much. I have read three letters from Judge Longstreet, published in the Field and Fireside.[1] it is not necessary to say I was pleased with them, for I have never seen anything from his pen that I was not pleased with. I hoped to see something more from him, but as South Carolina has already accomplished secession and the whole South seems to be moving that way, I presume he will have nothing more to say. Our Governor at first refused to convene the legislature but has yielded to the wish of the people at last, and it is well he did so, for they were determined to act in spite of him.[2]

Texas has suffered very much during the past year, both from the abolitionists and Indians,[3] the last Indian outbreaks occurred a few weeks since, and from the treatment the females received who was so unfortunate as to fall into their hands, it is supposed there must have been white men among them. Indians are known to be very cruel, but generally they take the women off or kill them at once. as far as I can learn they have never been known to violate their persons until this year—

One poor woman, a married lady, was treated awfully. After violating her person, they scalped & left her on the prairie, when found by her friends the poor creature had crawled through the rain to a hole of water. she lived long enough to tell her friends how she had been treated, gave birth to a child and died—

Two girls was found by some Gentlemen. they had been shamefully treated, stripped perfectly naked and left in their plight. The people on the frontier have sent round begging for help, and it has not been in vain. some have gone to their assistance and whipped off the Indians and relieved the people that were forted up. some young men from our town left last week for the frontier. I hope they will give the Indians and white demons among them such a drubbing that they will never dare to venture back again.

When I heard from Sister last all was well. Where is Libby and what is she doing? I would like very much to hear from her. Give my love to your good Mother, Dear, and all the children, Mrs. McMurphy, Stack, McCoy, and all my friends.

May God bless, protect, and save you all in Heaven is the prayer of your friend Mollie.

1. Augustus Baldwin Longstreet (1790–1870), a well-known lawyer, minister, and author, distantly related to the Civil War general James Longstreet. In 1861 he was president of the University of South Carolina and enthusiastically advocated secession. The *Southern Field and Fireside* was a popular magazine.

2. Sam Houston (1793–1863), a Virginia native and a founder of the Texan republic,

opposed secession but finally agreed to the legislature's order for a popular vote on the question. A majority voted to secede in February 1861, and Houston resigned in March.

3. Actually very few abolitionists lived in Texas by 1861. The Indians may be members of the Comanche nation.

Private Journal of Mary Owen Sims. Small Manuscript Collection, Arkansas History Commission.

Overcome with anxiety about the secession crisis, the widow Mary Sims blasts all politicians for destroying the Union for which men died in the Revolution.

1 January 1861. Again a new year has begun its course, but who can tell its end. Christmas is passed with all its frolic and fun and I have hired out all my servants, rented Forest Home to Bro. Williams who has recently sold his farm to a Mr. Harrison and have taken my abode at The Oaks with Mother.[1] Still it is not like home though Ma is very kind, but there is no place like home.

This is the arrangement I have made for this year, but God alone knows what will be next year. It seems that the whole political world has gone mad and our union which was bequeathed to us by our forefathers who purchased it with their blood. This boasted Republic that has been the admiration of the world and the pride of every American is on the eve of destruction. Mr. Lincoln, a leader of the Black Republicans, was elected last November and declares his intention of carrying out the principles of his party, that of prohibition of slavery in the territories and the Southern States have determined almost enmasse not to stay in the Union at all, but to withdraw and form a Southern Confederacy. South Carolina has already withdrawn and set up for herself. Mississippi and all the most Southern States are for following her example. Some of the Norther[n] States declare positively that the South shall submit to Lincoln. So if disunion does come Civil War, with all its accompanants — "lean, famine, quartering steel and climbing fire"[2] will be sure to succeed and if so by next year I may be a beggar — but oh, God grant that men may have some reason and that this great calamity may not befall us; for thou alone can avert it.

We have a most dreary day this the first Lord's day of 1861. Ma has a very sick servant (May) which gives us much uneaseness. Dr. Ketchen stayed with her last night. I hardly know when I will assume my pen again as Willie will be sent off to school in a few weeks[3] and I shall be very busy in arranging his clothes and at the end of that time I intend spending some time with Sister who is near her confinement.

1. Sims owns four slaves and calls her place in Dallas County Forest Home. Her brother William Owen farmed nearby, and her widowed mother, Ann Owen, lived on a sizable farm in the same county.

2. Perhaps a Biblical reference to Revelation, which describes the punishments, among them famine and fire, inflicted on sinners at the end of the world.

3. Her son William was eleven years old.

Lizinka C. Brown to her kinsman David Hubbard, [early] January 1861, from Paris, France, to somewhere in Alabama. Brown-Ewell Family Papers, The Filson Club Historical Society, Louisville, Kentucky.

Lizinka Campbell married planter James Brown in 1839 when she was nineteen. The couple lived on their several plantations in the Old Southwest. After her husband's death in 1844, Mrs. Brown remained a widow for many years. Moneyed, well-connected, and shrewd, she felt comfortable writing to such powerful men as David Hubbard, one of her husband's relatives. A veteran of the War of 1812, congressman, and successful planter, Hubbard became a "fire-eater" during the secession crisis. Lizinka Brown views the South's prospects with more skepticism, however, and wants to prevent war in any case.

Dear Major, . . . It seems to me peaceable secession is impossible—how can the Territories be divided? If we cannot agree about them in the Union can we out of it? How can 8,000,000 at the South contend successfully against the 16,000,000 of the North? Is Andy Johnson crazy?[1] Or as they say here has he been bought? Brackenridge seems very quiet—what is he doing?[2]

Is there any real danger of famine in Georgia? Can the South make her own supplies of meat & bread? If not had she not better give in? In case of an attack on the forts by the Federal Gov. —is there any probability of the Cotton States laying an embargo on the export of Cotton for two or three months? If the South will only fight together & treat together it seems to me we might do yet—but it is useless to speculate about what you know already a great deal [more] than I do — One thing perhaps you do not know as well & that is that Mrs. Stowe[3] & the abolitionists have done their work so thoroughly that it is doubtful whether either England or France would dare to take the part of the slaveholders however much they desire it — as I believe L. Napoleon does.[4] There is great suffering in both countries however which is attributed to the drain of specie from England to America & the total absence of demand there for Fr. manufactures. If Lincoln gives Bell no office & if Andy Johnson deserts the South & turns traitor it would be no bad move for Bell to declare for the restoration of the Missouri Compromise & its extension to the Pacific, or secession.[5]

. . . it seems to me you should advise him to do it & tell him if he will, I will work for him with the Legislature next fall & as it will be the first time I have electioneered for anybody & I will do it with all my heart in a good cause. . . .

A letter received from Rev. Mr. Cobb yesterday said two white men & eight negro men had been hurt at Montgomery — no evidence against them, but the confession of one negro extorted by whipping. Is this so? I suppose Maj. Hubbard was there at the time — if the spirit of 1856–7 is abroad I would go home at once & live at the farm until it is over to save our negroes from the persecutions of the poor whites.[6] . . . Yours affectionately L. C. Brown.

1. Andrew Johnson (1808–75), a former governor of Tennessee, was elected to the U.S. Senate in 1857. In December 1860 Johnson denounced secession and remained with the Union. He was the only member from a Southern state who continued to serve in the U.S. Senate during the war. In 1864, he ran on the Republican ticket as Abraham Lincoln's vice president, and he became president when Lincoln was assassinated a year later.

2. John C. Breckinridge (1821–75), a former vice president and U.S. senator, had run for president in 1860 on the Southern Democratic ticket. After the election he tried to put together the Crittenden Compromise, which failed, and in early 1861 he returned to Kentucky. Later that year, he enlisted in the Confederate army.

3. Harriet Beecher Stowe, the author of *Uncle Tom's Cabin.*

4. Louis Napoleon, emperor of France from 1851 to 1870. Although he and his wife, Empress Eugenie, sometimes appeared to sympathize with the Confederacy, he followed England's lead on whether to establish diplomatic ties with the South. After the loss at Gettysburg in 1863, neither country extended diplomatic recognition to the Confederacy, much less made an alliance with it.

5. John Bell (1797–1869), the former Whig from Tennessee who ran for president in 1860 with Edward Everett on a Unionist ticket. After the shelling at Fort Sumter, however, he reluctantly came out in favor of secession.

6. This reference is unclear. Hubbard often championed the cause of poor whites in

Alabama politics, despite the fact that he had long been a member of the state's planter elite. Perhaps Brown, who still owned bondsmen in Alabama, is implying that whites may mistreat slaves now that war seems imminent.

Diary of Cornelia Anderson. Cornelia Anderson Watkins Papers, Division of Special Collections and Archives, Margaret I. King Library, University of Kentucky at Lexington.

In 1861 Cornelia Anderson was twenty-three years old, unmarried, and the youngest child of a wealthy planter and his wife in Haywood County, Tennessee. Her opinions waver as she ponders what actions her state should take, for she fears that secession means a deadly war. Yet as winter turns into spring, her antipathy toward President Lincoln grows. After her cousin volunteers for the Confederate service, she makes up her mind about where her loyalties lie.

2 February 1861. . . . —much Political talk—great diversity of opinion— some Union, others for secession—Old [Hop?] Bulletin wield quite an influence in the Union line [1] — dear me! it is quite bewildering, I must say, when we take different views of the subject—Only the Wise Jehovah can bring order out of this great confusion—may he not let his wayward children drift away to the breakers of destruction is my prayer—Incline tho the minds & hearts of thy people oh Lord to do the way that will redown to his honour & glory—to our peace & prosperity—. . . .

Monday March 4th—1861—Great crises—This day the Blak Republican President is inaugurated [2]—woe, woe on us—bright & sunny; a painful contrast to most of our hearts; there is nothing but darkness & gloom ahead—for who can tell the events this days work may bring forth—seven states seceeded [3] the south divided what will our enemies do, but attempt to coerce the brave independent spirit into their obnoxious measures— then comes rebellion—Great & Holy Father, I pray Thee pour oil upon the troubled waters—Bro R—went to town—I've been quite sick most of the day—Sat up 'till 12 o'clock—so busy transferring [4]—

Wednesday—[April] 17th Great political excitement—war declared, by "Grand Mogul Lincoln"—95,000 troops called out for three months, so says proclamation[5] Our men & forming companies rapidly, drilling day & night—all seem anxious for a battle, how thoughtless, for when it once commences, heaven only knows when & where it will end. Painted most of my little Boy today.[6]

Thursday—[May] 9th Cos L has come to bid us a hasty adieu, will leave for camp next Tuesday—seems in fine spirits—poor fellow, will have many sighs of pain & sorrow to escape his lips ere we see him again. I pray this may not be the last shake of the hand we will have this side the grave—all is suspense now—

Tuesday—[May] 14th Sis & I spent today at Mrs. C—she seemed cheerful, carried them strawberries, which we all hulled cozily by the fire—had a dish o' politics with Mr. Mc—Union still—wishes our state to remain neutral—I s'd neutrality is but another name for cowardice—dont think there will be fighting—we are too credulous now, if we believe the promises of our sworn enemies, when too, experience has proved them false so often—we must remember "Sumpter."[7]

1. Apparently a local newspaper, editor unknown.

2. A derogatory term for President Abraham Lincoln.

3. By March 4, South Carolina, Mississippi, Florida, Alabama, Georgia, Louisiana, and Texas had seceded. On May 7, 1861, the Tennessee legislature voted to leave the Union.

4. This reference is obscure.

5. After the Confederates captured Fort Sumter on April 14, Lincoln promptly called for seventy-five thousand volunteers to put down what he called an insurrection. In early March, the Confederate Congress had called for one hundred thousand volunteers.

6. Anderson painted as a hobby.

7. Meaning Fort Sumter. Anderson may believe, as some Southerners did, that Lincoln committed an act of war when he sent a federal ship to supply the men at the fort. Confederate President Davis ordered the bombardment, however, before the ship arrived.

Sarah F. Toler to her sister, 1 April 1861, from Richmond, Virginia, to Lynchburg, Virginia. Barnes Family Manuscripts, Miscellaneous Correspondence, Special Collections Department, Alderman Library, University of Virginia.

Sarah Toler, recently widowed and the impecunious mother of seven children, has just moved to the Virginia capital from the Tidewater. Fort Sumter's surrender in Charleston harbor forms a postscript to her account of an inheritance dispute in the wake of her brother's death and the subtle, ongoing struggle between her male and female relatives.

My Dear Sister,

It has been sometime since I wrote, but I hope you will not think hard of me when I tell you sickness has been the only cause of my not writing. My family has been quite afflicted with a new desese called the Rosola it is presently like the measels only I believe it is worse. Sue was very ill with it, Sam Sarah and Julia Ellen were very sick[1] and since I last wrote I have been very sick myself—

I hope this will find you all very well. Sam wrote to Charlie some time ago but we have not received a letter from Lynchburg for a good time—

I thank God I have made out the cold and wet disagreeable winter so far[2] but I will assure you it is a hard thing for me sometimes. Well my dear sister Brother Richard's negro man Dick stayed with us some three or four hours this evening week ago. It is the first time I have seen him since the death of his master. He told me Brother Richard had made his will since I left the country and will him and eight hundred dollars cash money to me and after he received that insulting letter from Joe Segar, he destroyed the will and left everything to Long Snead and the Hillyards.[3] Joe Segar had better been dead and where no one could reach him than ever to have written that infamous letter to Brother Richard. I have no doubt but what he died empressed with the Idea that I had said something to Joe Segar about him and God is my Judge I never said anything again him in all of my life to no one much less to some one that has never done any thing for me worth mentioning[.] if he had continued doing it only in a small way for us it would of been something to his credit but as it is what he has done seems worse than nothing[.] if ever I get able I mean to let him know in full what and where his fortune began and what I think of him and his[.] he came very near being shot a few days since by a Mr. Gallaher[.] I suppose you saw an account of it.

Well my dear sister I will stop that subject and commence one of a more interesting character. Bro. Richard left in his [will] for a nice and suetable tomb stone to be erected over our dear old Mother sister Susan and himself which has been done[.] they were ordered and made and put up by one of our best stone masons in the city of Richmond—Mr. Davies. they staid in his lot while makeing and after being made and I did not know it untill they had been carried away and I am glad I did not for if I had have gone and seen the name of my dear Mother I must have sunk under the scene though so dear to me.

O what would I give to visit the sacred spots so far from me and plant one flower to the memorys of the dear departed but I feel there is not any thing that I could do which would releave my sorrows in my untimely misfortunes. it would afford me a great pleasure to see you all once more but alas the privilege is taking away never to be restored. you could not immagine my distress at times I hardly know what to do and where to turn for one word of comfort to sustain me in all the trials of the world.

Sister has been out and spent three of four evenings with me since the death of Mr. Page. Mary Jane Barnie has another daughter some two or three weeks old.

Beck says I must conclude by asking you to write as often as you can[.] you must not give out the Ide of comeing down this summer. I will be delighted to have you and your sweet children with me bless my dear sister Sook.[4] I never expect to see her again. I have no means of comeing to see her and she has so many [children] around her I hardly believe she will make a start very soon though I wish she could —

Tell Charlie I have given him out[.][5] tell Ned he must write to aunt Sarah and I will answer his letters. Give our very best love to all and except a large portion for yourself from your devoted sister Sarah F. Toler.

P.S.

I forgot to mention that there was the greatest stir here last night you ever saw or heard of on the intelligence of the takeing of Fort Sumter.[6] Canons were fired from the time of the arrival of the news untill sunset and flags were raised some houses illuminated, sky rockets and fire works in all parts of the City and it two o'clock in the morning before it subsided. Tomorrow night there will be a grand torch light procession all through the City with all of the best music of the day. [The next line is blotted out.] I reckon you are tired so farewell for the present. S. F. T.

you must excuse bad writeing and any mistakes as my eyesight has failed me a good deal where is Joe I never hear from him now. I wish he would write occasionally. S. F. T.

1. Her children, who have been afflicted with roseola, an illness that resembled measles in its symptoms.
2. Meaning she has made ends meet.

3. Joseph Segar lived in Elizabeth City County and owned ninety thousand dollars' worth of real estate in 1860; Sarah Toler owned one hundred dollars' worth of property the same year. The Sneads and Hillyards are her kinfolk, but Segar's relationship to the Toler family is not clear.

4. A nickname for her sister Susan.

5. Meaning she has given up hope that Sook's husband, Charlie, will bring her to visit.

6. The Federal troops at Fort Sumter surrendered on April 13, so Toler either misdated the letter or wrote it over a period of two weeks, from April 1 to April 14.

Journal of Meta Morris Grimball. Southern Historical Collection, University of North Carolina.

Mrs. Grimball is now completely focused on the great crisis. Even as she enscribed this diary entry, a Federal ship was sailing for Fort Sumter in Charleston harbor; later on April 12, the Confederate bombardment would begin. All five of her sons would be there to witness it, and all of them would later serve in the Confederacy. On the very last day of peace, she asks God to protect her loved ones. She is also beginning to convince herself that the South is in the right.

12 April 1861.

All yesterday I was in a most terrible state of anxiety and misery about my boys, but I know my case is not different from others.[1] Mrs. Elliott, the mother of William's Captain, has her only child down there, Mrs. Lowndes her only son, & many others.[2] But mine are very fine boys and very dear to me, still they must do their duty to their state; and I put my trust in my God & their God, my Savior & their Savior. And I Pray for them & for myself. The Government at Washington seems full of duplicity, and in looking back on the conduct of the seceding states, there seems to have been a truthful and noble faith activating <u>them</u>.[3]

1. One of her sons, William, would die in 1864.

2. Probably some of the numerous descendants of William Lowndes (1782–1822), the former congressman, and Benjamin Elliott (1787–1836), a prominent Charleston lawyer.

3. At this point, the Confederacy contained seven states. After Fort Sumter, Virginia, Arkansas, Tennessee, and North Carolina would secede from the Union.

Mary Boykin Williams Harrison Ames, n.d. "Childhood Recollections." Typescript at South Caroliniana Library, University of South Carolina, quoted with permission of Mrs. Martha Daniels.

Mary Boykin Williams was only ten years old when the war broke out, but she remembers the spring of 1861 quite clearly. Both of her parents, Katharine Miller Williams and David Rogerson Williams II, came from South Carolina's planter elite, and her maternal grandfather, Stephen Miller, was governor of South Carolina in the 1830s. On the eve of the great conflict, the Williamses left their Florida plantation to live in the Appalachian Mountains, but even there the war's transformations began to reach into their sheltered lives.

. . . All that spring was full of wild interest and excitement to us, and in a very unknowing fashion we were very enthusiastic little "rebels," as we hear ourselves called now. And in May we left Florida, and for the first time our dear old Mammy, who was no longer strong enough to take care of another baby, even with an under-nurse, and it seemed the saddest moment of our lives bidding goodbye to Mammy, who had nursed Papa, and then us four older children.[1] When we got to Charleston on our way to North Carolina, such enthusiasm and excitement and rushing to and fro, such beautiful soldiers and horses and all the delights of brass bands, etc., and how we enjoyed it; but as so many of our friends and relatives were there we saw as much of it as we liked,[2] and we should have been content to stay a great deal longer. However, it turned out we were not to go to our new home in North Carolina that summer, for we heard the house was not nearly finished, and a young cousin of Papa's, who was on his way to the Army of Virginia, offered us his house, "Cool Springs," for the summer—and so to "Cool Springs" we went. All this summer seems, as I look back, only impressed on my mind as being very, very hot, and all the elders of the family entirely absorbed in everything but us, and also how very nearly distracted Miller drove poor Mr. Bormann by his restlessness and inattention,[3] for, with all his heart and mind, he was thinking of our cousin, E. B.,[4] who had a camp for us, and who was raising and drilling a company, or batallion, of soldiers; as it was, each of our afternoons was spent at Camp Boykin, and its delights were endless. Mama would go with us sometimes and sometimes Aunty, too.[5]

Then came the Battle of Mannassus, and we could hear on all sides of the sorrow and grief that had come to so many of our relatives, and so on during that awfully hot summer.

Finally, autumn came, and there were hopes that, as Florida was considered so exposed and unprotected, our mountain home would be finished; so we went on up to North Carolina and decided to spend a few weeks at the hotel till our house was ready. But we found that, having put ourselves in the hotel, we would have to stay there many months, for almost no work was being done on the new house. So we all settled down to our winter's work, Mama by this time being alone with us, and Mr. Bormann and Papa having returned to Florida.

Our winter was full of many pleasures to us, for we had never seen snow before, or ice, nor had any such amusements as snow-balling, etc., and we enjoyed that greatly; but as I recall the weary, sad face of our dear Mother, I know how hard a winter it was on her—and particularly after one evening when Mama called E. and me into her room and said she wanted to tell us not to be alarmed or frightened if she made us both come into her room for the night; and she then told us that the baby's nurse had told her that one of the maids in the yard and her lover, a negro from elsewhere, had been overheard arranging how they might enter and rob the house and then run off, and the plan was to do it that night, and poor dear old Silvie was so terrified for fear they would find out she had told on them it was quite pitiful.[6] I don't recall what steps Mama took to protect us, but I know that after that our lives were never so peaceful again, and any noise at night would wake us very easily, that is, Mama or me. E. slept across a narrow passageway from me that winter. She had the care of David, and I slept in the nursery with the baby, Kate,[7] as I had done for so long a time, and it used to be one of our jokes that almost nightly poor little David would fall out of bed and cry out "Please Enie take me in!" and end by coming across and begging me to put him in Enie's bed again. . . .

1. Serena (1848–76), Stephen Miller (1853–1938), and David (1858–1928), in addition to the author, who died in 1931. Such nostalgic memories of a "mammy" were common after the Civil War.

2. Her aunt Mary Boykin Miller Chesnut, who wrote the now-famous journal about the war, was in Charleston that spring.

3. Her brother Stephen Miller Williams studied with one Mr. Bormann, the family tutor.

4. Probably one of the many Boykin cousins who fought in the war.

5. The children called Mary Boykin Chesnut Aunty.

6. "E" is Enie, their nickname for Serena. Mrs. Williams may have been especially

frightened because her cousin Elizabeth Witherspoon was murdered by her slaves in September 1861.

7. Kate was born in 1860.

Mary Hibberd to her sister-in-law Jane Hibberd Keefer, 30 April, 1 May 1861, from Richmond, Virginia, to Springborough, Ohio. Jane Hibberd Keefer Papers, MS 684, box 1, folder 10, Ohio Historical Society.

A Quaker in her late middle age, Mary Hibberd was married to a farmer in rural Virginia. In the 1850s the Hibberds moved to Richmond so James Hibberd could start a business. In 1860 Mary Hibberd opposed disunion, calling it a movement led by sinful, faithless ingrates. By the spring of 1861, she was nearly convulsed with fear about the fate of her adult children scattered across the Upper South. She also conveys the terrifying atmosphere in the new Confederate capital. In this context, it is perhaps understandable that she decides that events are beyond her control and it is time to be "resigned" to secession.

Dear Sister,

I recieved thy brief letter and hasten to answer it for I know thee must feel a desire to hear and have been insisting on James answering thy letter, as far as I dare. he seems as if he did not no what he is about as well as the rest of us in these times of consternation and terror that has seized the community every where there seems to be but little trouble to find a theme either to write or speak on at present for if we begin on any othe[r] than the all absorbing one it ends in that, that of our beloved & doomed country. how does thee suppose we have been feeling, with our children in the midst of a mob of the worst kind and so near the fight to as they were.[1] I can tell thee I have to be very guarded in keeping myself composed and endeavoring to keep my mind stayed where it should be for if I give way atall I become sick and quite unnerved.

Thee is anxious to hear of my dear child Jane. Well we were told they had but 24 hours in Baltimore to prepare to leave the City. That was last 5th day. Aron got a dispatch which said then "We leave the City tonight."[2] that is all we know, that they are homeless, and what the result will be is only known by him who knoweth all things, and all we can do is to trust to his mercy. Oh, it is storming terribly out. I think it resembles the state of society for where is there a more rebellious and ungrateful people than the people of these United States for where has there been one under Heaven so favourable as we and now the lamb must suffer for it poor returns for such blessings.

[1 May 1861] Well, here I had to stop last night, for Allen[3] returned from town and call to me that he had 2 or 3 letters and oh what sad letters. I don't believe I can write inteligably for I was at 12 oclock in the night sitting up rubbing my forehead to induce sleep but all of no avail but it is of no use to dwell on my sorrows when there are so many that is feeling just as bad, so I will inform thee of the contents of their letters. they were from Henry and Tace and Lyd but Ah how different the stories Lyd all life and hope[4] and poor Tace her own troubles[5] and that of poor Janes to[o] she says she is almost crazy, for they did not get away from the City when they expected, for Gideon's mother took sick and says she cannot be moved. Tace says in such a time as this she thinks she ought to exert herself as much as possible for there lives are in danger every hour[.] she said she has never been able to hear from her untill the 27th since the mob and she says she thinks she is almost frightened to death but I think not, for all that has given me any comfort, is the knowledge that Jane is so cool and deliberate, but these awful mobs are calculated to move every nerve however secure we may feel. Tace wrote to her to come home at once as her father had telegraphed to them but she says she cannot leave Gideon for it is not likely she will ever see him if she does. Tace and Henry telegraphed after writing that they would leave this week but she said she could not bear to leave her dear Jane there to be killed. We get no truths here in the papers people have declined taking them. Allen says the news that come one day is contradicted the next but from Tace and Henrys letter they are having awful times lest such excitement she says she never read of soldier's marching every moment and in every directions And if Jane does come it will be at an awful expence. it costs 60 dollars now to get from Baltimore to Phila. oh dear I fear she will not get here Oh I could write thee all day and tell thee of fresh scenes I hear of but I cannot it is as much as I can do to get thru with my work and now my family will be so increased and we expect some from Loudon to[o][6] they are driving them from there or at least all the young men if not they must take an oathe of allegiance to the South there are 6 or 7 hundred now in Richmond and coming all the time. Tace says there are 400 from Baltimore in Phila. that she has a knowledge of.[7] Well they are flee-

ing in every direction fear and consternation has seized us but where can
flee to God is every wher alike and to him only can we go for refuge and
I think we will find it before it is over. James tells me to say to thee that
he did give the mill in charge to George Seibert but he does not appear
to act nor write either[.] [8] Isaac Kilmore wrote to James about it the other
day saying Monty could not be got out atall. James wrote to him he must
leave but w[h]ether he will or not he cannot tell he has not paid his rent
and now he cannot for Virginia money is not worthy any thing only 60 cts.
discount[.] [9] is it not awful he says he dont think it is worthwhile to expect
any from them or any other quarter for he thinks likely the property will
be confiscated. I dont like to write things so unfaviourable but cant help it
is beyond our controul at this time and we will just have to be resigned to
it is all the way I can see for us we can get no letters to or from Baltimore
at least none come. James say he has been doing all he can and will continue to[.] he wrote to Isaac Kilmore George Seibert and Monty last week
and perhaps they may succeed in getting him out and if they do they have
a very competent man to put in his place so Isaac Kilmore writes he seems
to feel more for you than any one else. James says when he hears from Isaac
he will write to thee at once. Well dear sister I hope thee can read this but
I fear it but indeed I never felt as if my senses were gone before that is I
feel stupid and like just nothing in the quiet and not opening my mouth or
heart to any living being but our condition I cannot deplore so much yet
when I consider the poor friends in Virginia[.] [10] they are taking their property very much they have distressed Samuel Janney but he says he will not
leave altho he expects to suffer very much[.] they took all James Walkers
horses. I hear he has a son over at the boarding school a nice young man.
I feel very much for him indeed and I am glad I can for it is said to be the
gift of Heaven oh I hope we may be allowed that if every thing else is taken
for when we lose that we are poorly off and I think it is departing very fast
from the community at large. They noh every thing now that dont say what
them they fixed upon several times to tar and feather our neighbor Aron
White and his soon poor Charles he was taken from the evil to come he
died the same day Rachael Ballard did and the same hour of the week before
on the same day of the week. Aunt Beulah Patterson died I suppose thee
has hea[r]d of it we have had many deaths this winter but these thee knew.
Mary McKinstry and Mary Hibberd just left Baltimore the day before the
mob if they had not gone then they could not have gone so Mary writes a
man that went with them stayed and had to pay an enormous price to go
in a private way [11] that the way now Mary could not get near all her proved

rents the agent went he had 6 houses and could get no rent and they were af[r]iad every moment that the starving ones would rise and enter there houses to get some thing to keep them alive what a state of things in Md.[12]

Henry says recieved a letter from Gid and Jane the 27th they report matters in a dreadful condition there Gideon's Mother is poorly and prevents them Coming. William Vicker, and Rachel will be at Richmond to his brothers this weak. poor Tace says Mother dont be more uneasy than thee can help several of our A[u]nt Chouts well as ever on first day, father and mother as well as usual all of the children send there love. Allen says tell Aunt Jane I have a fine Newfoundland dog for her if I can get him over any way twill be an excellent watch.

friends from here have enlisted Isaac Thomas Leutenant William Thistelwaite and others.[13]

Write soon, very soon if I hear anything new from Jane I will write.

1. Her adult children lived close to the northern edge of Baltimore harbor. On April 19 a secessionist crowd attacked troops from the Sixth Massachusetts Regiment as they headed down Pratt Street for the Camden Street railroad station. In the melee four soldiers and twelve civilians were killed, and over the next several days Unionists evacuated the city by the hundreds.

2. Jane is Hibberd's daughter and Keefer's niece and namesake, and Aron Hibberd is her brother-in-law. They may be headed for Ohio. The Quaker "fifth day" was Thursday.

3. Her adult son.

4. Possibly a sister-in-law, Lydia Dare, who lived in the Midwest.

5. The writer's daughter Tace Hibberd; Henry may be her husband.

6. A number of relatives lived in Loudon County, Virginia.

7. Hibberd evidently means that hundreds of Unionists have fled the Virginia countryside to Richmond and from Baltimore to Philadelphia.

8. James Hibberd owned a mill in Maryland with his sister Jane.

9. Before the Civil War many states issued their own currency, which other states could accept at a discount if they wished.

10. "Friends" in both senses, for these men are Quakers. Some of the Janneys were Unionists.

11. Meaning in a private conveyance, since many of the public roads were closed. McKinstry and Hibberd are her cousins.

12. Possibly meaning Baltimore's homeless population.

13. Evidently in the Confederate army. Most Quakers were pacifists, but several hundred nevertheless served in both armies during the war.

A Lady of Virginia [Judith Brockenbrough McGuire], Diary of A Southern
Refugee During the War *(New York: E. J. Hale & Son, 1867), 1–3.*

*Judith McGuire was the middle-aged spouse of Reverend John P. McGuire, prin-
cipal of the Episcopal High School near Alexandria, Virginia. In her diary she
poignantly evokes the transition from peacetime routines to preparations for war
as she closes up their school. With much bewilderment and anguish, she too begins to turn away from the Union.*

4 May 1861. I am too nervous, too wretched to-day to write in my diary,
but that the employment will while away a few moments of this trying
time. Our friends and neighbors have left us; every thing is broken up. The
Theological Seminary is closed; the High School dismissed. Scarcely any
one is left of the many families which surrounded us. We are left lonely indeed; our children are all gone—the girls to Clarke, where they may be
safer,[1] and farther from the exciting scenes which may too soon surround
us; and the boys, the dear dear boys to be drilled and prepared to meet
any emergency.[2] Can it be that our country is to be carried on and on to
the horrors of civil war? I pray, oh how fervently do I pray, that our Heavenly Father may yet avert it. I shut my eyes and hold my breath when the
thought of what may come upon us obstrudes itself; and yet I cannot believe it. It will, I know the breach will be healed without the effusion of
blood. The taking of Sumter without bloodshed has somewhat soothed my
fears,[3] although I am told by those who are wiser than I, that men must fall
on both sides by the score, by the hundred, and even by the thousand. But
it is not my habit to look on the dark side, so I try hard to employ myself,
and hope for the best. To-day our house seems so deserted, that I feel more
sad than usual, for on this morning we took leave of our whole household.
Mr. ———— [4] and myself are now the sole occupants of the house, which
usually teems with life.[5] I go from room to room, looking at first one thing
and then another, so full of sad associations. The closed piano, the locked
bookcase, the nicely-arranged tables, the formally-placed chairs, ottomans
and sofas in the parlor! Oh for someone to put them out of order! And
then the dinner-table, which has always been so well surrounded, so social,
so cheerful, looked so cheerless to-day, as we seated ourselves one at the
head, the other at the foot, with one friend,—but one,—at the side. I
could scarely restrain my tears, and but for the presence of that one friend,
I believe I should have cried outright. After dinner, I did not mean to do

it, but I could not help going into the girls' room, and then into C.'s. I heard my own footsteps so plainly, that I was starled by the absence of all other sounds. There the furniture looked so quiet, the beds so fixed and smooth, the wardrobes and bureaux so tightly locked, and the whole so lifeless! But the writing-desks, work-boxes, and the numberless things so familiar to my eyes! Where were they? I paused, to ask myself what it all meant. Why did we think it necessary to send off all that was so dear to us from our own home? I threw open the shutters, and the answer came at once, so mournfully! I heard distinctly the drums beating in Washington.[6] The evening was so still that I seemed to hear nothing else. As I looked at the Capitol in the distance, I could scarcely believe my senses. That Capitol of which I had always been so proud! Can it be possible that it is no longer <u>our</u> Capitol? And are our countrymen, under its very eaves, making mighty preparation to drain our hearts' blood? And must this Union, which I was taught to revere, be rent asunder?[7] Once I thought such a suggestion sacrilege; but now that it is dismembered, I trust it may never, never be re-united. We must be a separate people—our nationality must be different, to insure lasting peace and good-will. Why cannot we part in peace?

1. Her daughters and some of the female students journeyed to Clarke County in the Shenandoah River Valley, where McGuire had relatives.

2. Several of her sons and nephews served in the Confederate army.

3. As she indicates, no lives were lost in battle during the shelling of the fort in April.

4. Meaning her husband, who voted for secession in the state convention in Richmond in May 1861.

5. The McGuires had several house slaves, who were still working in the household or on the grounds.

6. The Union capital was a few miles away across the Potomac River.

7. Her father fought in the American Revolution.

Diary of Amanda McDowell. Curtis McDowell Papers, Tennessee State Library and Archives.

Twenty-one years old in 1861, Amanda McDowell taught school with her father, an impoverished middle-aged instructor at Cumberland Institute in White County, Tennessee. That fateful spring she tries to persuade herself to support the Confed-

eracy, but she can not rid herself of the conviction that secession is wrong and the war unjust.

4 May 1861.

We got the mail today. I got a letter from Fayette.[1] he was well and in fine spirits when he wrote it. There is a great deal of news in the papers about the war. Little thought have I had that I should ever live to see civil war in this our goodly land, but so it is. The southerners are so hot they can stand it no longer and have already made the break. There will be many a divided family in this once happy Union. there will be father against son and brother against brother.[2] Oh God! that such things should be in a christian land, that men should in their blindness rush so rashly on to ruin and not only rush to ruin themselves but drag along with them so many thousands of innocent and ignorant victims, for there are thousands who will rush into the fury with blind enthusiasm, never stopping to question whether it be right or wrong, who if they only understood it properly would stay at home with their families and let those who started it fight it out. But the ignorant mass are so easily excited that one enthusiast who can make mountains of molehills and raise a bustle about nothing can so stir them up and excite that they will run headlong into almost anything that is proposed to them. They are taking on considerably at Sparta.[3] Have raised a secession flag and are organizing companies at a great rate. Why Christian men who live here in peace and plenty with nothing to interrupt their happiness should prefer to leave their peaceful homes and all the ties which bind them to their families and rush into a fight in which they cannot possibly gain victory and in which they may lose their lives is more than I can see. But of course my judgment is not much anyway. But in my feeble opinion they will have cause to repent their rashness. I do not think that the killing of one another is going to better it any. But on the contrary I fear it will make it worse. God grant that it may not prove so serious a matter as we are all fearing. I say fearing I do not fear anything in particular. I can conceive of the horrors of civil war, and I know it is dreadful but I do not fear that I will hurt me. And for my folks I am not uneasy. I know they will not go into it till they are convinced that it is their duty, and when they are firmly convinced that it is their duty to fight for their Country, it becomes me not to interfere with them about it, or grieve at their so doing, for I love my country I <u>think</u> as well as any who live in it could love it. And although I shudder to think any of them either being killed or killing another yet

I should consider it my duty to take it with the best grace possible. And when I consider that it is my duty to do a thing I generally do it. . . .

9 June 1861. Sunday afternnon.
I am not in a writing mood this evening but it is the last chance I shall have soon, I expect. Mary will go home with Jack in the evening and then I shall have less time than ever. She has been wanting to so badly all the time. Jack came home on Friday, and intended to start back this evening but father has not been well for several days as he would not leave till he was better, he has been about all the time but was afraid that there was something severely the matter with him, he is better this evening. The mail never came till today. I got a letter from aunt Deborah, uncle Wm is dead. I am sorry indeed for aunt and the children but not for him for aunt said that he died happy, only regretting the condition of his family and business, which he left in a very unsettled State, but said that he left thousands of dollars uncollected, and she never expected to get at half. The times are hard and business almost stopped on account of the war.

Yesterday was the great day of election in Tennessee. I guess it is voted "out of the Union" by this time. But it would not have been had the people been allowed to vote their true sentiments. At least I do not believe it would. Nearly all the Union men in this neighborhood stayed at home, not wishing to get into a brawl and deeming it a hopeless cause.[4] And what did go did not vote. Jack and Wade went down to Quebec town[5] in the afternoon to see how they were progressing. Jack said that there were about twenty Union men standing there but none of them ventured to vote for fear of their lives. Frank Coatney voted Union, said he would do it at the risk of his life and did it but things got so hot that he had to leave the ground. And Jack said they marked him and were going after him last night. And another man there swore that he did not think he would ever vote again, since it was of no use that a man could not do as he wished like honest men ought to do, that their liberties had already been voted away by the "big bugs"[6] of the country and for his part he did not know that [he] should ever vote again. . . .

15 June 1861.
I have not the heart to write anything. The Mails came today but broughtt nothing much. I suppose we now are of the Southern Confederacy. I think we oughtt as well be numbered with the Nations that were, at once. Great

enthusiasm prevails now but I am afraid the tide will be turned before long. Oh what a fair country and what a glorious government have Politicians ruined. I feel sometimes like saying, "Oh! that my heart was a fountain of waters that I might weep it away." for this my ruined Country. For it is now beyond a doubt a lost and ruined Country. I do not think any thing short of Divine interposition could now save it. And I do not think even if such miricals were common that there is enough good in the land to save it. . . . But I know that though the good may suffer in this world that there is a rest in heaven after death where the wicked cease from troubling and the weary are at rest. I am not of the good, but I rely upon my Savior for help, and I shall try in my humble way to do my duty to the best of my knowledge. And if we are now one of the Confederate States, and the Government should call upon me to give up my best friends and best interest for the good of my country, I should consider it my duty to do it without a murmur, although I consider the whole business wrong.

Yet it is probably the best that we can do. Fayette sent me a letter by Mary Ann's father today, he talks of Volunteering. I suppose he knows more about what is his duty then I do. I should hate to see him start to war at any time or under any circumstances but doubly so under the present State of affairs, for I do not think it is right to fight against the government, unless we had been oppressed by it. And we have never in my judgement been oppressed in the least, but perhaps I do not know. I shudder to think of associations he will have to have. I fear that his temperament will will not resist all the temptations that will be continually thrown around him.[7] But if he thinks it is his duty to go I say for him to go and May his God go with him is my earnest prayer.

20 July 1861. Saturday morning.
I do not know what to do with myself. there is no one here but we three[8] and Sallie Pointer, Mr. Carr came after M. A. yesterday and his little girl & Sallie and Jack and Charlie Pointer[9] came with him. they are all gone back but Sal we prevailed on her to stay a few days with us. Fayette has volunteered and is to start on Wednesday.[10] I do not know whether he will come home or not. Jack said they would both be here tomorrow he expected. The mails have all stopped and Jack can do no good. he printed a paper this week. I had rather Fayette had waited a while. I cannot bring myself to believe that it is a just war. If we were invaded or in danger of invasion

or oppression or wrong in any way, I could bid him Godspeed with a much better grace. But I believe it to be an unjust and unholy war.[11] I am I own loth to see him engage in it. I know it is hard though for a young man with any spirit to stay away now they make so much noise. I do not think he will stand it long. I am afraid Mary will grieve herself to death.[12] I love her as dearly as I love myself. . . .

1. One of her brothers.
2. Her father, Curtis, and brother Jackson supported the Union, while Fayette was a Confederate. She is not related to Susanna McDowell, whose letter appears in the chapter on race in this book.
3. A small town nearby.
4. On May 7 the Tennessee legislature voted to secede from the Union and on June 8 submitted the resolution to the voters for approval. As McDowell indicates, the vote took place in a violent, intimidating atmosphere.
5. A small village in White County, today known as Quebeck.
6. A nineteenth-century idiom for the rich and powerful.
7. She probably means drinking, gambling, and prostitution.
8. Her father, her sister-in-law Mary Ann, and herself.
9. Her neighbors, one of whom runs a small newspaper.
10. He joined the Confederate army.
11. Many believing Christians shared an understanding of the meaning of a "just" war, first elaborated by St. Augustine. By the mid-nineteenth century, it was defined as a war declared by a legitimate authority, carried out to promote peace, undertaken as a last resort, and waged with moderation and wisdom.
12. Her sister-in-law, Fayette's wife.

Martha Duland to her friend Mary Cox Collins, 13 April 1861, from Columbia City, Kentucky, to Lexington, Kentucky. Collins Family Letters, Division of Special Collections and Archives, Margaret I. King Library, University of Kentucky at Lexington.

In 1861, Martha Duland was in her early forties, a devout Presbyterian, and married to a coach painter. Neither she nor her husband owned slaves, and they were about to embark on new careers as missionaries. She employs the family metaphor, as many women did, while discussing the rift between the sections, and like many women she abhors the secession movement. She also prays for divine guidance to prevent the awful prospect of war.

My dear Friend,

I received your very kind letters of March 22nd, and of April 3d. By the first, I was pleasantly surprised, at so early a reply; when I had been so long in writing to you. We were pleased to hear of the health of your family, and while we were sorry to hear, of your pastor's health having been interrupted, we hope it may become permanently restored, by a sea voyage. The labors of a faithful pastor are truly invaluable.

I gave your love to the children. Willie seemed quite pleased to hear you had a little boy. he is just about the age of our Charlie, and Willie loves his brother very much. they are always together. Willie thinks he would like to be a good boy, and some day become a good minister. The present aspect of things in our country, would indicate stormy times before that time would come round. It seems as if we were approaching a fearful crisis. The secession movement is deeply lamentable, and the contemplation of a civil war brings with it a thousand horrors. it becomes us as Christians to humble ourselves and call upon our God that he may in his infinite mercy avert from us this danger, and bind us together as a nation, and that we become again as one common brotherhood, knowing no North and no South.

The one dollar Mr. C. enclosed as coming from a minister's son, was duly forwarded to our good brother — .

As to your letter of the 3d enclosing 30.00 as we understood 10 to each of the families, I refered to, and 10 to ourselves. I acknowledge has placed me in a position that I do not Know what to say, or how to reply. I felt so dissatisfied with myself for writing so freely to you, that if I had, had time to write another sheet, I would not have sent that, and left out the particulars of which I spoke. And you may judge of my feelings on receiving your reply. We feel truly thankful to you and your husband, for the great kindness, and sympathy you express. Husband forwarded the aid you sent to those brethren, we have not heard from them yet, but know it must have come most opportunely to them, as well as to us.

Please express our gratitude to those who have so generously united with you in contributeing to our wants as missionaries. May the blessing of him who has said "In as much as ye have done it unto the least of these my brethren ye have done it unto me," rest with you.

Please to Mr. Collins that we regretted very much that the Review did not reach us,[1] until after Mr. D. started to Presbytery he esteems it very highly and will cheerfully to all in his power to extend its circulation. The Presbytery met rather in an out of the way place off the railroad, or I would have forwarded the review. Mr. Duland will see as ma[n]y of the ministers as he can, and write to Mr. C. his success, at his earliest convenience. We deeply sympathize with your in your reverses, and hope for you, great success in your new enterprise.[2]

Please write often. Your letters are refreshing. And excuse my poor ones. Yours sincerely, Mrs. J. E. Duland.

1. The *Danville Review,* a newspaper edited by Mary Collins's husband, Richard.
2. Richard Collins gave up his paper in Maysville because of financial problems and founded the *Review* in 1861.

Recollections of Letitia Dabney Miller, c. 1926, Mrs. Cade Drew Gillespie Papers, Small Manuscripts, Special Collections, University of Mississippi.

The daughter of an attorney, Letitia Dabney grew up in the village of Raymond, Mississippi, in the 1850s. Both of her parents were Virginians by birth, and they owned half a dozen slaves in 1860. During the secession crisis, Dabney happened to be away from home on an extended visit with two of her women relatives in Charleston. There, dissenting views are not welcome, not even from a nine-year-old girl.

. . . My father and uncle were what is called Old Line Whigs, and as such were violently opposed to Secession and all the Democratic Party stood for. I had heard Jeff Davis and Secession denounced in my home,[1] and like a little parrot I repeated these sentiments in school.[2] One of the teachers took me aside and told me not to utter such sentiments; they would make me very unpopular and I might have to leave school. I was frightened and held my tongue. There were no men in our home so I can't remember hearing politics discussed there. In April we were hurriedly taken to the Battery one day to see the shelling of Fort Sumter. We went to the house of a friend. The roof was flat, surrounded by a parapet. On this a small telescope had been mounted. The grown-ups used it constantly, but each child was permitted to look now and then. I saw smoke and flame pouring up from the fort, and the men walking on walls of air. . . .

1. In Mississippi, that is.
2. While she was visiting Charleston.

Susan C. Stone Barton to her daughters Emily Barton Brune and Eva Barton, 18 April 1861, from Fredericksburg, Virginia, to Baltimore, Maryland. Brune-Randall Family Papers, MS 2004, Manuscripts Division, Maryland Historical Society Library.

By the spring of 1861 Susan Barton reluctantly came to advocate secession. Yet she wants every avenue to be exhausted before the nation goes to war, and she fears that the conflict will endanger her loved ones. Her stinging remarks on the Virginia governor are obviously based on close personal observation.

My dear Em & Eva, I tried to write to you yesterday, but was prevented, & am now glad to have Em's letter to acknowledge as well as yours Eva, which I had been anxiously looking for. it was a subject of gratulation that I had recieved one from you the very day before the communication was stopped — I fear it will not be very long before there will be more serious impediments than high waters & broken railroads — The prospect is dark before us, & I have many anxious & sorrowful feelings, & often haid no comfort but in the recollection that "the Lord reigneth," and His outstretched arm is able to stop the storm of angry powers, if he sees it is well — & has promised that all things work together for good to those who love [and] trust in Him. Don't distress yourself about me dear Em you must remember, I am more hopeful about all things than you, & although I see the prospect of greater evils before us than ever before, I have much assurance of ours being a righteous cause, that I hope wisdom will be given to our rulers, to counteract all the wiles & evil intentions of our enemies, or rather assailants. I do not even like to admit that I feel they are enemies — I had hoped we should all (Maryland included) have been allowed to form a separate peaceable government, & after the excited feelings of the North had died away <u>possibly</u> might have united again — but with their bitter hatred to the South there could be no union, & perhaps on both sides it existed, but if it did, I was not aware of it, but we only want to be left alone —

Virginia has the satisfaction of feeling she had done every thing to restore peace, which she could not have had, if she had gone out when South Carolina did[1] & as I thought she ought — As if this state of things had then come, she would not have the consolation of thinking she had exhausted every peace measure & had not brought war on ourselves. I am sorry Maryland is

not with us, & possibly it is best, one bone of contention, having the Capitol, may be avoided, as it was her grant to the Government & not Virginia's.[2]

I enclose Gov. Letcher's Proclamation & reply which we think dignified.
He must have been sober when he wrote or had good advisers.[3] The Convention has adjourned & it is said the vote was nearly unanimous.[4] —there
are reports that Harper's Ferry has been taken & recaptured by a [com-
pany?] from Washington. at any rate I trust my sons will be preserved, &
that they may not have to go away from home defences—the little band of
volunteers are just passing, it is sad to see them—William & Liz & I expect
Cary will be up tonight at night (Friday). I do not think Cary will go on
to meet the Nortons, under different circumstances [I] have no doubt she
would be glad to do so—

Until today I had not thought of Eva's not staying as long as she wished
or thought best, but I fear there may be some difficulties about the intercourse, as there is a threatening in Washington of the mails of the seceding
States being withheld or stoped—all intercourse between here & Washington may be stopped too—James Jenifer expects to come on shortly, if he
has not left, he would be a good escort—

Molly thinks Walter may come too—she has been as kind & attentive in
saving me trouble as you or Carrie could have been & I tell her as troublesome as the latter with her care to prevent my taking cold—I should be
very sorry for you dear Em to be alone, but there is no danger you are exposed to, & cannot always have one of the girls—

I feel sorry for Mr. Brune, but it would be almost as painful to him to
separate from the North as from Va., & perhaps it is best however we may
regret it.[5] My love to him, & Mrs. Wm. Brown & all at Mrs. Collins.

1. South Carolina seceded on December 20, 1860, and Virginia on April 17, 1861.

2. Meaning that the state of Maryland, rather than Virginia, donated the land for
the new national capital at the dawn of the century.

3. John Letcher (1813–84), the prosecession governor of Virginia, took office in
1859.

4. The vote was actually eighty-eight for and fifty-five against.

5. Frederick W. Brune (1813–78), Eva Brune's husband, was a native of Baltimore
and had studied law at Harvard. George William Brown, the secessionist mayor of
Baltimore, was his brother-in-law and former law partner.

Emma Mordecai to her sister-in-law Sara Hays Mordecai, 21 April 1861, from Richmond, Virginia, to Philadelphia, Pennsylvania. Alfred Mordecai Papers, Library of Congress.

In 1861, Emma Mordecai was a forty-eight-year-old schoolteacher, unmarried, and a member of a well-known Richmond family. Her father, Jacob, was an educator and a moderately successful merchant, and her brother Alfred Mordecai, Sara Hays's husband, served as a major in the United States Army in New York. Whereas Jacob Mordecai was an observant Jew, only two of his thirteen children remained in the faith. Emma Mordecai was a fervent Unionist until the attack on Fort Sumter, but she is starting to change her mind about the impending war, as are her other women relatives.

This week without exaggeration has seemed a month long, my dear Sara, and it is impossible to realize that it was only last Sunday that we parted with you all so suddenly and sorrowfully. We rejoiced to have brother George to help us bear the change in our circle,[1] tho' we were all gloomy enough, the condition of the country weighing too heavily on all spirits to allow of cheerfulness any where. Great events have transpired since then. The news of the taking of Ft. Sumter, the secession of Virginia and the warlike operations going on every where have kept us in a constant state of intense and painful excitement.

Yesterday a dispatch from Georgetown informed us that Fanny, her mother, brother, and children would be in Richmond at 2:30 by the Central rail road, giving us all a startled feeling, tho' it was what might be expected at any moment. They all reached here safely, and it is the impression that it was the last day the boat between Washington & Alexandria would be allowed to run. Fanny says the condition of things in the District has become intolerable to any southerner. Edmund will resign[2] and so will Mr. Rives at once, and they will both be here on Monday.[3] It is pretty certain that Edmund will be employed by Capt. Schott who is it is said erecting fortifications somewhere in lower Virginia. The proceedings of our Convention and the arrangements of our state Government are kept from the public, and tho' all our volunteer companies are kept full equipped — knapsacks parked and all ready to start at a moments warning, not even their commander knows what their destination is to be, and of several companies who have left the City it is not known where they have been ordered.

Richmond was illuminated on Friday night in celebration as well of the secession of Virginia as of the taking of Ft. Sumter but there was no noisy exultation nor joyful spirit in the perfectly decorous throng that filled the streets. A deep earnest enthusiasm greatly tempered with sadness was the prevailing feature. It has cost us throes of agony to sunder our ties with our beloved common country but the southern spirit is now thoroughly aroused, and southern rights and independence will be contended for until obtained or until extermination puts an end to the contest. The most hopeful Unionists in Virginia have now given up, that since coercion has become the policy of Lincoln's administration, combined resistance is our common duty, and sorrowfully but earnestly advocate separation. The change made sister Caroline sick with sorrow,[4] and she kept her bed and fasted the day that war was proclaimed—but she rose an entirely converted woman, and is now satisfied that the South is doing all it is left for her to do—resisting oppression & villainy with a firm and lofty spirit. She sends her warm love to you & says you must not love her any the less for the change.

Your sweet affectionate letters gave us all great gratification. It was most amiable in you to be plea[sed?] with such a visit—it seemed to me it [was?] so stupid that I was almost ashamed of it—I know it did us good to have you with us, but I did not think the feeling reciprocated. Mr. Stern, & Miss Blair & her brother came Monday evening to see Laura[5]—I was sorry enough she was not here to see them—Brother has been more depressed in the last week than since the beginning of our trouble. I suffered most when the Union was first broken, and while hoping and fearing for restoration and reconstruction. Fanny is staying at Joe's and her mother & brother at Mrs. Cannills a cousin of Mrs. F. of the Clemens in Philadelphia. We are anxiously looking for dear Brother Alfred's answer to sister Ella's[6] letter—We all regret that she did not forward to him brother Sol's letter[7] but she will not be prevailed upon to do so until she hears from him. I have just been up to entreat her to let me send it with this but she cannot be persuaded. Rob has been in twice since you went away and was much disappointed at not seeing you again—

Willie & George[8] were sorry they could not come in Saturday evening—but Willie has been much troubled with an affection of the throat and was afraid of being caught in the rain—The weather yesterday & today has been beautiful but unusually cold—everything seems unnatural in this most unhappy season—I hope nothing prevented your leaving Philadelphia when you proposed doing so, and that you are safely at home. Ann Halyburton & Miss Deborah Louch were here yesterday—Everybody anxiously inquires what is Major Mordecai going to do—and we answer we do not know.[9]

—Judge Halyburton has not yet sent in his resignation, waiting for the secession to be ratified by the people, but as this is several weeks off, he will probably not wait so long. Ann has just finished dispatching Willie fully equipped to his company—She was just as quiet and cheerful as usualy and said she always hoped for the best. Many mothers here are in tears—miserable with apprehension—Rose [10] thinks that Johnny who belongs to a company at the University went with it to Harper's Ferry [11] but she has not heard from him. She is perfectly willing for her sons to go. Georgy is crazy to join a company—Willie is willing to wait until he is called on—he belongs to the militia. Sister Ellen sends her love to you and says she hopes you got her letter, and the key safe.[12] The Express with your trunk and her dress from Baltimore drove up Monday morning soon after breakfast. The dress was perfectly satisfactory in all respects.

Dear Sara I feel as if I were writing you a very incoherent letter, but I feel so perturbed all the time that I can do nothing composedly—When I think of you all, which we do constantly, it is with sorrow and anxiety—but I will not dwell on any of our uncertain prospects. Our dear Mother [13] says—I must say everything that is kind and affection to you and yours. She has not been as comfortable since you went away, altho' she is satisfied that her anxious wish for Virginia to secede has been gratified. It was a mournful agitated day with us all, the day it was announced. Many men shed tears at the removal of the flag—many more felt moved but seemed themselves—Those most anxious for the action heard it with a pang—All now seem relieved & ready for action. What words can express the criminal folly of the Government in bringing about such a state of things. Let us not allow political differences to interfere with family affection and individual good feeling. Let our prayers be for the right and just. God bless you all. Your ever aff. sister Emma.

1. Her brother, a businessman who had converted to the Episcopalian church.

2. Meaning the District of Columbia. Edmund Myers, her half-brother, a railroad executive who would soon become an officer in the Confederate army.

3. William Cabell Rives (1793–1868), a Virginian, attended the state convention that voted on secession. Rives initially opposed secession but later served in the Confederate Congress.

4. Probably her half-sister Caroline Myers, who was in her late sixties.

5. Her sister Laura.

6. Her half-sister Ella Myers.

7. Her brother Solomon Mordecai, a physician, lived in Mobile and was a secessionist. He converted to Protestant Christianity before his death.

8. Two of her adult nephews.

9. In May 1861 Alfred Mordecai quit the U. S. Army and would not fight on either side in the war.

10. Rosina Young Mordecai, spouse of Augustus and sister-in-law of Emma Mordecai, who converted to the Christian religion.

11. The federal arsenal in northern Virginia (now West Virginia) attacked by John Brown in 1859.

12. Probably Ellen Mordecai, the writer's sister, also an educator who converted to Christianity.

13. Rebecca Myers Mordecai, Jacob's second wife, who died in 1863.

Fanny Cox Broderick to her sister Mary Cox Collins, 25 April 1861, from Maysville, Kentucky, to Lexington, Kentucky. Collins Family Letters, Division of Special Collections and Archives, Margaret I. King Library, University of Kentucky at Lexington.

Kentuckian Fanny Broderick, a businessman's wife, dreads the possibility of secession and war. In the spring of 1861 her male relatives are choosing opposite sides, and every day brings terrible news about the nation's collapse. So Broderick begins to prepare for hard times ahead.

My Dear Sister,

I received your letter this morning, I had been writing a few lines to Richard about getting a garden Syringe for Uncle Geo. Forman but Mr. Broderick could not wait long enough for me to reply to yours then as I should not have written so soon but I wished to let you know that we would send some things down on Monday with the roses as you wish. I will send but a few and those small as [another?] year if you feel more settled I can let have you more. the future appears so dark that we cannot feel the same interest in anything that we did. I have never realized to the same extent how uncertain every [thing] is, "that we know not what a day may bring forth." My fears have never been aroused until now. I have been confident that the evils feared would be averted but there seems little hope now, for passion instead of reason rules now.

I think you should not decide too hastily about staying where you are this summer. it may be so that it will be best for you all to come here. If

Jeff Davis is determined to take possession of Cincinnati (which I for one don't think he'll ever do),[1] you would certainly not stay, but I shall not give up the hope of having you with us if things remain so unsettled, at least for a time, for we are quiet here compared to what it is with you. I don't know how you bear it. Your nerves must be much stronger than mine but mine are easily unstrung.

I am glad Ed is going to the farm. John will go down next week to be with him, their sympathies are too much with the north to remain in Kentucky if she secedes and they will have plenty to do and that is a great advantage in these times of excitement. Will Ed rent his house or leave it empty? How do the Hunters get along?[2] I should think they would feel uneasy for fear Garnett would join the secessionists as many of the Students have done in different places, you must give my love to them all.[3]

I had a very pleasant visit to the country and to Washington. I had not seen Phebe for three weeks so of course to be with her for so many days was very pleasant. She will not be home until Saturday week when she will have been absent five weeks. I am glad she will so soon be through as I fear she would not continue well to study as closely as they say she does.

I would have sent this week for the frames for her pictures but everything looks so gloomy that I thought we might need the money for bread and meat soon. So I would wait a while longer, but it will be quite a disappointment to her.

We have received a letter from Uncle George for Mother which we took the liberty of opening, he seems very feeble. Cousin George's son has joined the army and is in Florida — but the letter will be sent to you soon, for Uncle requested us to, as he is not able to write much.

Tomorrow I shall be busy house cleaning and next week I hope to get through after that I shall have more leisure. On looking at your letter you say I must send the roses on Monday and I have said I would, but you must mean Tuesday so I shall send them then.

Kiss the children for me and tell them we hope that the war will be ended before it is time for them to come up and that they may not be disappointed in their visit.

Give my love to all enquiring friends. your affectionate Sister Fanny.

1. Jefferson Davis (1808–89), the former U.S. Senator from Mississippi, who was chosen president of the Confederacy in February. As Broderick surmises, he did not try to capture Cincinnati.

2. Possibly Virginian Robert M. T. Hunter (1809–87), who had many relatives in

Kentucky. After a long career as a states rights Democrat in national politics, he served as Confederate secretary of state and then as Confederate senator from Virginia.

3. Possibly Hunter's kinsman James Mercer Garnett (1840–1916), then a student at the University of Virginia, who fought in the Confederate army.

Clara Dunlap to her sister, 6 May 1861, from Camden, Arkansas, to no address. Fred J. Herring Collection, Small Manuscript Collection, Arkansas History Commission.

Clara Dunlap was twenty-five years old, the daughter and sister of slaveowners. Her husband John Dunlap, a merchant, had no slaves of his own, but several men in his family owned bondsmen. By the spring of 1861 she has embraced the Confederate cause, and as her brothers prepare to join up, she lambasts Abraham Lincoln. White women scarcely ever used profanity in writing, even this comparatively mild language, which suggests just how hostile she feels toward the president. Dunlap is well on her way to becoming one of the "she devils" that so many Northern troops encountered when they invaded the Confederacy.

Dear Sister,

Yours of the 18th I received several days since, & I can assure you I was truly glad to hear from you, & from home, & that all were in the enjoyment of good health; & oh what a real blessing it is; I never before in my life, reallized, what a great blessing health was so much, as now; I am getting to beleave that every one has to be afflicted; one way or another the better to appreciate it <u>fully</u>, as I do now.

I am happy to say your letter found all well; I was over at brother John's yesterday, brother G & sis M—& all their children were there; all were well; we had a nice strawberry dinner. S's strawberry vines are doing fin[e]ly this year, better than mine or brother G's either; & the finest berries I most ever saw, Sis M's baby is growing very pretty indeed, brother J. thinks he's the prettiest one of the children; Sallie's boy still grows, has several teeth, George re[a]d a letter from Irene, not long since, & will answer it soon; I should like so much to see Grand-ma's garden Just now; I know, from Irene's description it must be pretty. Sis M & I were speaking of it, & wondering how she could in so short a time, make such a nice garden, & then to think she is now confined to her bed & cannot go to see how pretty she has made it. I am in hope's though when warm weather comes she will be able to get out. My garden is doing better, vegetable's are begining to grow will soon have peas, — have had one mess of Irish potatoes, & have upwards of a hundred & fifty chickens; John has a fine stand of corn, growing very fast, cotton has come up & looks well; he has <u>185</u> acres in cultivation this year besides his potatoe patch & pea patch; you know it will keep him <u>very</u> busy, to work it well. We were all much surprised to hear of Bettie Ziglar's marrying; I did not think she was that old; I am glad to learn that Doc L. is doing so well; if he keeps on, he will soon win him self a <u>name</u>; though he is very young yet, I recon Mrs. Lassiter wont mind it so much now, about his leaving home, as he is trying so hard to do his duty faithfully.

I think our State is <u>arroused at last,</u> to thinking of <u>war,</u> I think they have 8 or ten companies now at Little Rock, they will soon start to Virginia, to assist Jeff Davis,[1] & <u>not</u> old Abe,[2] as he thought they would; at least he has the presumtion to demand, assistance from us; but I must give you our Governor's[3] reply to Mr. <u>Abraham</u> (as they call him) in answer to his demand for troops to fight the Southern States; Governor Rector telegraphed back to him, to "<u>Go to hell, God dam him</u>",[4] I almost hate to repeat it, but I guess old Abe is begining to think by this time; that he might as well be <u>there</u> as here; for all the South & Ark. included, cares, well he deserves the worst that can befall him. I guess he thinks we out here, are <u>hoosier</u> sure enough; or that we have a <u>hoosier</u> Governor[5] one, & wĭth all that we are pretty independent in our way of speaking & there he will think just about right. a great many of our young men in this neighborhood & in Cam[den]. has gone & a good many others speak of going in the next regement that's formed. John is more excited than I ever saw him, speaks strongly of going in the next company that asks, so does brother G, he told sis Mollie the other day; if her father was only out there; that he would go off with those brave young men, that were going to defend their country; & it made him feel so bad to stay behind & sis M says the tears would roll down his face while he was speaking; he is <u>very</u> much excited too; very much. brother J is more cool but determined. Oh I almost forgot brother G told me to ask you & Irene to save him some more tulip seed, if you pleased, he had some very pretty ones this year, but wants a variety. Nearly all of my fruit trees died last summer, when we had that drouth,[6] but have 5 cherries trees 4 or 5 pairs, as many apple's & peach trees, & one little blue-plumed scion living; all the others died, all my grafts died, too, brother J told me to tell Ma she must not mind his pleagueing her, & not get mad & scold him too much, & when she moves out here, he will give her one of his best cows

298 / *Our Common Affairs*

& calves to start with, says he is always joking every body & she must not [mind?] what he said. I told him though I did hope she would send him a good scolding; so that he would know better next time. Sis M & S both told me to be sure & send their best love to you & Ma, G'Ma, Sis C, Irene & all enquiring friends, Sis M says you must write soon. Well Neal I am writing so often now, I dont have as much news to write as I did when I wrote more seldom, you must write soon. Give my love to Ma Sis C, G'Ma & all enquiring friends, Tell Mrs. Howard were I twice the distance, I could never forget her many acts of kindness, to me & you, & to you alone since I left, I think her too true a friend to forget so easily, that neither <u>time</u> or <u>distance</u> can make me forget one who was proved so true a friend as She has to us. Give my love to her & Rebecca in particular, tell R I should like to be there to compare <u>babies,</u> Jimmy is learning to eat right well now, gets prettier every day so <u>John</u> says, I dont think he would hardly own that there ever was a baby so pretty or so smart—as <u>Papa's hoosier</u> as he calls him. Tell all the negroes howdy. Tell Laura not to name her baby. (I guess she has one in this time) until I send her a name,[7] tell mammy[8] my baby loves <u>biscuit</u>—& <u>rice</u> & <u>flour doins,</u> beter than cornbread do write soon C & tell me all the news; from Your affectionate sister Clara Dunlap.

P.S. John sends his respects to you all. A convention of delegates met yesterday at Little Rock to pass an order of <u>secession</u>.[9]

1. The Confederate president, recently installed in Richmond, the new Confederate capital.

2. President Abraham Lincoln.

3. Henry Massie Rector (1816–99), a Democrat, was elected governor in 1860. In February 1861 he seized Federal arsenals in Arkansas to outmaneuver the state's Unionists. In retaliation, they limited his term to two years, and he had to step down in 1862. For the rest of the war he served as a private in a reserve unit.

4. By all accounts, Rector's reply dated April 22 read as follows: "In answer to your requisition for troops from Arkansas to subjugate the Southern States, I have to say that none will be furnished. The demand is only adding insult to injury. The people of this commonwealth are freemen, not slaves, and will defend, to the last extremity, their honor, lives and property against Northern mendacity and usurpation." It was a tough message, but evidently contained no profanity.

5. A term of unknown origin that apparently became part of American slang in the 1830s; used to mean a rustic, a backwoodsman, or an innocent.

6. An archaic term for drought.

7. Whites sometimes insisted on naming slave infants, but most slave parents also gave their children names of their own to be used within the black family.

8. A term that whites began using in the late antebellum era for black women who nursed the children of their masters.

9. The state officially seceded on May 6, 1861.

Jane T. Quigg to her cousin Mary E. Sipp, 2 June 1861, from South Easton, Pennsylvania, to somewhere in the Mid-Atlantic states. Jane Townsend Quigg Papers, MS 1926, Manuscripts Division, Maryland Historical Society Library.

Jane Quigg wed a Methodist minister when she was in her teens, and throughout the 1850s she followed him to pastorates all over the Mid-Atlantic states. In letters to fellow Southerner Mary Sipp, she complained that her northern-born husband was trying to turn her into a Yankee too. On the eve of the war's first major battle, her political attitudes are in flux. She loves her native region but reviles the secessionists who led it out of the Union.

Dearest Mary,

It is the sunset hour of a genial summer sabbath day. Surely the sabbath's sacred hours was never more needed to calm the fevered pulse, and quiet the excited imagination, then now amidst the extraordinary occurrences and cares of these times. A great calamity has befallen our once happy land indeed. We have reached prosperity by such peaceful paths, that it is extremely difficult to realize these days of war and tumult as belonging to us. Although I love the South, and my sympathies and my prayers have been with her, yet I must say that indignation against those who have so wantonly plunged us all into such ruin fills my heart. I cannot help wishing that destruction may befall those who have so insulted our flag under whose folds we were born, and under whose protection we have lived so long and so happily. Dear old Maryland, how she is being buffeted in the storm. You may be sure I felt extreme concern for her safety, and for the welfare of those loved ones on her soil. Since it seems probable that she will stay with the remains of the Union I breathe much more freely, yet she is not safe but many parts are torn and distracted by actual conflict between the parties. Brothers Sam'l and Lem'l remained in the city while many were fleeing from it,[1] but their business is utterly prostrate, and they must share in the universal distress. I hear from them regularly. Their lasts letters stated that they were still able to make their payments but unless things improved they could not hope to do so much longer. Lem'l said only seven dry-goods houses were left standing in the city. There own is one. I visited Baltimore at Conference time, yet there was then no sign of the storm which has since swept so furiously the city.

My dear Mother's health has been very precarious. She took a cough before she left here last Summer, and it has clung to her, and increased until she has become very much debilitated and all the recent reports have been gloomy enough to excite my worst fears. We are all hoping to see her recover at least some measure of the strength she has lost, and pray that her life may be prolonged. We, each of use owe much to our Mother. Her life has been devoted to her children's interests, and we have always found her counsel and direction, safe.

My friends are on the side of the union, but you may be sure they do not exculpate the North from all blame, in bringing about the present state of affairs. They are between two fires, and they feel the force of the flame very seriously. I am very glad you were not in Virginia when the strife commenced. I often think how fortunate that you left it to return not again. I was surprised to hear that you had become reconciled to teaching for the rest of life. Now Mary you may be able to do as much good in that capacity, and perhaps more, but I cannot feel reconciled to the fact that one so adapted to make domestic life happy should settle down in the conviction that it is for others but not yourself to have Husband and children and home. Now I often wonder if you have not destined yourself to this. I don't believe there is any need of your treading life's pathway alone, and had you company, you would not feel that it may be short, but you would have so much to live for, that you would live in spite of yourself. Now I confess the thought of death brings more reluctance with it, than before these ties were formed. I think sometimes it would be dreadful to die and leave these little children especially. My Husband could get another wife, but they could not have another Mother. yet it is only when my faith is weak, that these suggestions meet me, and when stronger I find so much blessing and Joy in my home and with my loved ones, that only gratitude fills my heart, to the exclusion of forebodings of evil.

Mr. Quigg is so full of patriotism, that I am sometimes tempted to think, that he will either seek a chaplaincy in the army, or volunteer to preach, pray, or fight, just whichever there is the most call for. I have promised to put no obstacles in the way of whatever he conceives be be his duty. Pennsylvania would not do for me however in his absence. It is endurable with him, but without him my native sands and plains would be my refuge. The Eastern Shore of Maryland as you know is rather isolated, so that I suppose war's din is scarcely likely to be heard about its peaceful rural districts. Yet is very hard to know what part will be exempt before the finale of the struggle. "God bless our native land."

You will remember that this is our last year in South Easton, and we may be more inconveninent to you hereafter, so I hope you will visit me here. I am exceedingly sorry to hear that your health has suffered so much. I sincerely hope your energies will rally, and your wonted health return. How far are you from New York, and how do you reach it from Middletown? So your Mother is near Paterson again. I remember Uncle Rionier and Aunt Jane perfectly. Give warm love to your Mother for me, and say to her, that when you come again to see me I would like to see her also.

Our boys have grown very much, and all day long beat imaginary drums and shoot imaginary foes. Howard says, "Why do men kill each other in war? Is it not a sin?" Ally is very chubby, and Gracie also. She is two years old now, and is very interesting. Her Father pets her a great deal, and she loves him dearly. Cousin Susan is old fashioned. Lou is larger than I am, and as black as Africa's own daughter.[2] Please write very soon dear Mary, and write a good deal, for I want to know all about you and yours. Lovingly ever yours, Jennie.

1. Meaning the city of Baltimore. Quigg was born and reared in Maryland.

2. The Quiggs hired some house slaves when they lived in the South but owned no slaves of their own. In 1860 a free black teenager named Louisa Duffy worked for the family in Pennsylvania. This remark is both casually racist and rather strange. Perhaps Sipp has never met Duffy, so Quigg feels she must describe her appearance.

AFTERWORD

Diary of Amanda McDowell. Curtis McDowell Papers, Tennessee State Library and Archives.

As the deadly conflict finally draws to a close, Amanda McDowell, now aged twenty-five, feels a quiet sense of triumph over the fire-breathing secessionists of 1861. Her denunciation of secession's tyranny goes beyond the antipolitical tone of the antebellum era and the fear that so many women expressed during the secession winter. Whether this represents a passing outburst or a new current in white Southern women's culture remains to be seen.

17 April 1865.
The girls keep my ink and things carried off so that I cannot get to write when I want to.[1] There is great news. I have been looking for a grand smash up for some time. things have been so still. And guess from all accounts the great Southern Confederacy is about "gone up for ninety days," as the boys say.[2] The news is (and it is corroborated and told over by every new arrival from *Nashville*) that Lee, his whole army, Petersburg, Richmond, and some say Davis himself is taken. The latter item is hardly true, but the rest is true I expect.[3] Some are already rejoicing over the downfall of their oppressors. For truly Secession has been the greatest tyrent that ever reigned over this

country. For my own part I try not rejoice at anyone's downfall only so far as I think it will be for the good of their own souls. But I do rejoice in the prospect for peace. Some think it will certainly be made. I fear we are going to be disappointed, but will live in hope. Newton Camron got home yesterday. He has been in prison, but was exchanged and made tracks for home A year or two ago. he was awfully disgraced. P. come home home from the Southern army. I wonder how his pulse beats on the subject now. he says Stephen Williams will be at home in a few days.

1. Meaning her students. McDowell continued to teach school during the war.
2. This phrase meant that a man had enlisted in the army for a three-month tour.
3. Confederate General Robert E. Lee (1807–70) surrendered to Union General U. S. Grant at Appomattox Courthouse, Virginia, on April 9, 1865, but, as McDowell surmises, the Union army did not capture Jefferson Davis until May 10 as he fled through southern Georgia.

INDEX

Cobb, Samuel, 208

Cole, Laura, 19, 21, 96–98, 229–31

Collins, Mary Cox, 251–52, 286–88, 294–96

Collins, Richard H., 192–94

Collins, Sallie R., 18, 25, 41n. 65, 120–21

Compromise of 1820, 216–17, 269

Conrad, Anne (Nancy) Addison Carr, 18, 56–57, 59–61, 68–69, 98–100

Conrad, Elizabeth W. Powell, 56–57, 59–61, 68–69, 98–100

contraception, 14–15, 132–33

Cook, Elizabeth W., 114–16

cooking: by slaves, 143, 147, 150, 153, 161; by whites, 9, 59, 79, 116, 123, 126, 129–30, 146–47, 153, 154, 161, 201

Cott, Nancy, 4, 28

counterculture, 6–7, 32n. 14

courtship, 60, 163, 171, 184; advice on, 101, 175; between cousins, 99; enjoyment of, 86, 91–92; studies more important than, 158

Crawford, Jane Gaston, 169–72

Crawford, Martha E. Foster, 106–7

culture: white female, 1–41; white male, 11–12

Cunningham, Louisa Bird, 20, 235–36

Davies, Maria Dyer, 18, 149–51, 199–200

Davis, Hester Ann Wilkins, 20, 247–48

Davis, Jefferson, 288, 295, 297, 303

Deas, Nancy Izard, 10, 125

death, 98–99, 117, 126; of friends and neighbors, 72, 126, 157–58, 261; of relatives, 68, 96–97, 117, 199, 225, 253, 262, 272–73, 279, 284; of slaves, 33, 180

demography, 14–15

Diary of a Southern Refugee During the War, 281–82

divorce, 15, 110–13, 135–38

domestic violence, 13, 23, 65–68, 110–13, 136–37, 208

Donelson, Eliza E. D., 45, 52

Donelson, Mary Purnell, 52–53

Douglas, Stephen, 250, 262

dreams, 5, 104, 105, 131, 160, 163, 189

dress, 86, 147–49, 177, 200, 201, 227; as fashion, 26–27, 121, 161–62, 220, 222; purchasing cloth for, 138–39

duels, 45–46, 224

Duland, Martha, 286–88

Dunbar, Sarah, 46–48

Dunlap, Clara, 22, 296–99

Dyer, Martha Tabb Watkins, 127–28

Early, Elizabeth Brown Rives, 18, 57–58, 185–87

Early, Mary Virginia, 57–59, 185–87

Eastin, Eliza D., 52–53

Eastin, Mary, 45

education, 64, 197, 206, 207; of boys, 108–9; of girls, 5–6, 58, 85, 94–96, 108, 117, 163, 177, 205, 239–41, 257, 259; importance of, 76–77, 158; of men, 11, 53, 66, 182; of women, 3, 19–20, 54–55, 215

Eliot, T. S., 16

epidemics, 98–99, 184

essentialism, 25–26

Evans, Augusta Jane, 26

Evans, Eli, 27

family life, 6, 11, 12, 14–15, 43–80 passim

Faragher, John Mack, 21

Farnham, Christie Ann, 5–6

fashion. *See* dress

Faust, Drew Gilpin, 9

Few, Mary, 85–87, 211–14

Finley, Sarah Ann, 15

Fishback, Susan H. S., 20, 252–54

Fletcher, Lucy Muse Walton, 18, 22, 151–54, 264–65

Flynt, Jonathan Ralph, 223–26

Forman, Martha Browne Callender, 126–27

Fort Sumter, 22, 264, 271, 273, 281–82, 288, 291–92

Fox-Genovese, Elizabeth, 4–5

Franklin, Mary G., 10, 25, 145–46

free blacks, 5, 9, 17, 201, 263, 301

Freehling, William W., 13

Friedman, Jean E., 4–5, 27

friendship, 24, 26, 81–122

frontier, Southern: friendship on, 103–6, 114–16; lawlessness on, 24, 183–85; prospect of living on, 181–83; secession on, 265–67; slavery on, 204–5, 257–60; work on, 127–28, 141–45, 156–57

Gaillard, Marianne, 237–39

Galbreath, Margaret, 19, 217–19

Gaston, Jane. *See* Crawford, Jane Gaston

Gaston, Martha, 21, 169–72

Geertz, Clifford, 15, 36n. 33

Gilchrist, Julia A., 18, 117–18

Gone with the Wind, 3

Gordon, Caroline M., 69–70

Gordon, Virginia Meade, 62–65

Library of Congress Cataloging-in-Publication Data

Our common affairs : texts from women in the Old South / edited by
    Joan E. Cashin.
        p.   cm.
    Includes index.
    ISBN 0-8018-5306-0 (hardcover : alk. paper).

    1. Women—Southern States—History—Sources.   2. Southern States—
History—1775–1865—Sources.   I. Cashin, Joan E.
[HQ1438.S630973   1996]
305.4'0975—dc20

                                         95-51431